D0836399

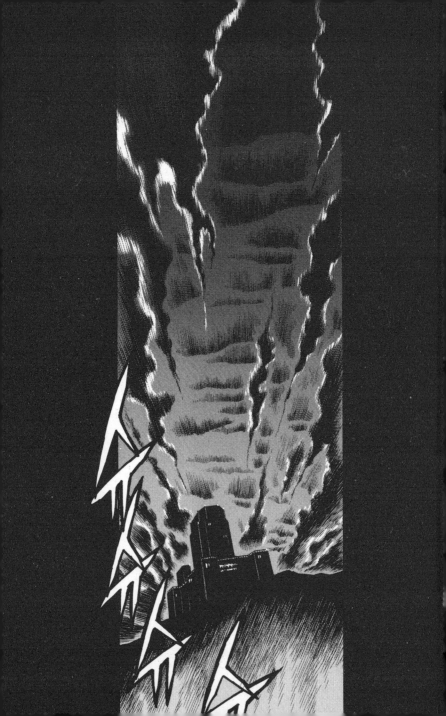

VOLUME 14

STORY AND ART BY
WOO

HAMBURG // LONDON // LOS ANGELES // TOKYO

Rebirth Vol. 14
created by Woo

Translation - Jennifer Hahm
English Adaptation - Bryce P. Coleman
Associate Editor - Aaron Sparrow
Copy Editor - Suzanne Waldman
Retouch and Lettering - Caren McCaleb
Production Artist - Jason Milligan
Cover Design - Jorge Negrete

Editor - Bryce P. Coleman
Digital Imaging Manager - Chris Buford
Pre-Press Manager - Antonio DePietro
Production Managers - Jennifer Miller and Mutsumi Miyazaki
Art Director - Matt Alford
Managing Editor - Jill Freshney
VP of Production - Ron Klamert
Editor-In-Chief - Mike Kiley
President and C.O.O. - John Parker
Publisher and C.E.O. - Stuart Levy

A  Manga

TOKYOPOP Inc.
5900 Wilshire Blvd. Suite 2000
Los Angeles, CA 90036

E-mail: info@TOKYOPOP.com
Come visit us online at www.TOKYOPOP.com

ISBN: 1-59532-029-6
First TOKYOPOP printing: June 2005
10 9 8 7 6 5 4 3 2 1
Printed in the USA

STORY THUS FAR

At the behest of Master Tae, Deshwitat and the team travel to a far-off land, one filled with strange customs and constant danger—New York City. It is here that they hope to obtain the power Deshwitat will need to stop the now god-like Kalutika and his apocalyptic designs. Suddenly, the group is attacked by a group of rogue vampires, and Millenear is kidnapped. The team's only lead is a grizzled vampire named Draistail. He offers to help Deshwitat defeat the evil vampires' master, Mr. Grey, in the upcoming Vampire Lord Tournament. Deshwitat scoffs at the offer, but is forcibly prevented from pursuing the abductors. However, Rett and Beryun, accompanied by a vampire hostage, depart on a perilous rescue mission...

DESHWITAT

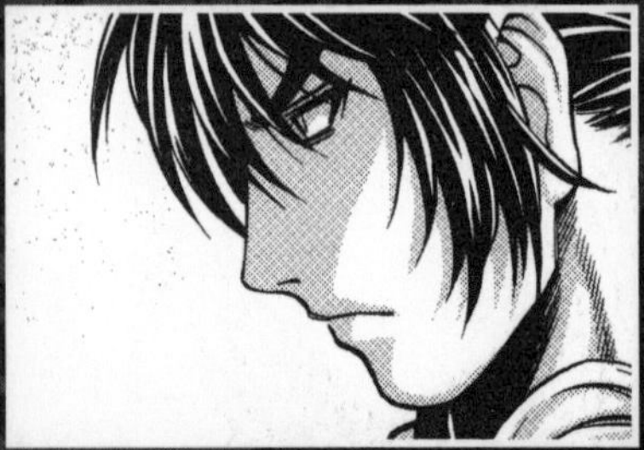

HE IS ON A BLOOD-QUEST FOR REVENGE AGAINST A MAN HE ONCE CALLED "FRIEND."

RETT

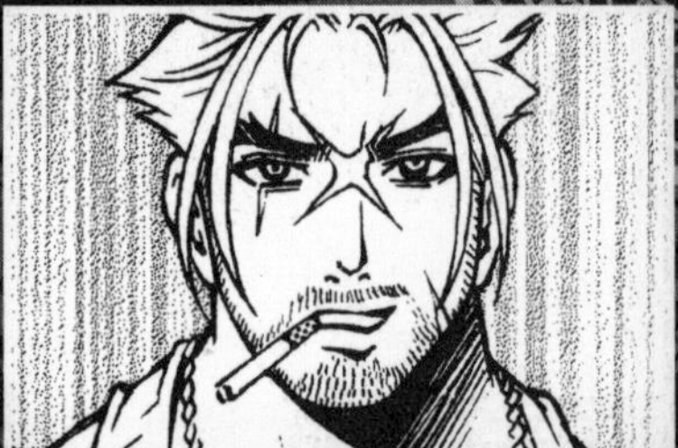

DESH'S MOST TRUSTED AND FEARSOME ALLY. HE WAS CURSED WITH IMMORTALITY.

MILLENEAR

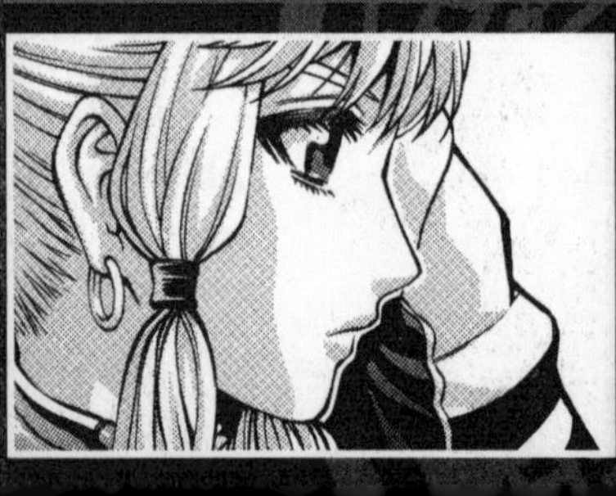

A FORMER EXORCIST, SHE STRUGGLES WITH HER GROWING FEELINGS FOR DESHWITAT.

REMI

HER FATHER'S BLOOD REVIVED DESHWITAT, WHOM SHE MUST NOW RELUCTANTLY HELP.

BERYUN

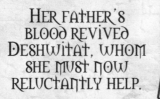

AN ARTIFICIALLY CREATED LIFE FORM. HER STILL WATERS RUN DEEP AND DEADLY.

EIJI

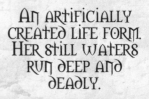

THE RAMBUNCTIOUS, YOUNG JAPANESE NINJA ASSIGNED TO ASSIST DESH'S TEAM.

MASTER TAE

LEADER OF A BUDDHIST SECT, SHE BELIEVES DESHWITAT MAY BE HUMANITY'S SAVIOR

DRAISTAIL

A CAGEY, OLD VAMPIRE WHO INSISTS DESHWITAT LEARN VAMPIRE FIGHTING TECHNIQUES.

RANG

CAPTURED AFTER THE VAMPIRE ATTACK, SHE'S BEEN TRICKED INTO BETRAYING HER LEADER

MR GREY

The villainous, would-be King of all vampires, he now holds Millenear captive.

KALUTIKA

Deshwitat's betrayer, he is a god-like being bent on the destruction of mankind.

REBÍRTH™

Vol 14

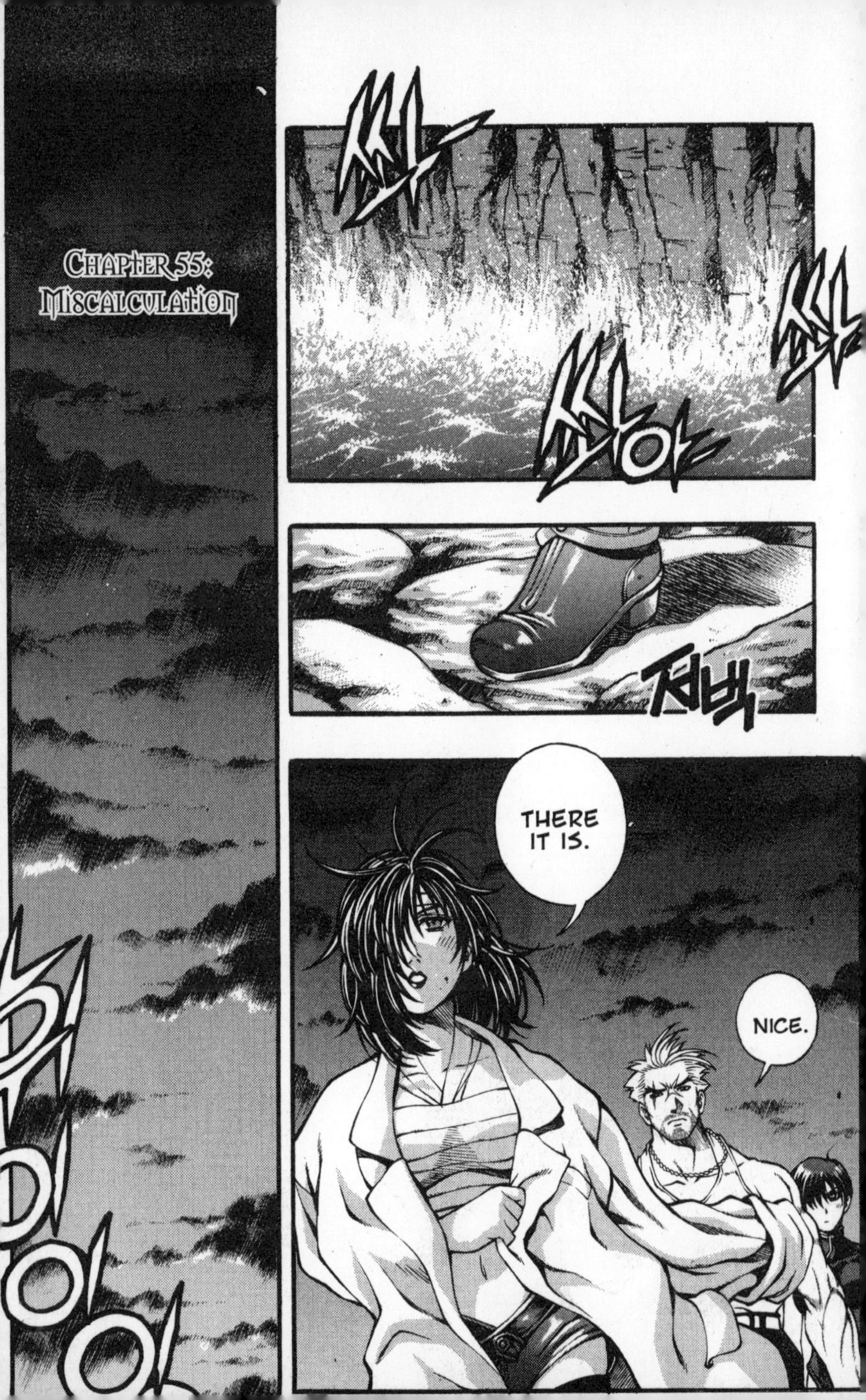
Chapter 55:
Miscalculation
THERE IT IS.
NICE.

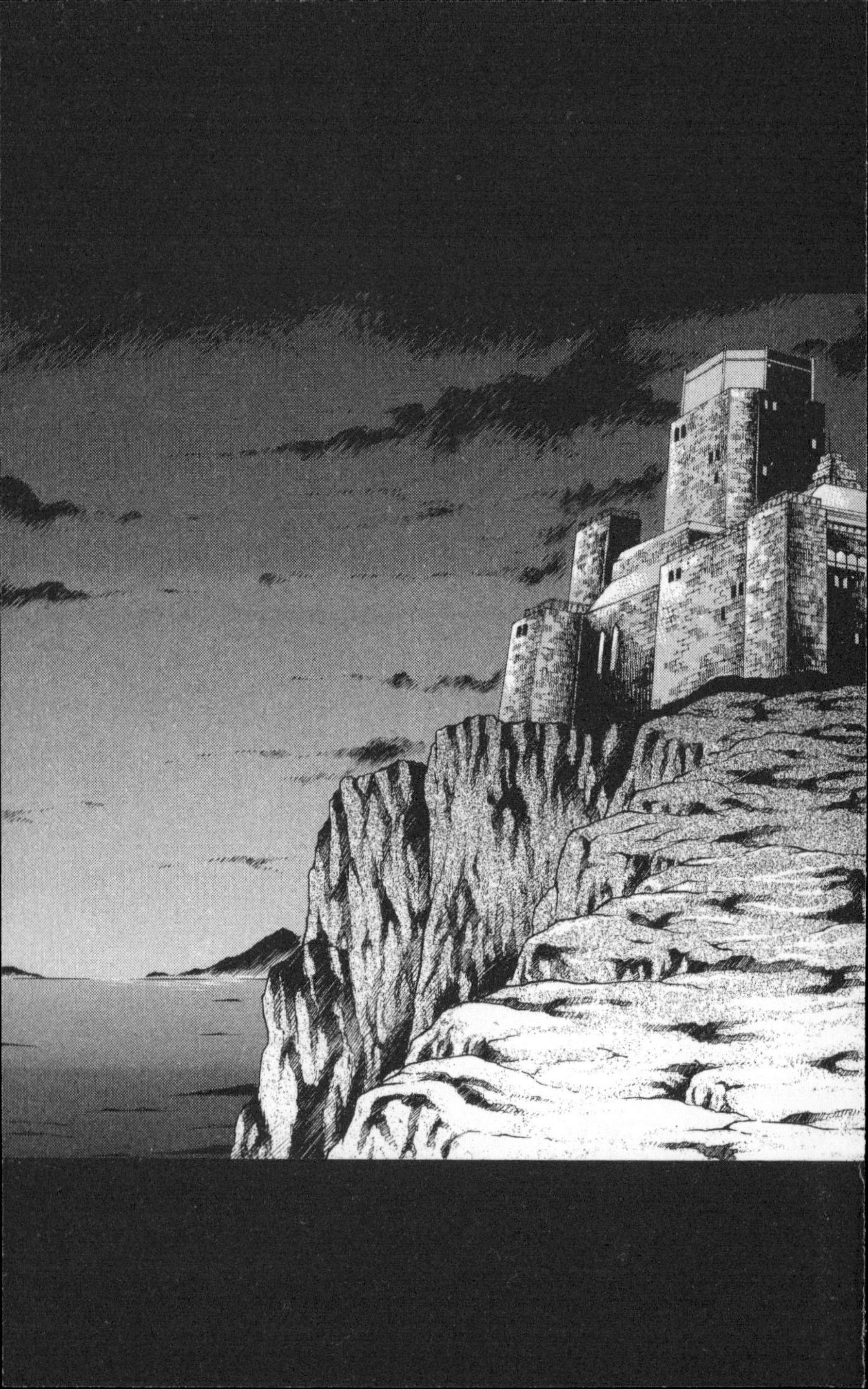

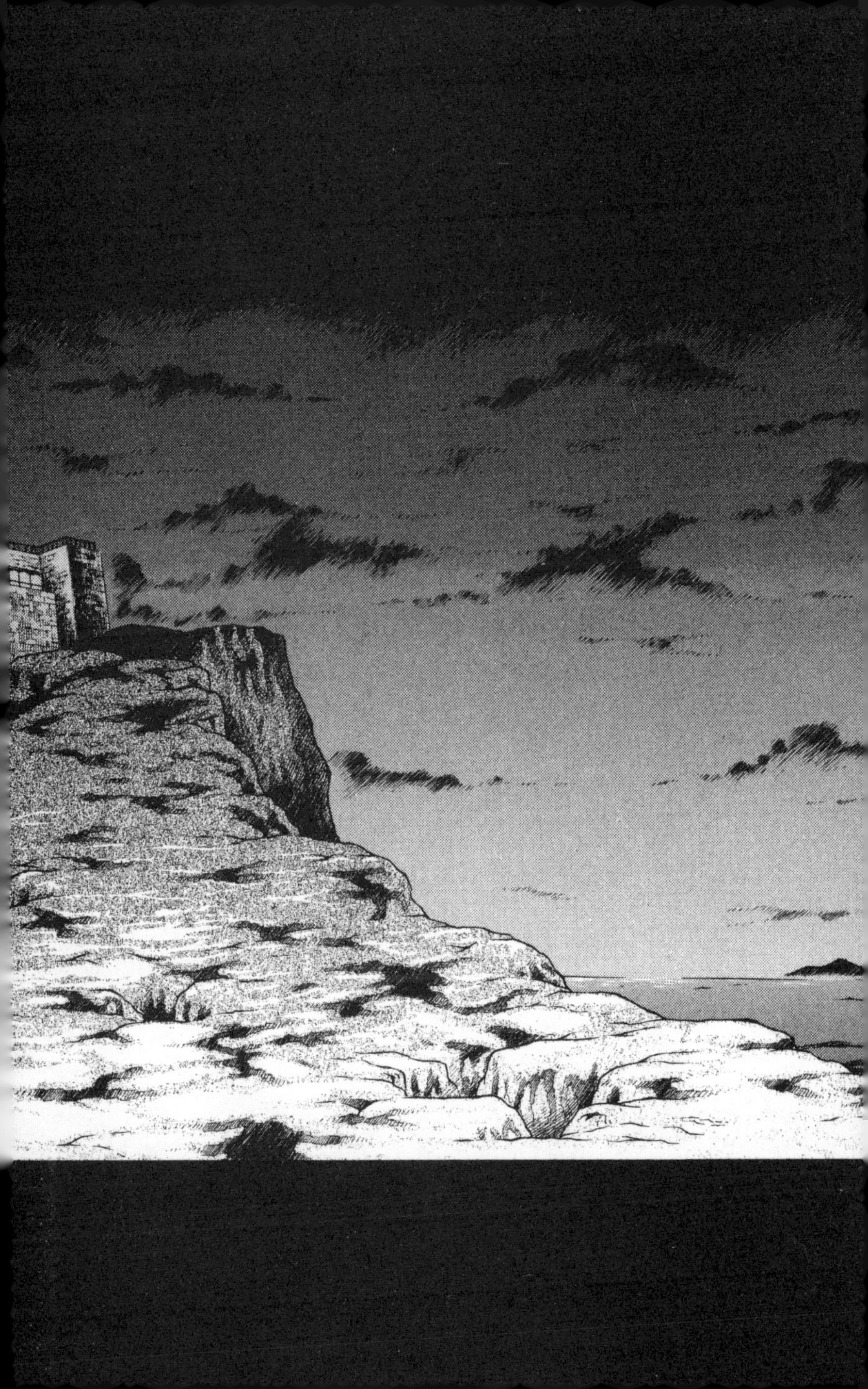

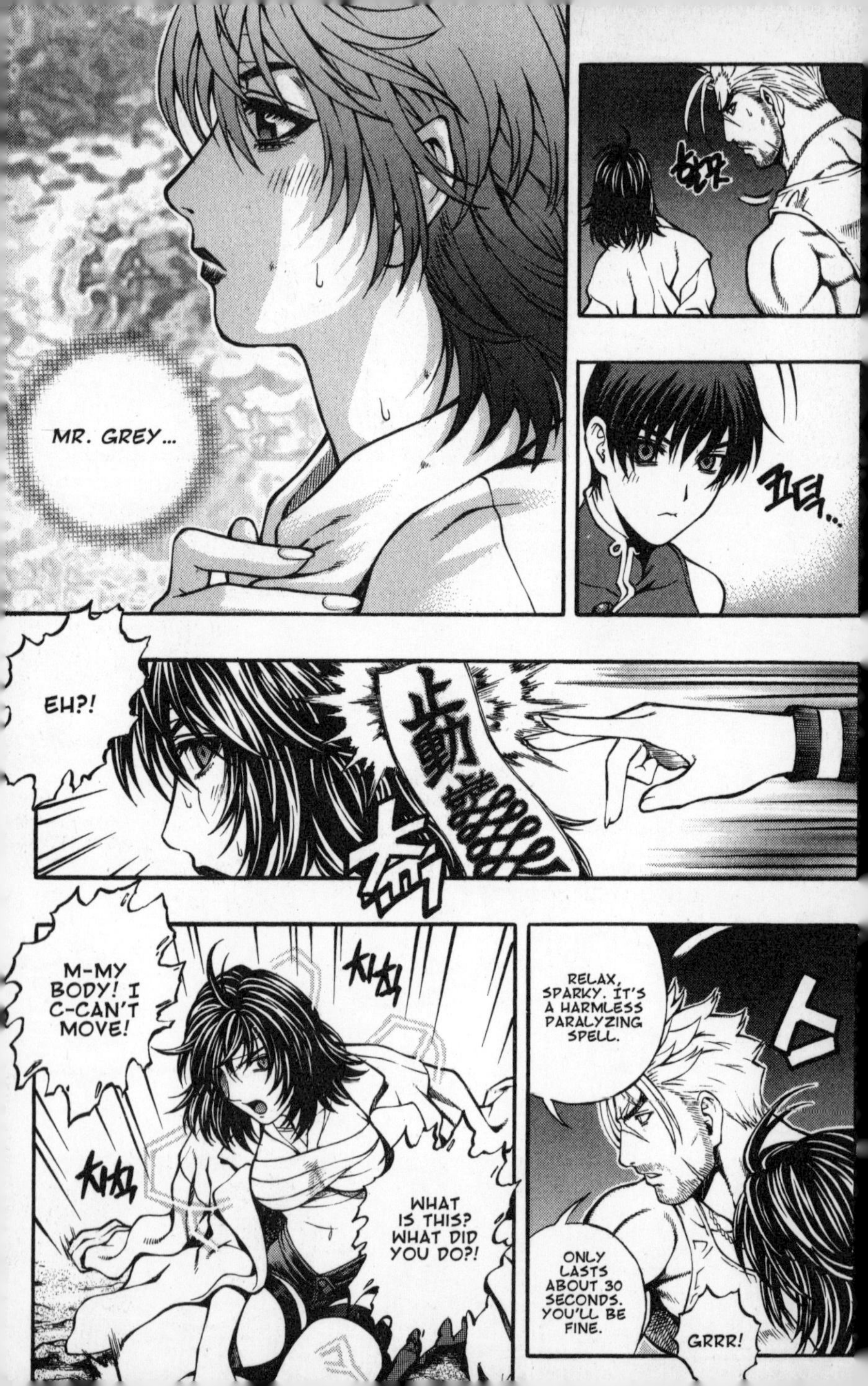
MR. GREY...
끄덕...
EH?!
M-MY BODY! I C-CAN'T MOVE!
WHAT IS THIS? WHAT DID YOU DO?!
RELAX, SPARKY. IT'S A HARMLESS PARALYZING SPELL.
ONLY LASTS ABOUT 30 SECONDS. YOU'LL BE FINE.
GRRR!

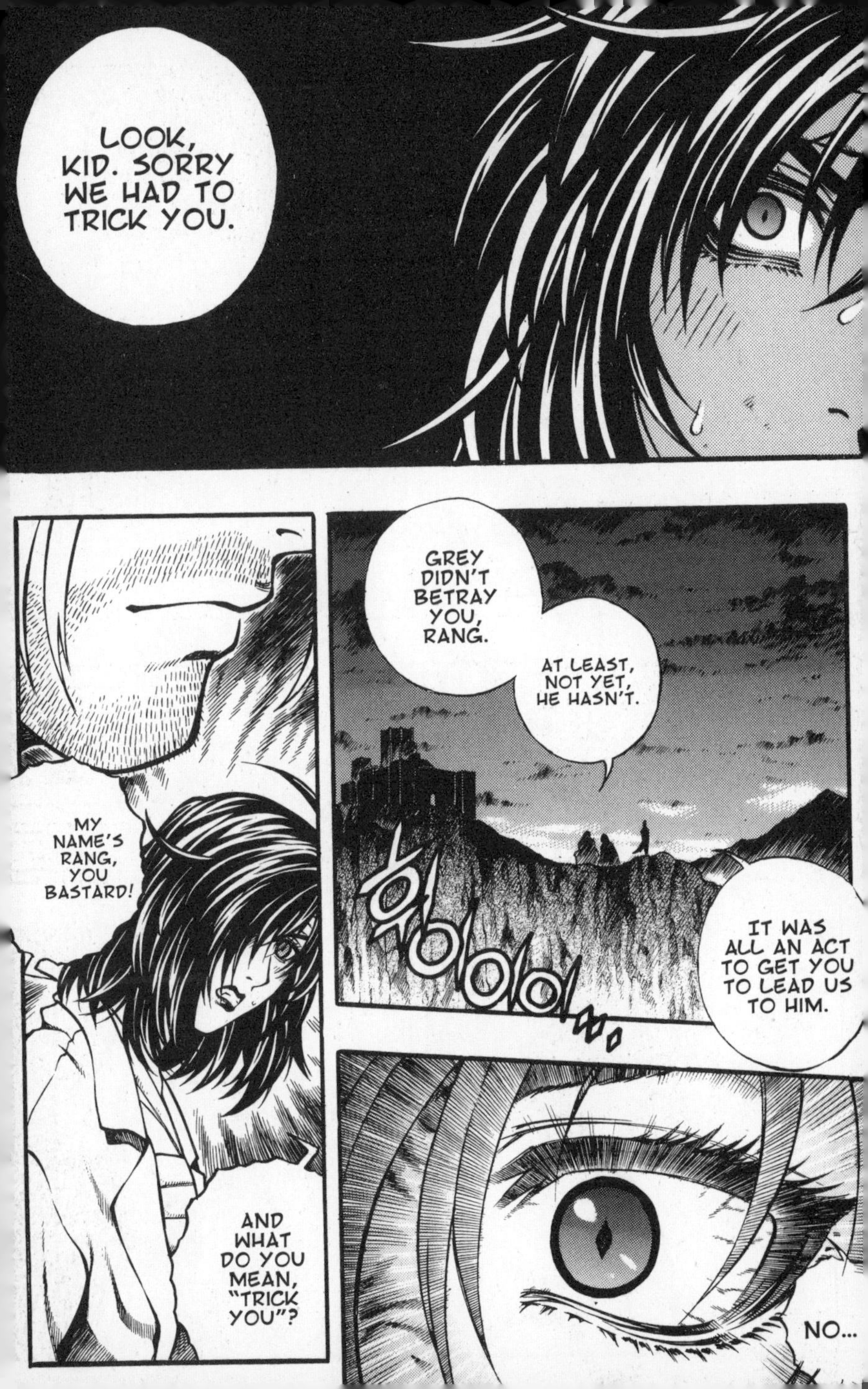
LOOK, KID. SORRY WE HAD TO TRICK YOU.
MY NAME'S RANG, YOU BASTARD!
AND WHAT DO YOU MEAN, "TRICK YOU"?
GREY DIDN'T BETRAY YOU, RANG.
AT LEAST, NOT YET, HE HASN'T.
IT WAS ALL AN ACT TO GET YOU TO LEAD US TO HIM.
NO...

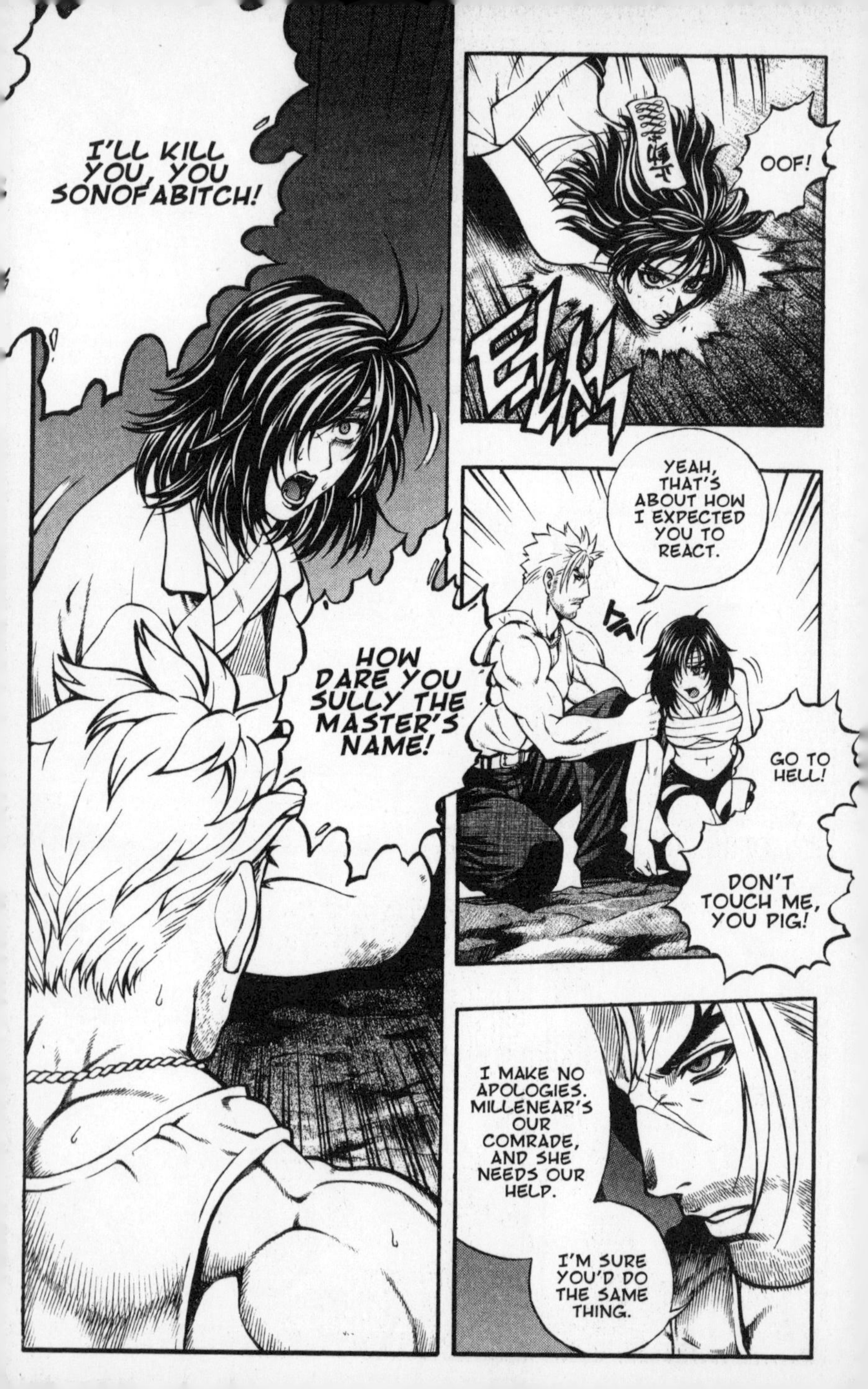
I'LL KILL YOU, YOU SONOFABITCH!
HOW DARE YOU SULLY THE MASTER'S NAME!
OOF!
YEAH, THAT'S ABOUT HOW I EXPECTED YOU TO REACT.
GO TO HELL!
DON'T TOUCH ME, YOU PIG!
I MAKE NO APOLOGIES. MILLENEAR'S OUR COMRADE, AND SHE NEEDS OUR HELP.
I'M SURE YOU'D DO THE SAME THING.

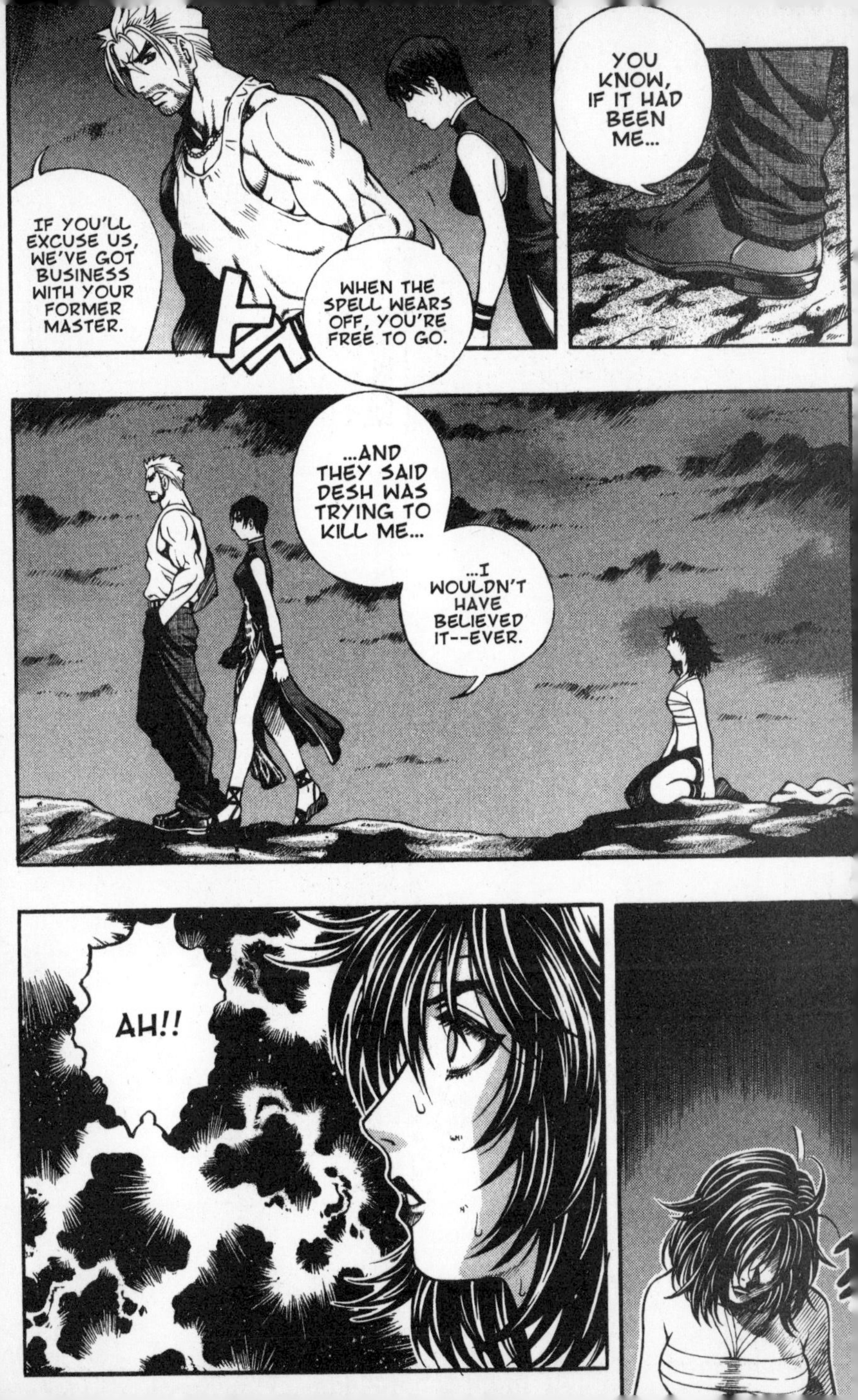
YOU KNOW, IF IT HAD BEEN ME...
IF YOU'LL EXCUSE US, WE'VE GOT BUSINESS WITH YOUR FORMER MASTER.
WHEN THE SPELL WEARS OFF, YOU'RE FREE TO GO.
...AND THEY SAID DESH WAS TRYING TO KILL ME...
...I WOULDN'T HAVE BELIEVED IT--EVER.
AH!!

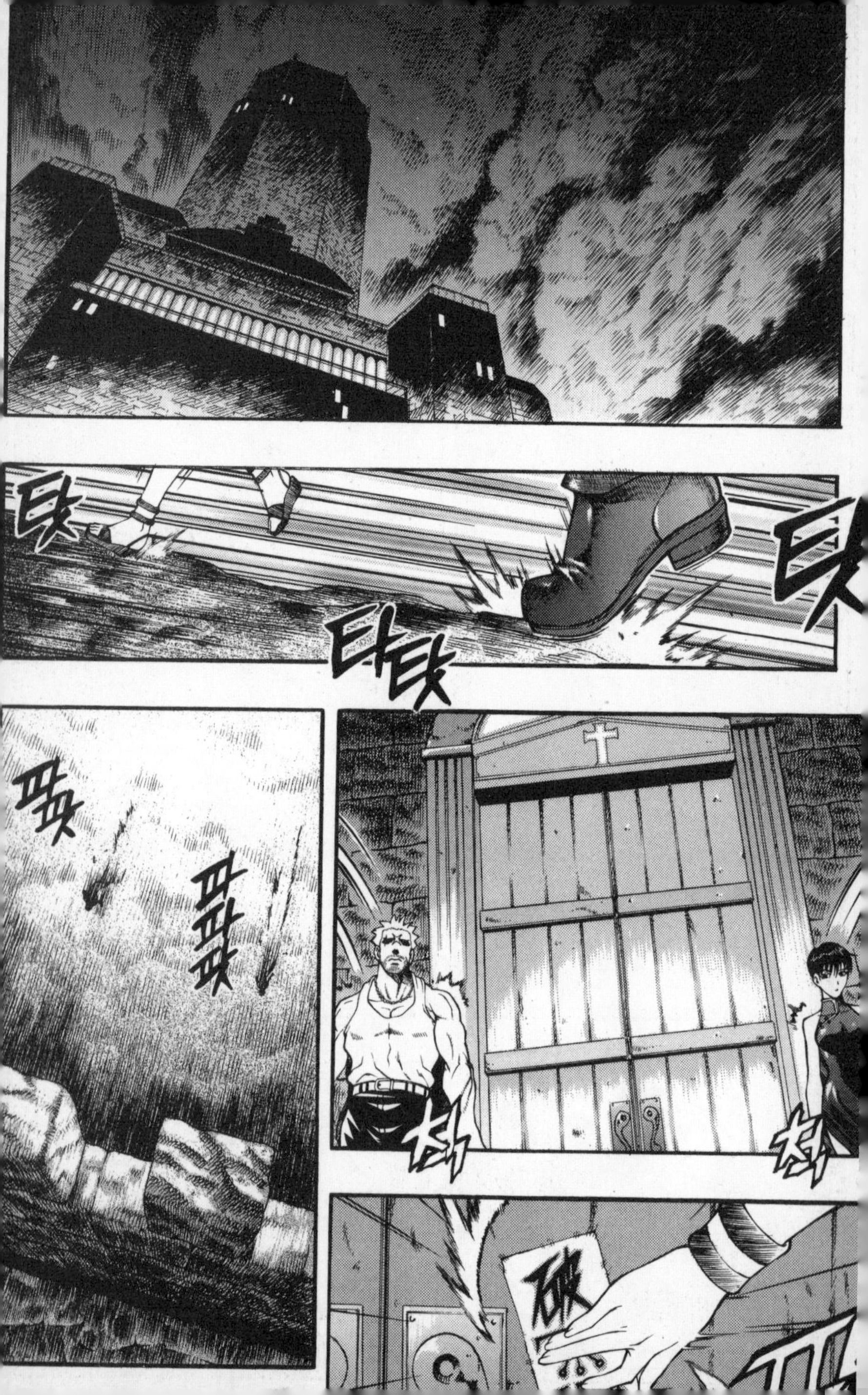
탁
탁
타탁
팍
팍팍
척
척
破

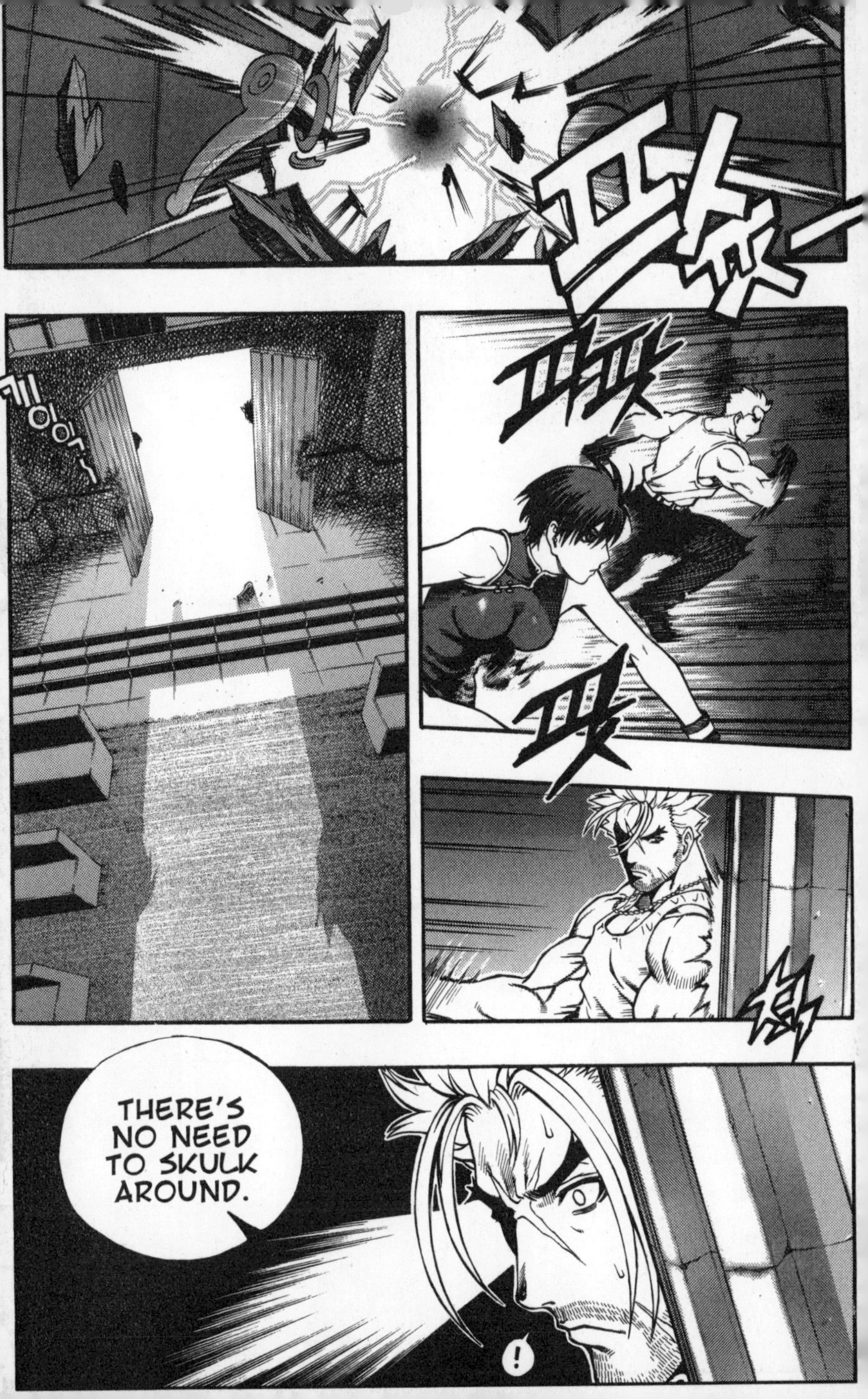
THERE'S NO NEED TO SKULK AROUND.
!

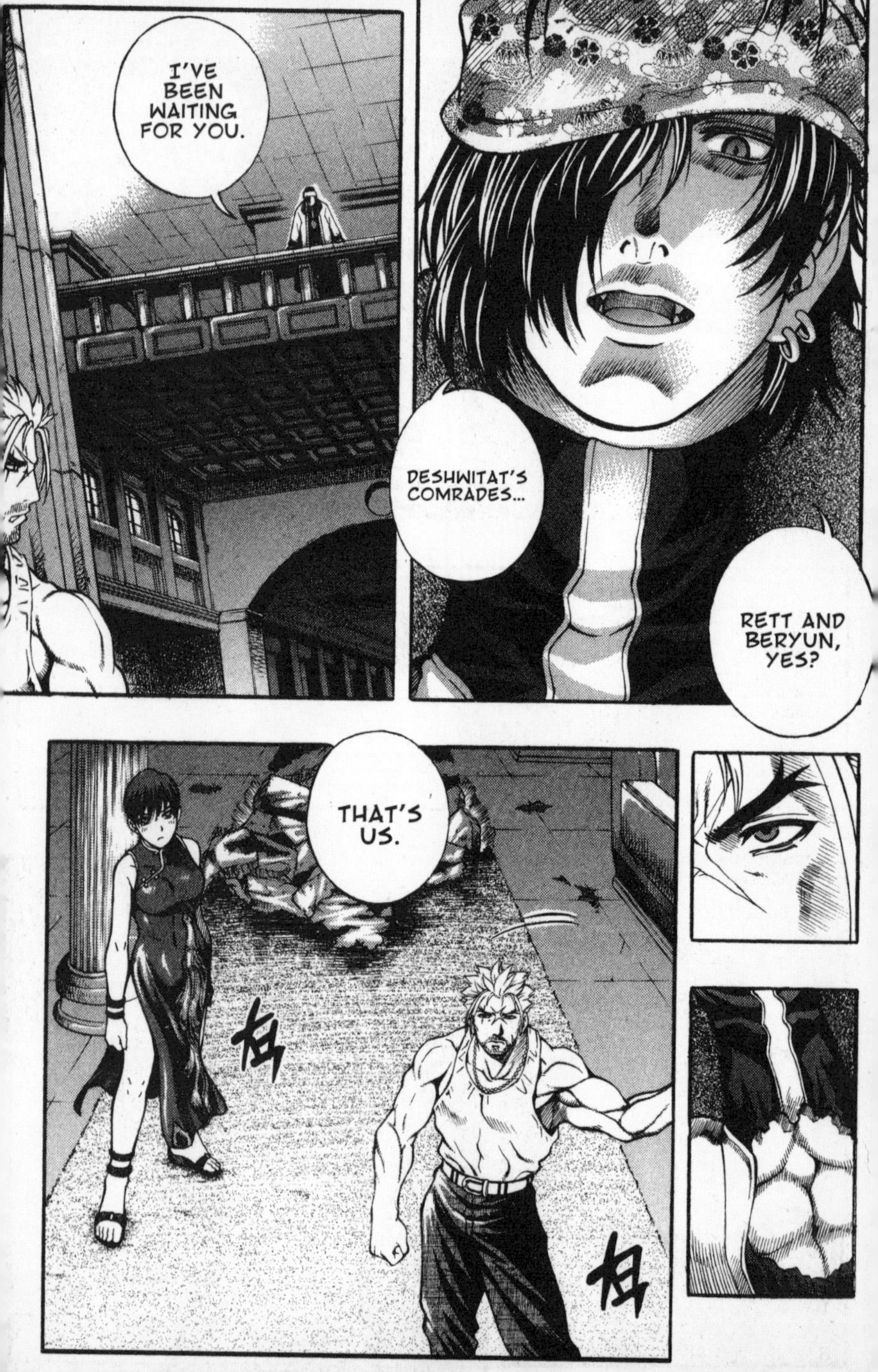
I'VE BEEN WAITING FOR YOU.
DESHWITAT'S COMRADES...
RETT AND BERYUN, YES?
THAT'S US.

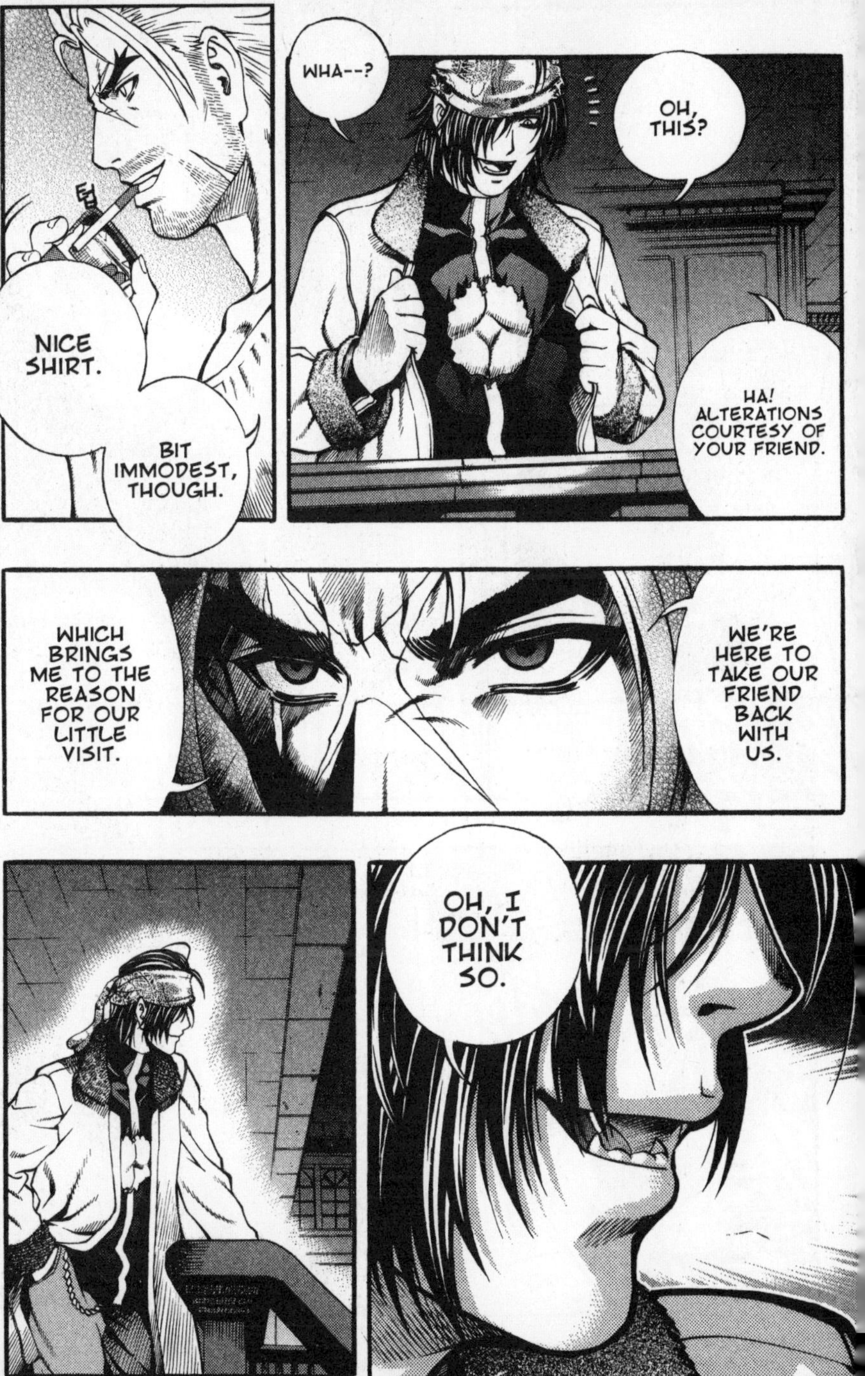
NICE SHIRT.
BIT IMMODEST, THOUGH.
WHA--?
OH, THIS?
HA! ALTERATIONS COURTESY OF YOUR FRIEND.
WHICH BRINGS ME TO THE REASON FOR OUR LITTLE VISIT.
WE'RE HERE TO TAKE OUR FRIEND BACK WITH US.
OH, I DON'T THINK SO.

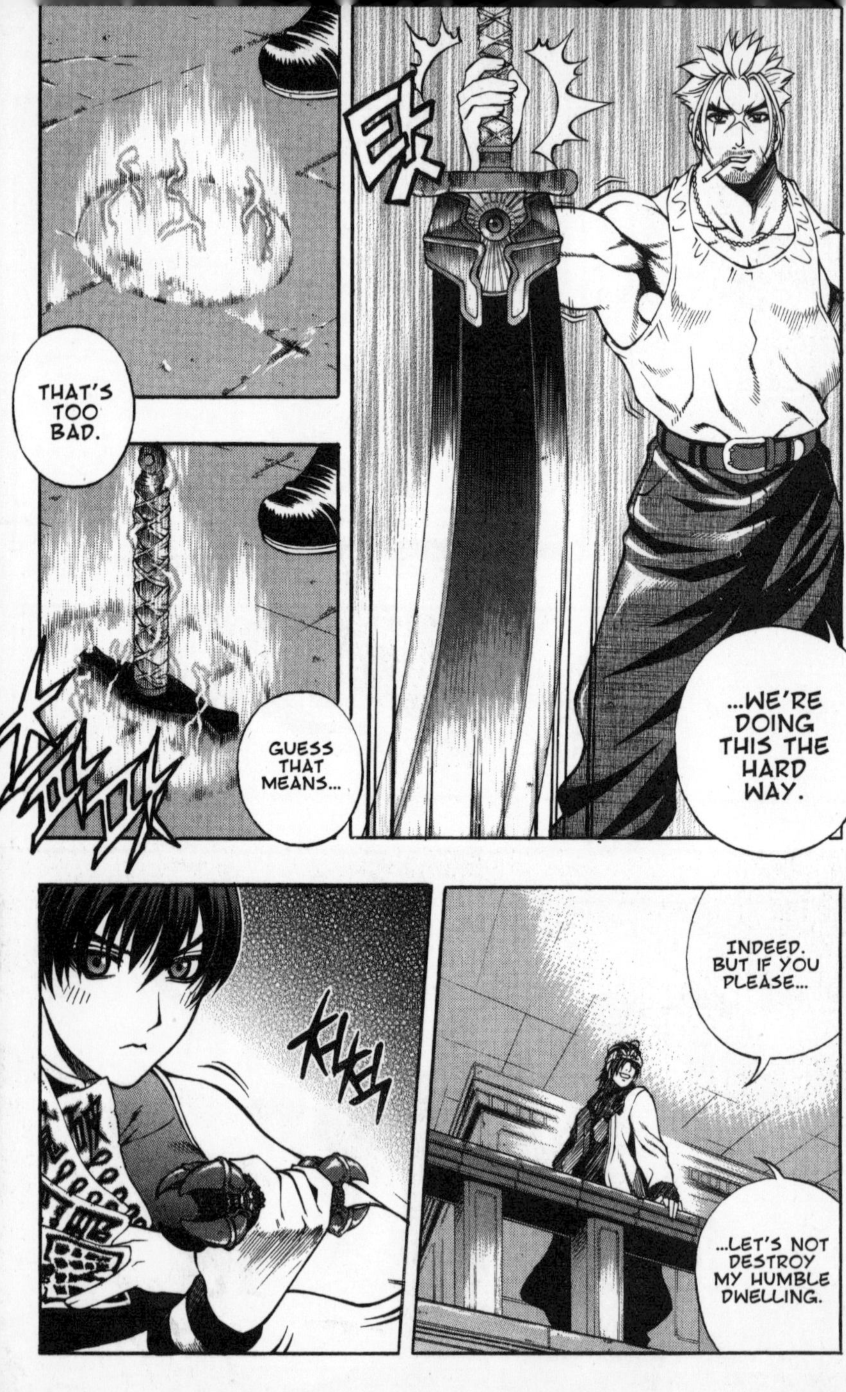
THAT'S TOO BAD.
GUESS THAT MEANS...
...WE'RE DOING THIS THE HARD WAY.
INDEED. BUT IF YOU PLEASE...
...LET'S NOT DESTROY MY HUMBLE DWELLING.

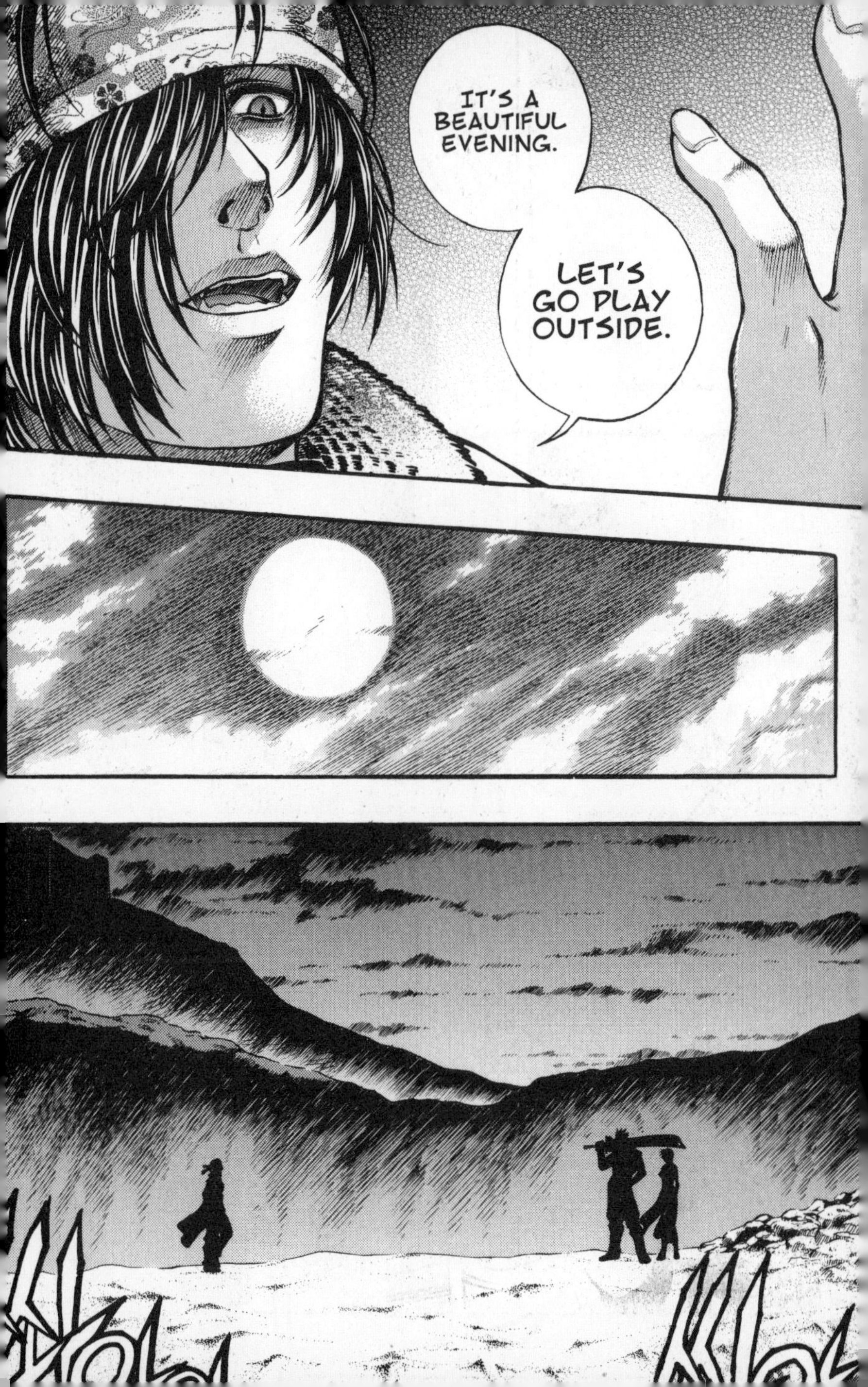
IT'S A BEAUTIFUL EVENING.
LET'S GO PLAY OUTSIDE.

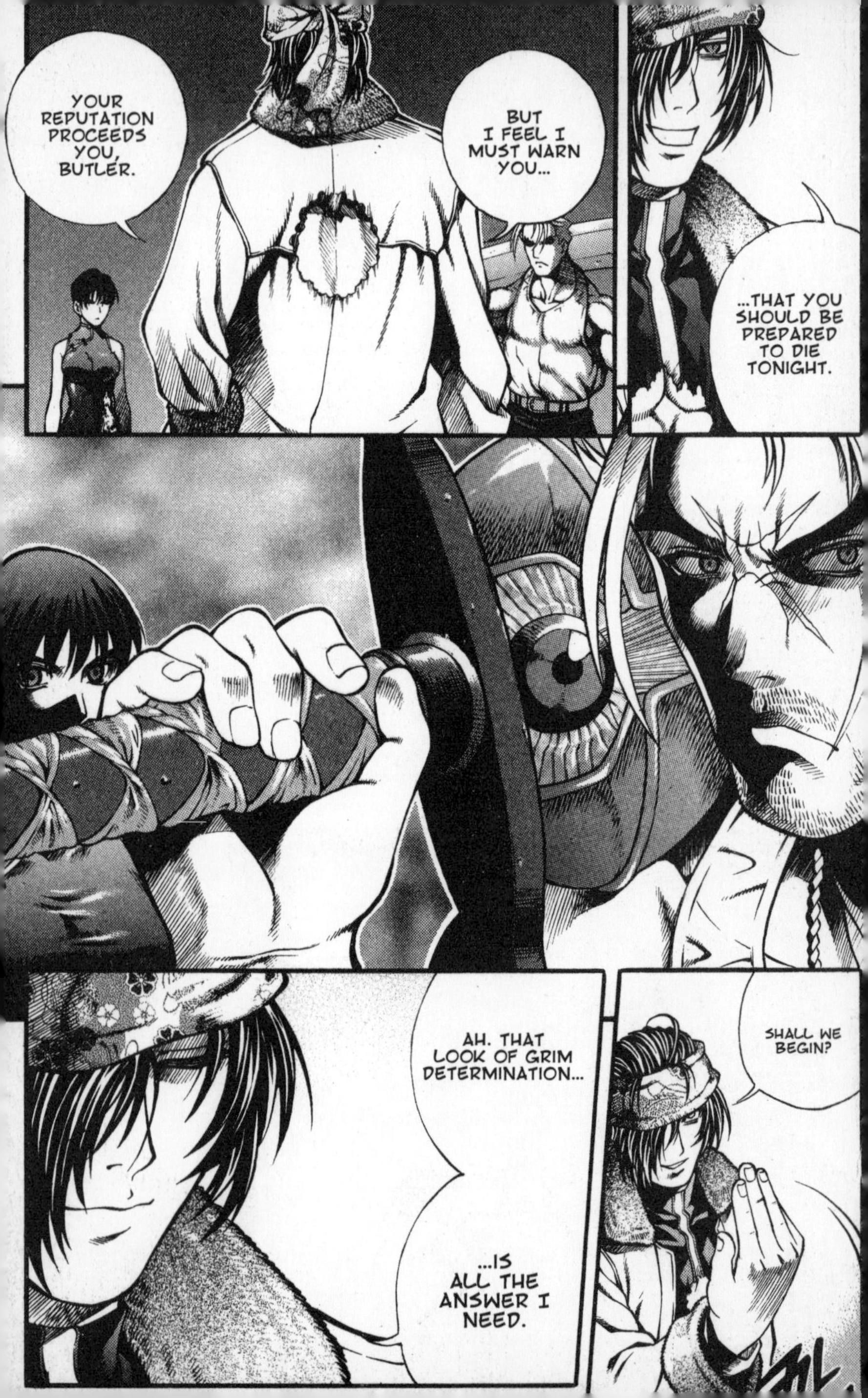
YOUR REPUTATION PROCEEDS YOU, BUTLER.
BUT I FEEL I MUST WARN YOU...
...THAT YOU SHOULD BE PREPARED TO DIE TONIGHT.
AH. THAT LOOK OF GRIM DETERMINATION...
...IS ALL THE ANSWER I NEED.
SHALL WE BEGIN?

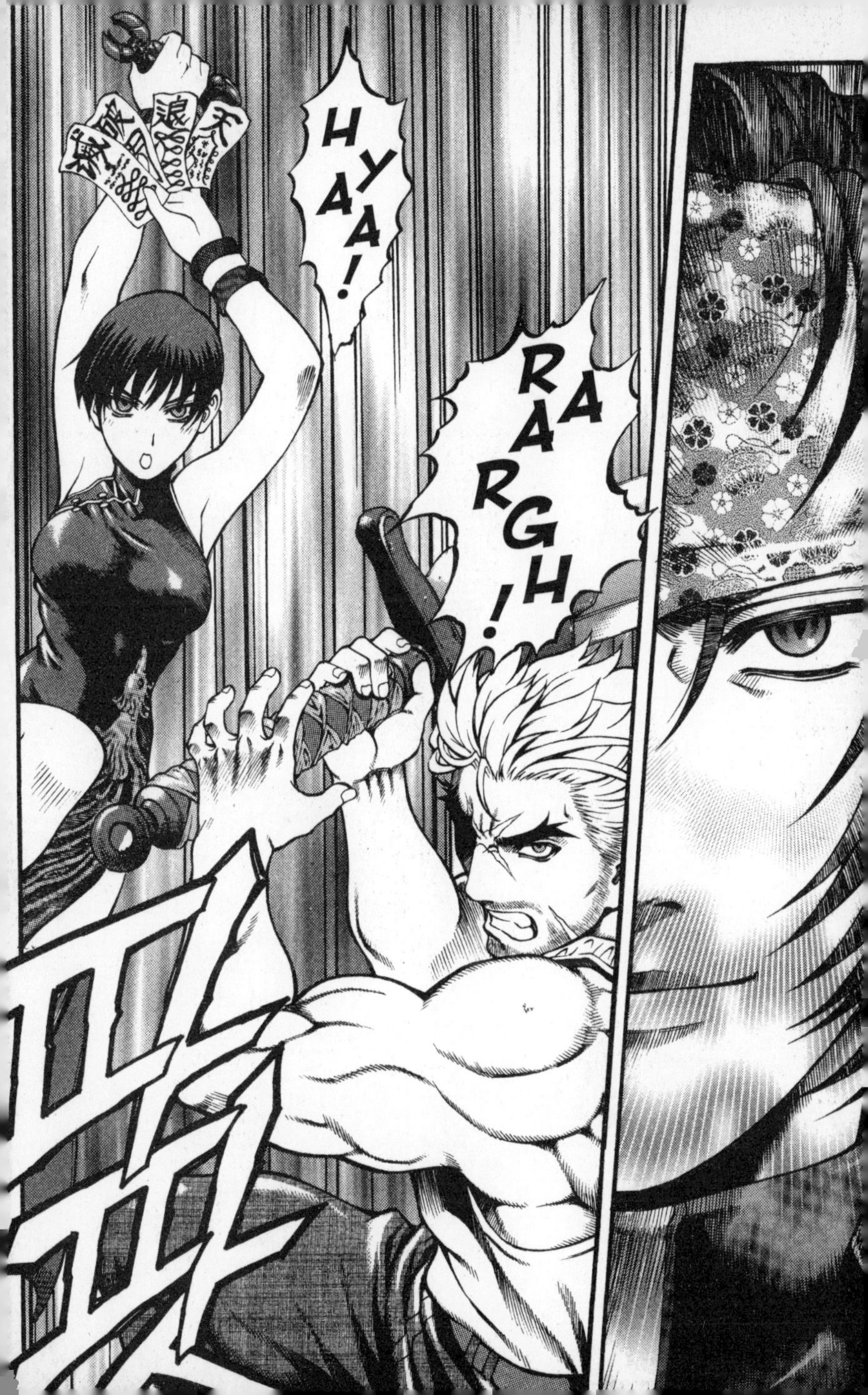
HYAA!
RAARGH!

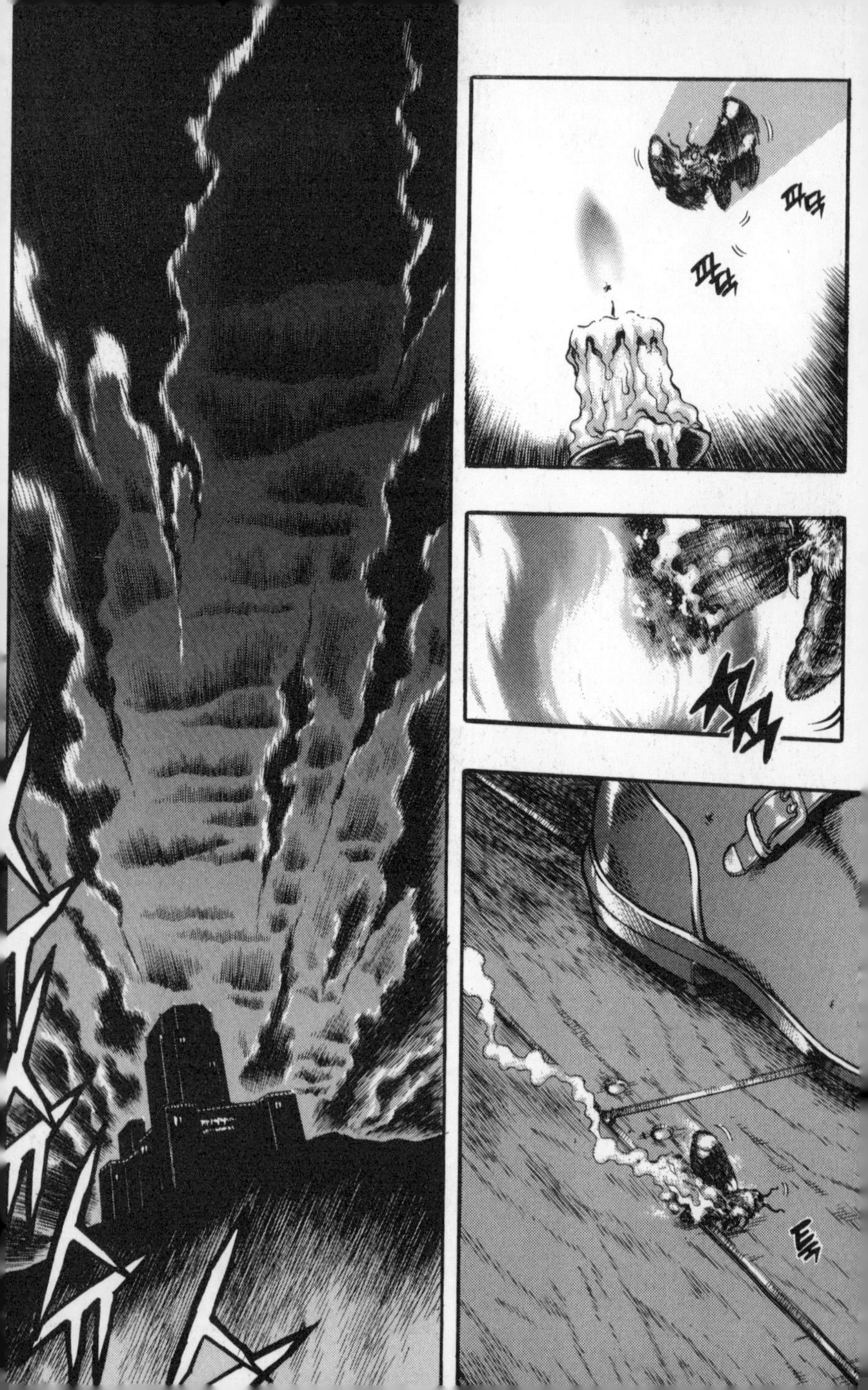
파닥
파닥
틱

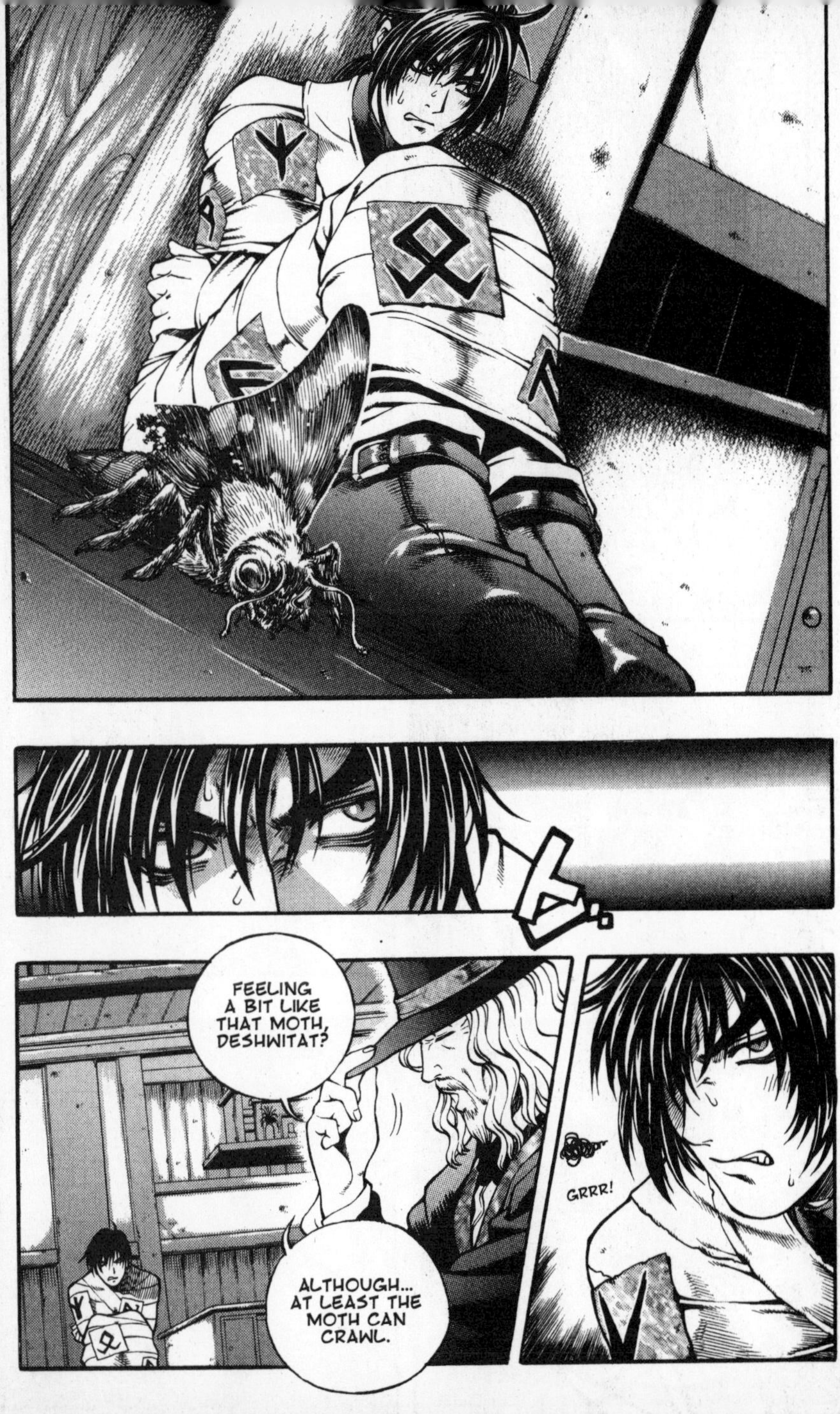

FEELING A BIT LIKE THAT MOTH, DESHWITAT?
ALTHOUGH... AT LEAST THE MOTH CAN CRAWL.
GRRR!

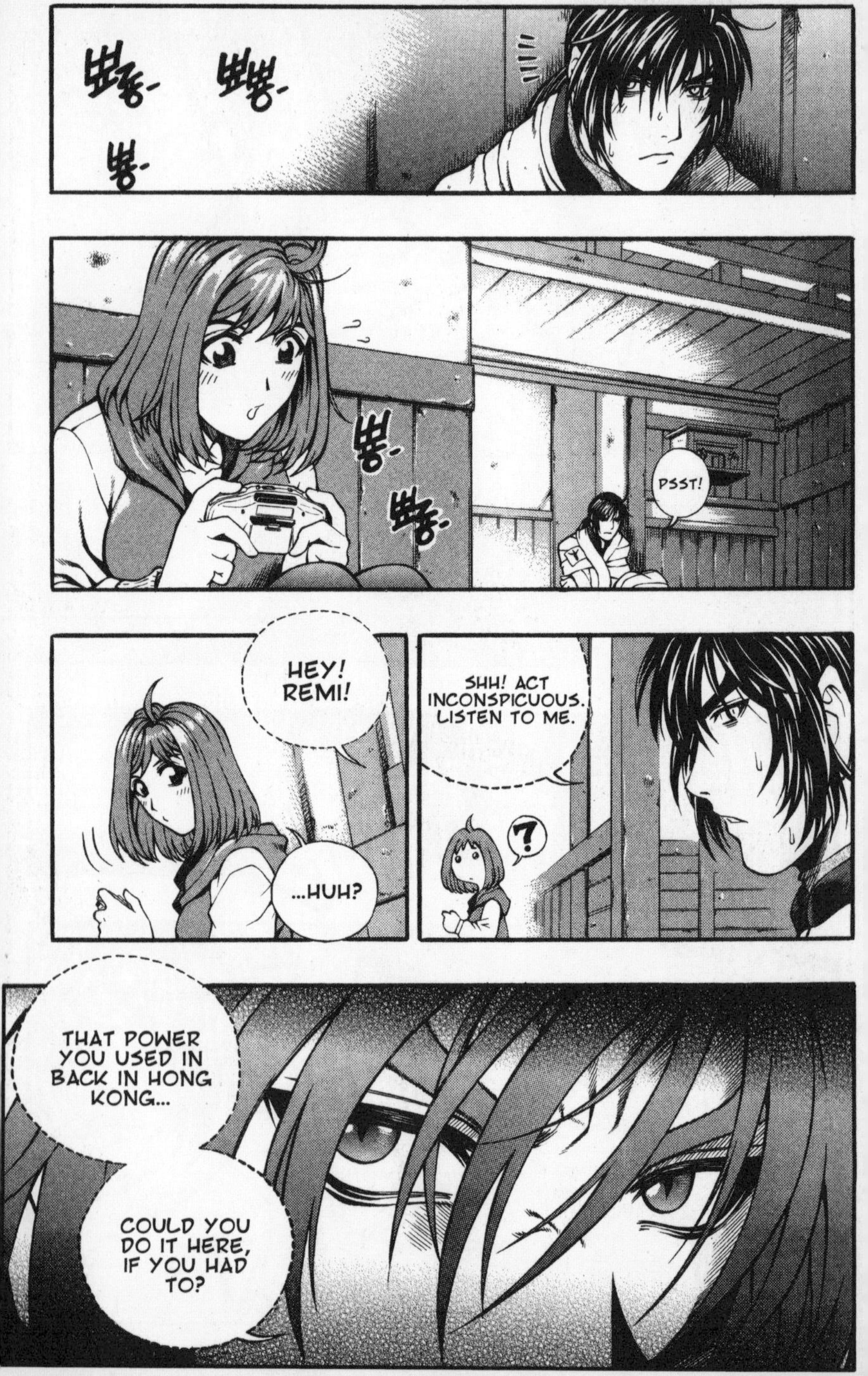
PSST!
HEY! REMI!
...HUH?
SHH! ACT INCONSPICUOUS. LISTEN TO ME.
?
THAT POWER YOU USED IN BACK IN HONG KONG...
COULD YOU DO IT HERE, IF YOU HAD TO?

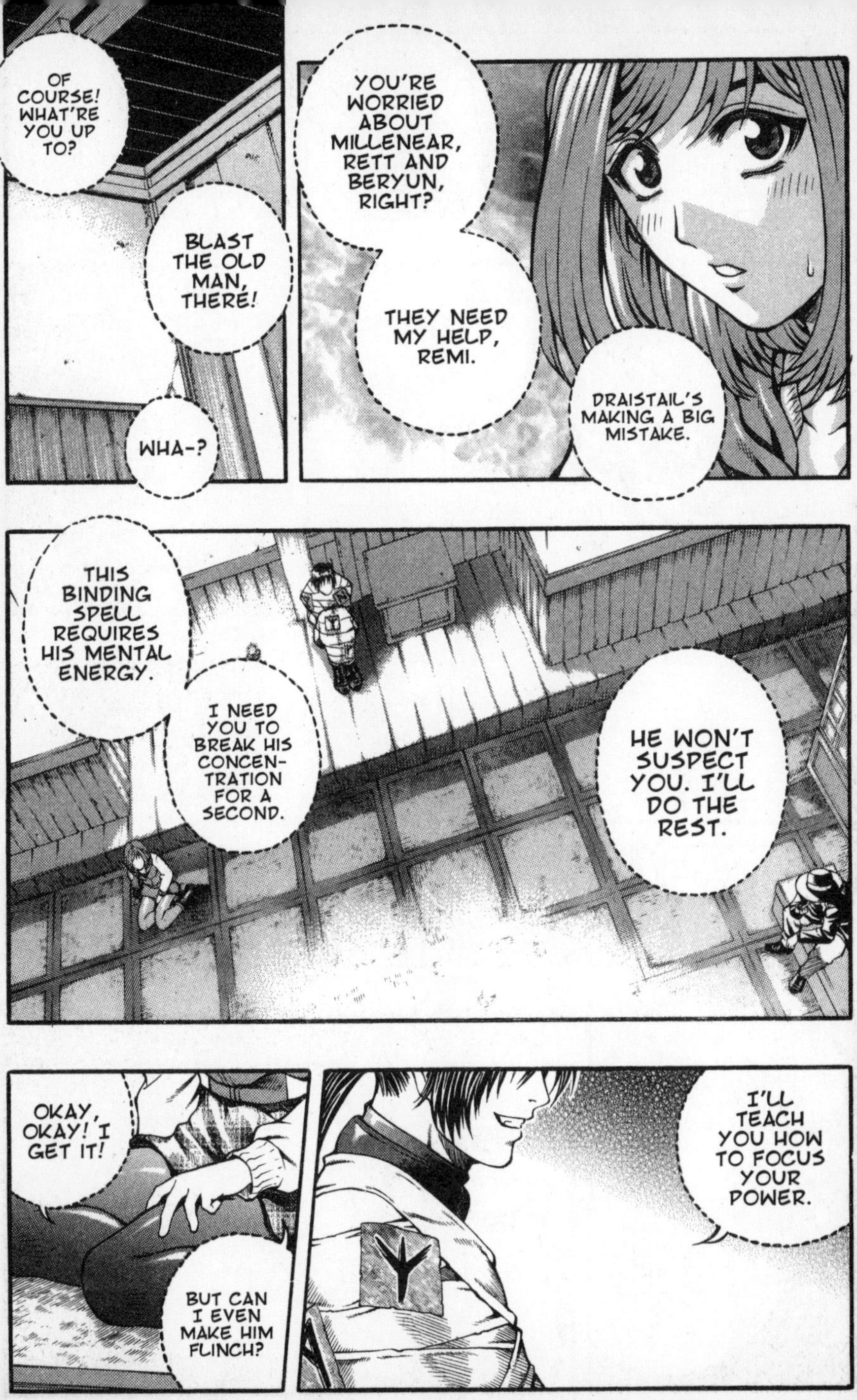
YOU'RE WORRIED ABOUT MILLENEAR, RETT AND BERYUN, RIGHT?
THEY NEED MY HELP, REMI.
DRAISTAIL'S MAKING A BIG MISTAKE.
OF COURSE! WHAT'RE YOU UP TO?
BLAST THE OLD MAN, THERE!
WHA-?
THIS BINDING SPELL REQUIRES HIS MENTAL ENERGY.
I NEED YOU TO BREAK HIS CONCEN-TRATION FOR A SECOND.
HE WON'T SUSPECT YOU. I'LL DO THE REST.
I'LL TEACH YOU HOW TO FOCUS YOUR POWER.
OKAY, OKAY! I GET IT!
BUT CAN I EVEN MAKE HIM FLINCH?

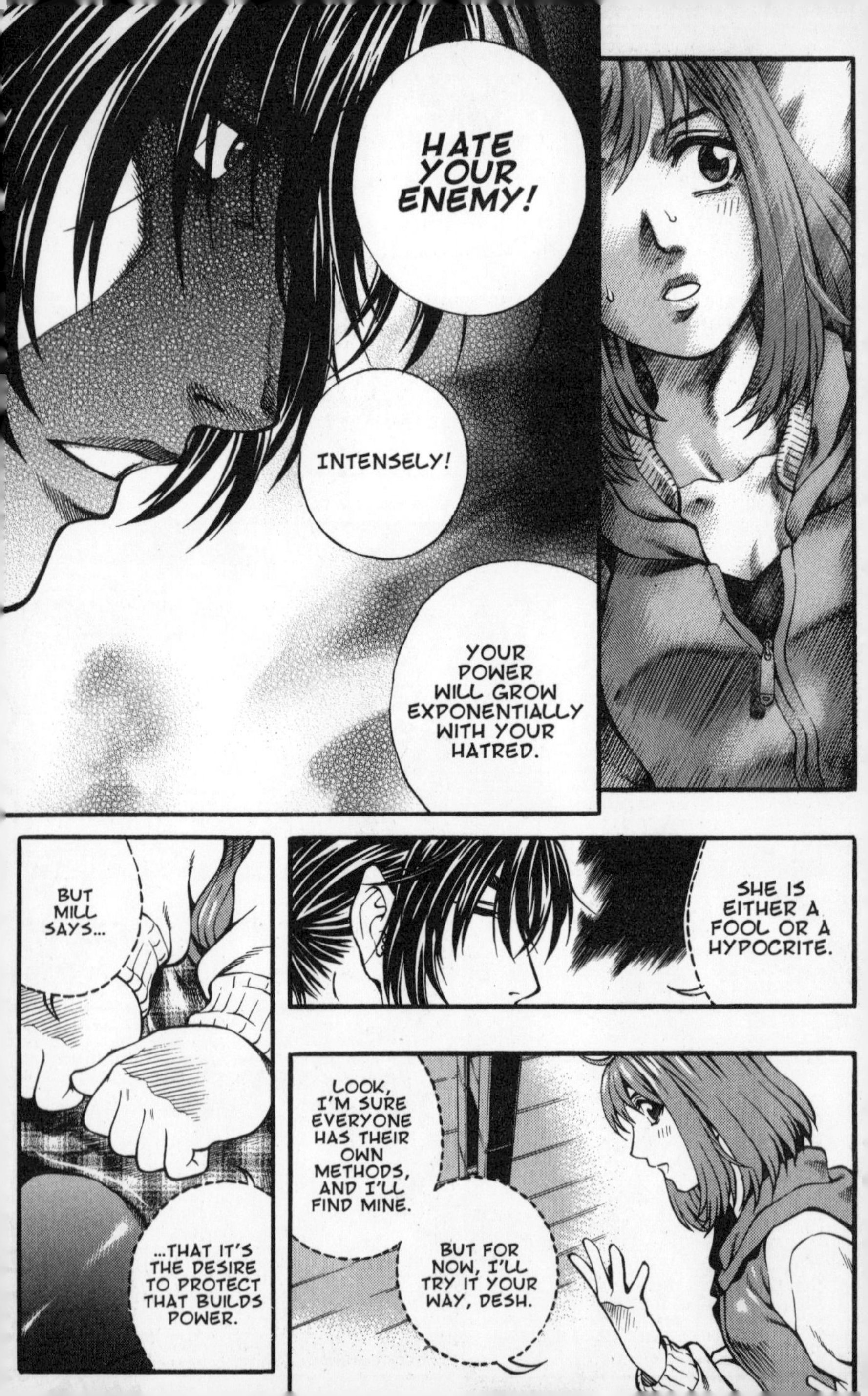
HATE YOUR ENEMY!
INTENSELY!
YOUR POWER WILL GROW EXPONENTIALLY WITH YOUR HATRED.
SHE IS EITHER A FOOL OR A HYPOCRITE.
BUT MILL SAYS...
...THAT IT'S THE DESIRE TO PROTECT THAT BUILDS POWER.
LOOK, I'M SURE EVERYONE HAS THEIR OWN METHODS, AND I'LL FIND MINE.
BUT FOR NOW, I'LL TRY IT YOUR WAY, DESH.

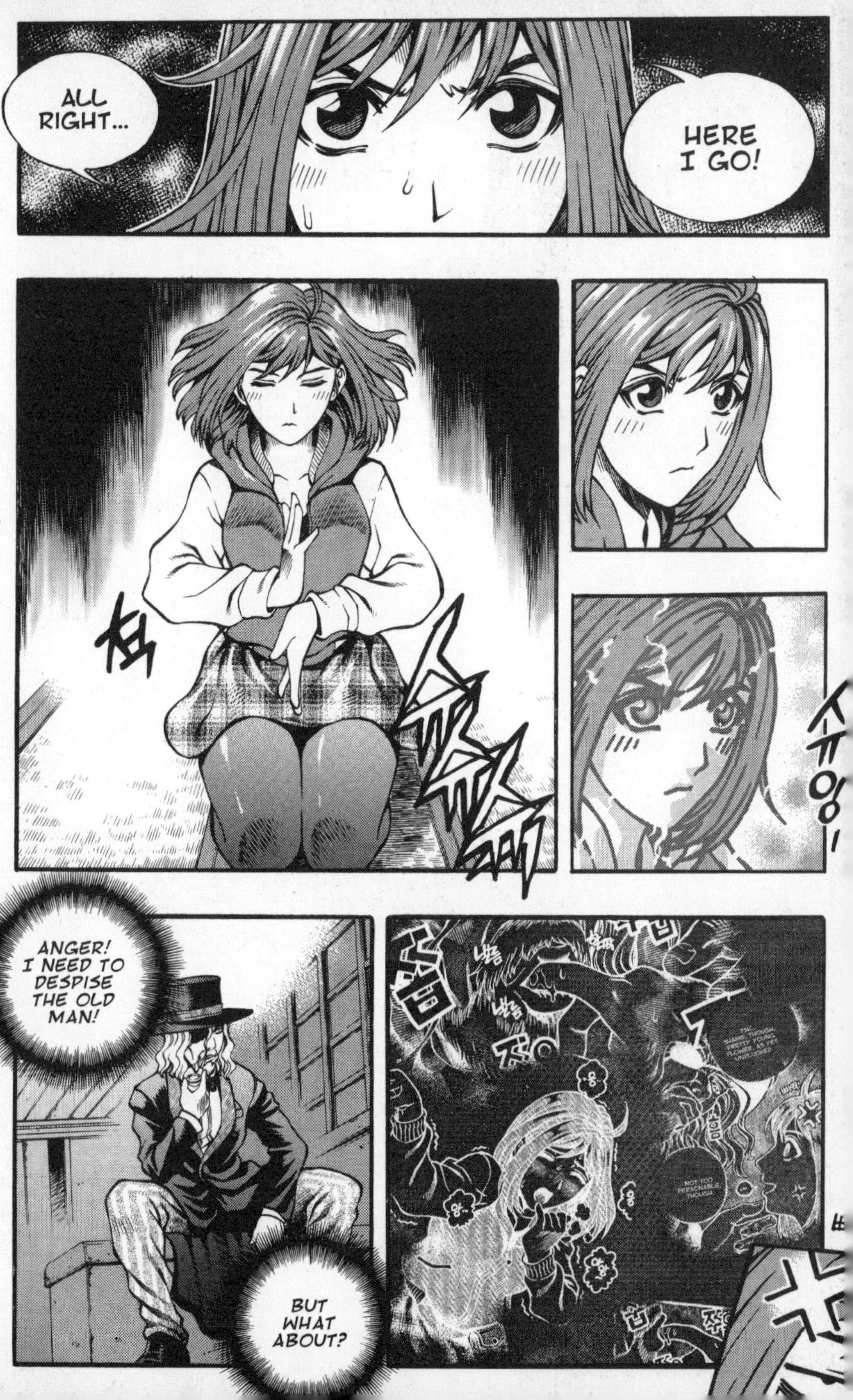
HERE I GO!
ALL RIGHT...
ANGER! I NEED TO DESPISE THE OLD MAN!
BUT WHAT ABOUT?
TSK. SHAME, THOUGH. PRETTY YOUNG FLOWER AS YET UNPLUCKED
NOT TOO PERSONABLE THOUGH

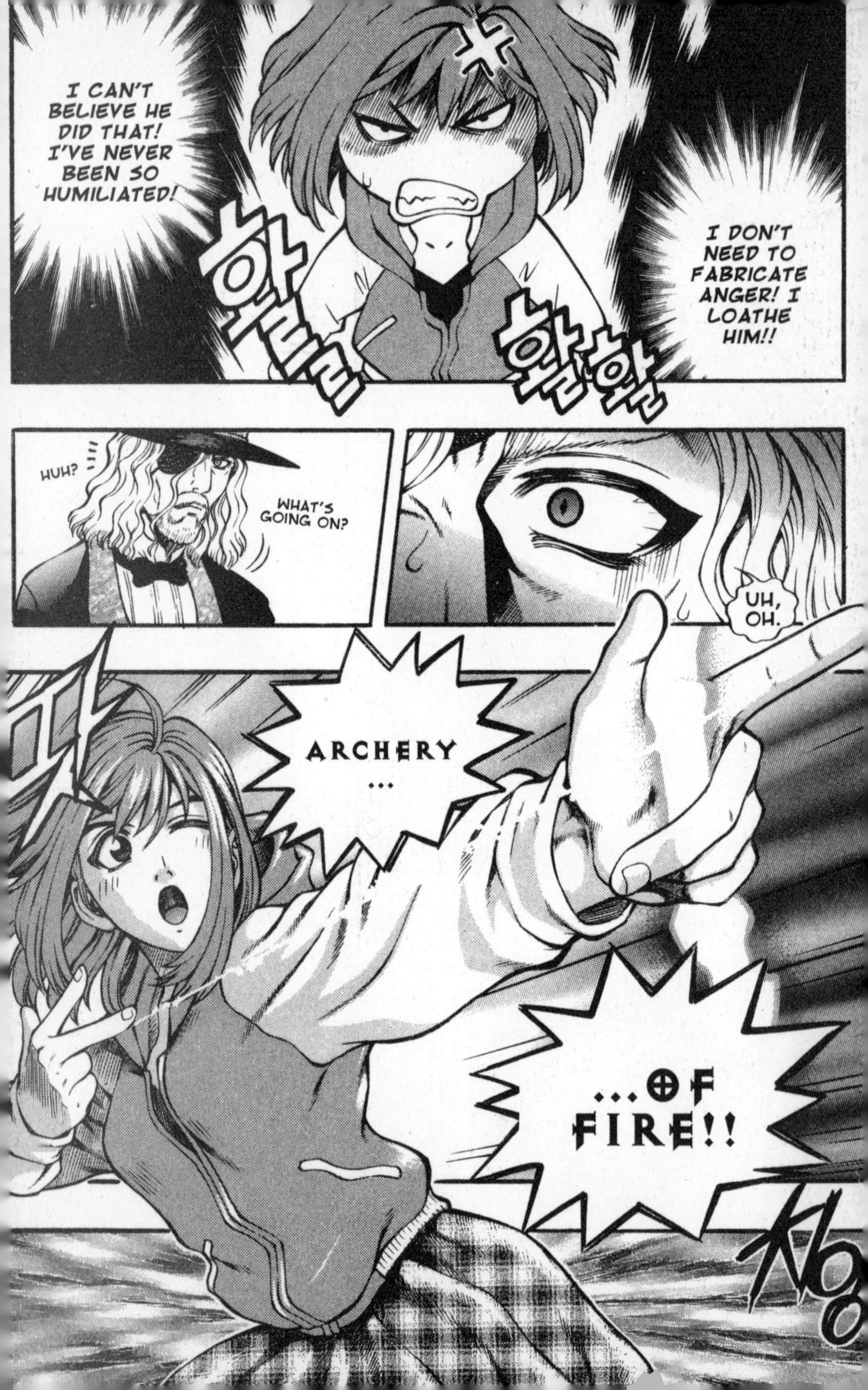
I CAN'T BELIEVE HE DID THAT! I'VE NEVER BEEN SO HUMILIATED!
화르르
활활
I DON'T NEED TO FABRICATE ANGER! I LOATHE HIM!!
UH, OH.
HUH?
WHAT'S GOING ON?
ARCHERY ...
...OF FIRE!!

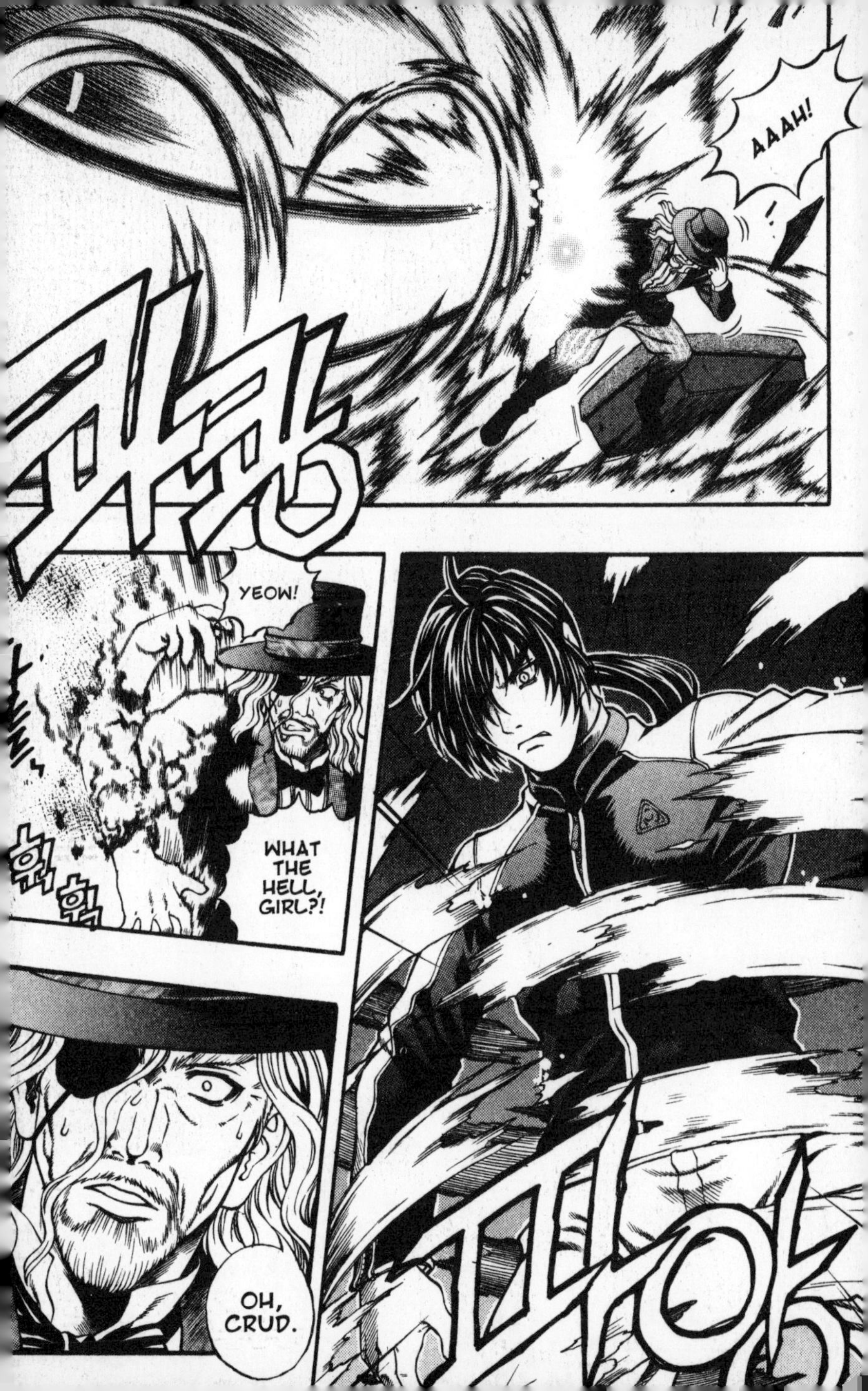
AAAH!
YEOW!
WHAT THE HELL, GIRL?!
OH, CRUD.

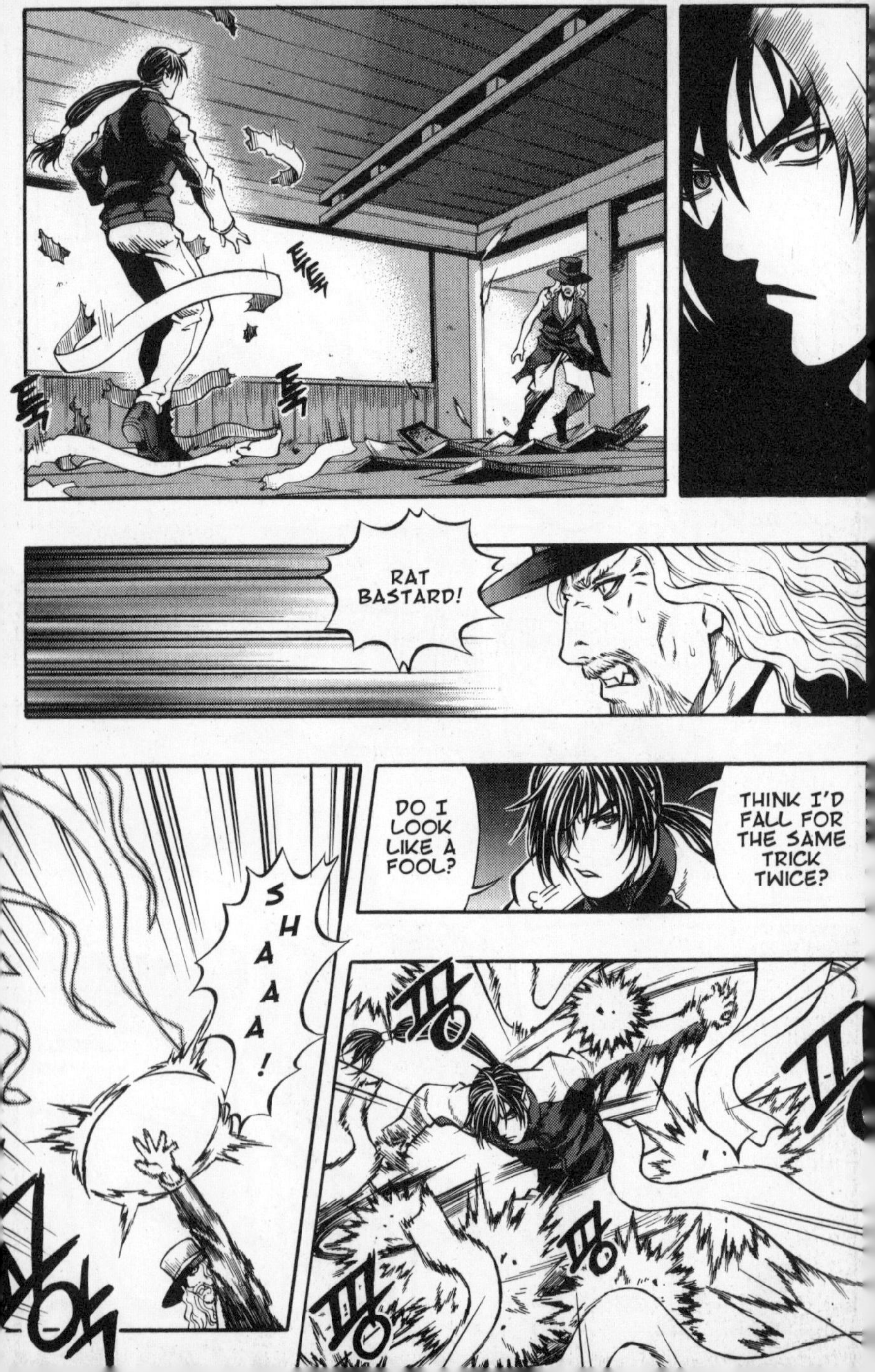
RAT BASTARD!
DO I LOOK LIKE A FOOL?
THINK I'D FALL FOR THE SAME TRICK TWICE?
SHAAAA!

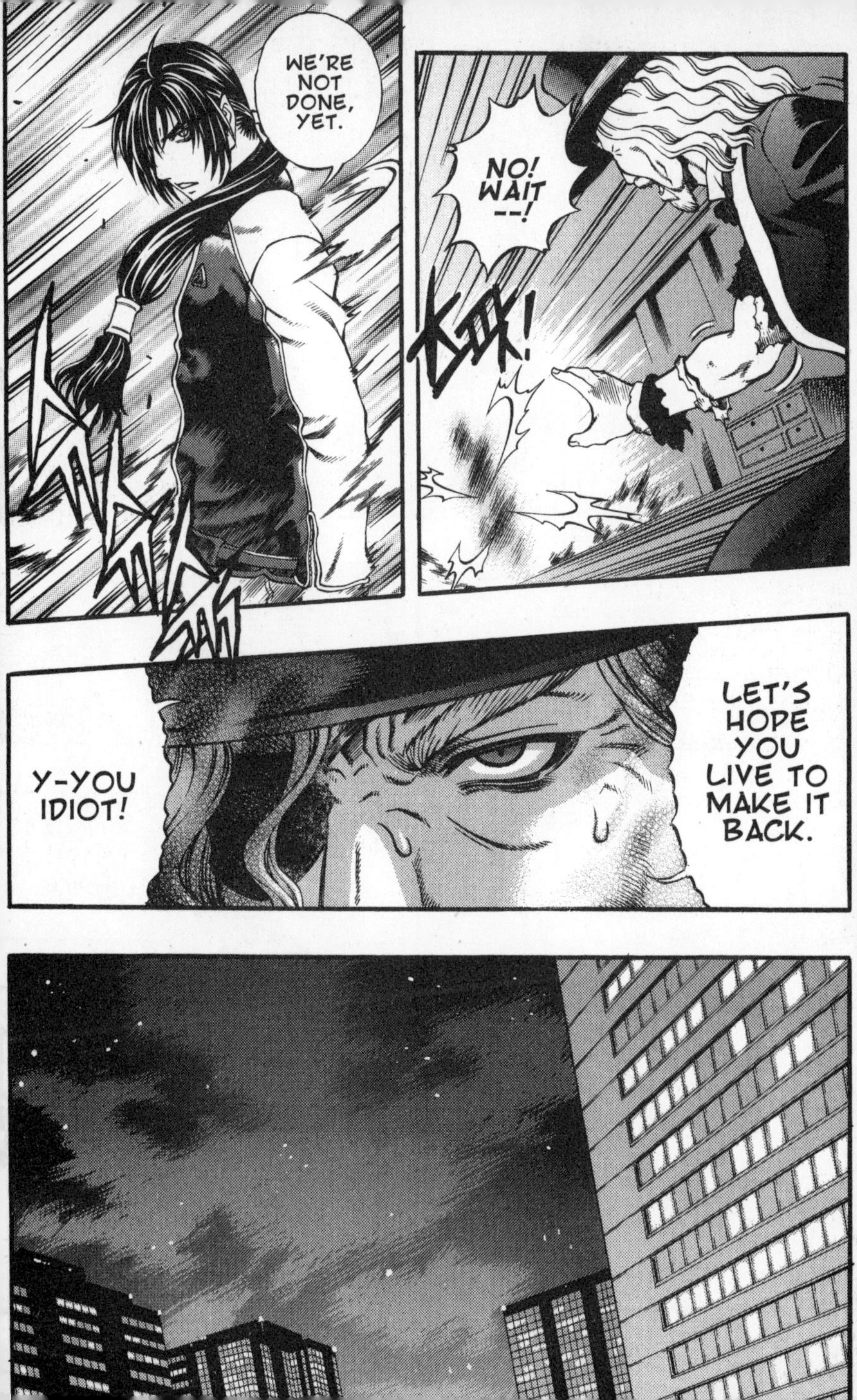
WE'RE NOT DONE, YET.
NO! WAIT--!
Y-YOU IDIOT!
LET'S HOPE YOU LIVE TO MAKE IT BACK.

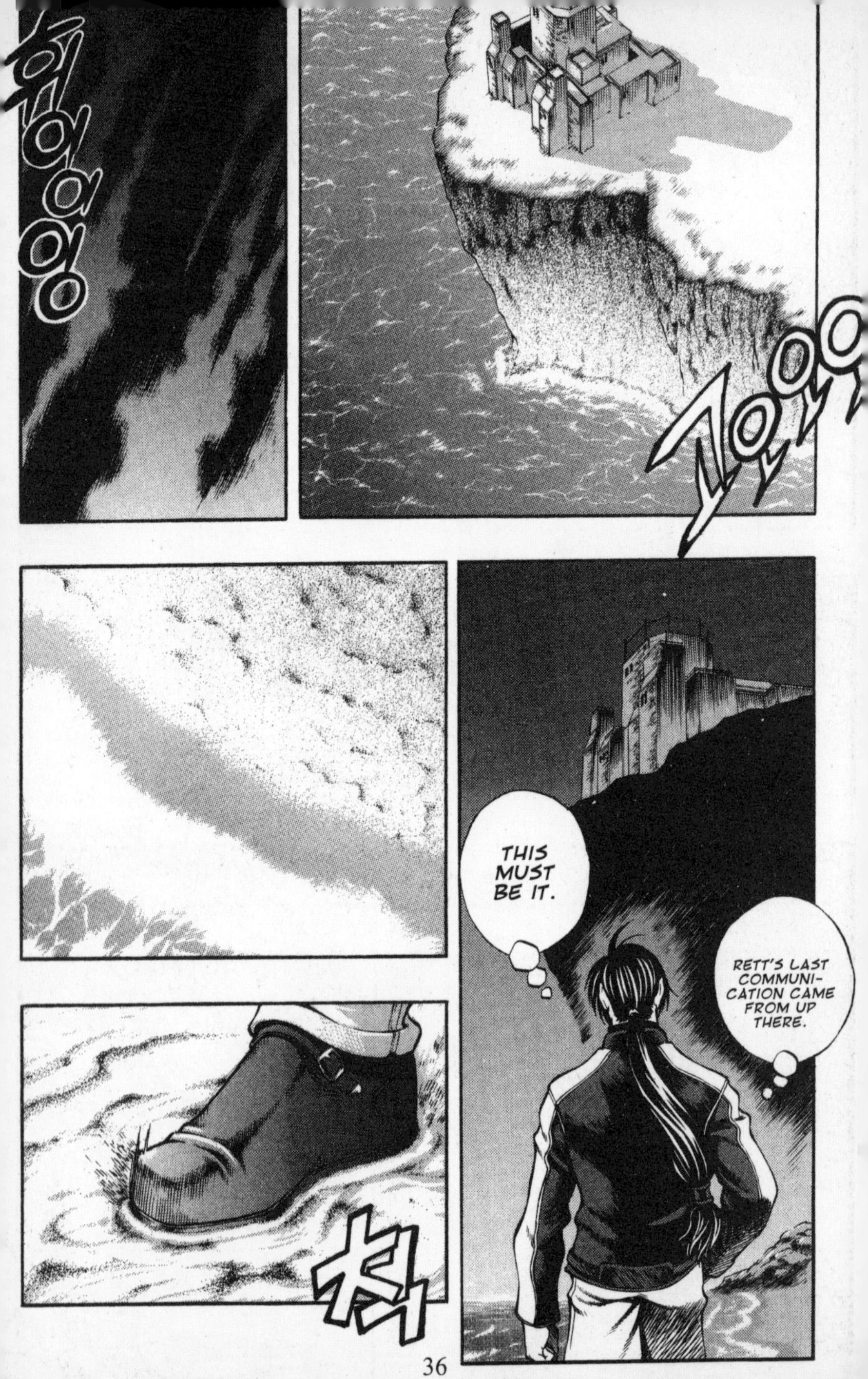
휘이이잉
THIS MUST BE IT.
RETT'S LAST COMMUNI-CATION CAME FROM UP THERE.
척

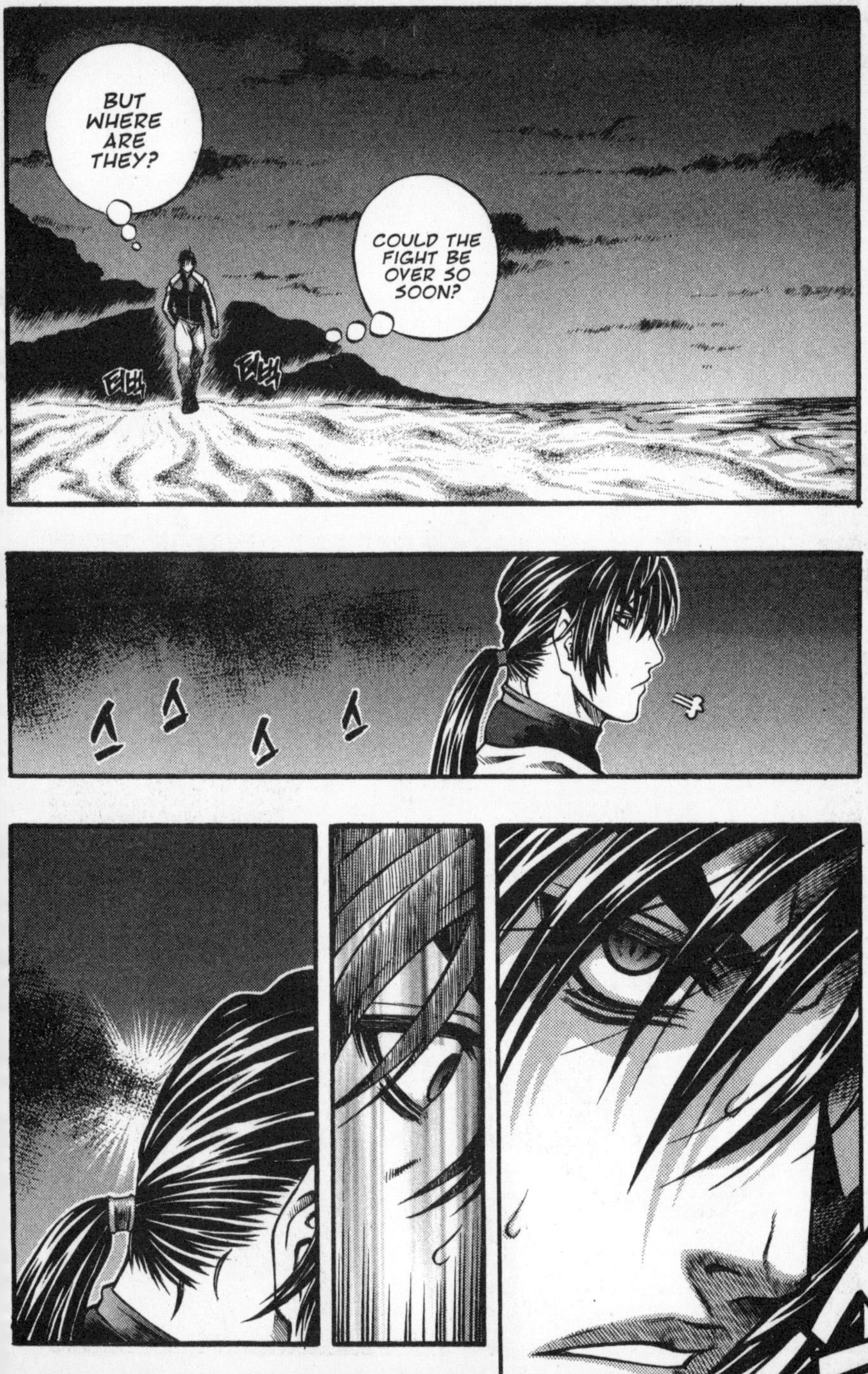
BUT WHERE ARE THEY?
COULD THE FIGHT BE OVER SO SOON?
터벅
터벅
스
스
스
스

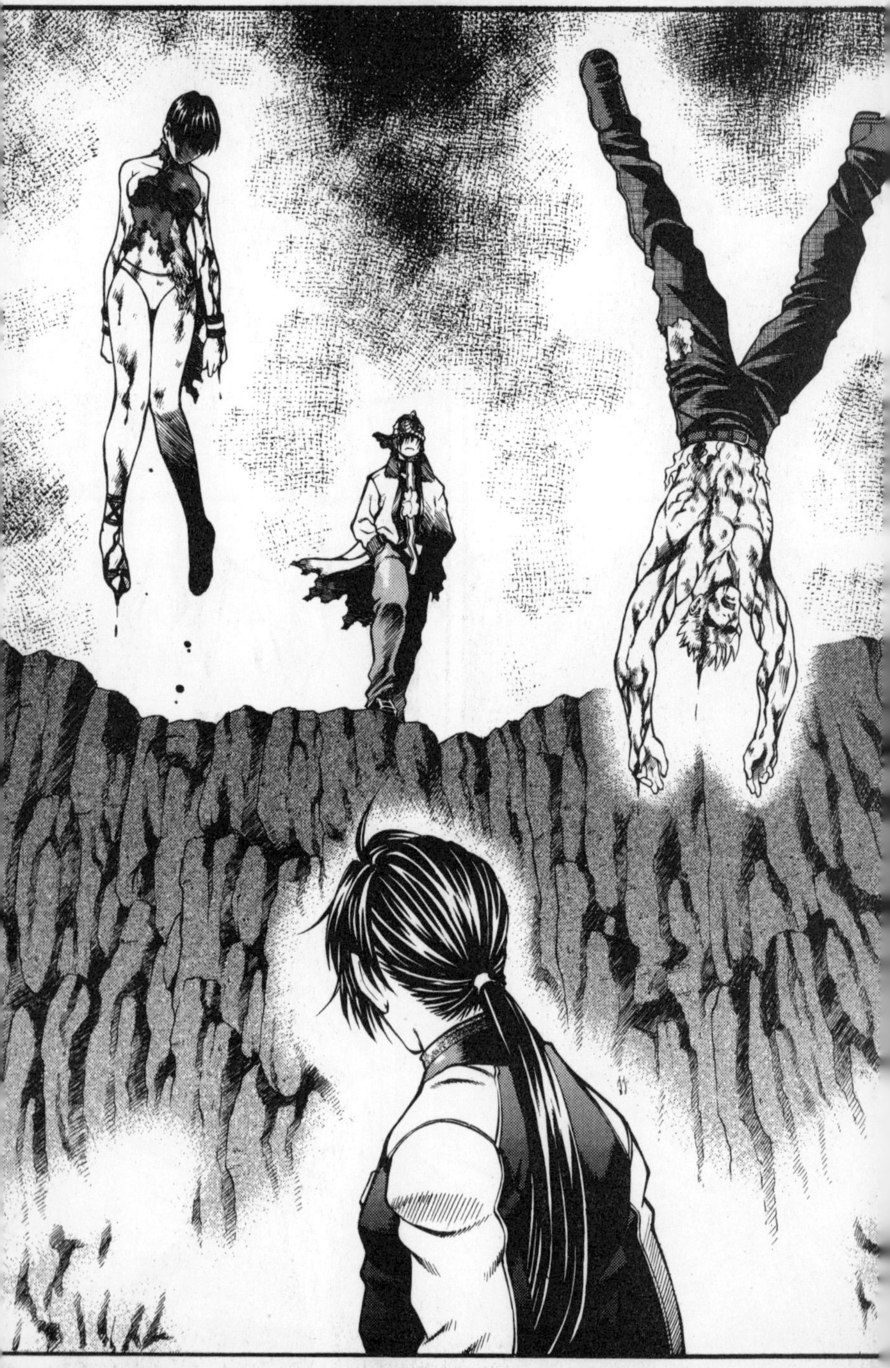

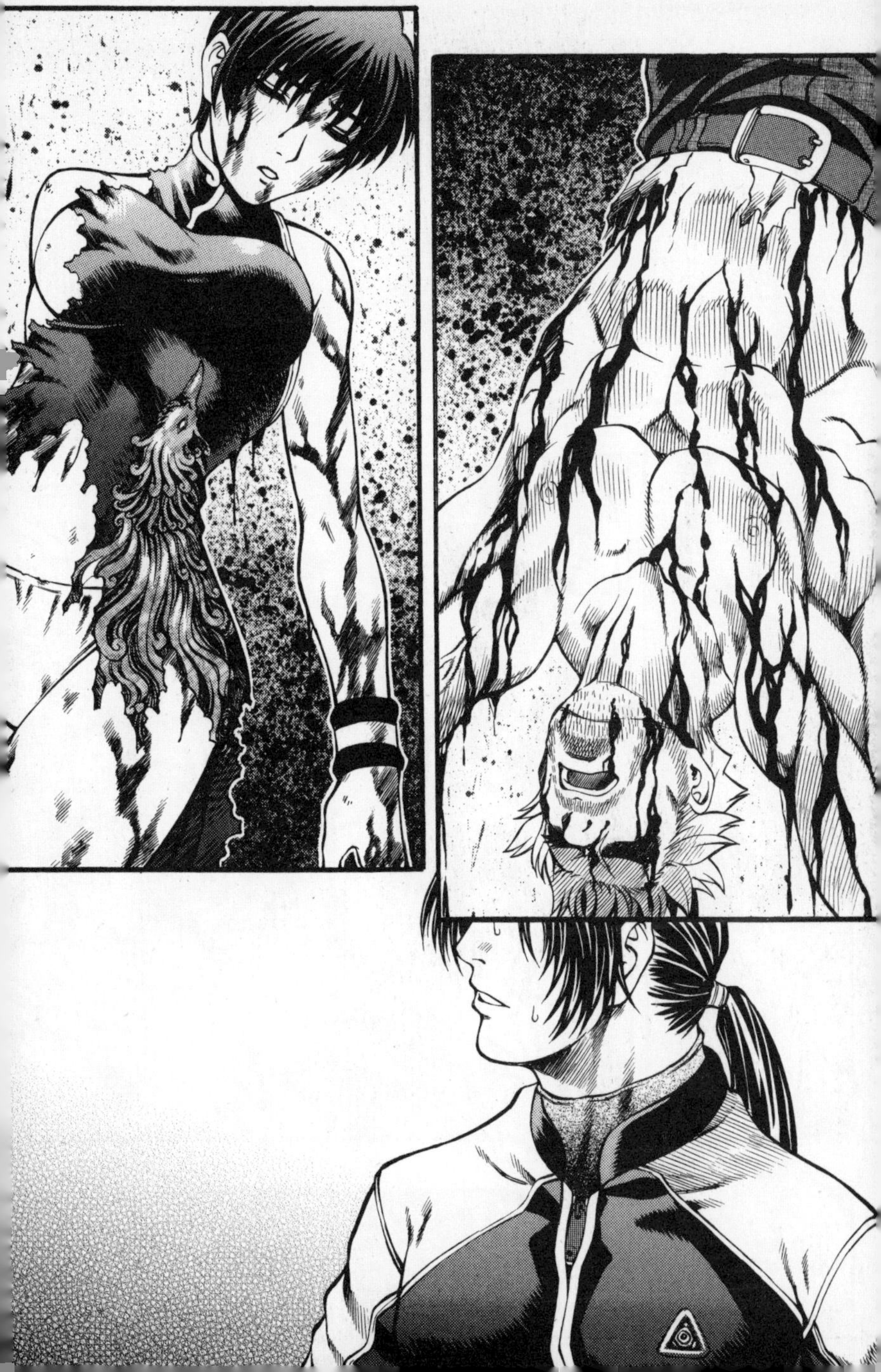

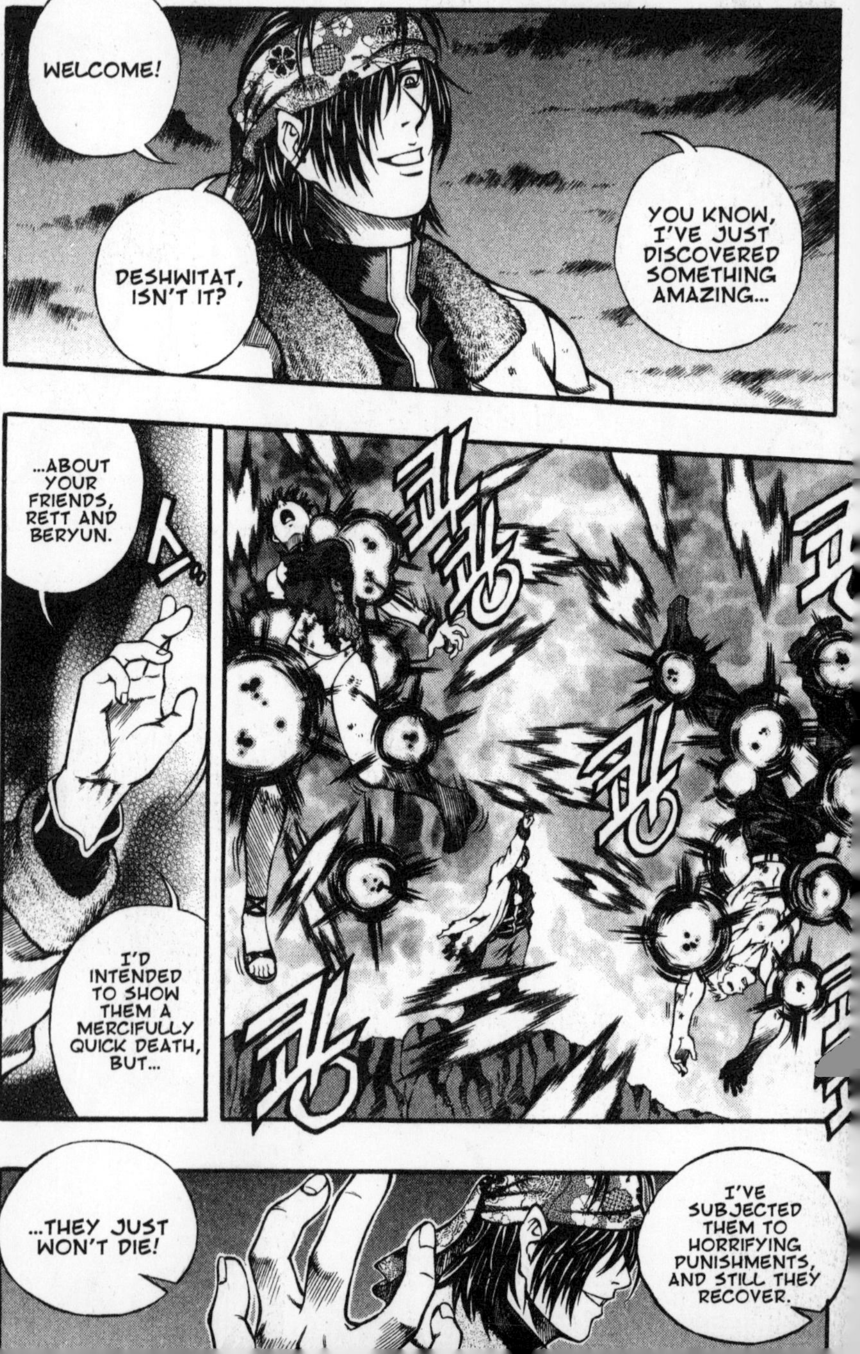
WELCOME!
DESHWITAT, ISN'T IT?
YOU KNOW, I'VE JUST DISCOVERED SOMETHING AMAZING...
...ABOUT YOUR FRIENDS, RETT AND BERYUN.
I'D INTENDED TO SHOW THEM A MERCIFULLY QUICK DEATH, BUT...
...THEY JUST WON'T DIE!
I'VE SUBJECTED THEM TO HORRIFYING PUNISHMENTS, AND STILL THEY RECOVER.

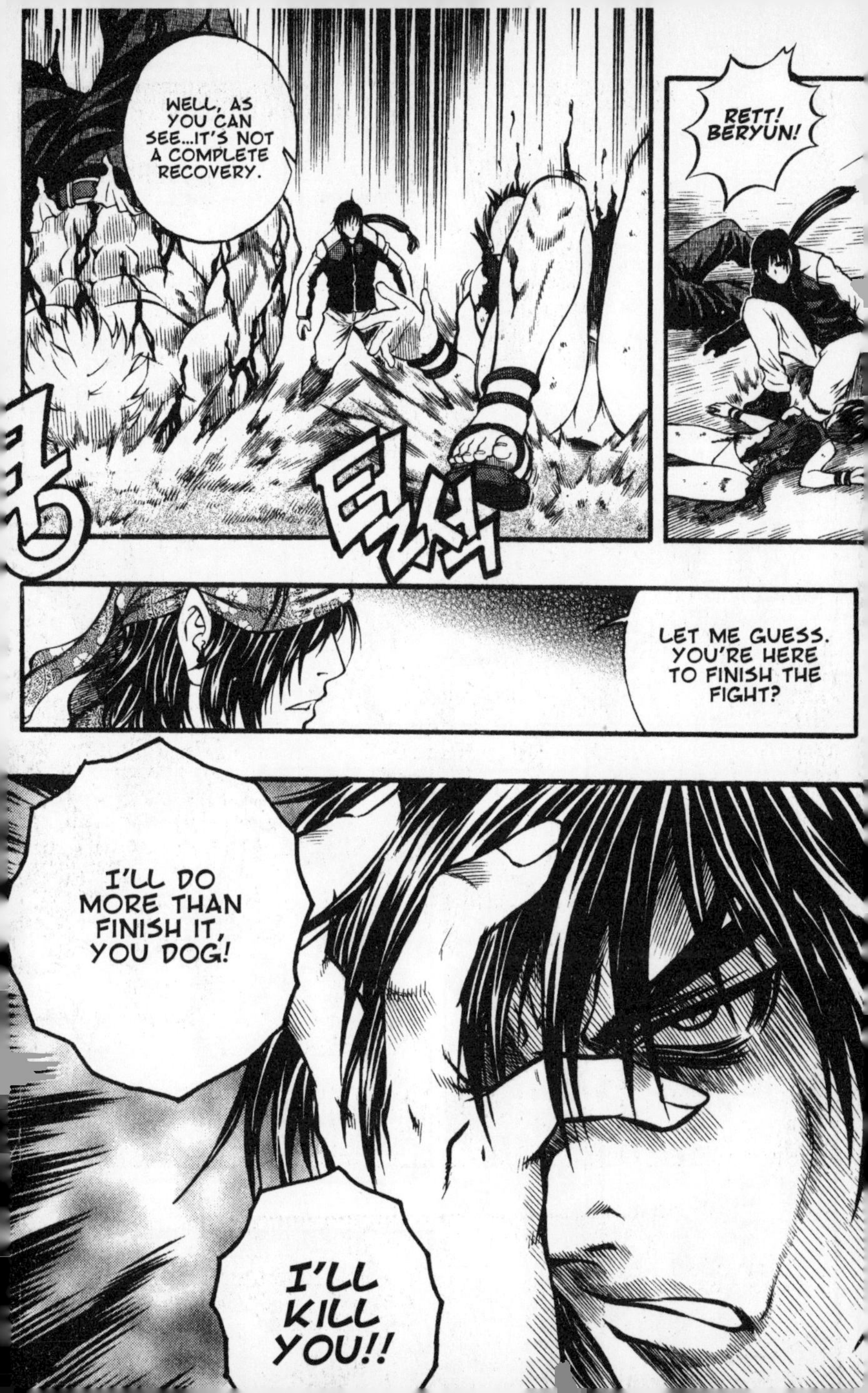
RETT! BERYUN!
WELL, AS YOU CAN SEE...IT'S NOT A COMPLETE RECOVERY.
LET ME GUESS. YOU'RE HERE TO FINISH THE FIGHT?
I'LL DO MORE THAN FINISH IT, YOU DOG!
I'LL KILL YOU!!

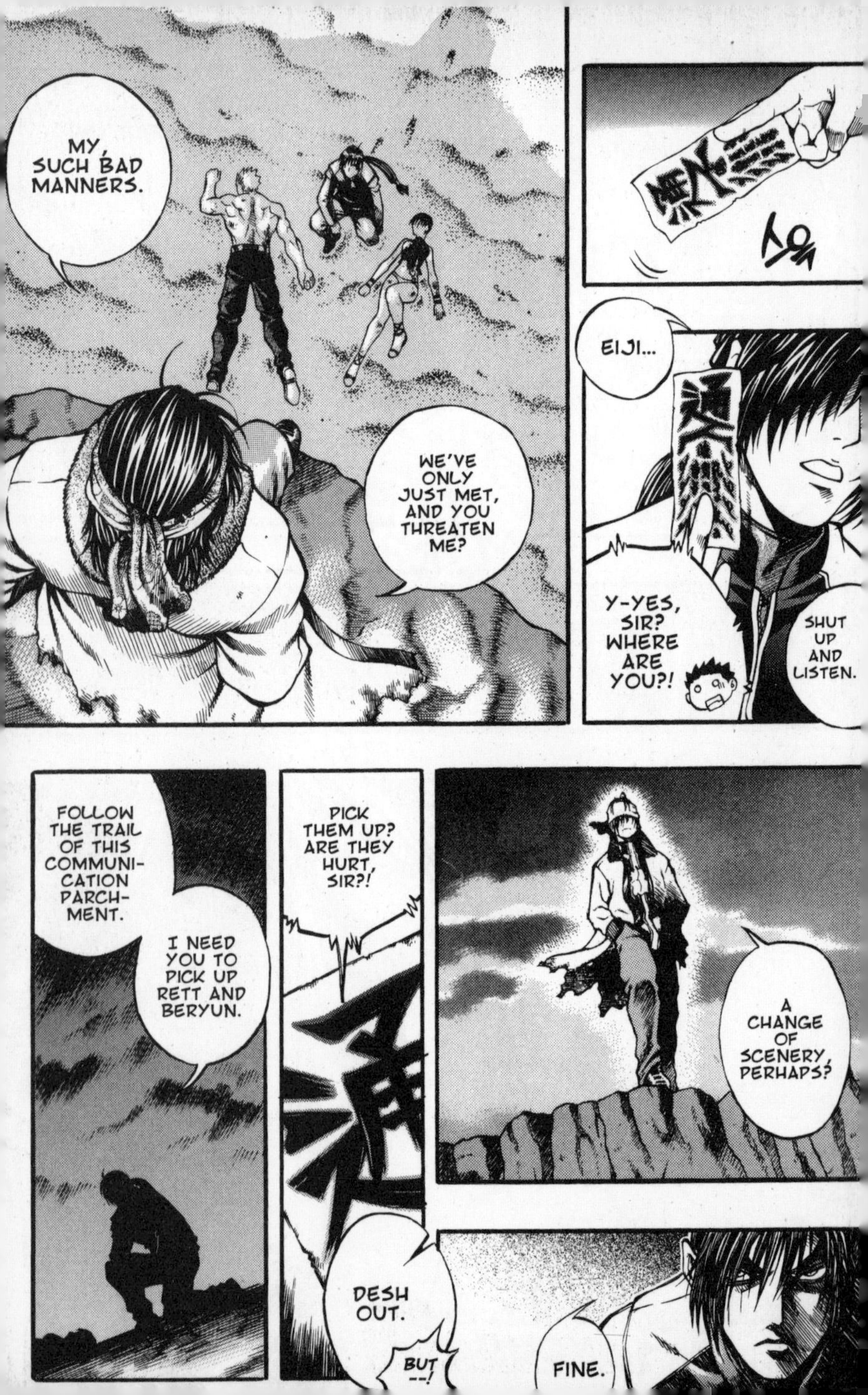
MY, SUCH BAD MANNERS.
WE'VE ONLY JUST MET, AND YOU THREATEN ME?
EIJI...
Y-YES, SIR? WHERE ARE YOU?!
SHUT UP AND LISTEN.
FOLLOW THE TRAIL OF THIS COMMUNICATION PARCHMENT.
I NEED YOU TO PICK UP RETT AND BERYUN.
PICK THEM UP? ARE THEY HURT, SIR?!
DESH OUT.
BUT --!
A CHANGE OF SCENERY, PERHAPS?
FINE.

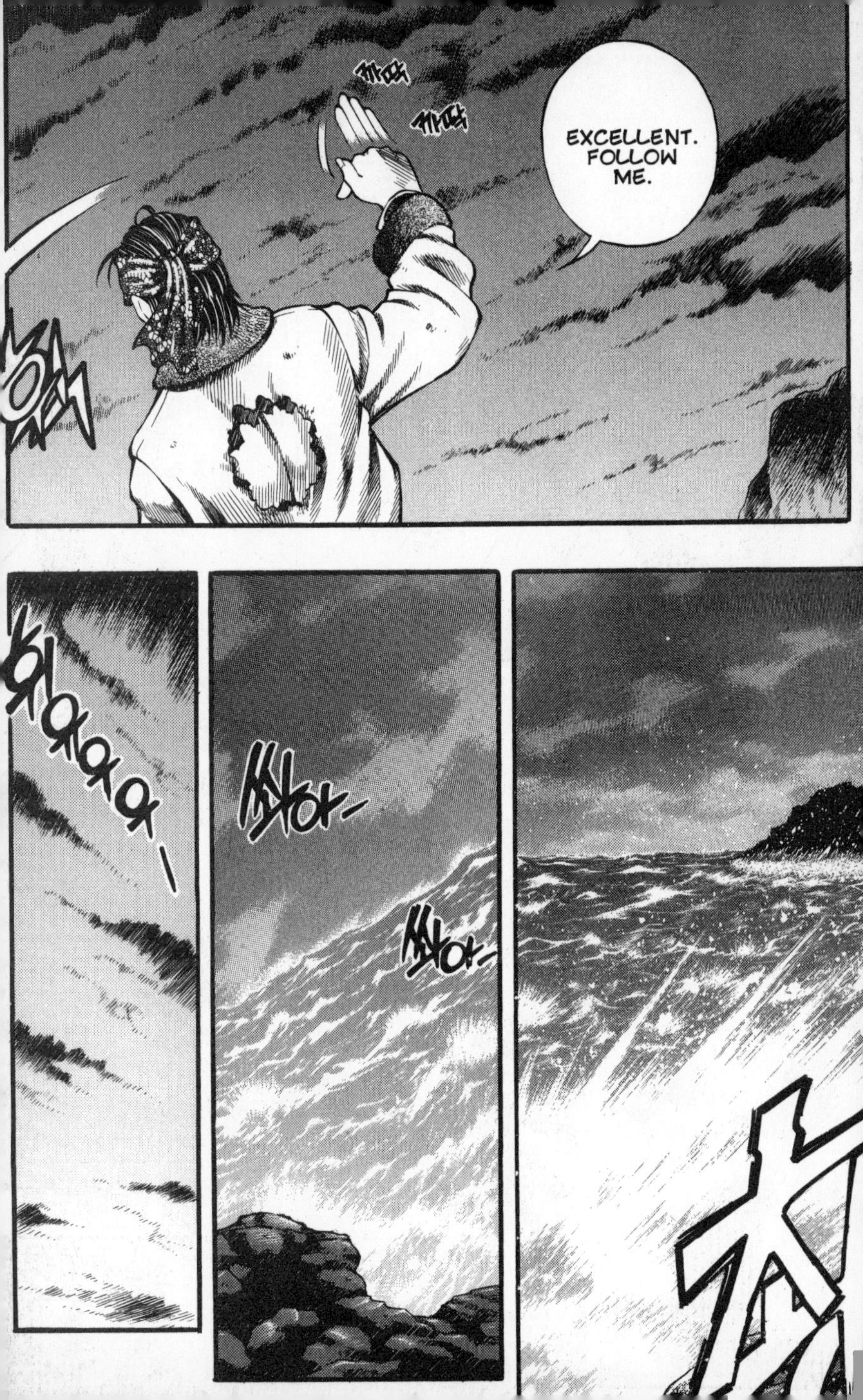
EXCELLENT. FOLLOW ME.

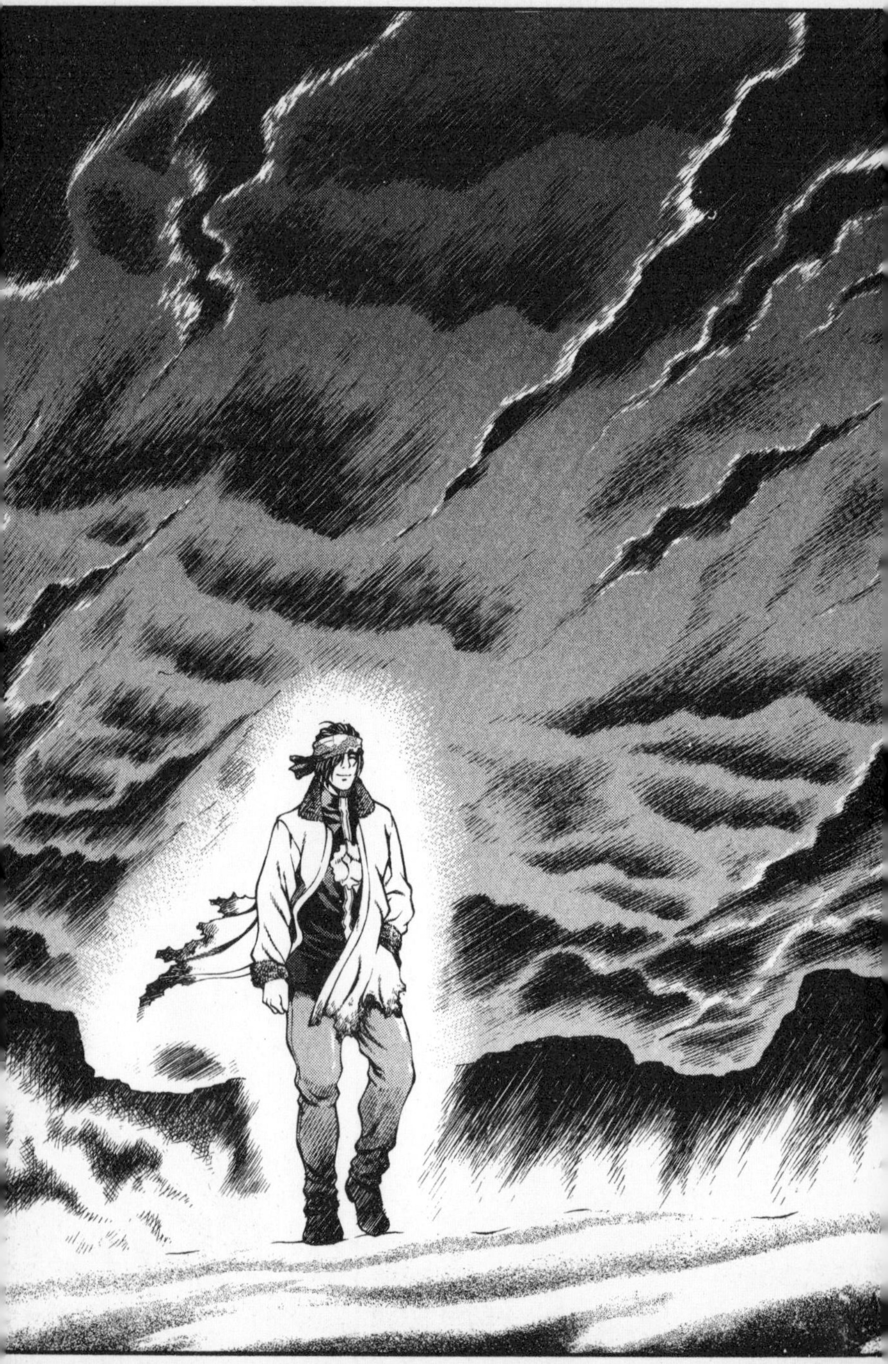

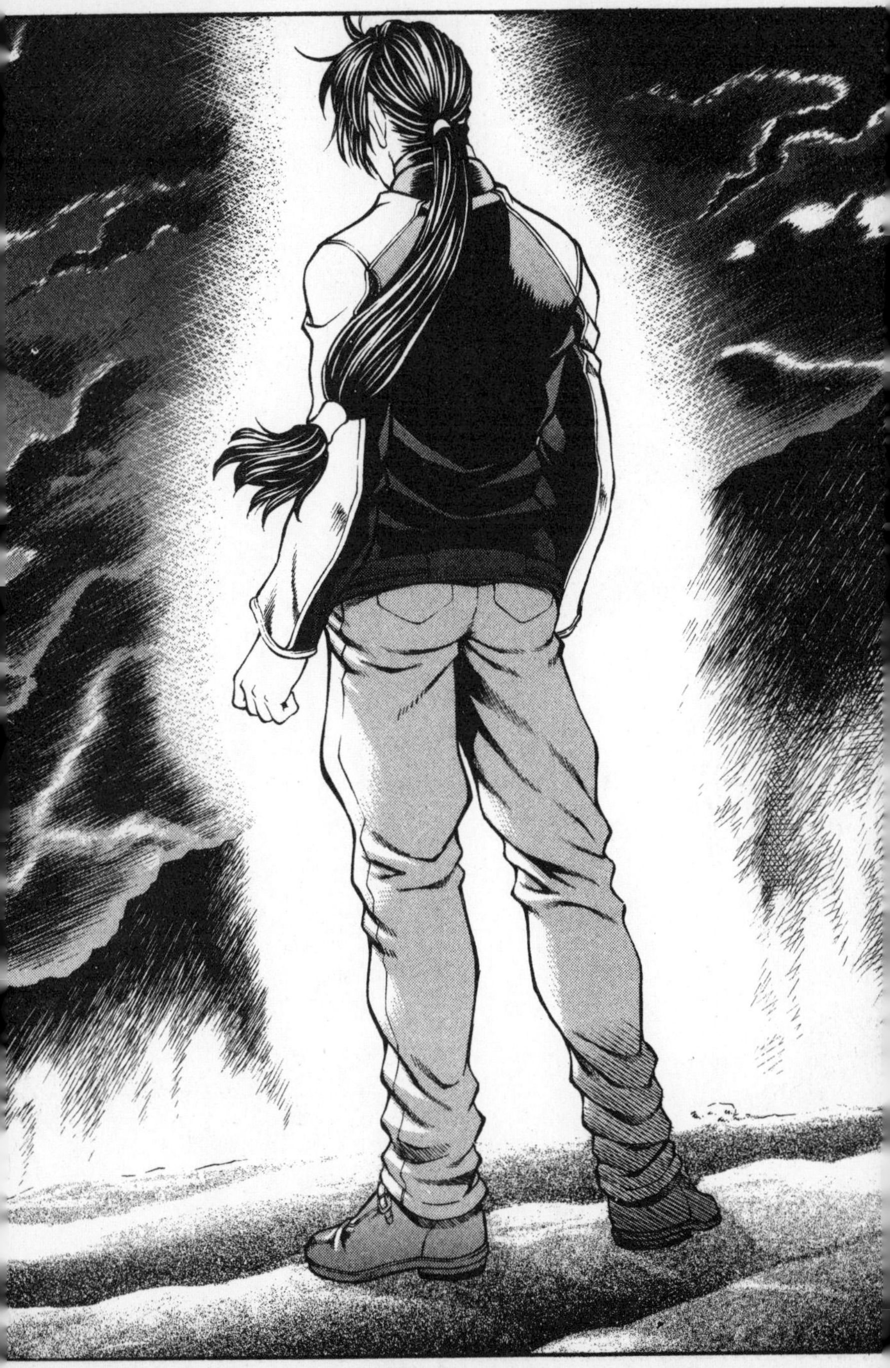

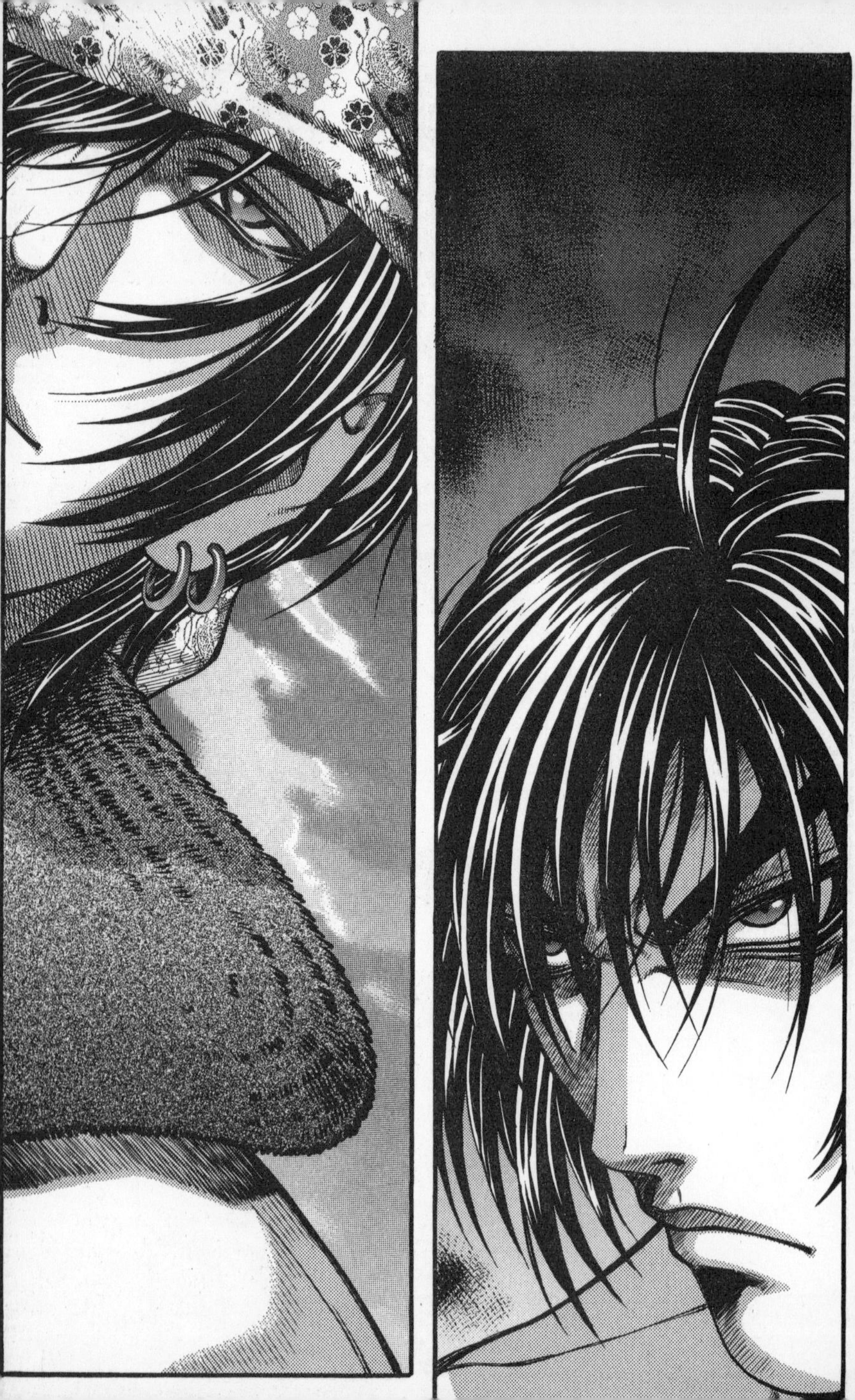

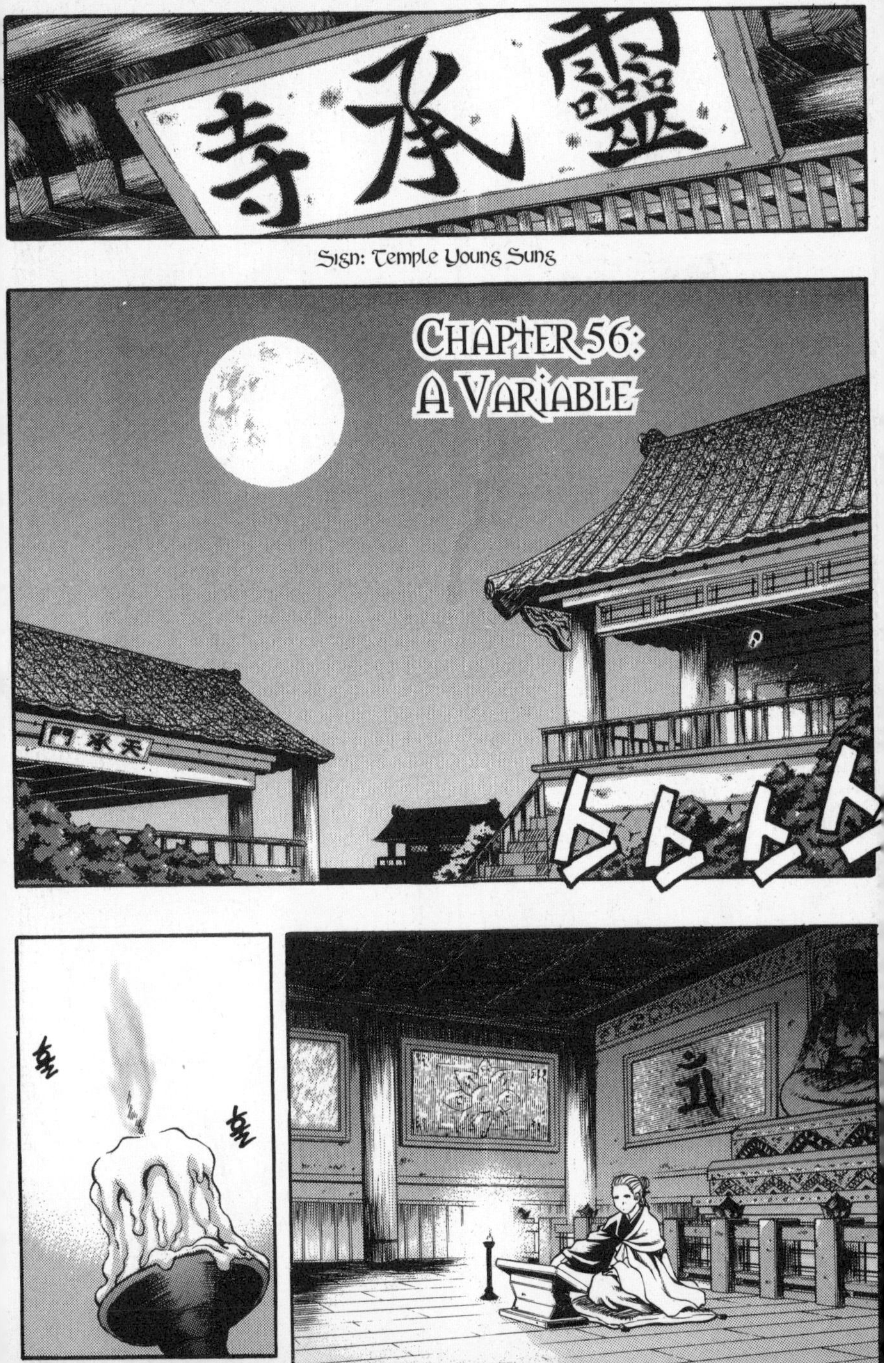
靈承寺
Sign: Temple Young Sung
Chapter 56:
A Variable
天承門
トトトト

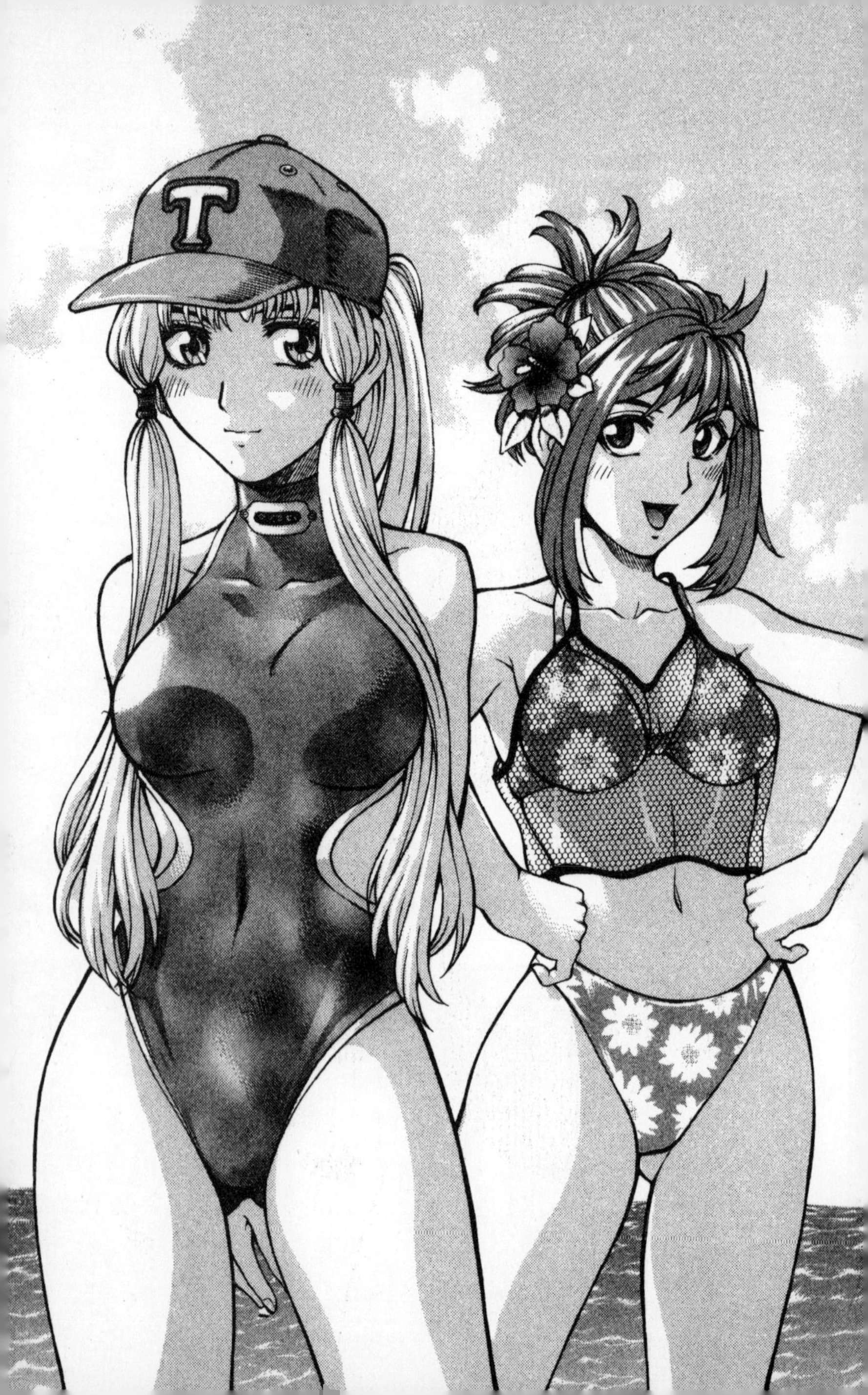

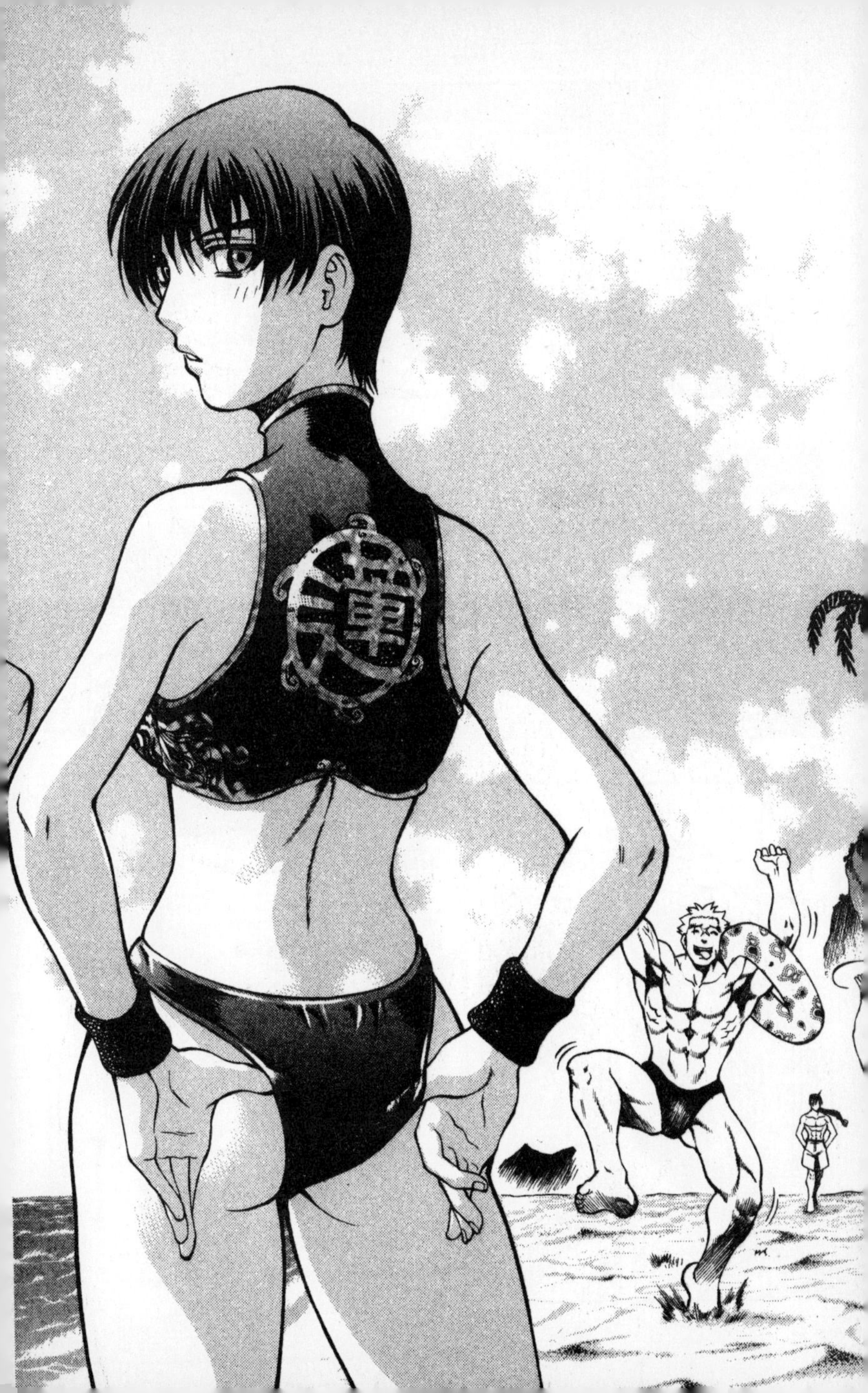

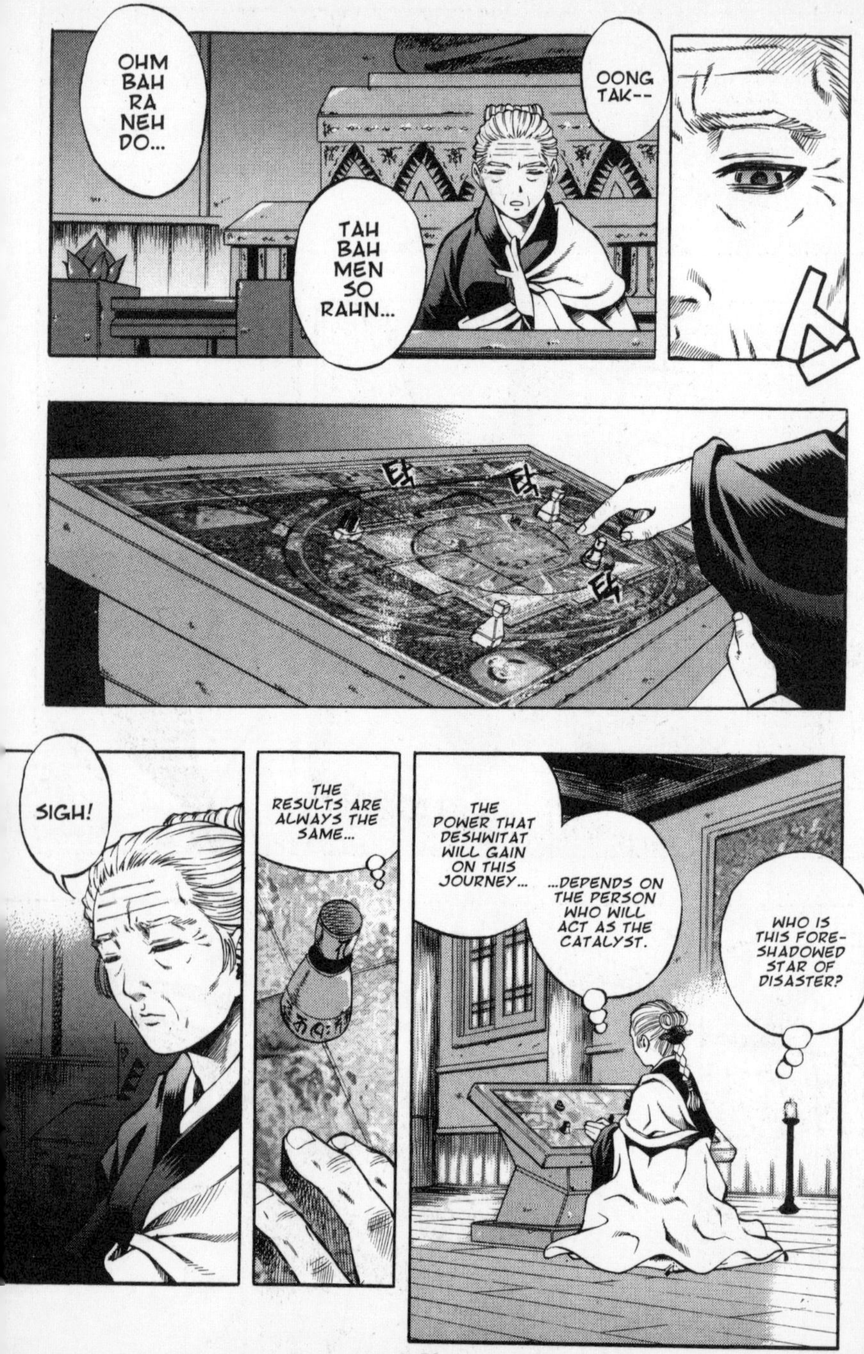
OHM BAH RA NEH DO...
TAH BAH MEN SO RAHN...
OONG TAK--
SIGH!
THE RESULTS ARE ALWAYS THE SAME...
THE POWER THAT DESHWITAT WILL GAIN ON THIS JOURNEY...
...DEPENDS ON THE PERSON WHO WILL ACT AS THE CATALYST.
WHO IS THIS FORE-SHADOWED STAR OF DISASTER?

BY ALL COUNTS THEIR PATHS SHOULD HAVE ALREADY CROSSED BY NOW.

THERE MUST BE A CAUSE FOR EACH EFFECT. IF I LOOK CLOSELY I SHOULD SEE IT.

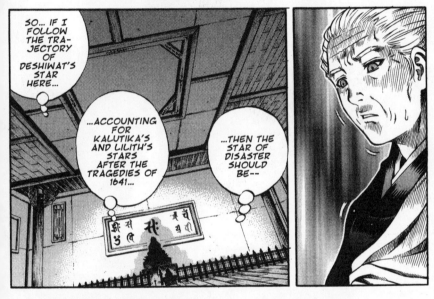

SO... IF I FOLLOW THE TRAJECTORY OF DESHIWAT'S STAR HERE...

...ACCOUNTING FOR KALUTIKA'S AND LILITH'S STARS AFTER THE TRAGEDIES OF 1641...

...THEN THE STAR OF DISASTER SHOULD BE--

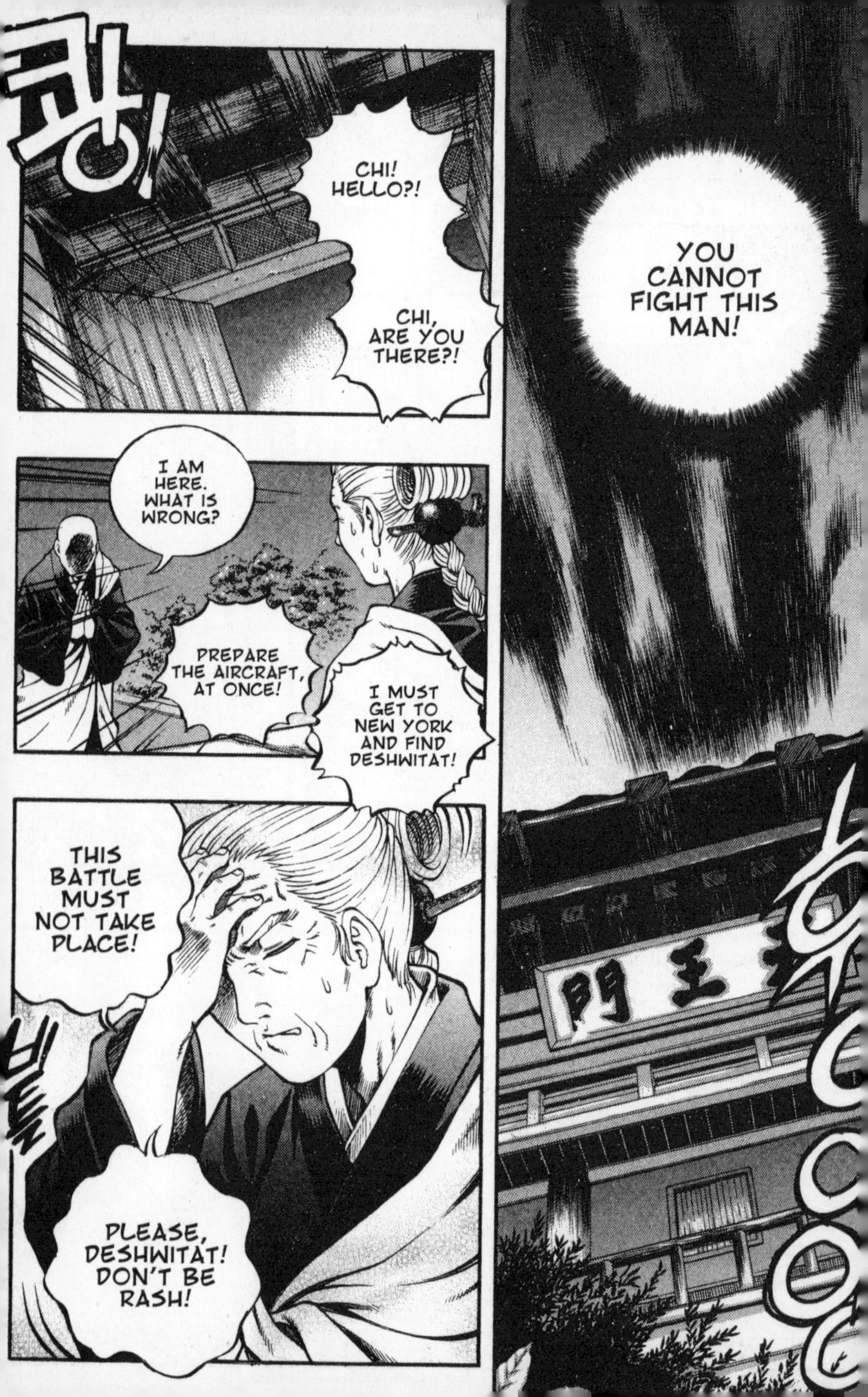

쾅!
CHI! HELLO?!
CHI, ARE YOU THERE?!
I AM HERE. WHAT IS WRONG?
PREPARE THE AIRCRAFT, AT ONCE!
I MUST GET TO NEW YORK AND FIND DESHWITAT!
THIS BATTLE MUST NOT TAKE PLACE!
PLEASE, DESHWITAT! DON'T BE RASH!
YOU CANNOT FIGHT THIS MAN!

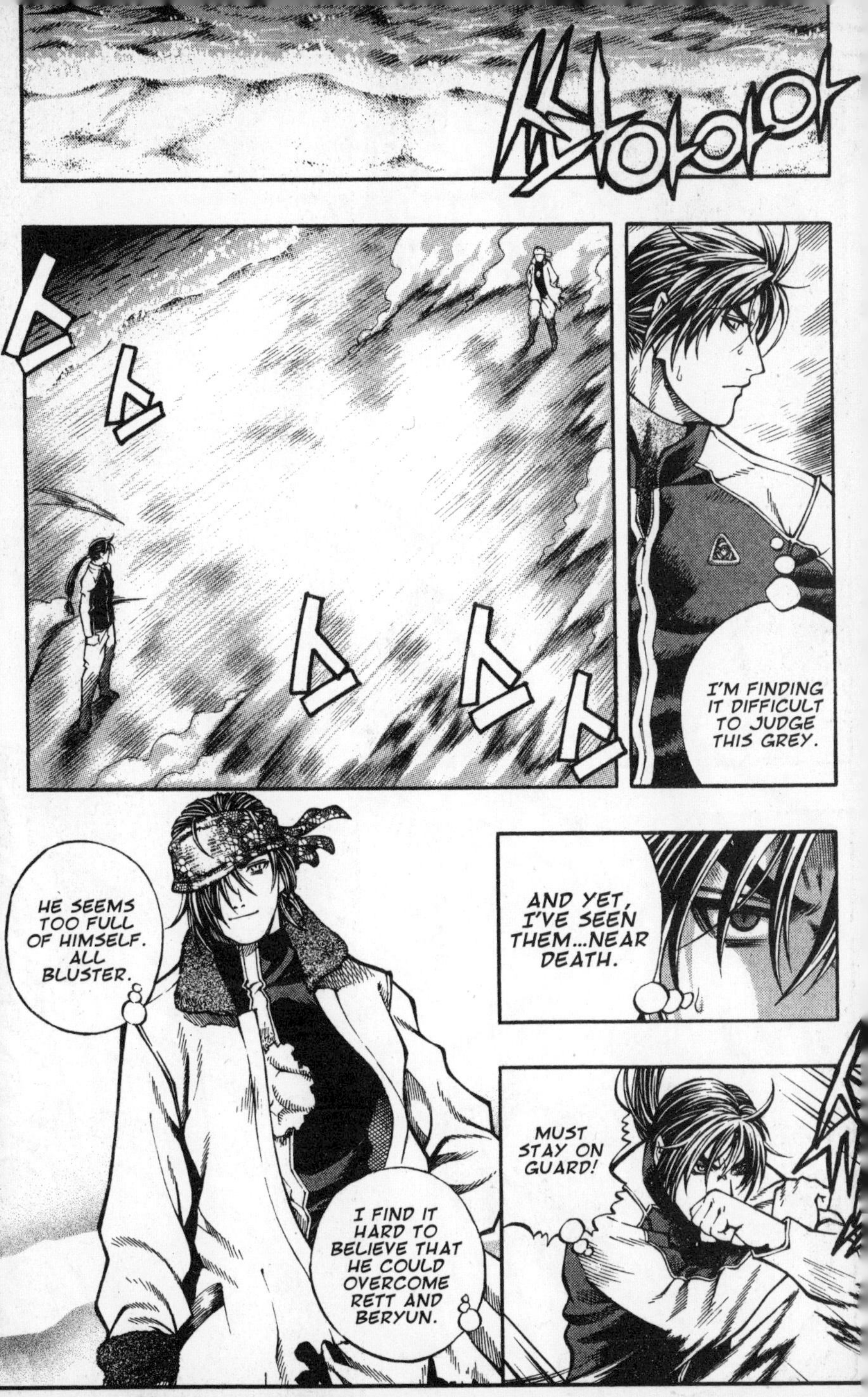
I'M FINDING IT DIFFICULT TO JUDGE THIS GREY.
HE SEEMS TOO FULL OF HIMSELF. ALL BLUSTER.
I FIND IT HARD TO BELIEVE THAT HE COULD OVERCOME RETT AND BERYUN.
AND YET, I'VE SEEN THEM...NEAR DEATH.
MUST STAY ON GUARD!

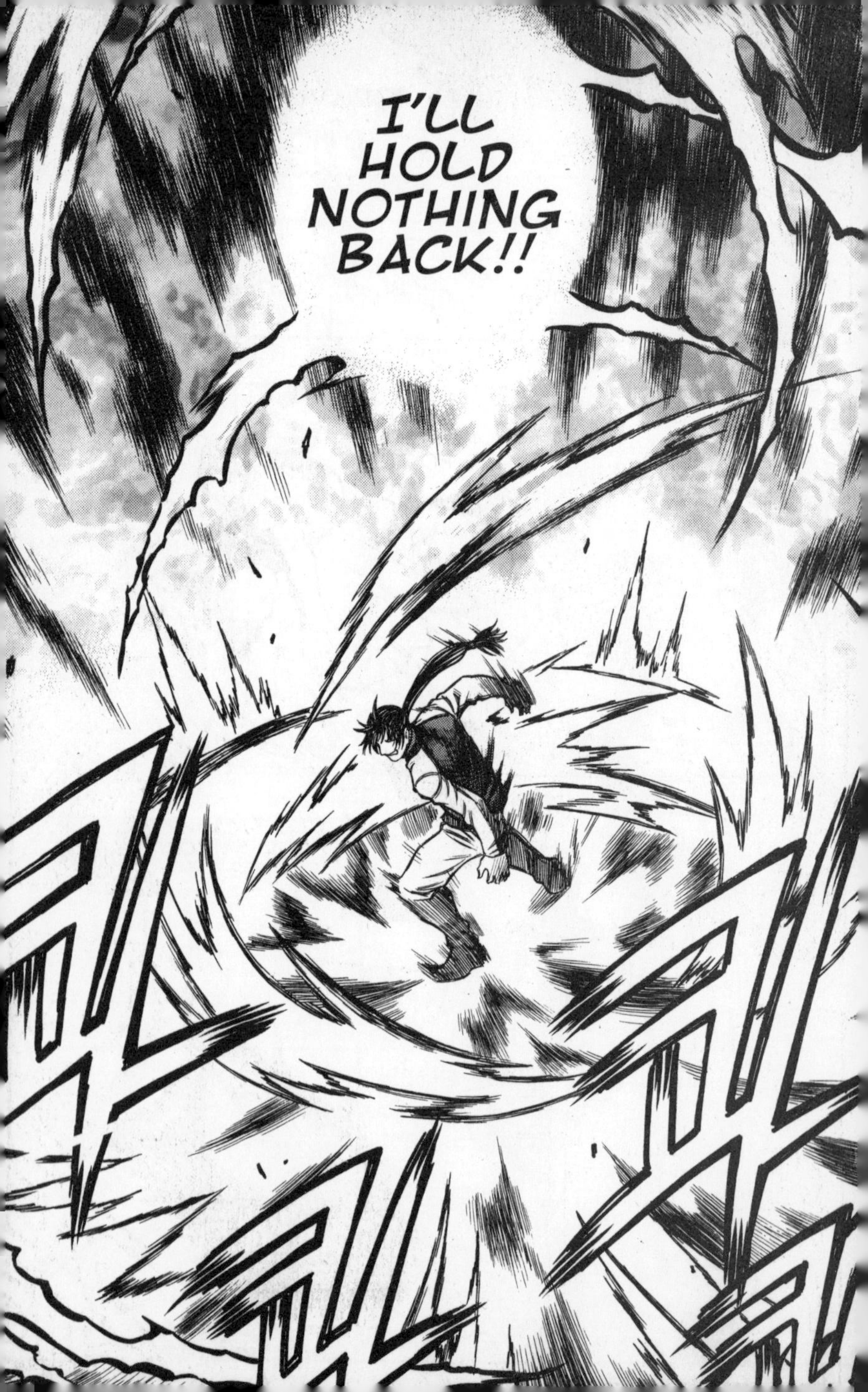
I'LL HOLD NOTHING BACK!!

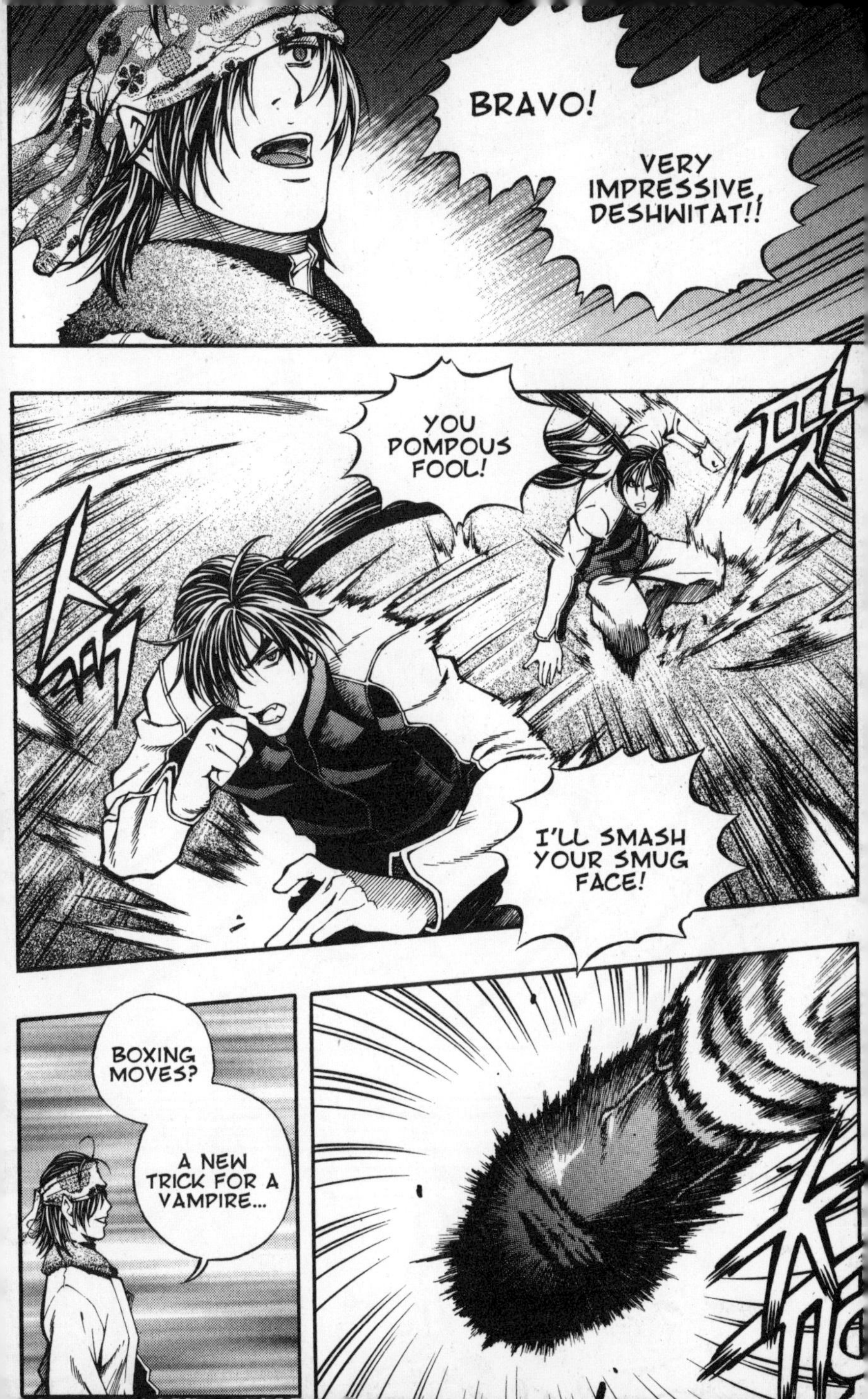
BRAVO!
VERY IMPRESSIVE, DESHWITAT!!
YOU POMPOUS FOOL!
I'LL SMASH YOUR SMUG FACE!
BOXING MOVES?
A NEW TRICK FOR A VAMPIRE...

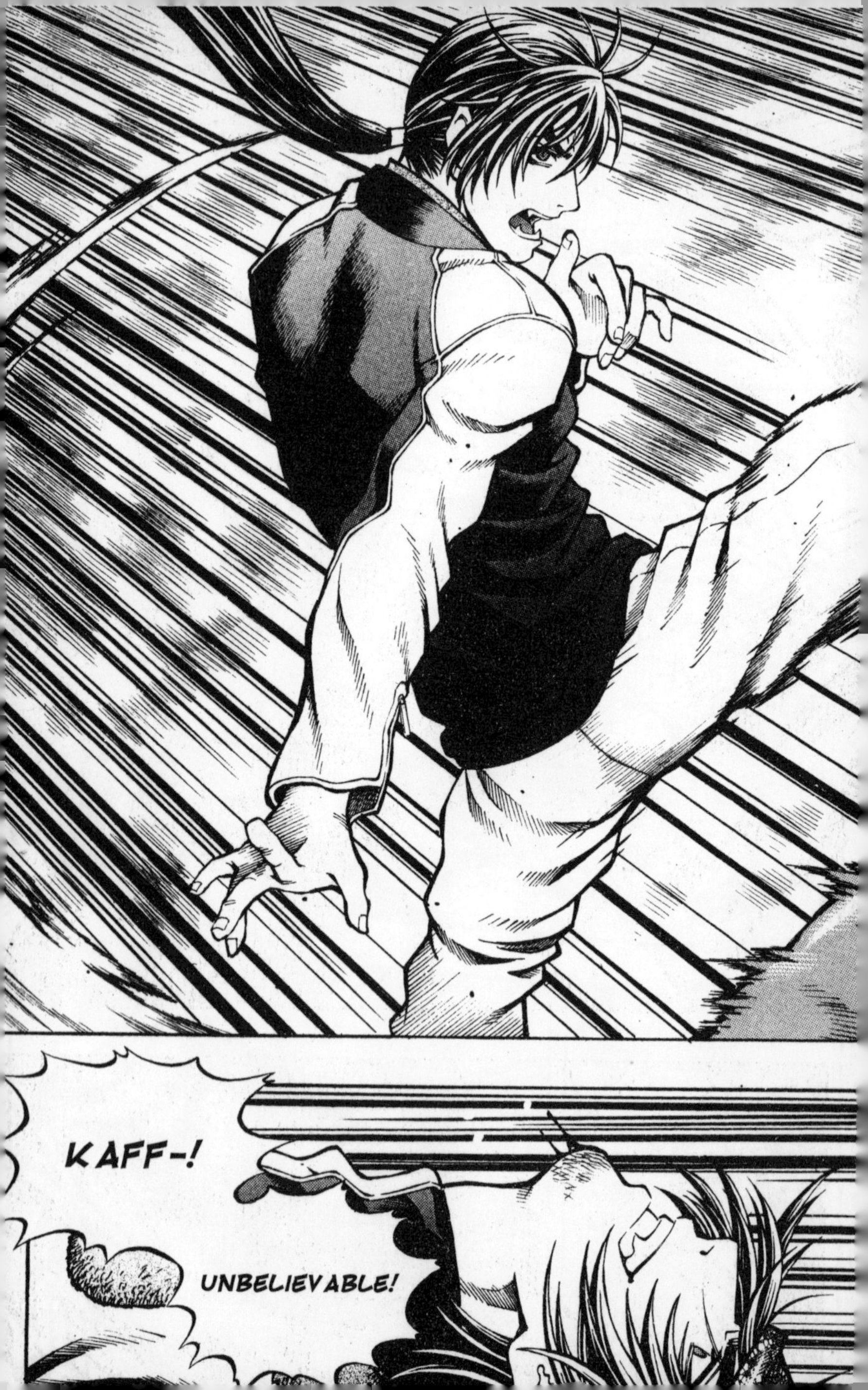
KAFF-!
UNBELIEVABLE!

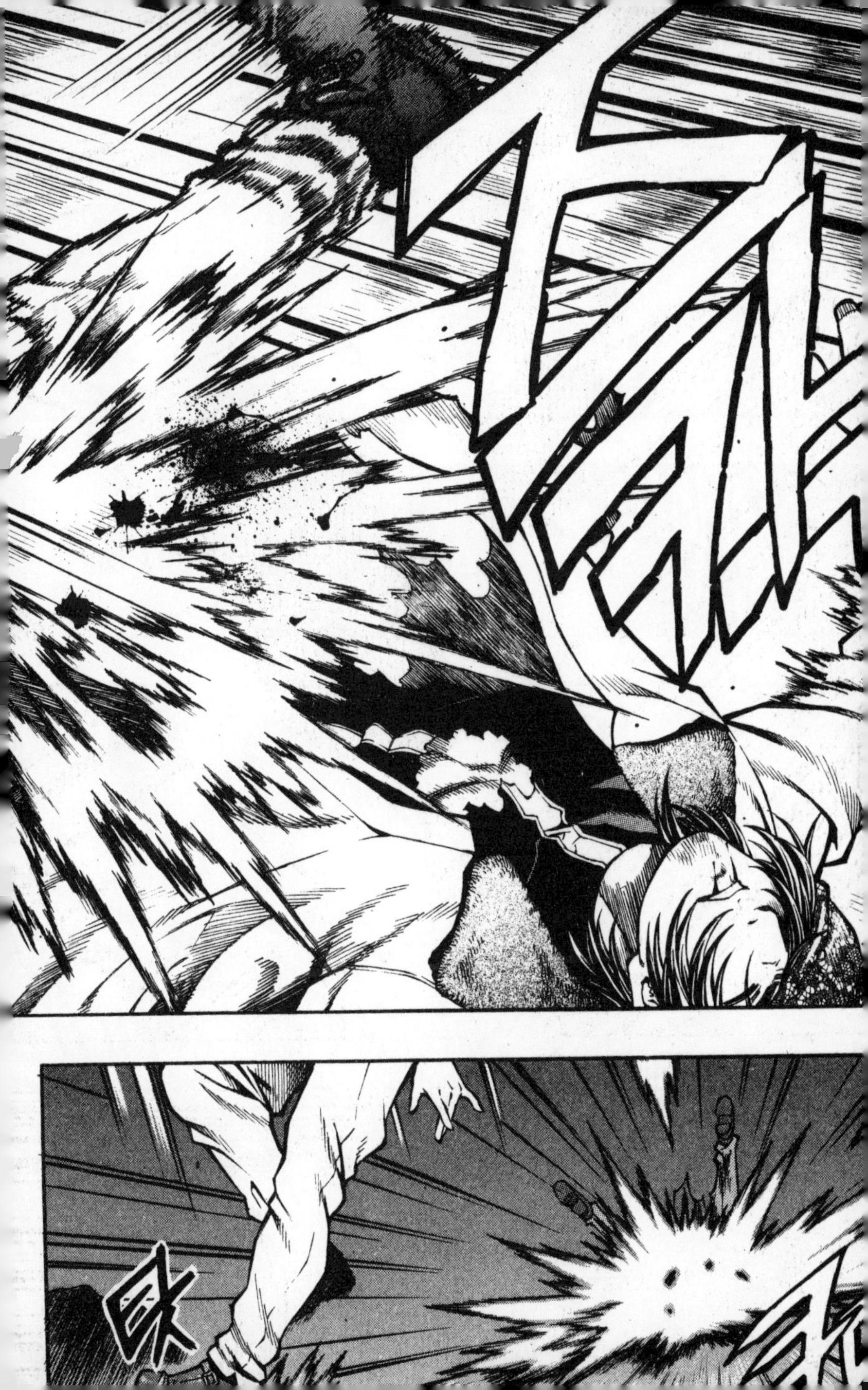

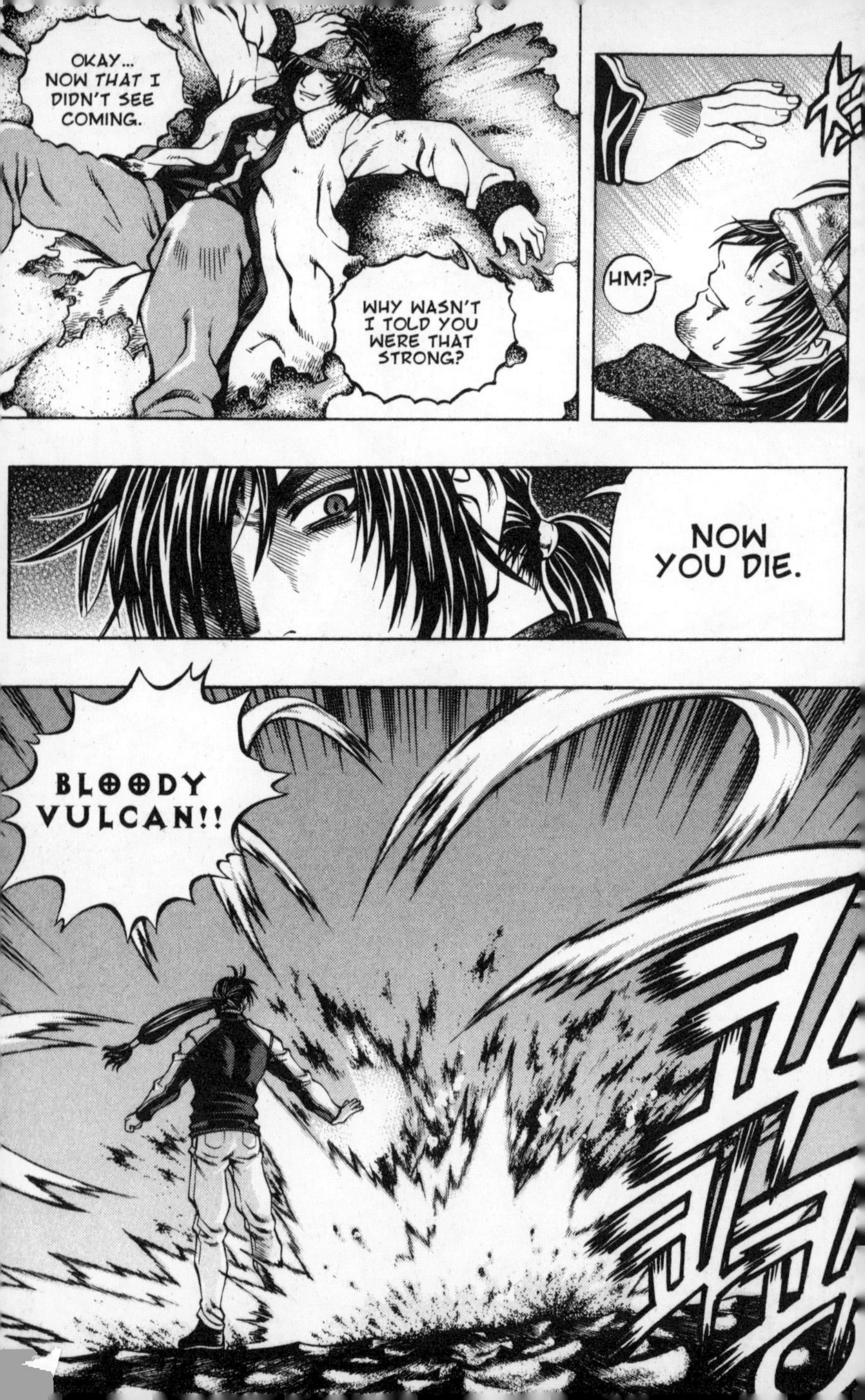
OKAY... NOW *THAT* I DIDN'T SEE COMING.
WHY WASN'T I TOLD YOU WERE THAT STRONG?
HM?
NOW YOU DIE.
BLOODY VULCAN!!

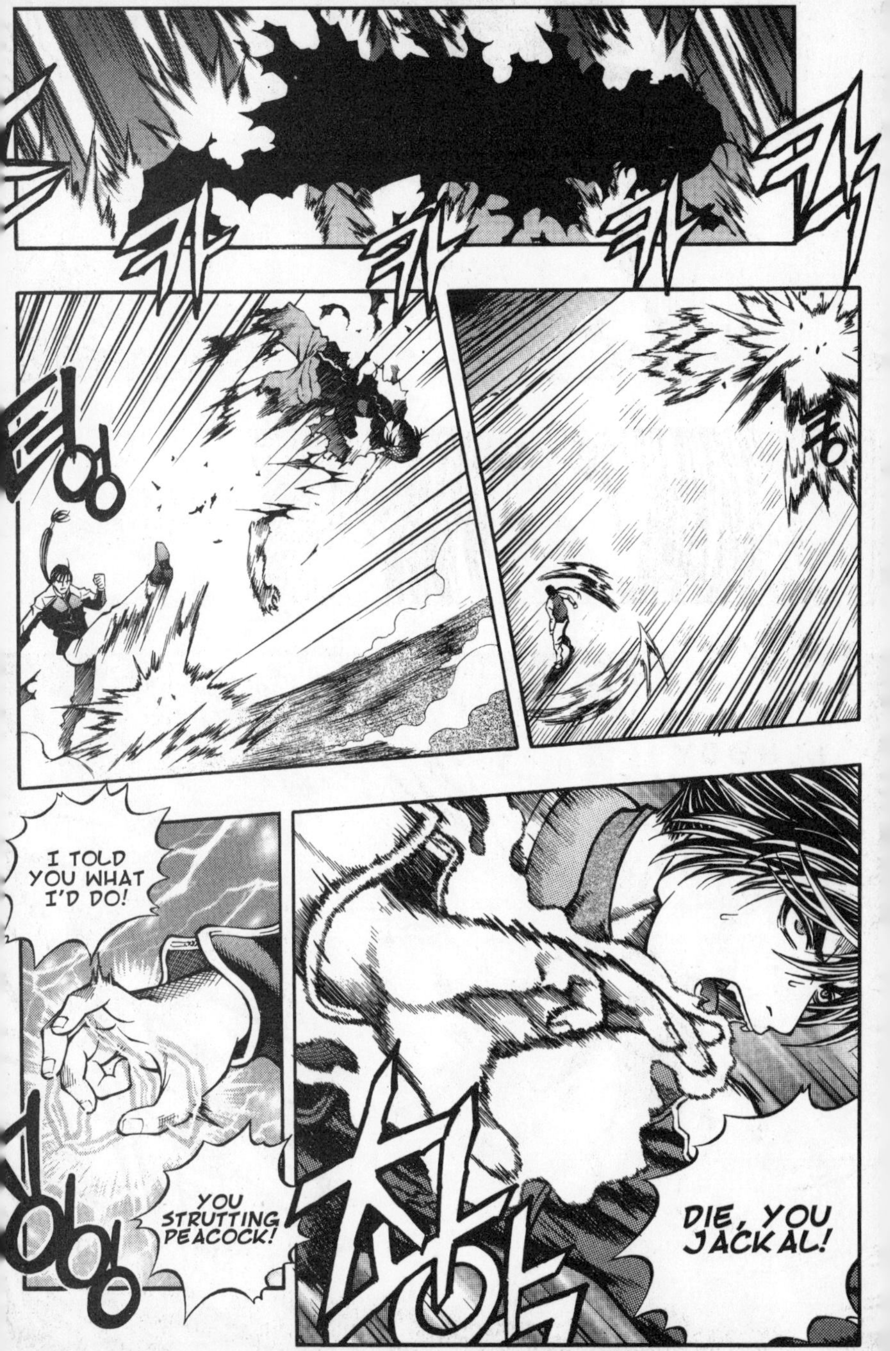
I TOLD YOU WHAT I'D DO!
YOU STRUTTING PEACOCK!
DIE, YOU JACKAL!

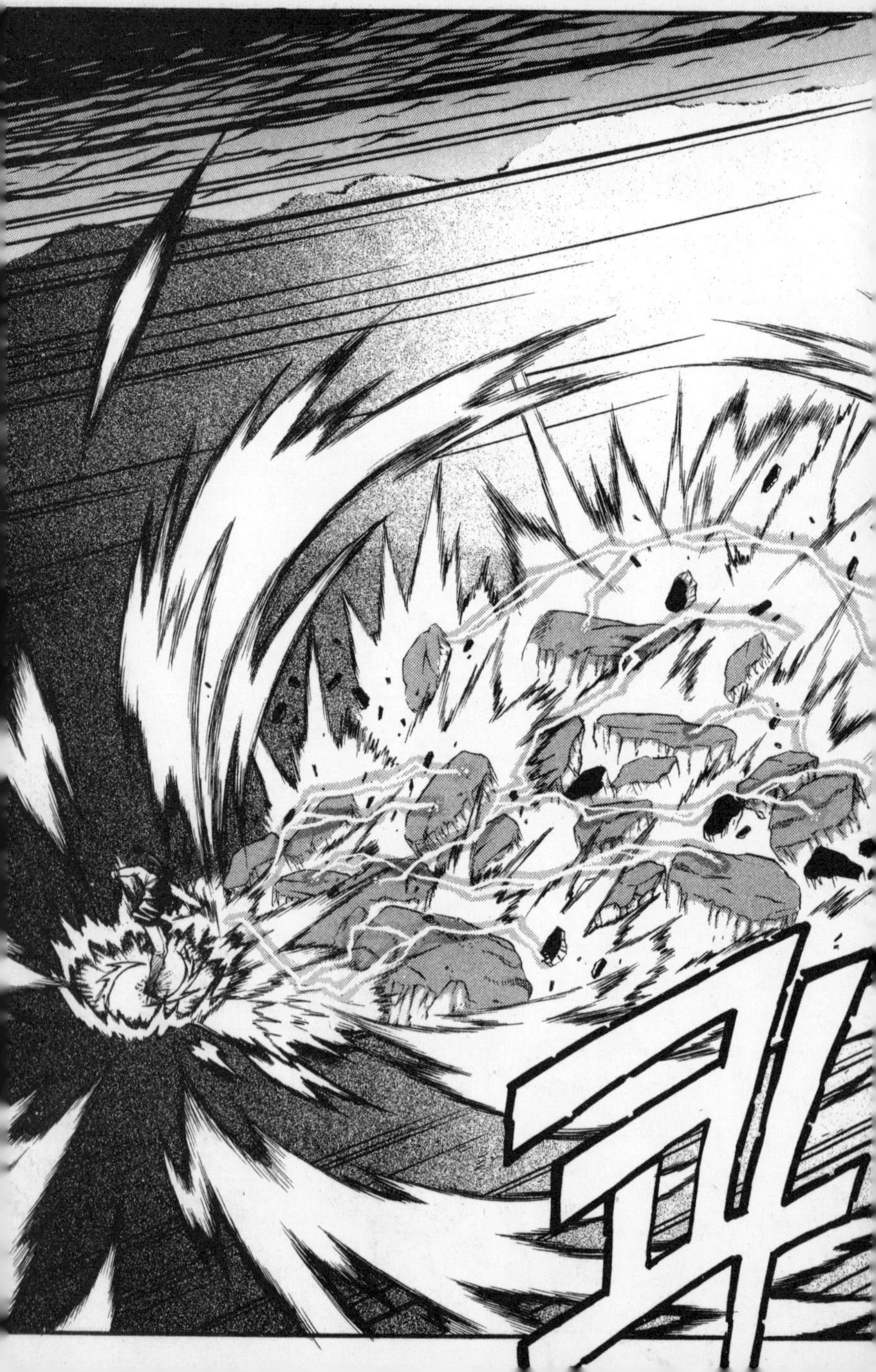

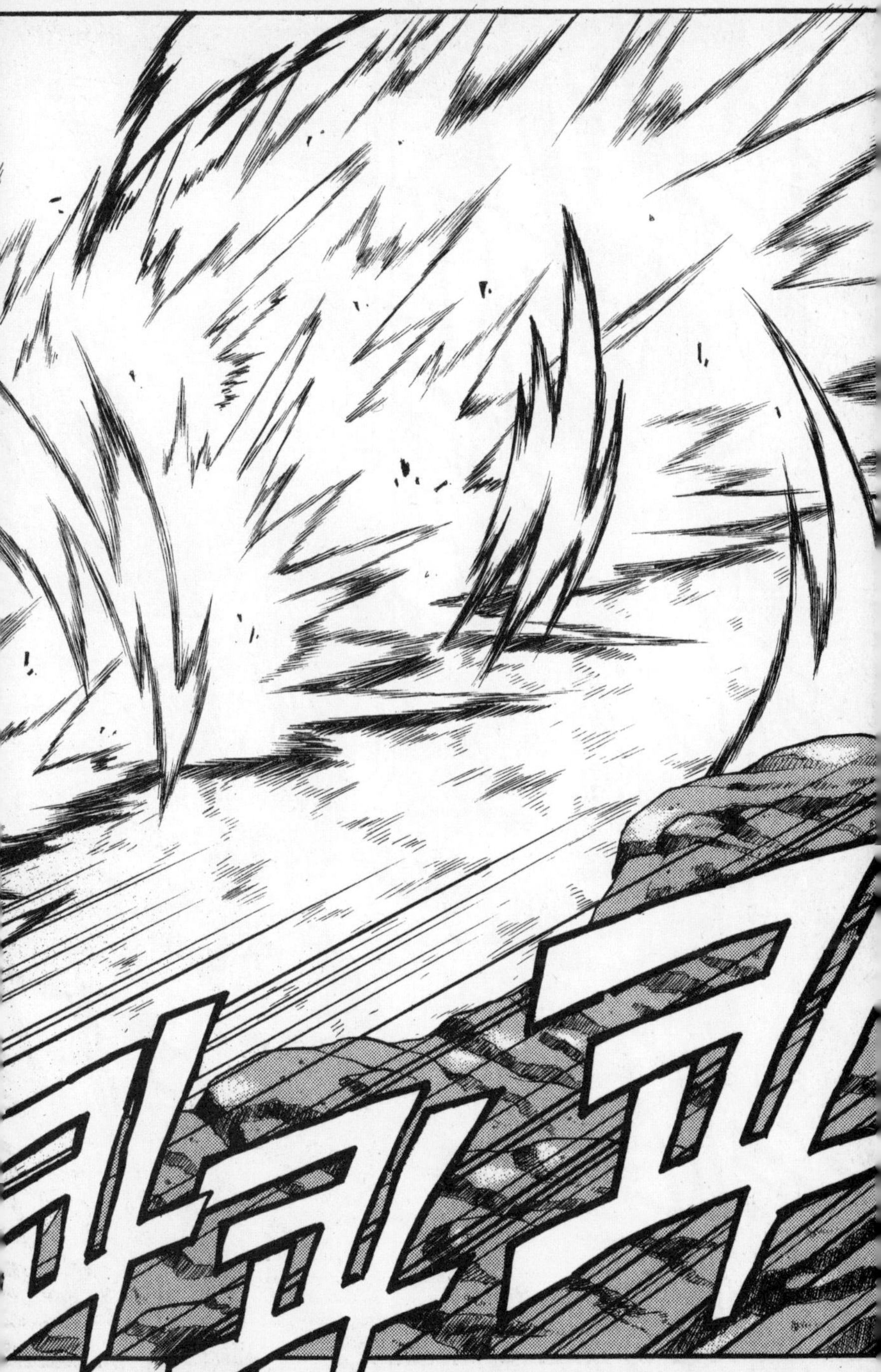

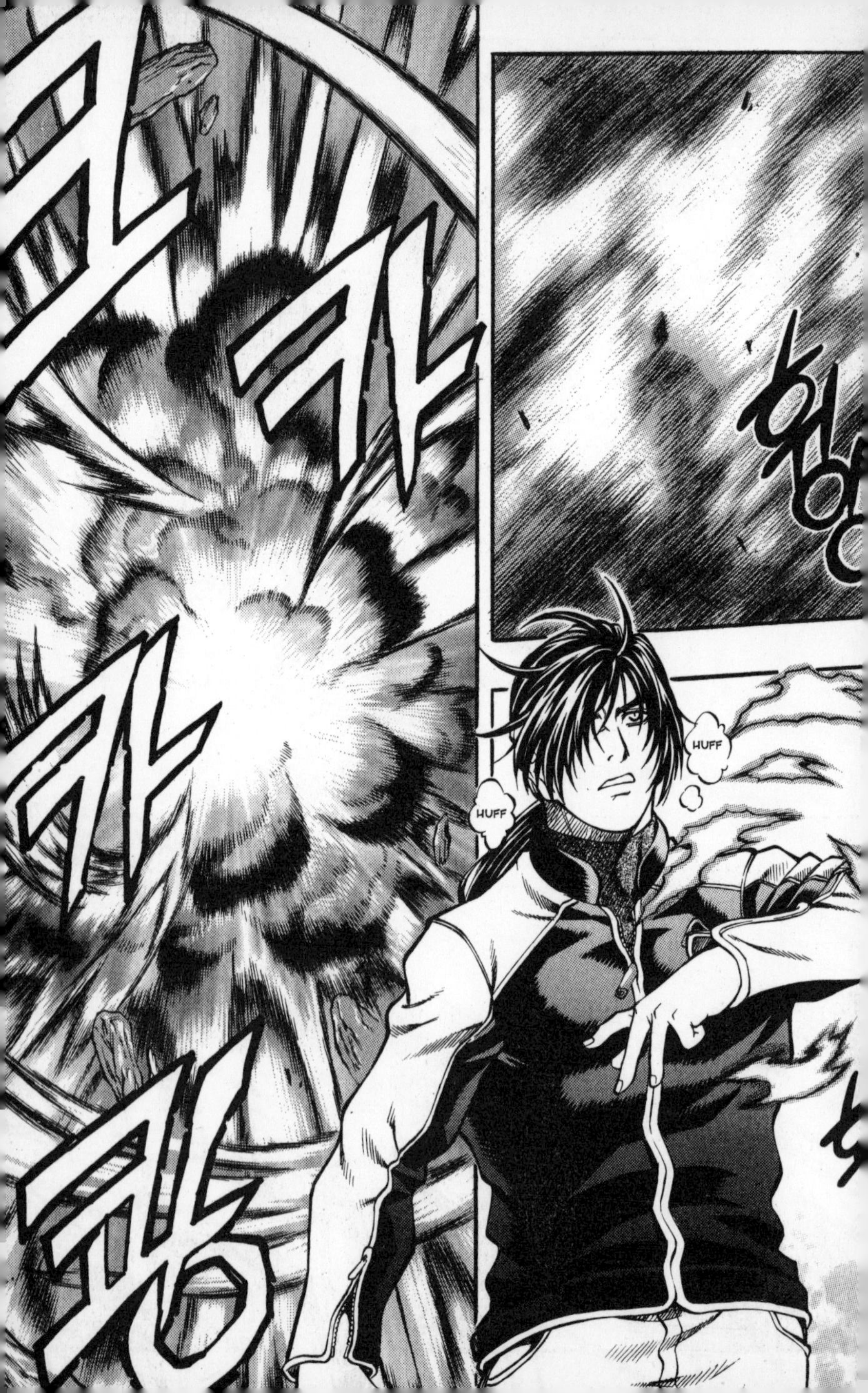
HUFF
HUFF

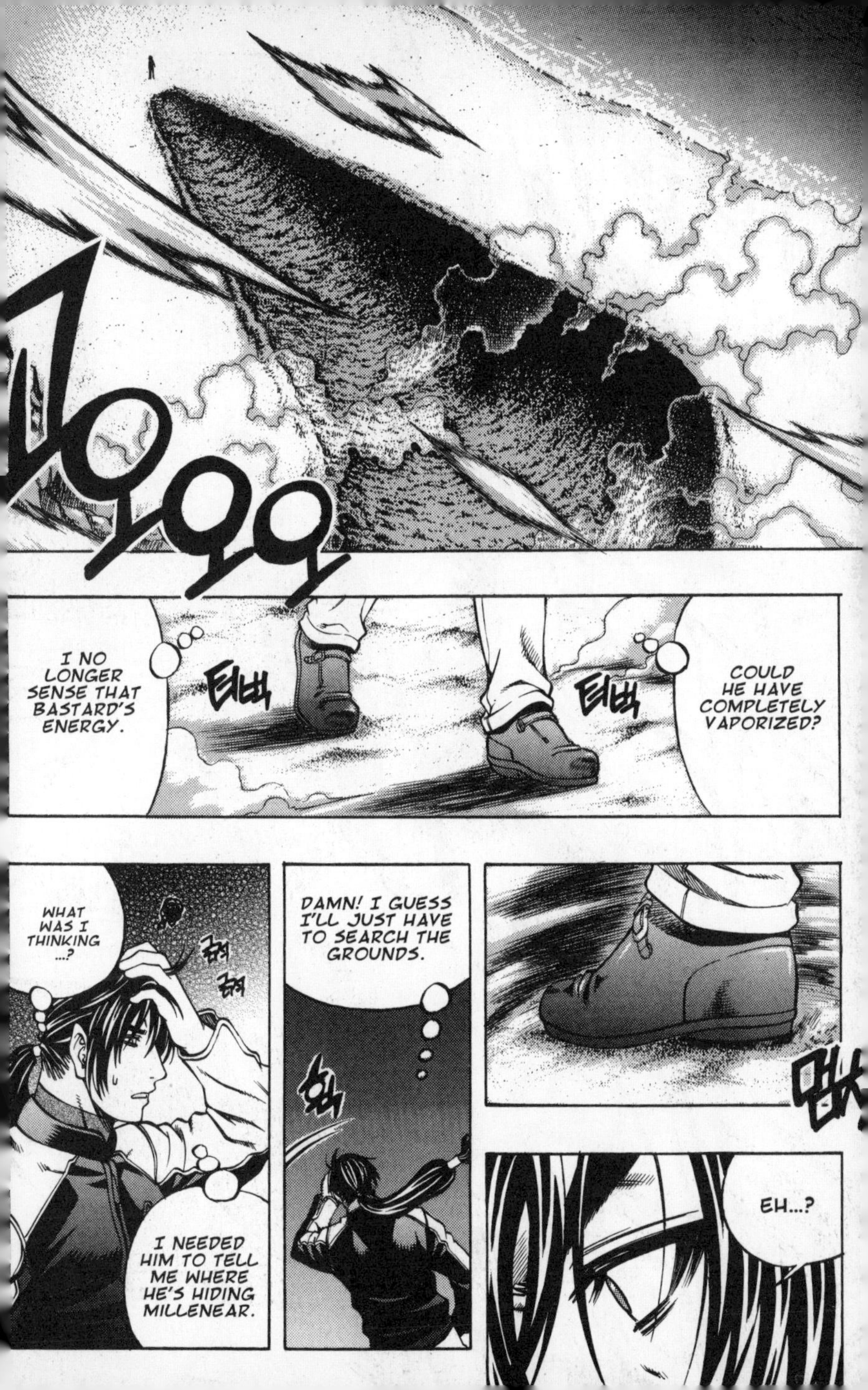
I NO LONGER SENSE THAT BASTARD'S ENERGY.
터벅
터벅
COULD HE HAVE COMPLETELY VAPORIZED?
WHAT WAS I THINKING ...?
I NEEDED HIM TO TELL ME WHERE HE'S HIDING MILLENEAR.
DAMN! I GUESS I'LL JUST HAVE TO SEARCH THE GROUNDS.
EH...?

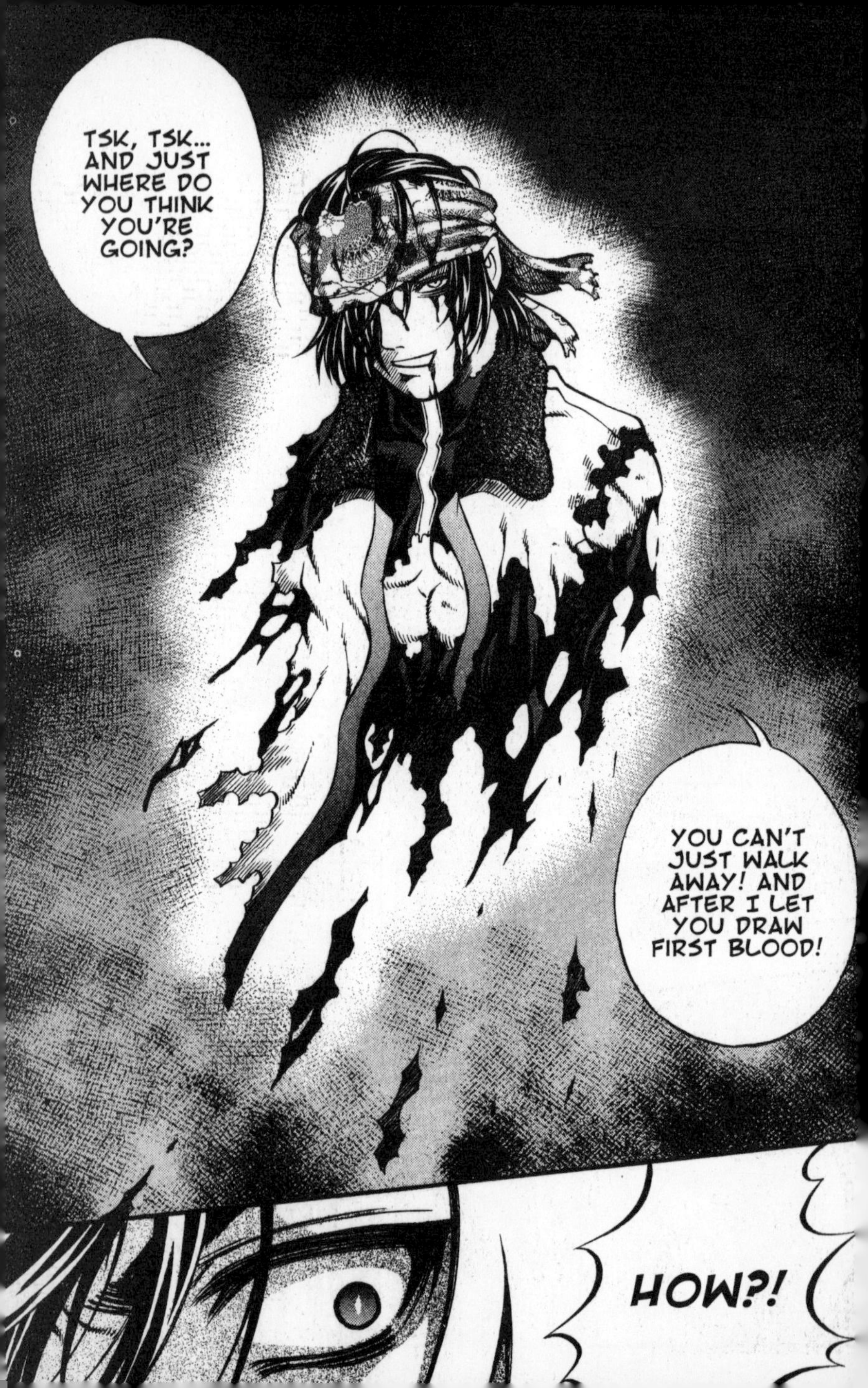
TSK, TSK... AND JUST WHERE DO YOU THINK YOU'RE GOING?
YOU CAN'T JUST WALK AWAY! AND AFTER I LET YOU DRAW FIRST BLOOD!
HOW?!

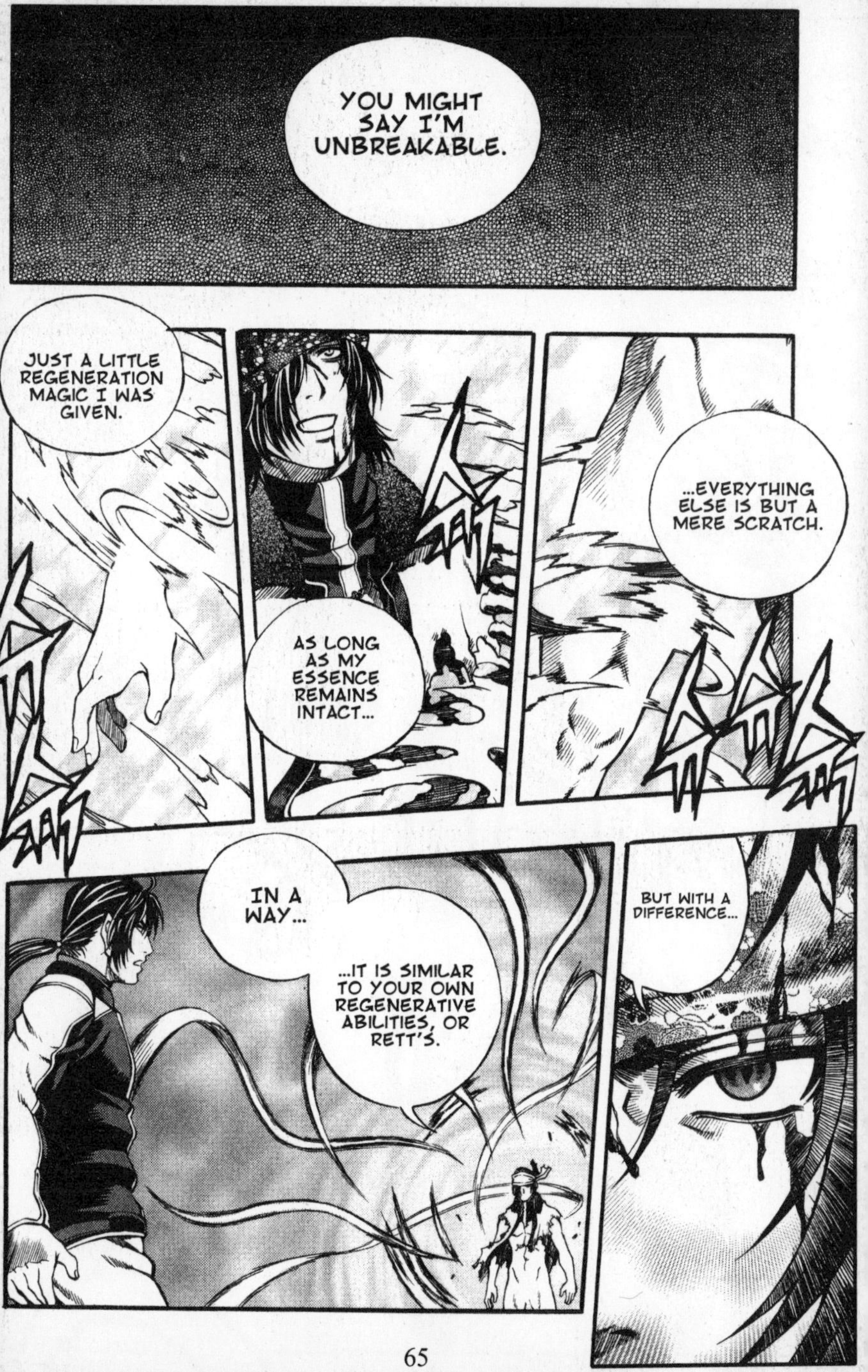
YOU MIGHT SAY I'M UNBREAKABLE.
JUST A LITTLE REGENERATION MAGIC I WAS GIVEN.
AS LONG AS MY ESSENCE REMAINS INTACT...
...EVERYTHING ELSE IS BUT A MERE SCRATCH.
IN A WAY...
...IT IS SIMILAR TO YOUR OWN REGENERATIVE ABILITIES, OR RETT'S.
BUT WITH A DIFFERENCE...

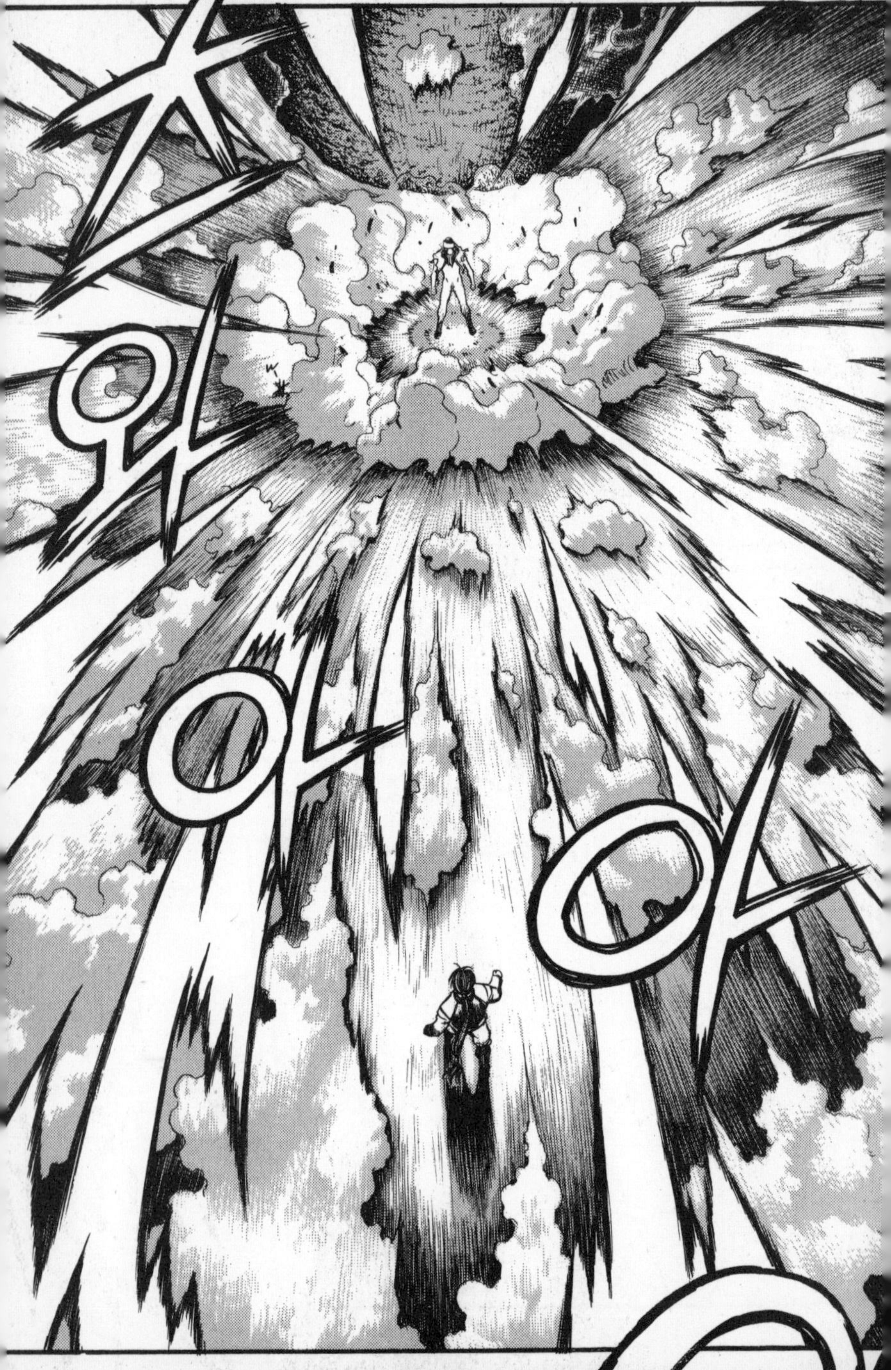

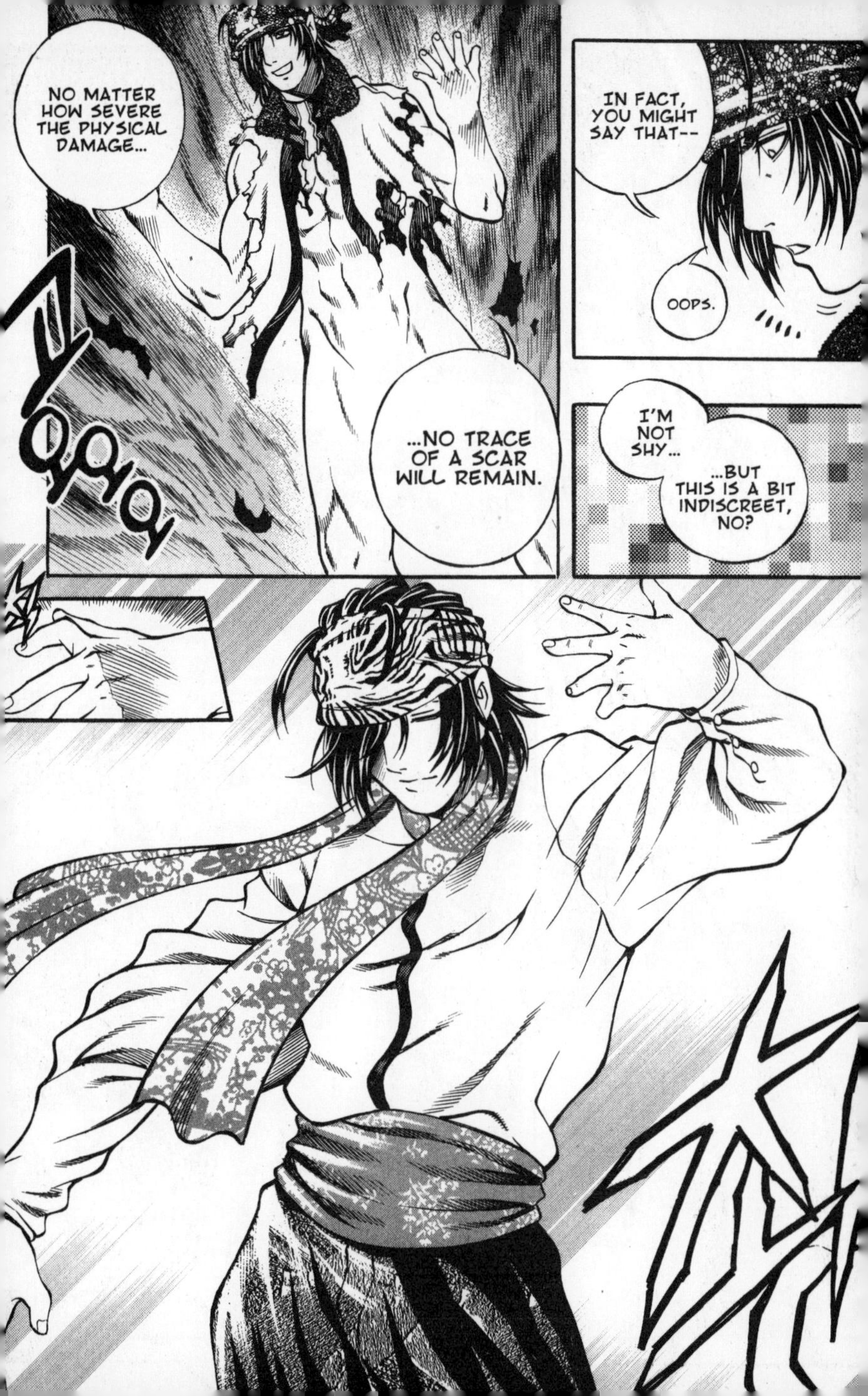
NO MATTER HOW SEVERE THE PHYSICAL DAMAGE...
...NO TRACE OF A SCAR WILL REMAIN.
IN FACT, YOU MIGHT SAY THAT--
OOPS.
I'M NOT SHY...
...BUT THIS IS A BIT INDISCREET, NO?

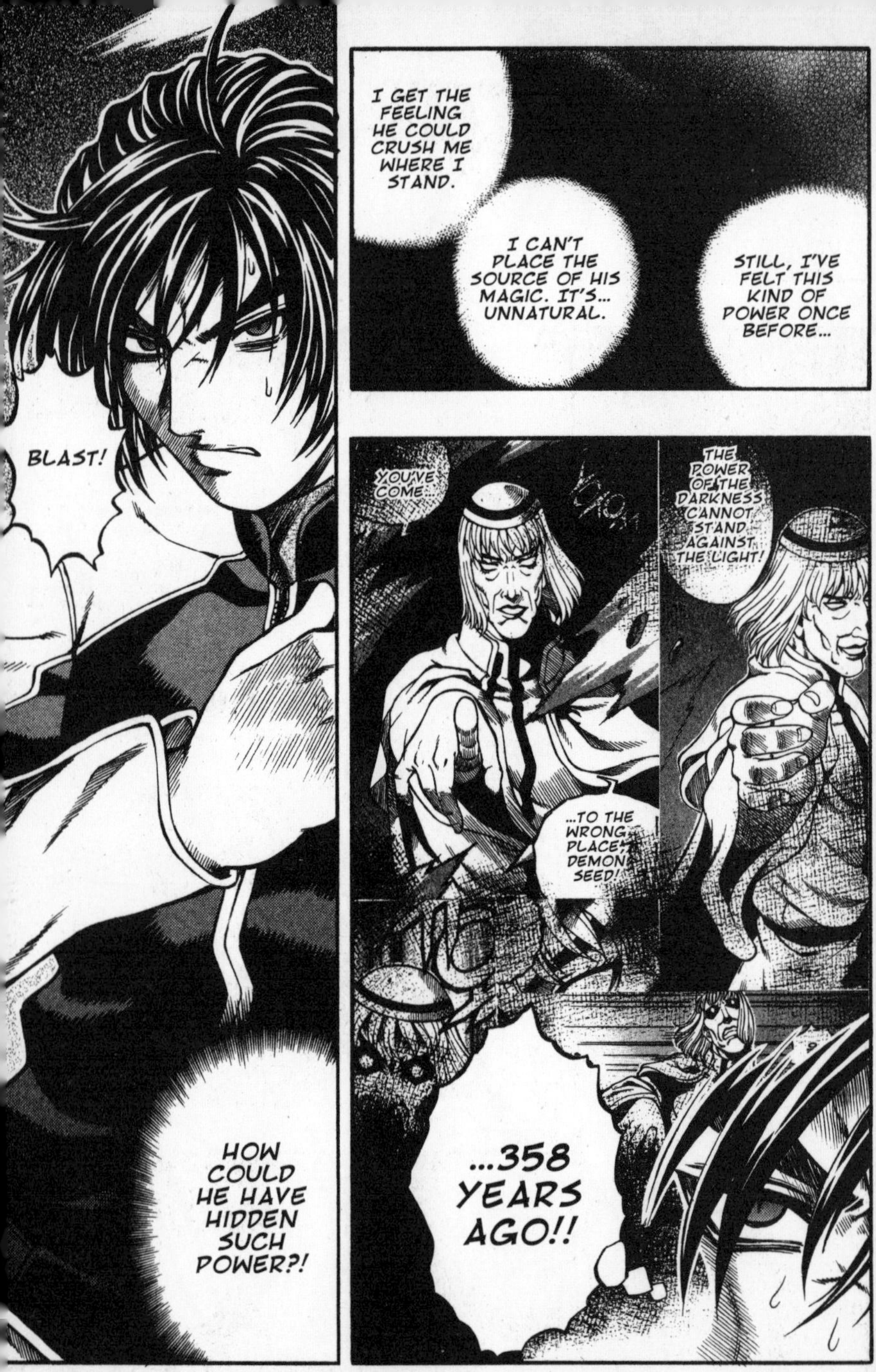
BLAST!
HOW COULD HE HAVE HIDDEN SUCH POWER?!
I GET THE FEELING HE COULD CRUSH ME WHERE I STAND.
I CAN'T PLACE THE SOURCE OF HIS MAGIC. IT'S... UNNATURAL.
STILL, I'VE FELT THIS KIND OF POWER ONCE BEFORE...
YOU'VE COME...
...TO THE WRONG PLACE, DEMON SEED!
THE POWER OF THE DARKNESS CANNOT STAND AGAINST THE LIGHT!
...358 YEARS AGO!!

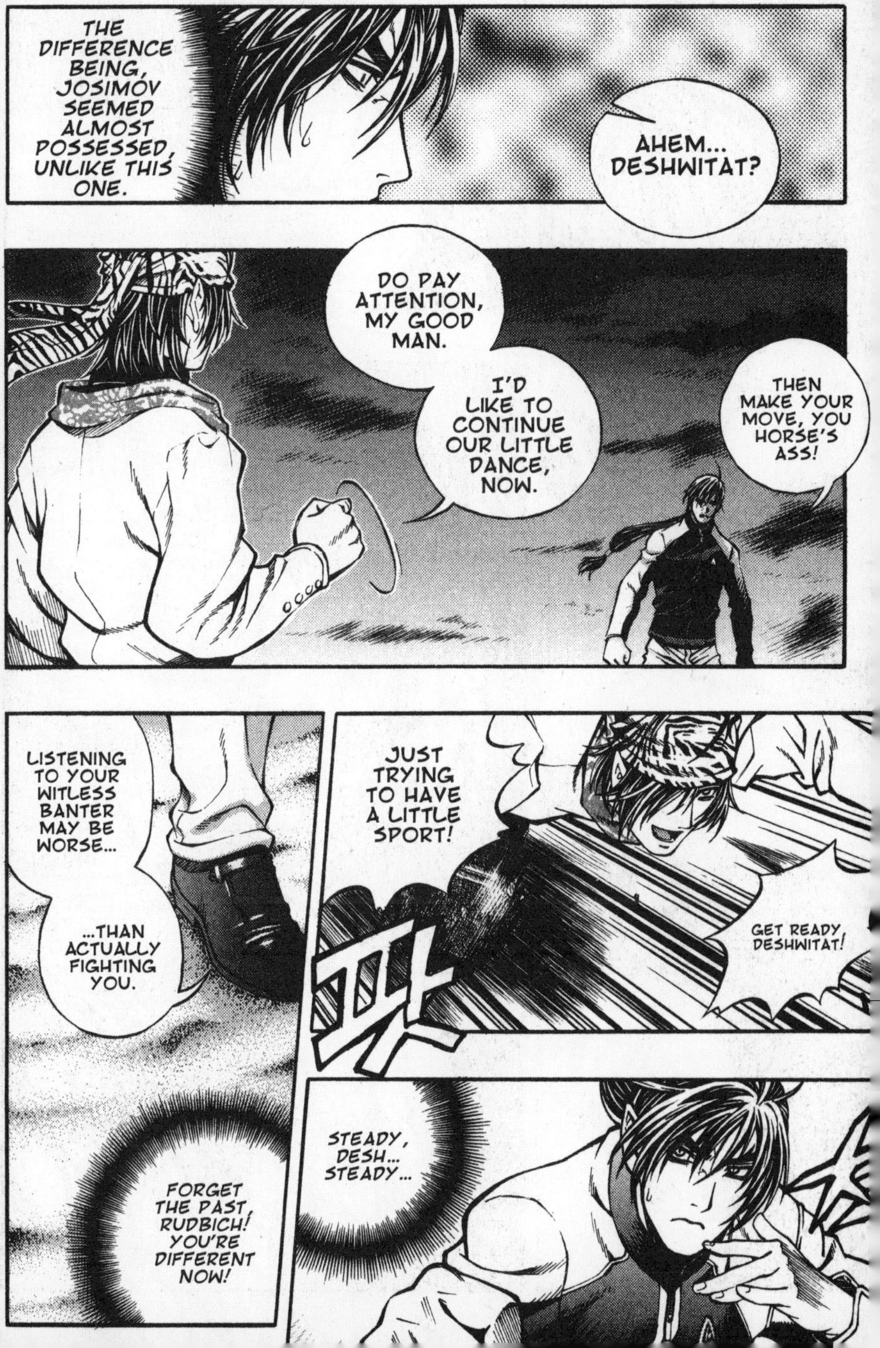
THE DIFFERENCE BEING, JOSIMOV SEEMED ALMOST POSSESSED, UNLIKE THIS ONE.
AHEM... DESHWITAT?
DO PAY ATTENTION, MY GOOD MAN.
I'D LIKE TO CONTINUE OUR LITTLE DANCE, NOW.
THEN MAKE YOUR MOVE, YOU HORSE'S ASS!
JUST TRYING TO HAVE A LITTLE SPORT!
GET READY, DESHWITAT!
LISTENING TO YOUR WITLESS BANTER MAY BE WORSE...
...THAN ACTUALLY FIGHTING YOU.
STEADY, DESH... STEADY...
FORGET THE PAST, RUDBICH! YOU'RE DIFFERENT NOW!

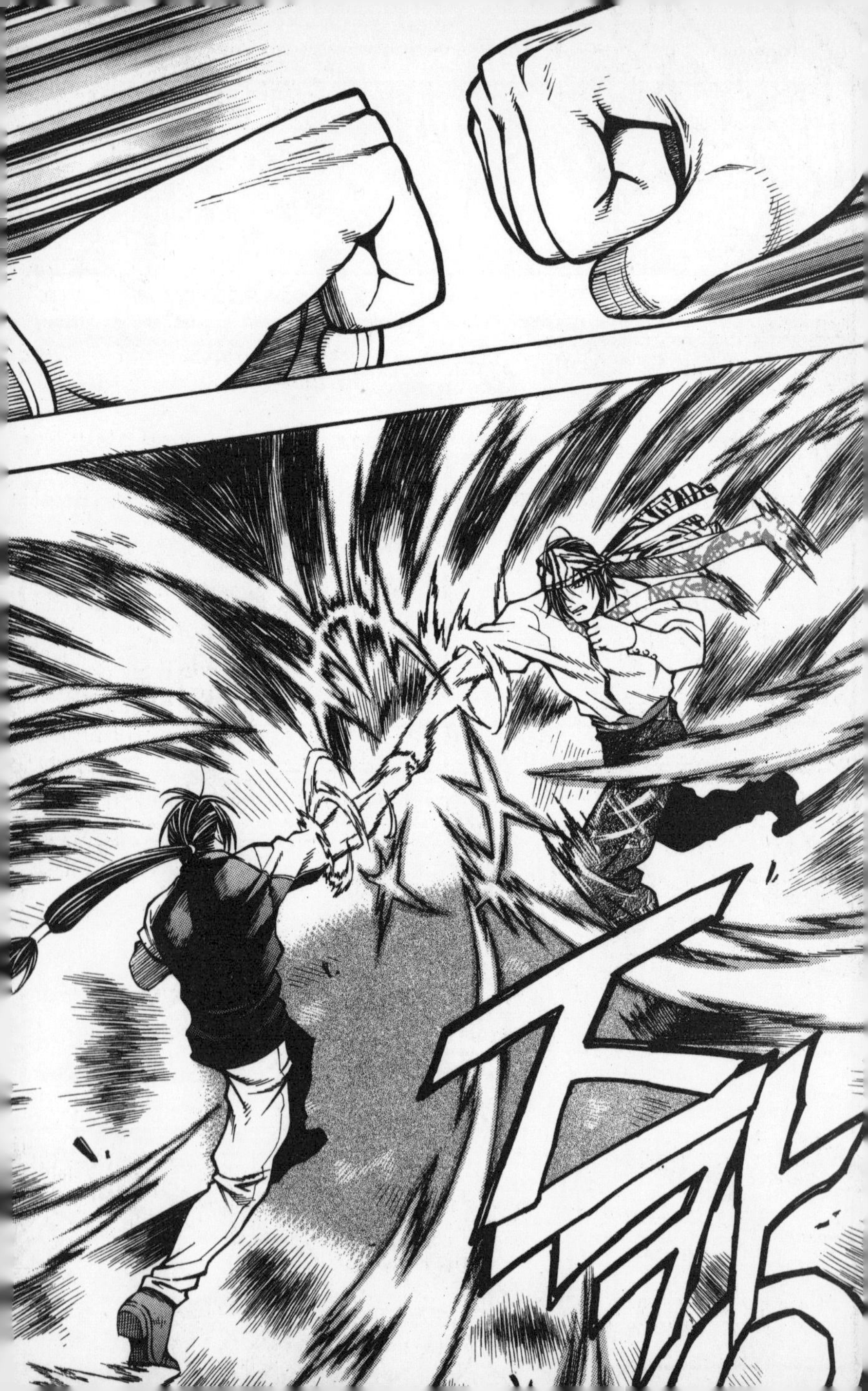

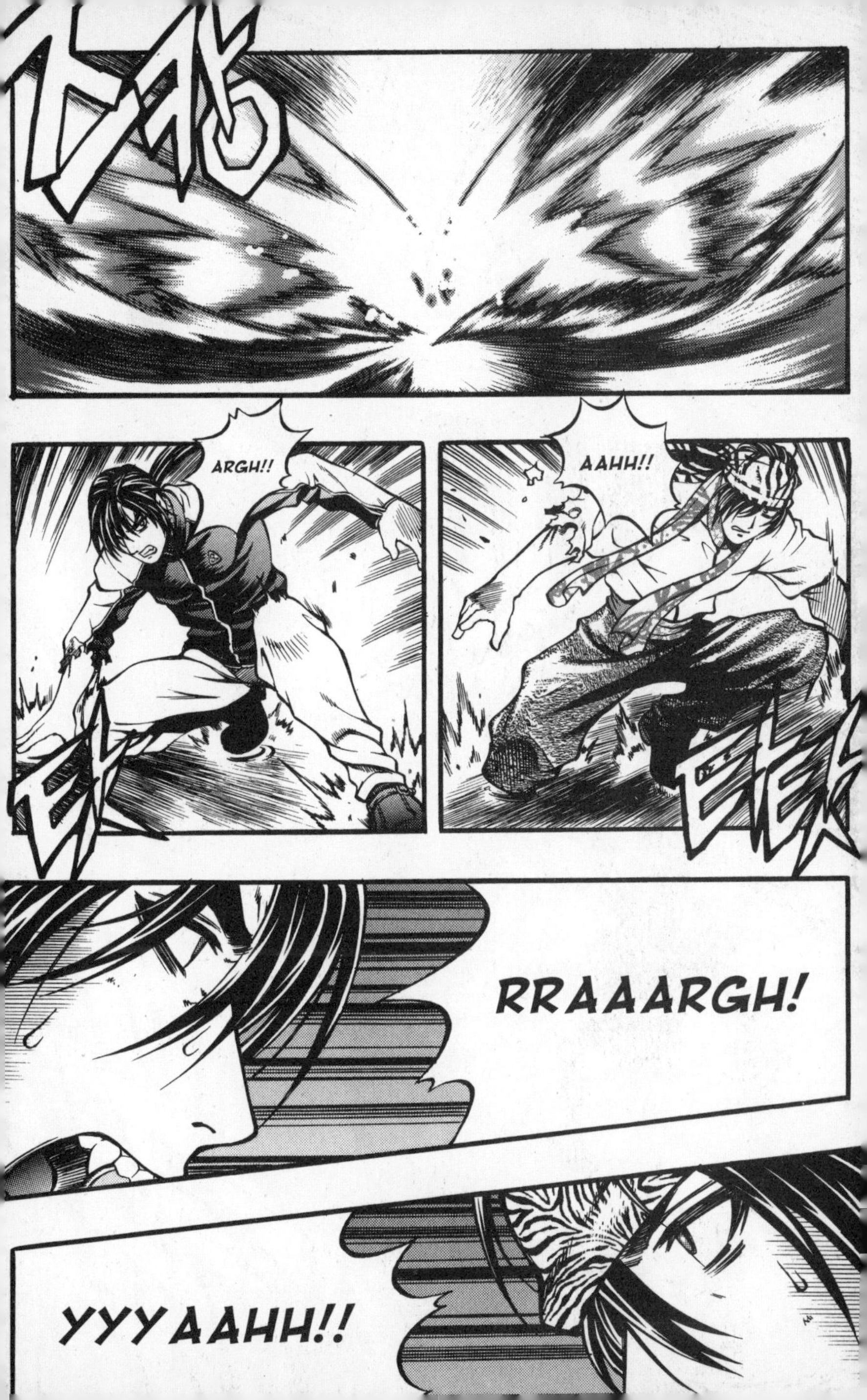
ZAK
ARGH!!
AAHH!!
RRAAARGH!
YYYAAHH!!

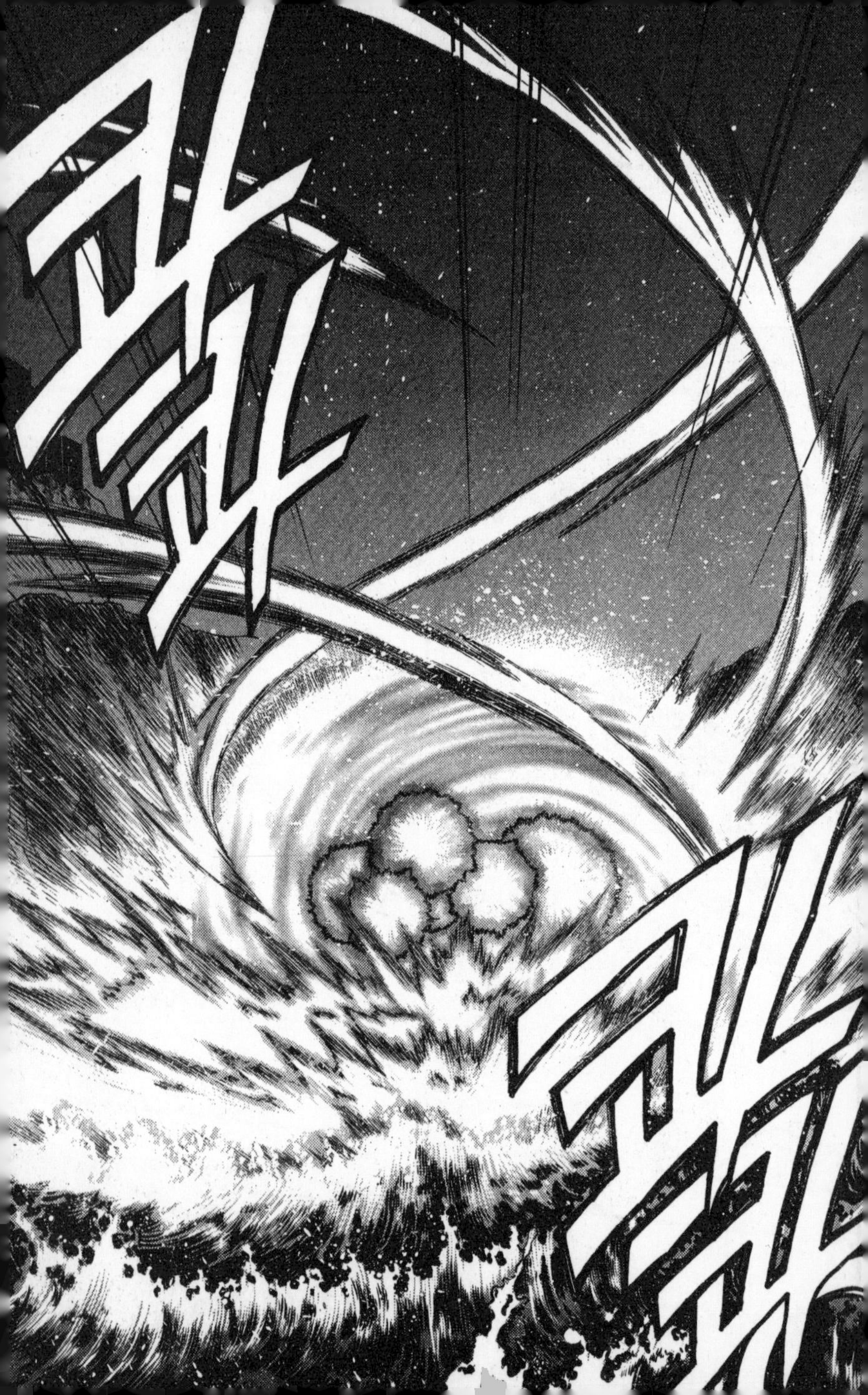

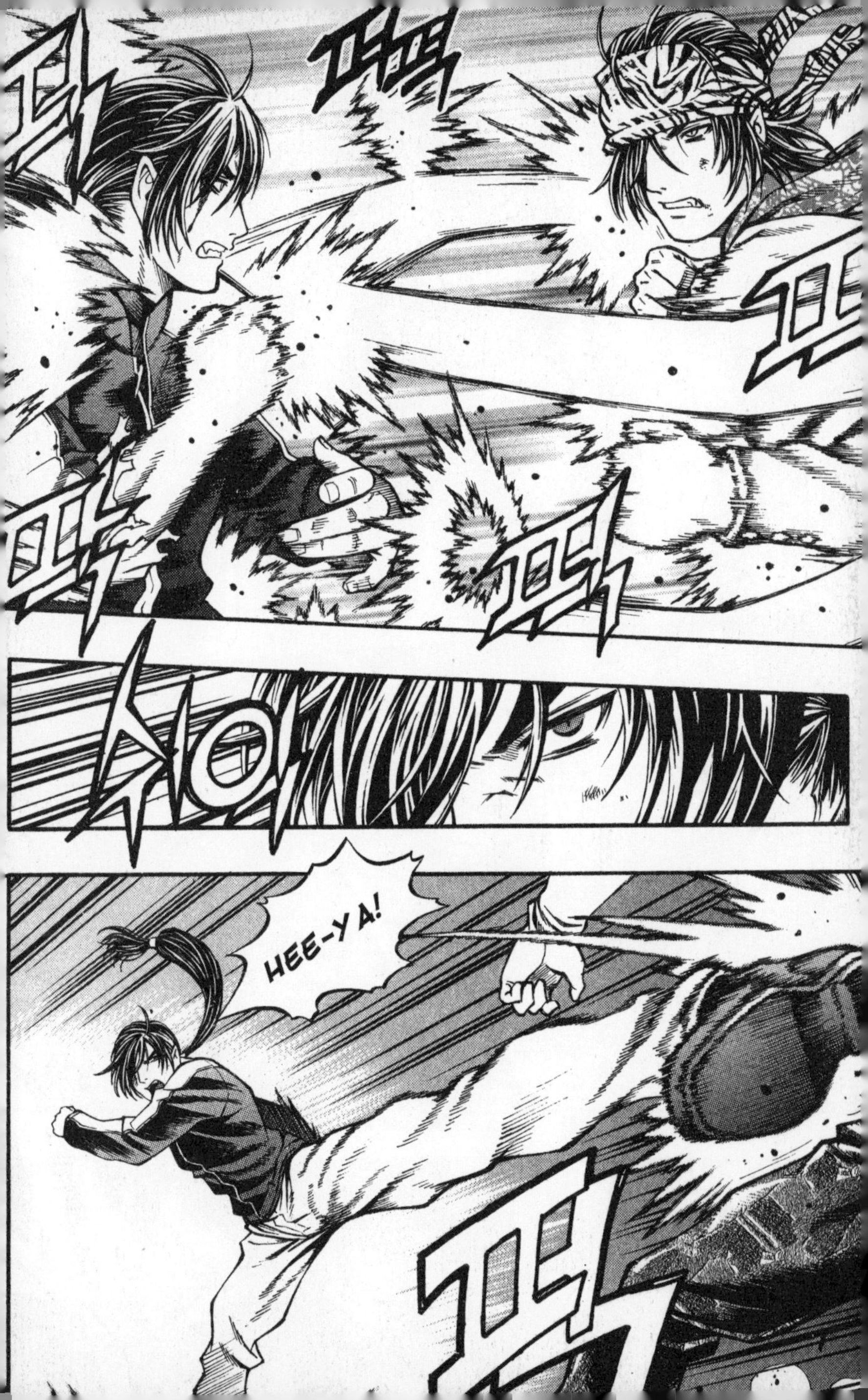
HEE-YA!

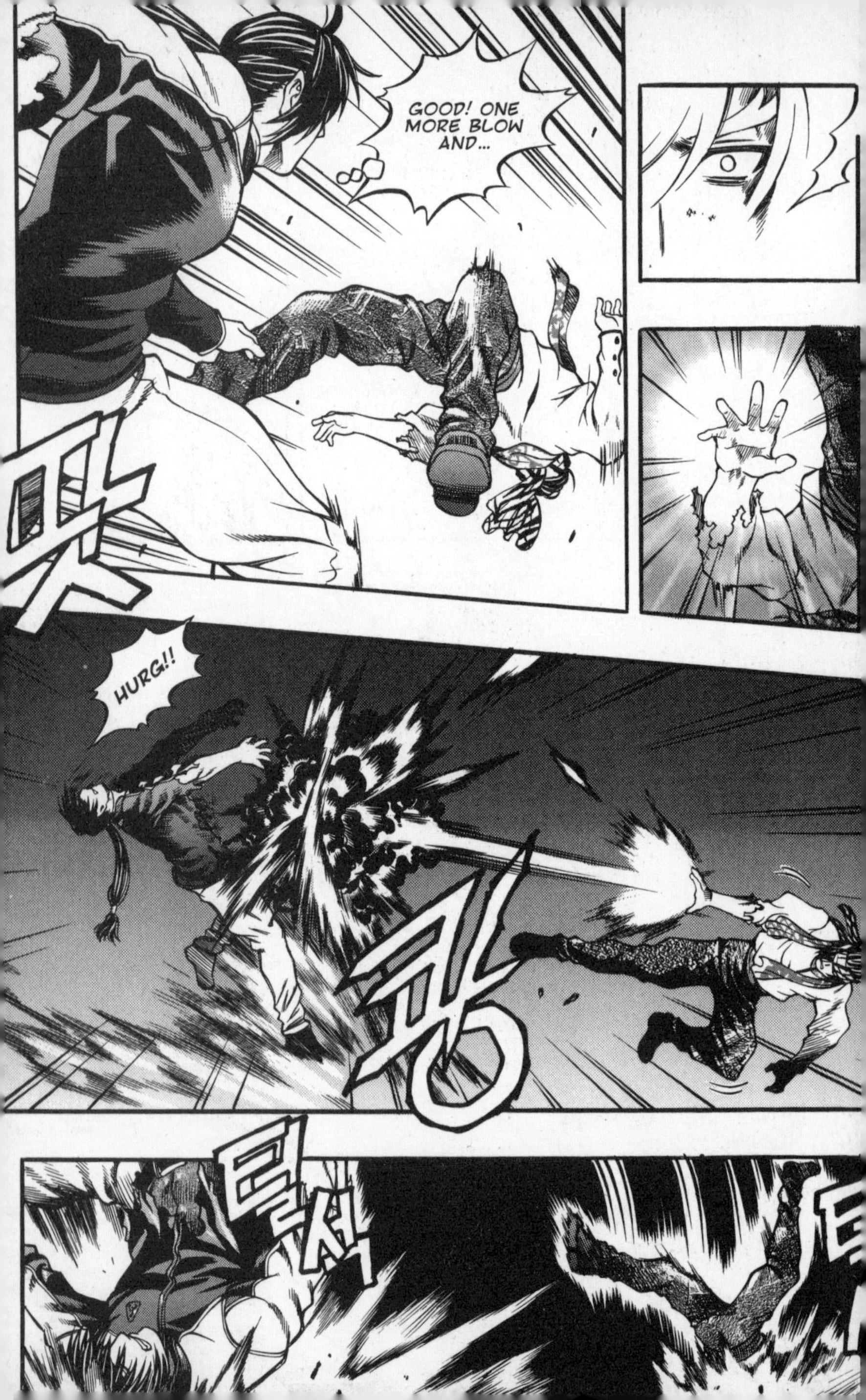
GOOD! ONE MORE BLOW AND...
HURG!!

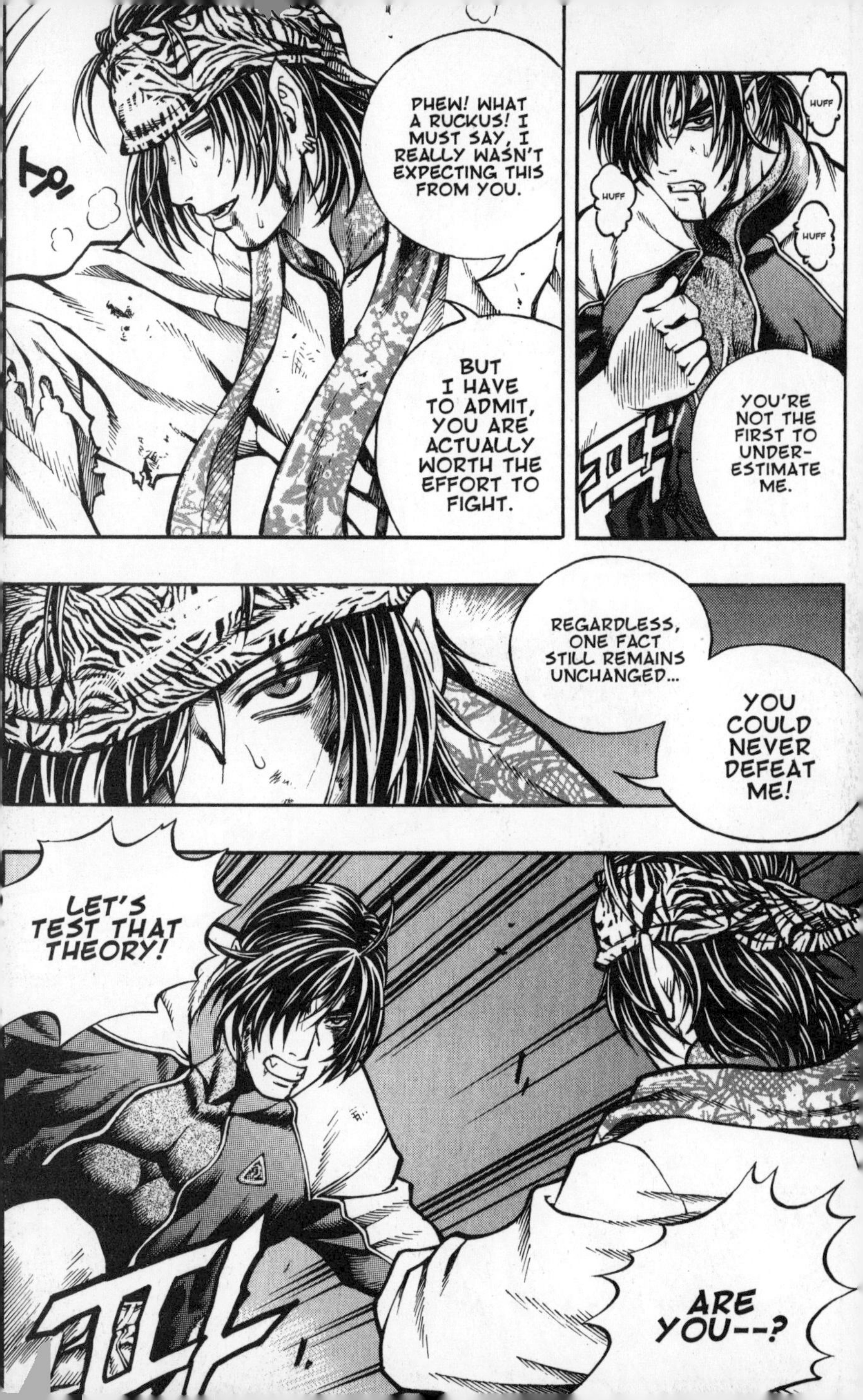
PHEW! WHAT A RUCKUS! I MUST SAY, I REALLY WASN'T EXPECTING THIS FROM YOU.
BUT I HAVE TO ADMIT, YOU ARE ACTUALLY WORTH THE EFFORT TO FIGHT.
HUFF
HUFF
HUFF
YOU'RE NOT THE FIRST TO UNDER-ESTIMATE ME.
REGARDLESS, ONE FACT STILL REMAINS UNCHANGED...
YOU COULD NEVER DEFEAT ME!
LET'S TEST THAT THEORY!
ARE YOU--?

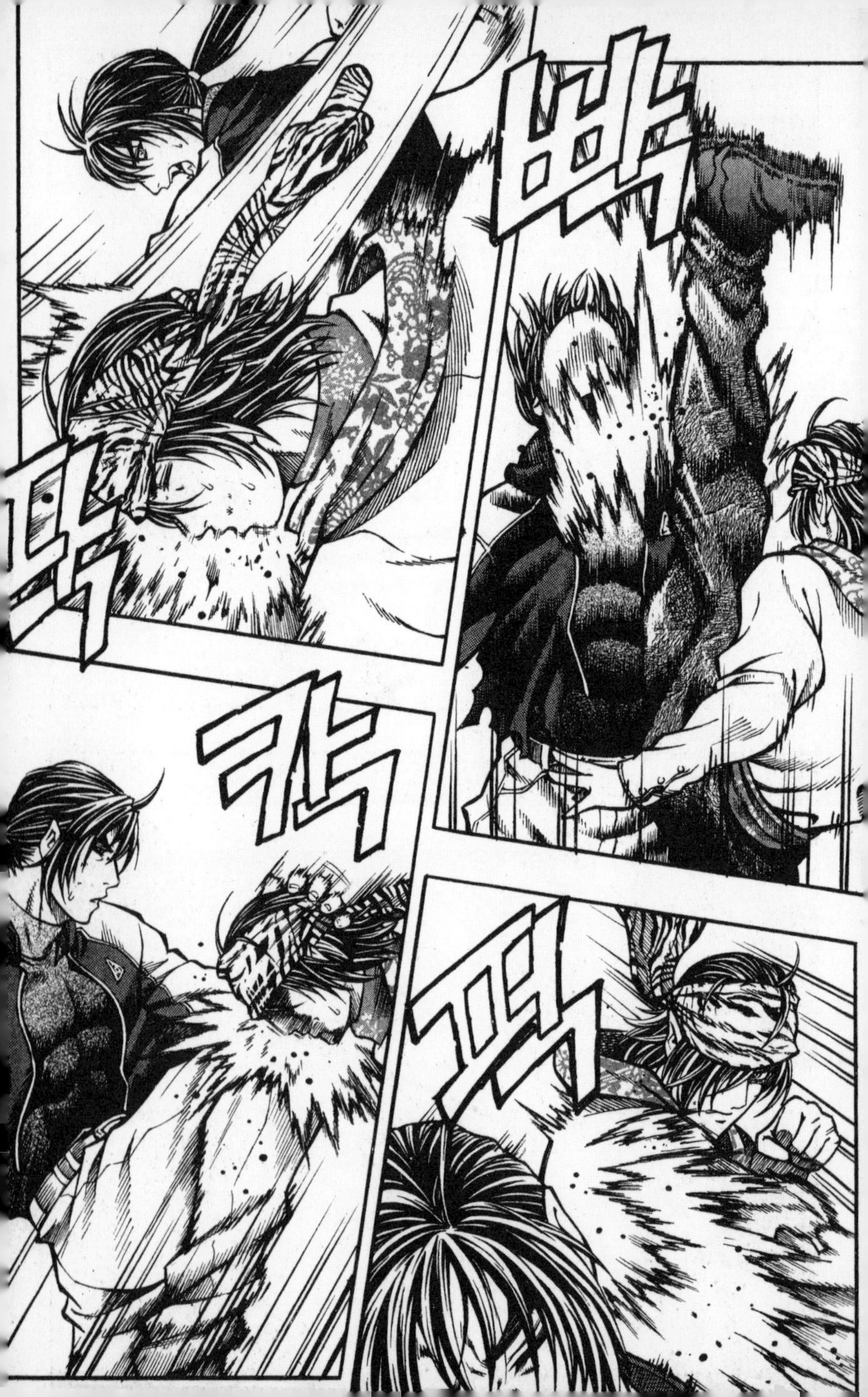

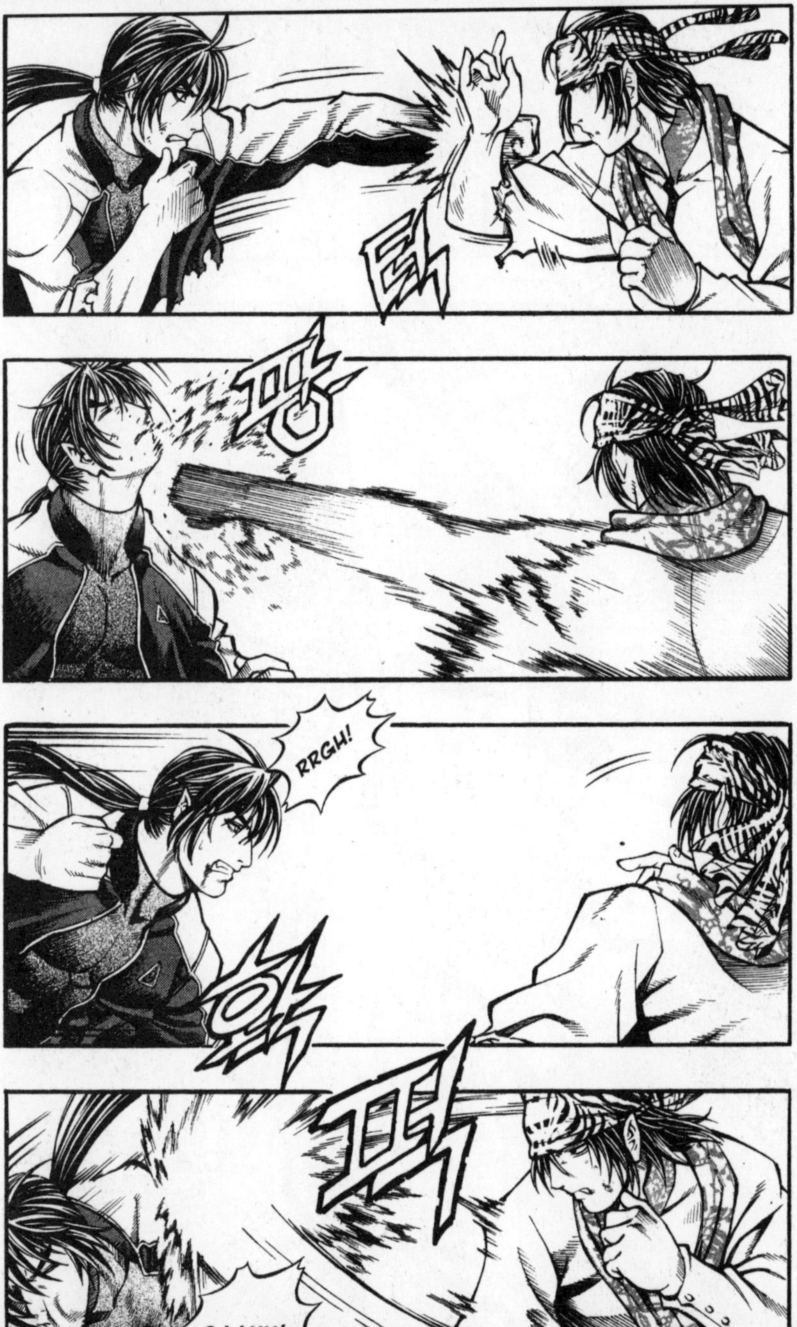
RRGH!
GAAHH!

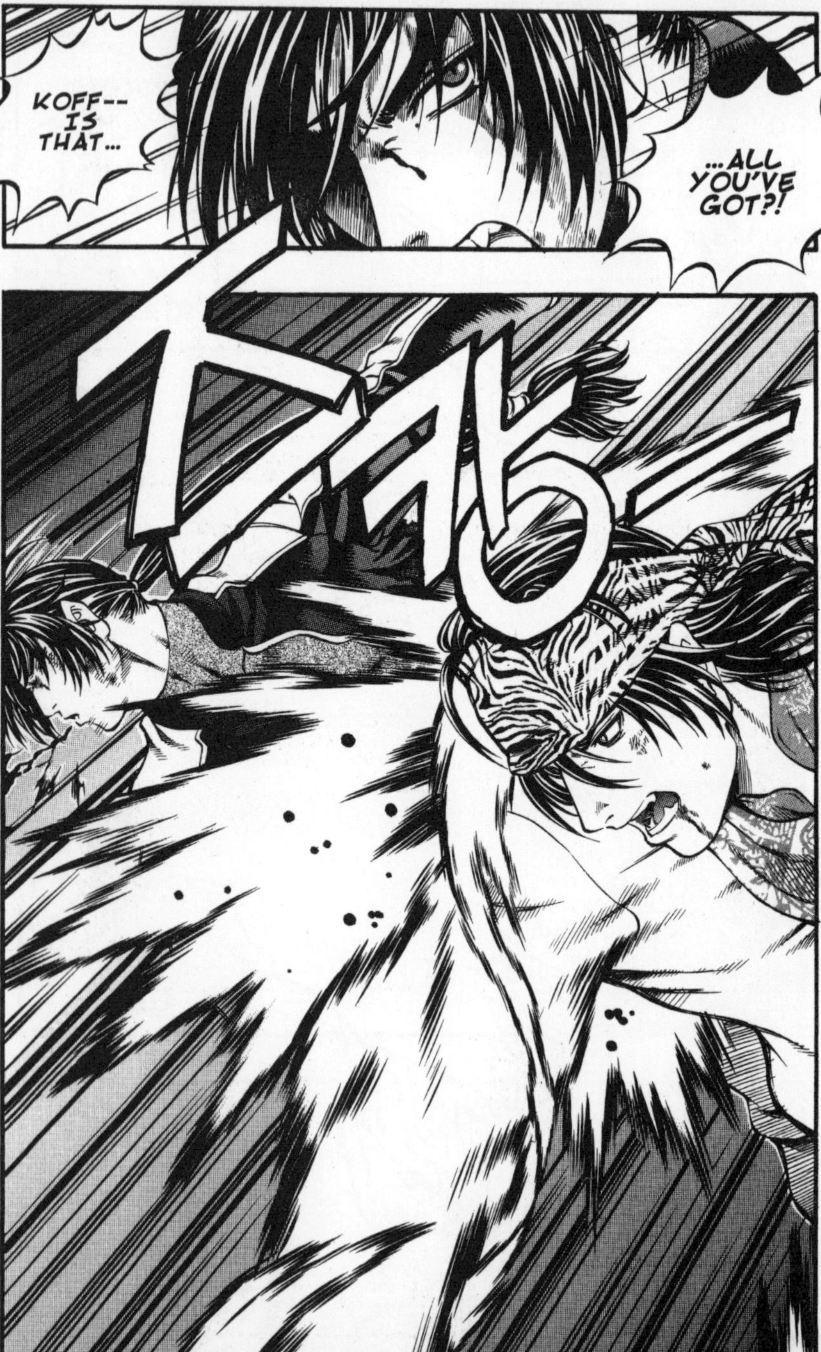
KOFF-- IS THAT...
...ALL YOU'VE GOT?!

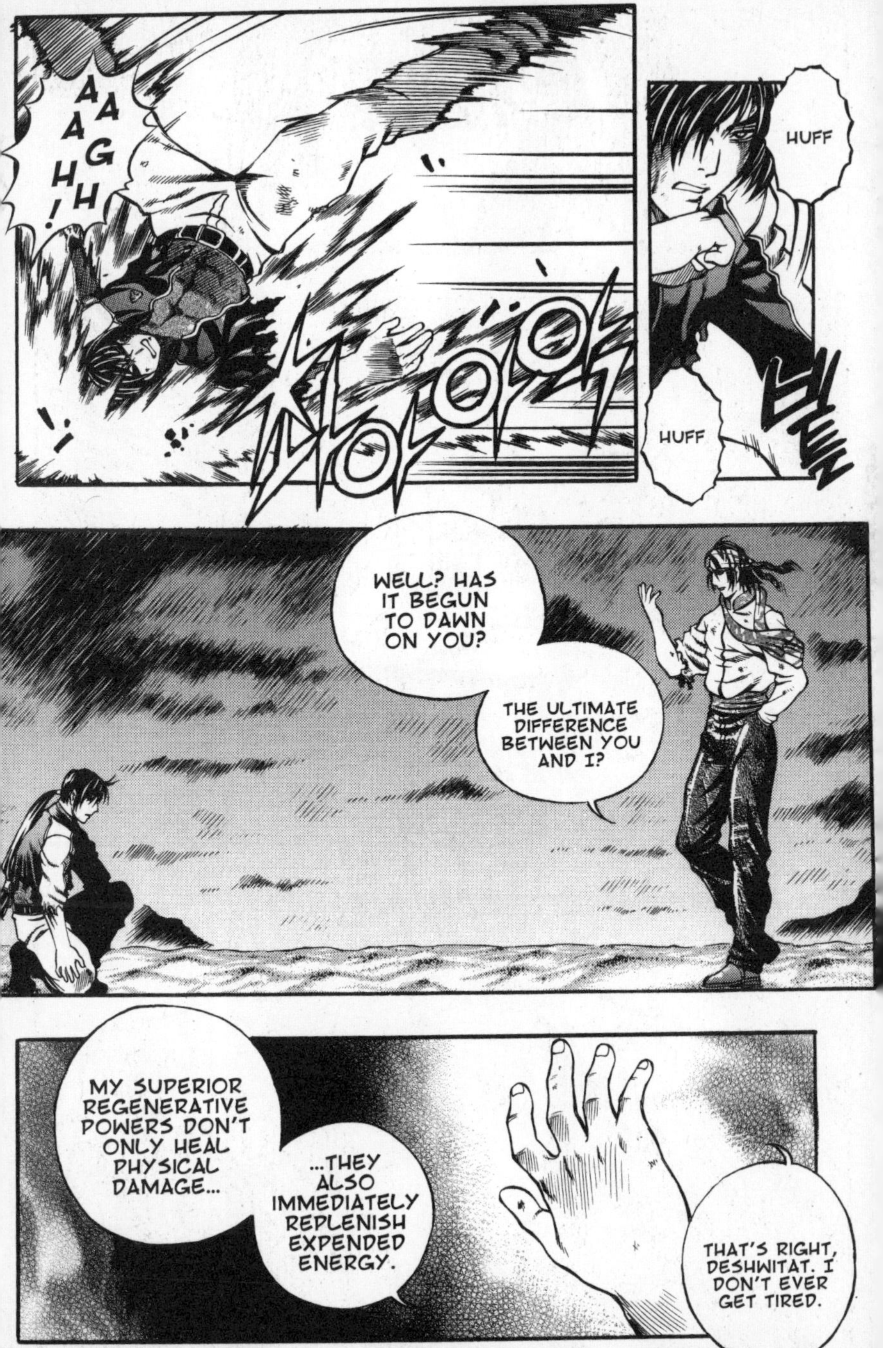
AAAGHH!
HUFF
HUFF
WELL? HAS IT BEGUN TO DAWN ON YOU?
THE ULTIMATE DIFFERENCE BETWEEN YOU AND I?
MY SUPERIOR REGENERATIVE POWERS DON'T ONLY HEAL PHYSICAL DAMAGE...
...THEY ALSO IMMEDIATELY REPLENISH EXPENDED ENERGY.
THAT'S RIGHT, DESHWITAT. I DON'T EVER GET TIRED.

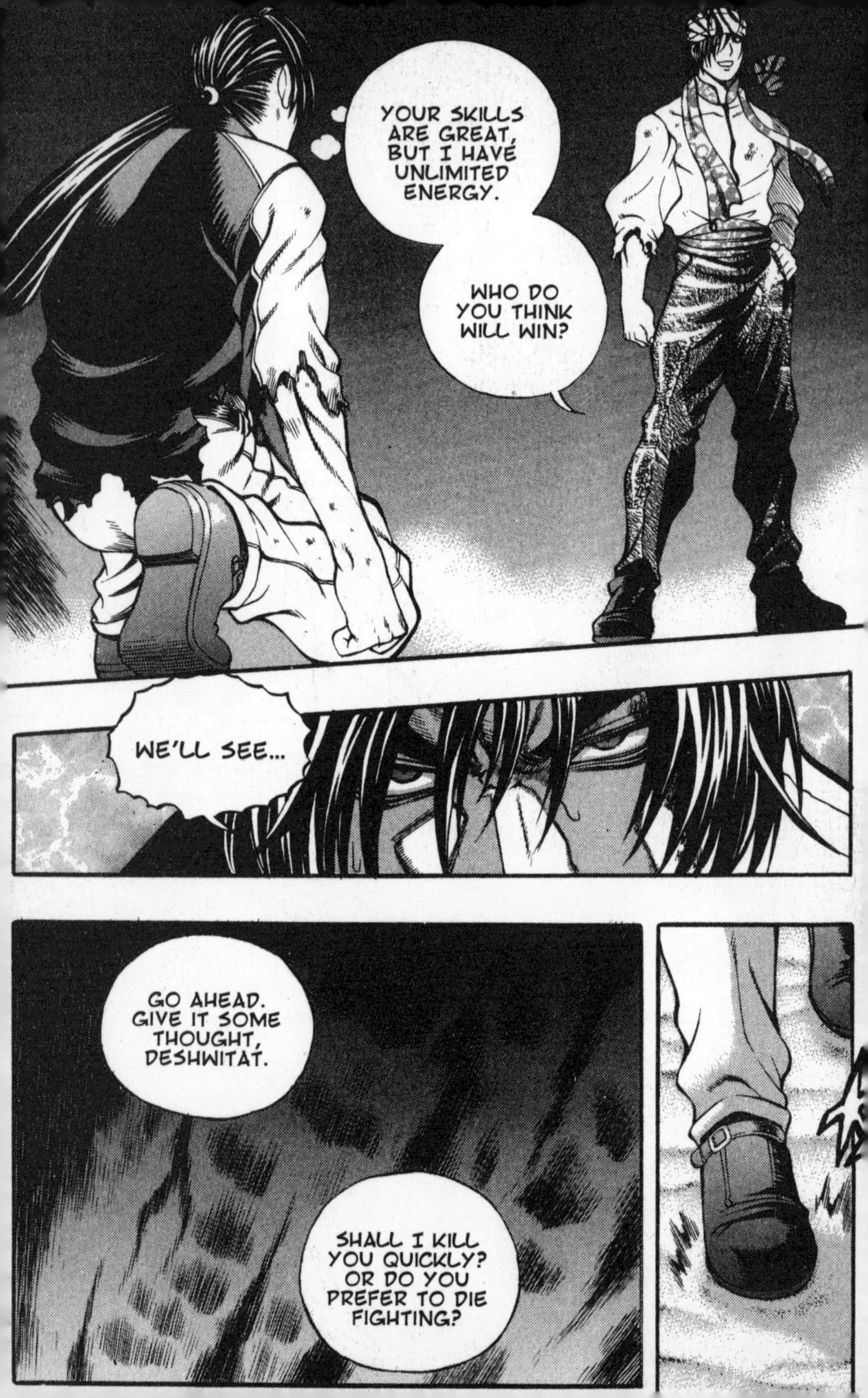
YOUR SKILLS ARE GREAT, BUT I HAVE UNLIMITED ENERGY.
WHO DO YOU THINK WILL WIN?
WE'LL SEE...
GO AHEAD. GIVE IT SOME THOUGHT, DESHWITAT.
SHALL I KILL YOU QUICKLY? OR DO YOU PREFER TO DIE FIGHTING?

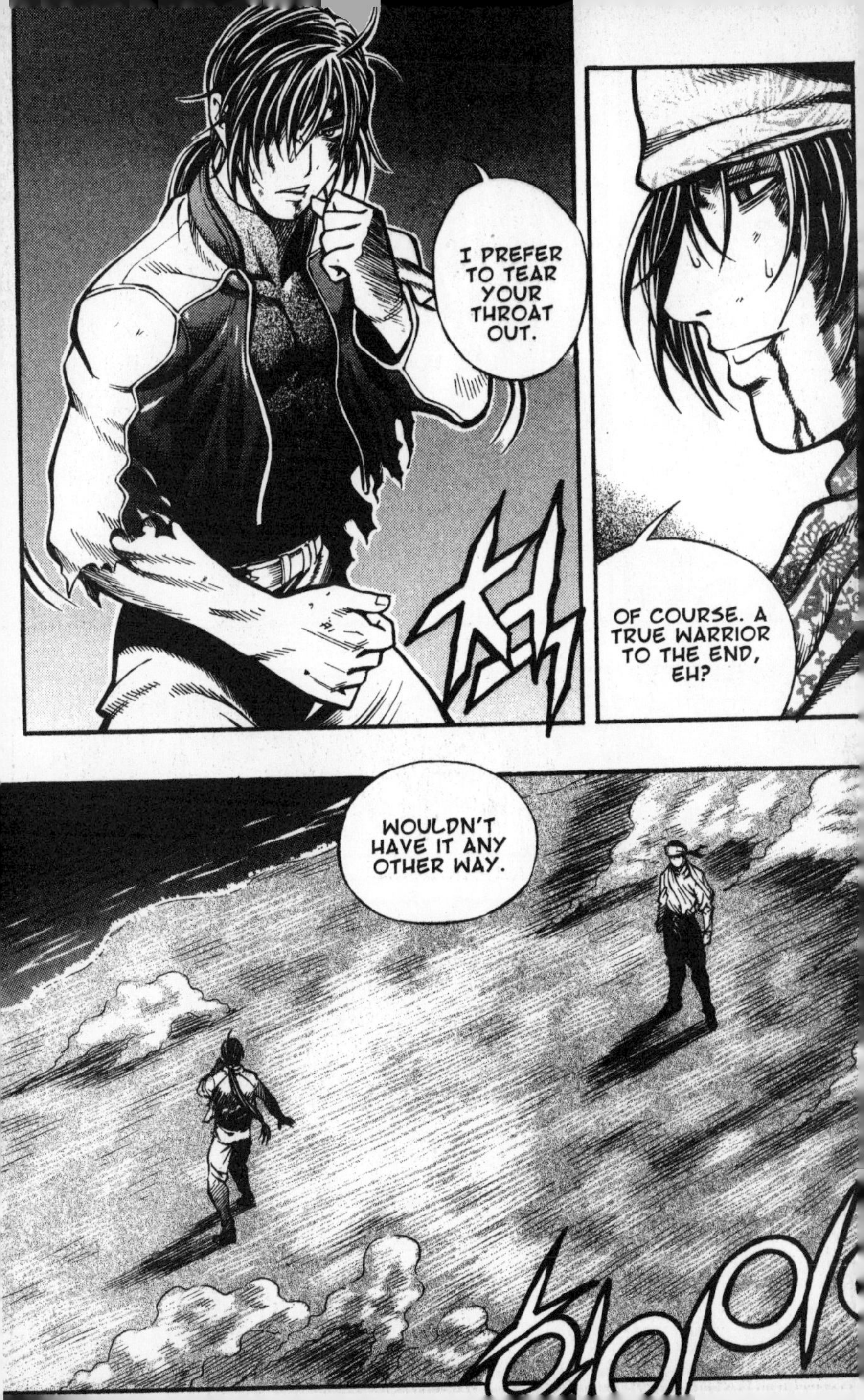
I PREFER TO TEAR YOUR THROAT OUT.
OF COURSE. A TRUE WARRIOR TO THE END, EH?
WOULDN'T HAVE IT ANY OTHER WAY.

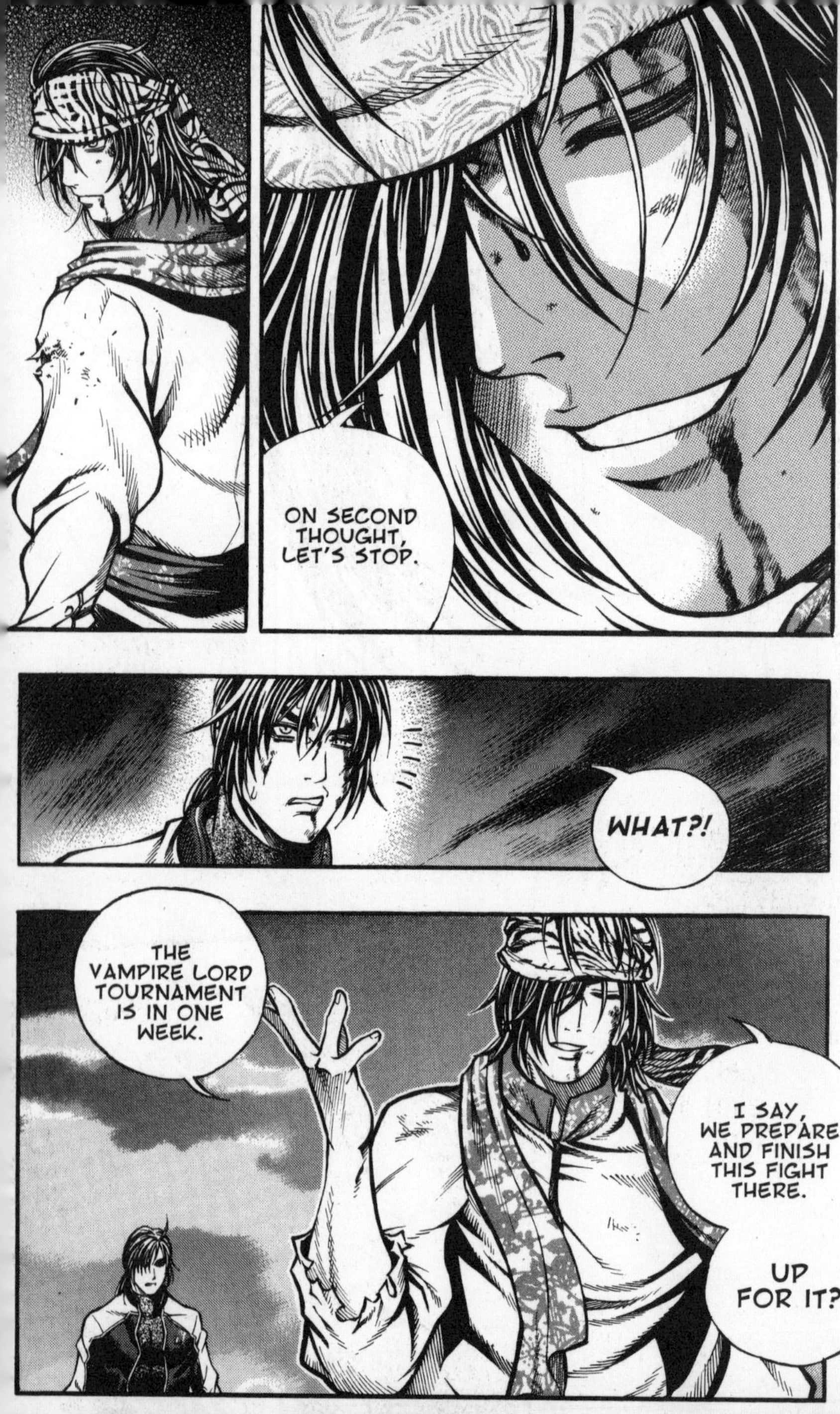
ON SECOND THOUGHT, LET'S STOP.
WHAT?!
THE VAMPIRE LORD TOURNAMENT IS IN ONE WEEK.
I SAY, WE PREPARE AND FINISH THIS FIGHT THERE.
UP FOR IT?

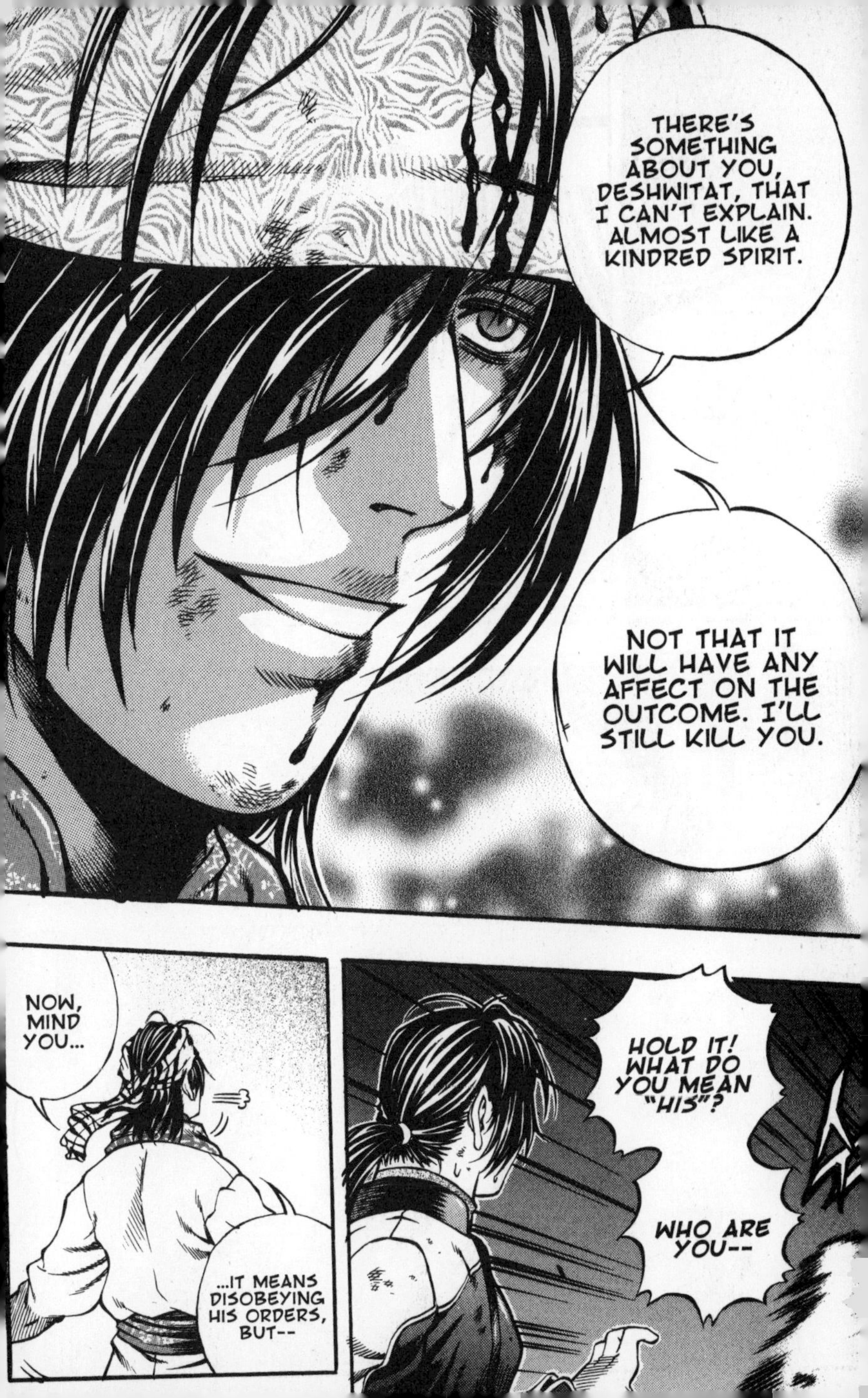
THERE'S SOMETHING ABOUT YOU, DESHWITAT, THAT I CAN'T EXPLAIN. ALMOST LIKE A KINDRED SPIRIT.
NOT THAT IT WILL HAVE ANY AFFECT ON THE OUTCOME. I'LL STILL KILL YOU.
NOW, MIND YOU...
...IT MEANS DISOBEYING HIS ORDERS, BUT--
HOLD IT! WHAT DO YOU MEAN "HIS"?
WHO ARE YOU--

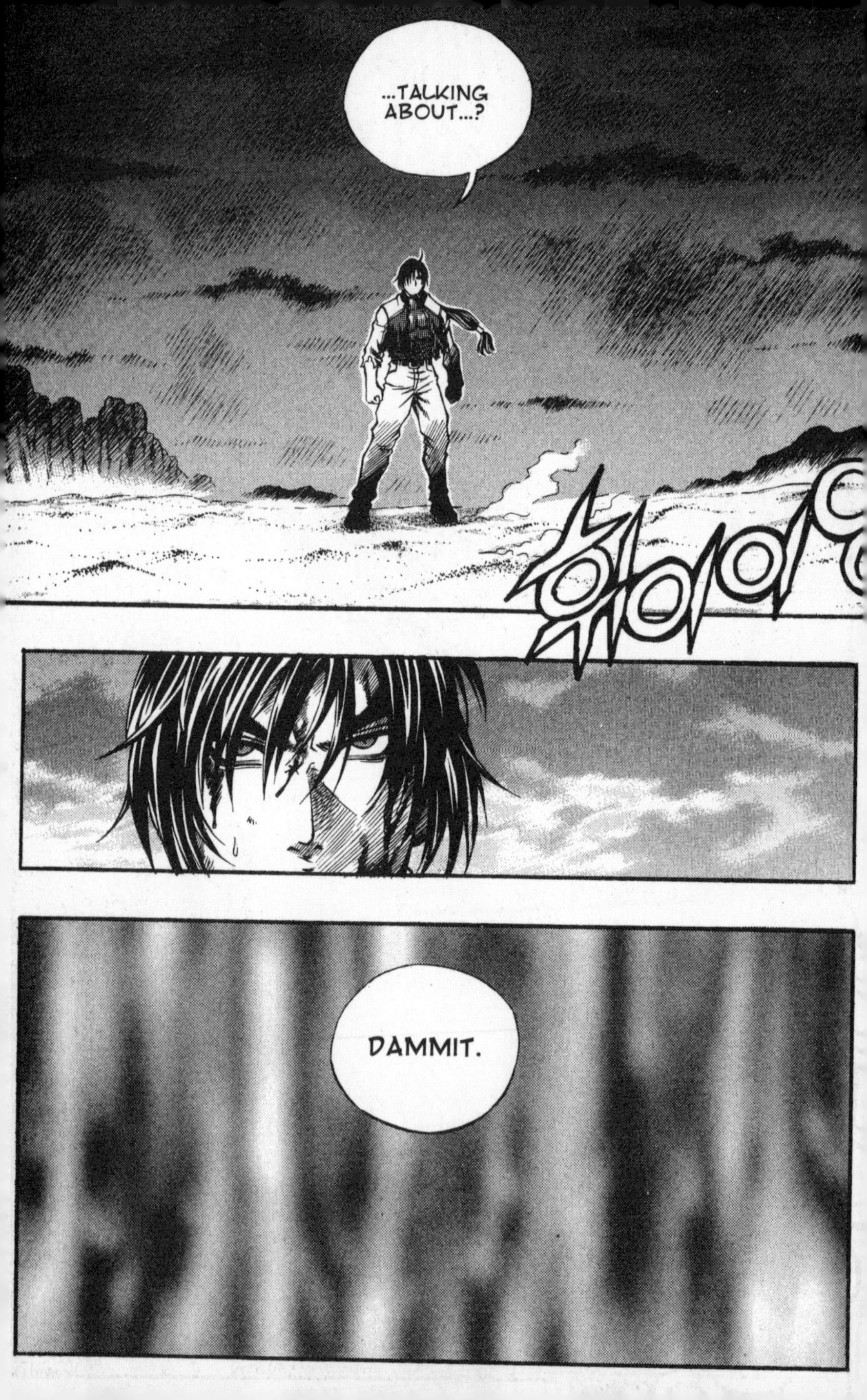
...TALKING ABOUT...?
DAMMIT.

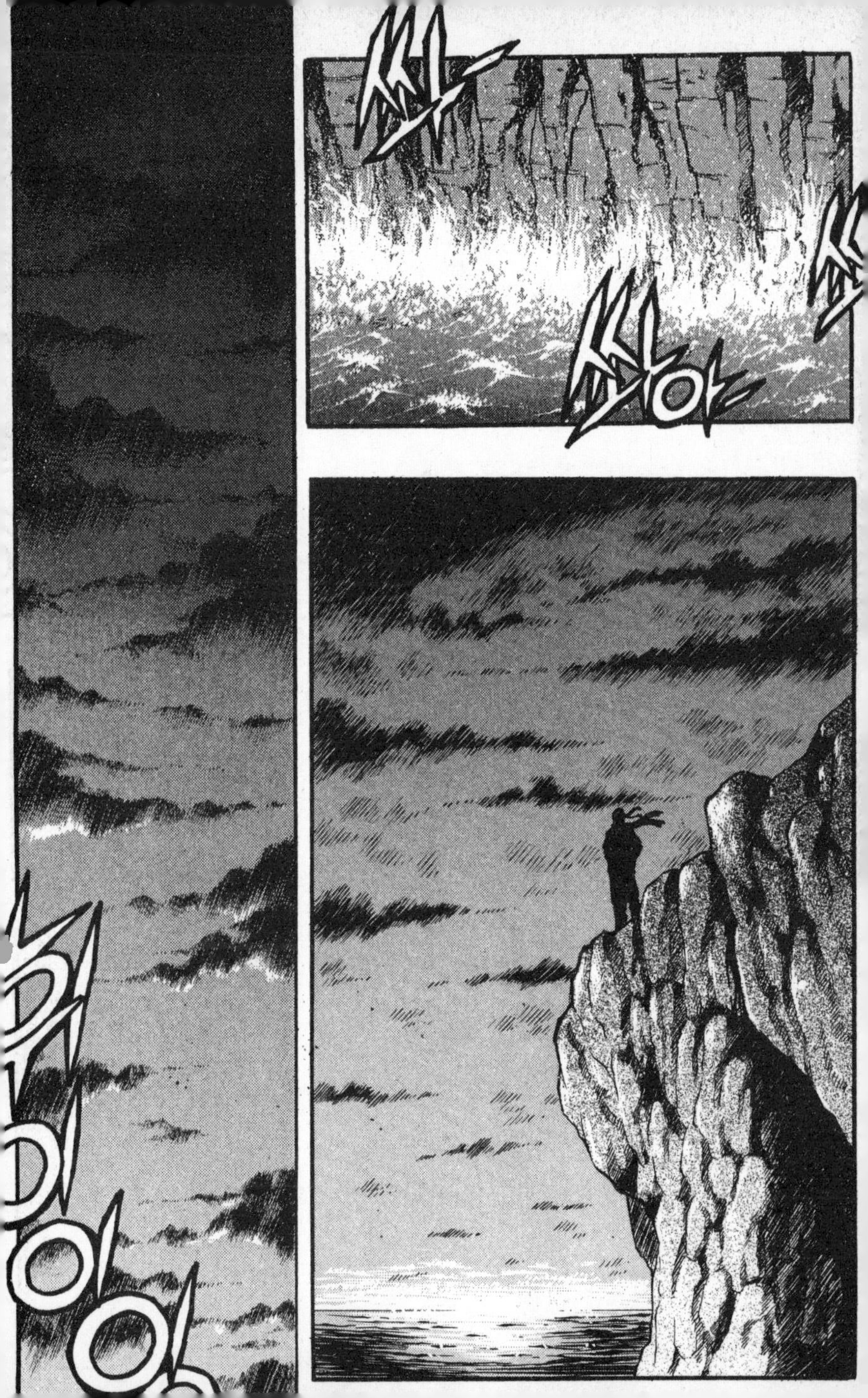

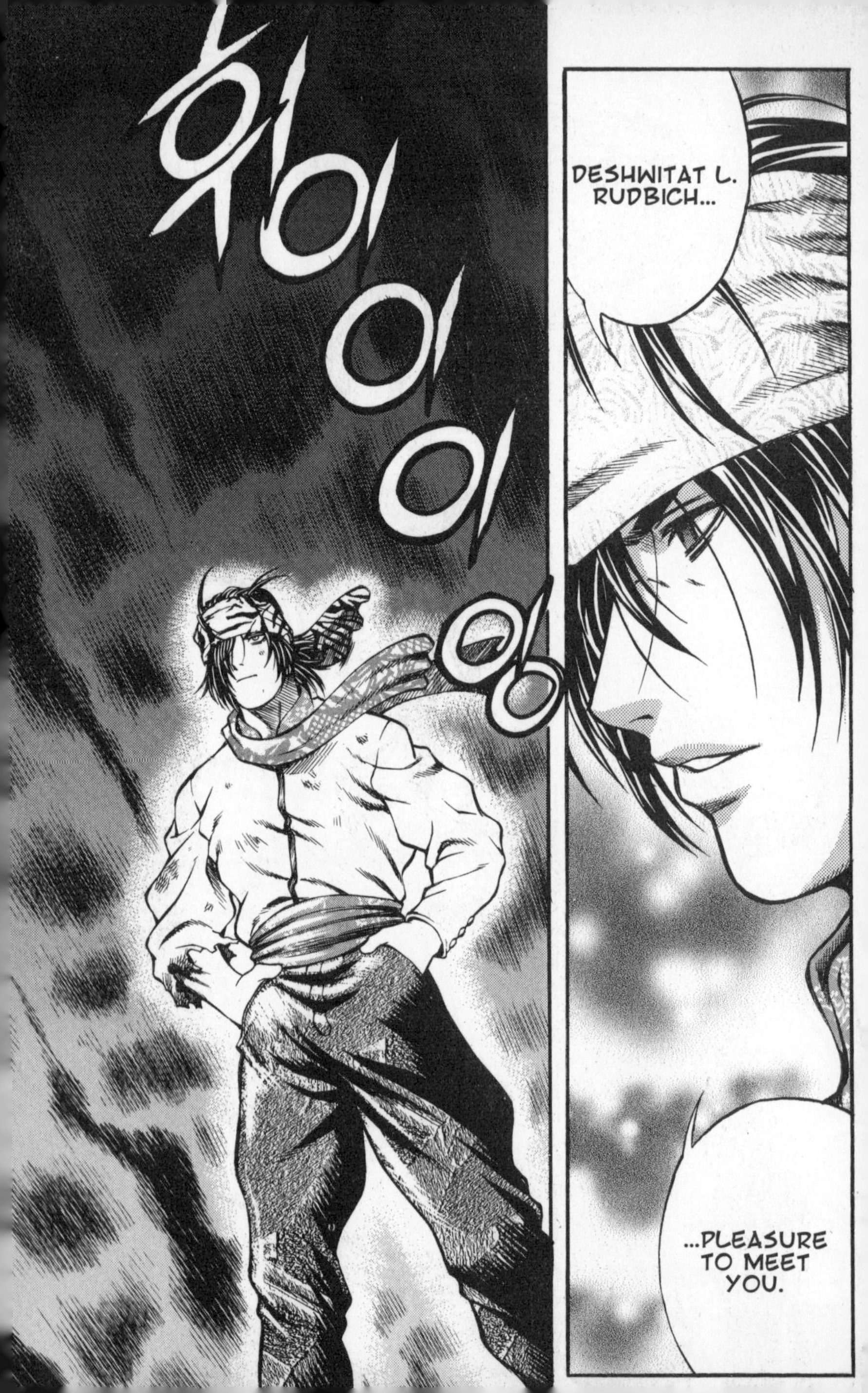
휘이이이잉
DESHWITAT L. RUDBICH...
...PLEASURE TO MEET YOU.

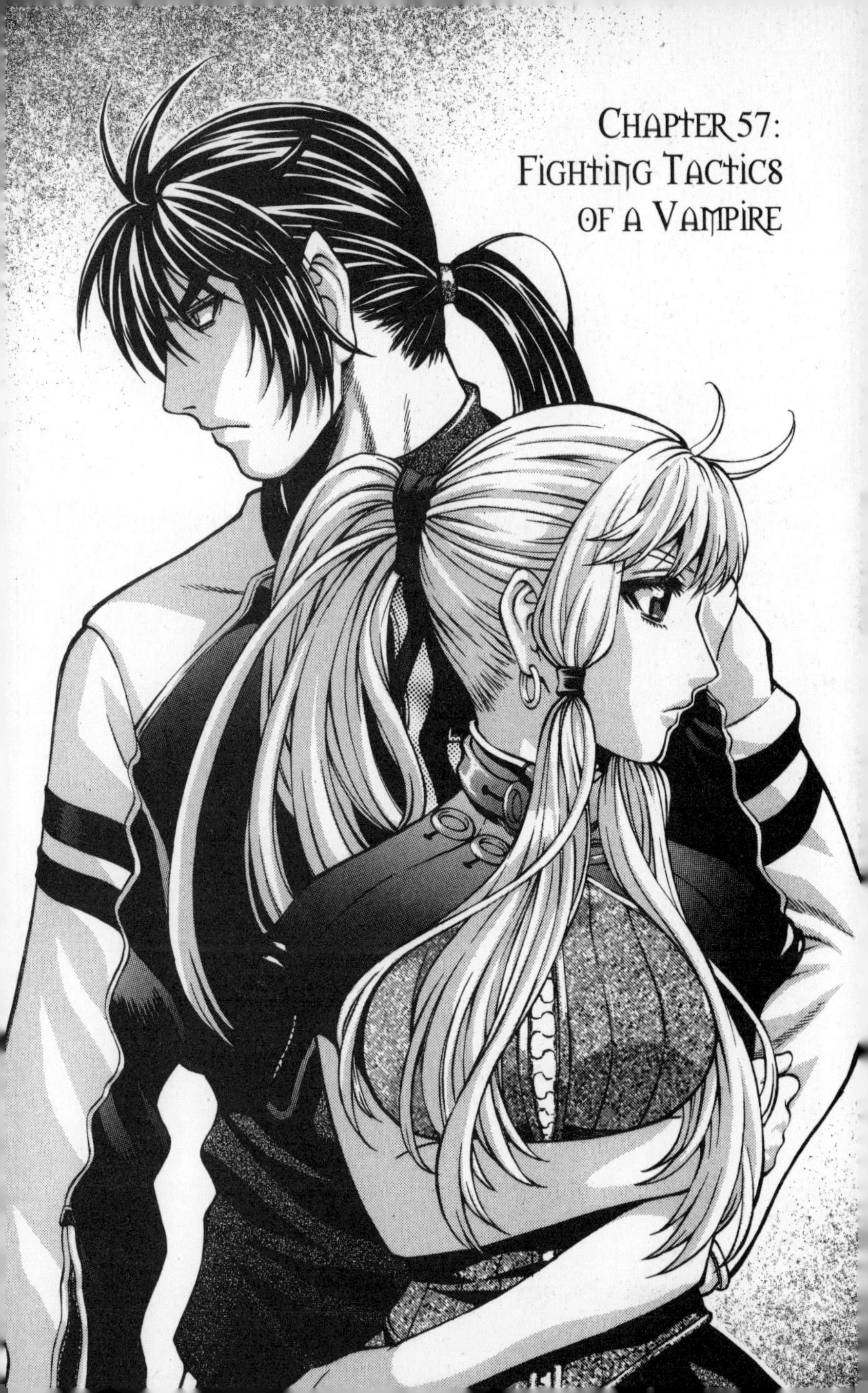
Chapter 57:
Fighting Tactics
of a Vampire

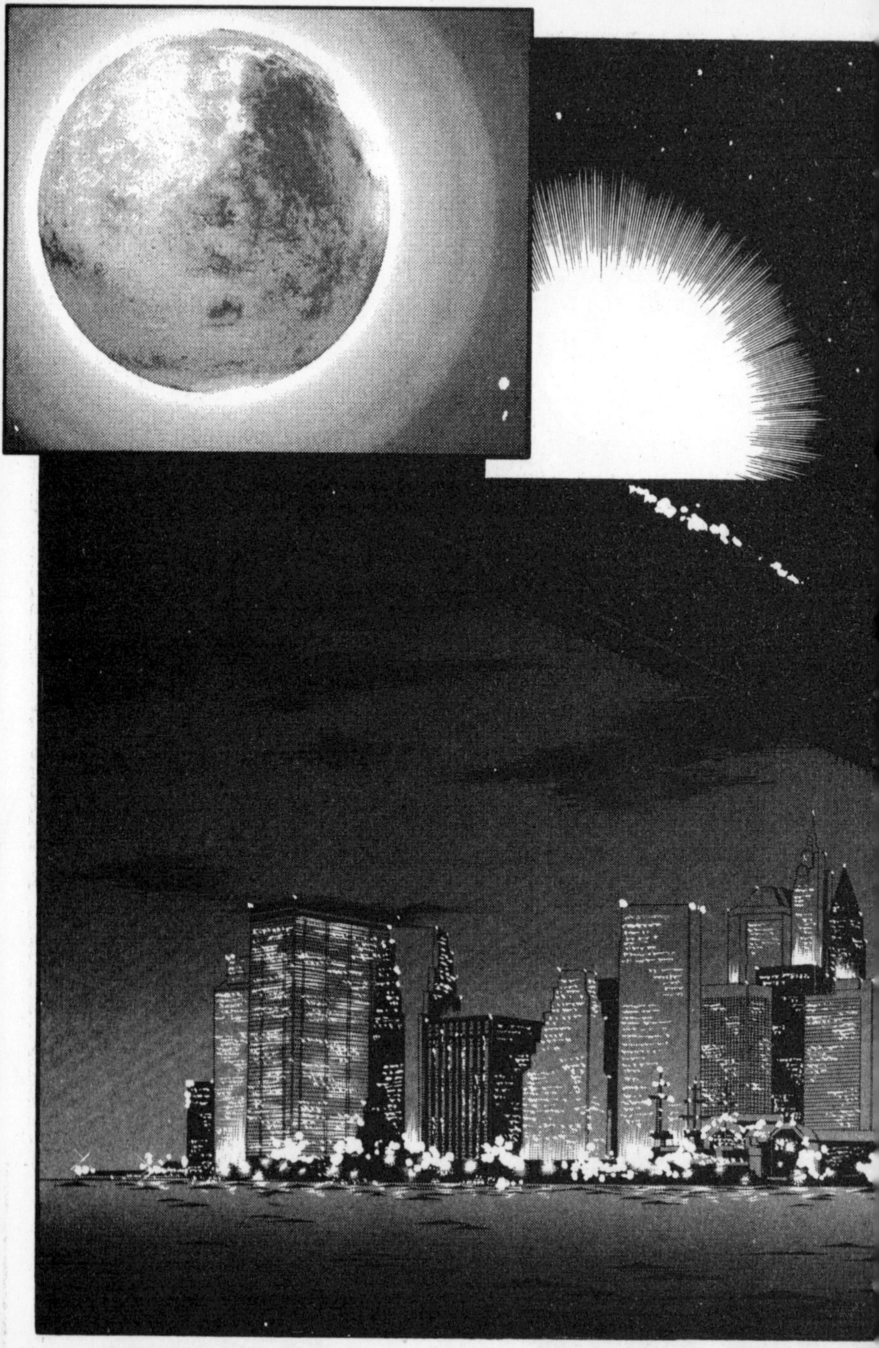

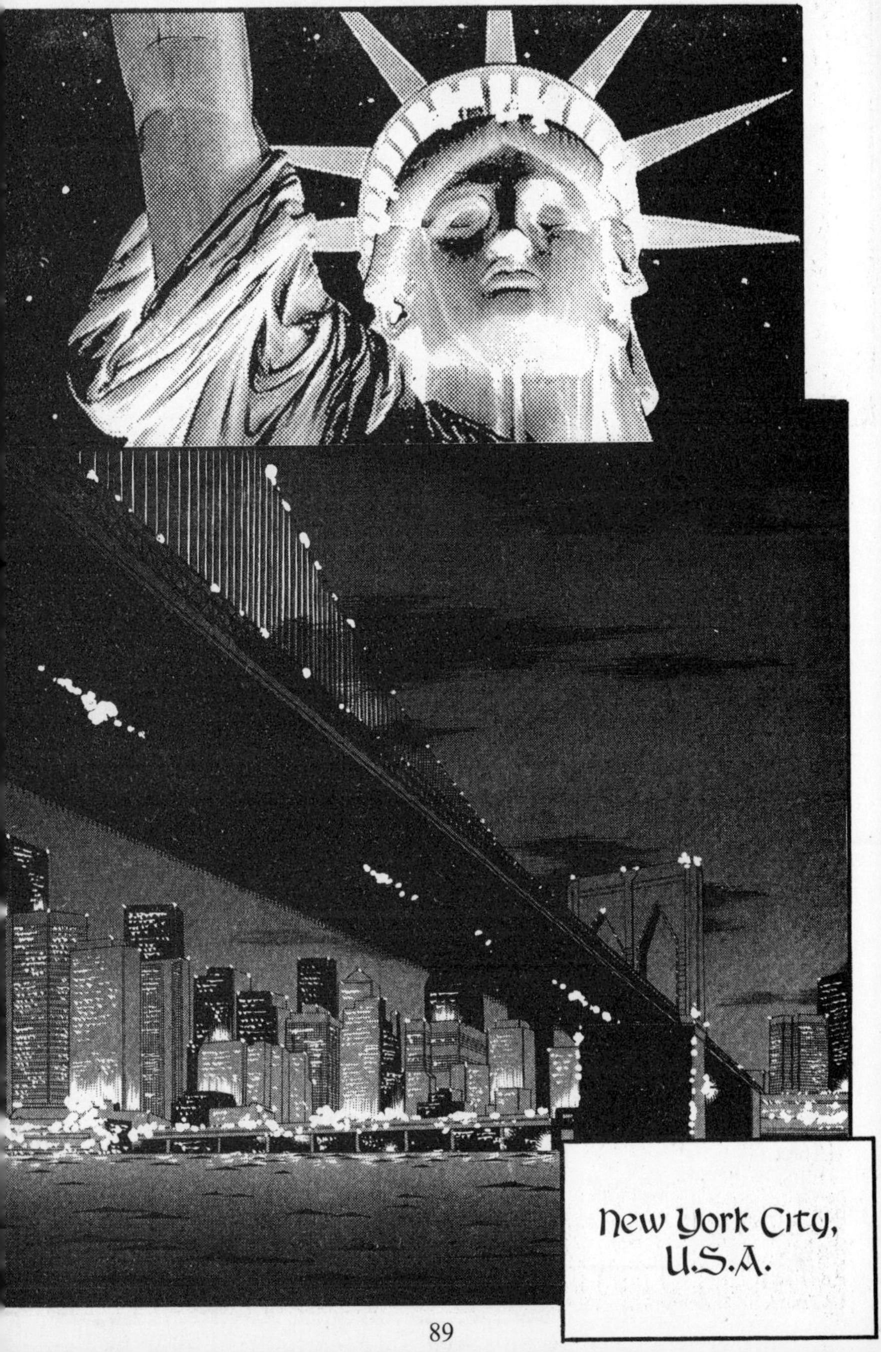
New York City,
U.S.A.

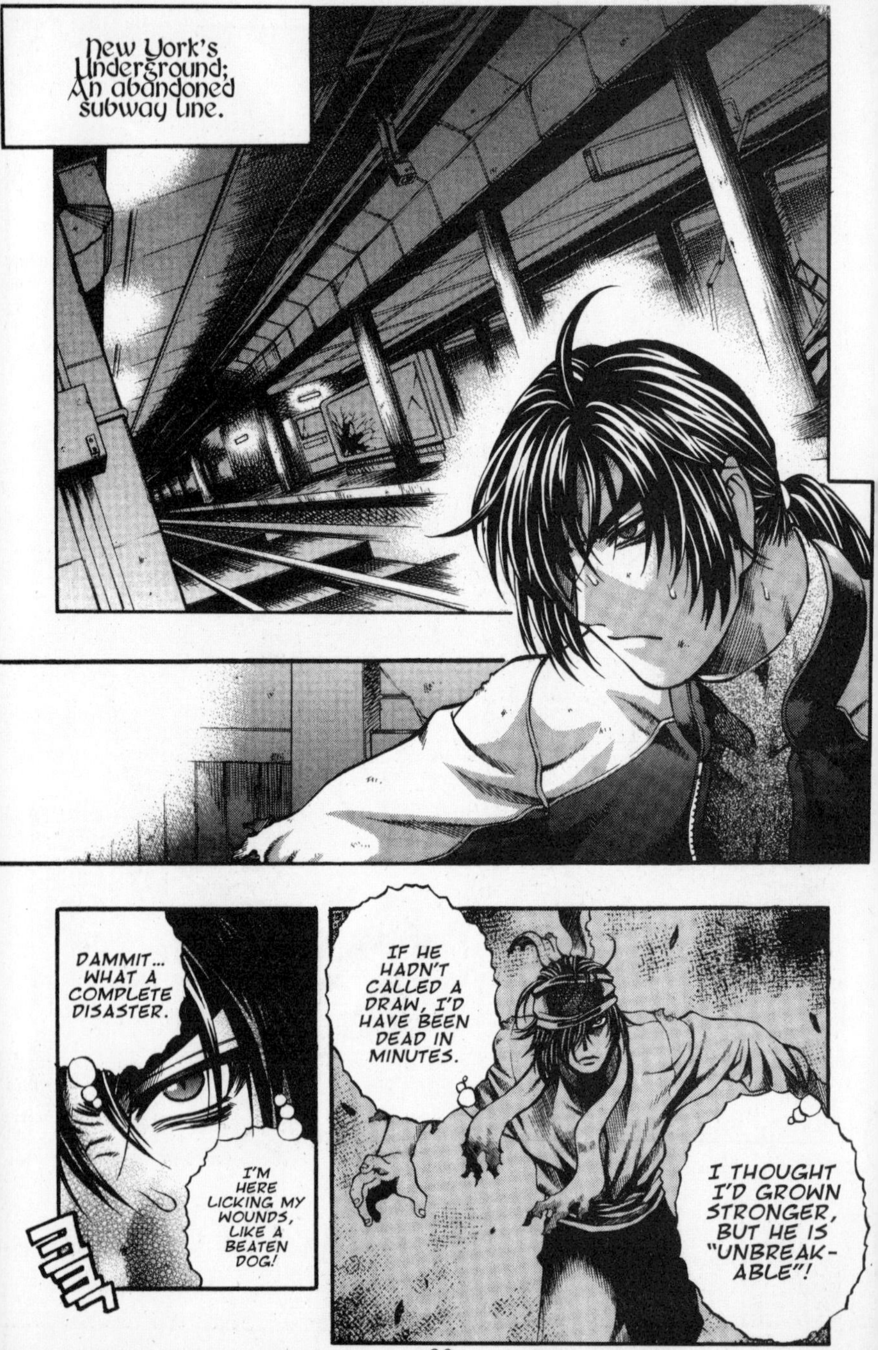
New York's Underground; An abandoned subway line.
DAMMIT... WHAT A COMPLETE DISASTER.
I'M HERE LICKING MY WOUNDS, LIKE A BEATEN DOG!
IF HE HADN'T CALLED A DRAW, I'D HAVE BEEN DEAD IN MINUTES.
I THOUGHT I'D GROWN STRONGER, BUT HE IS "UNBREAK-ABLE"!

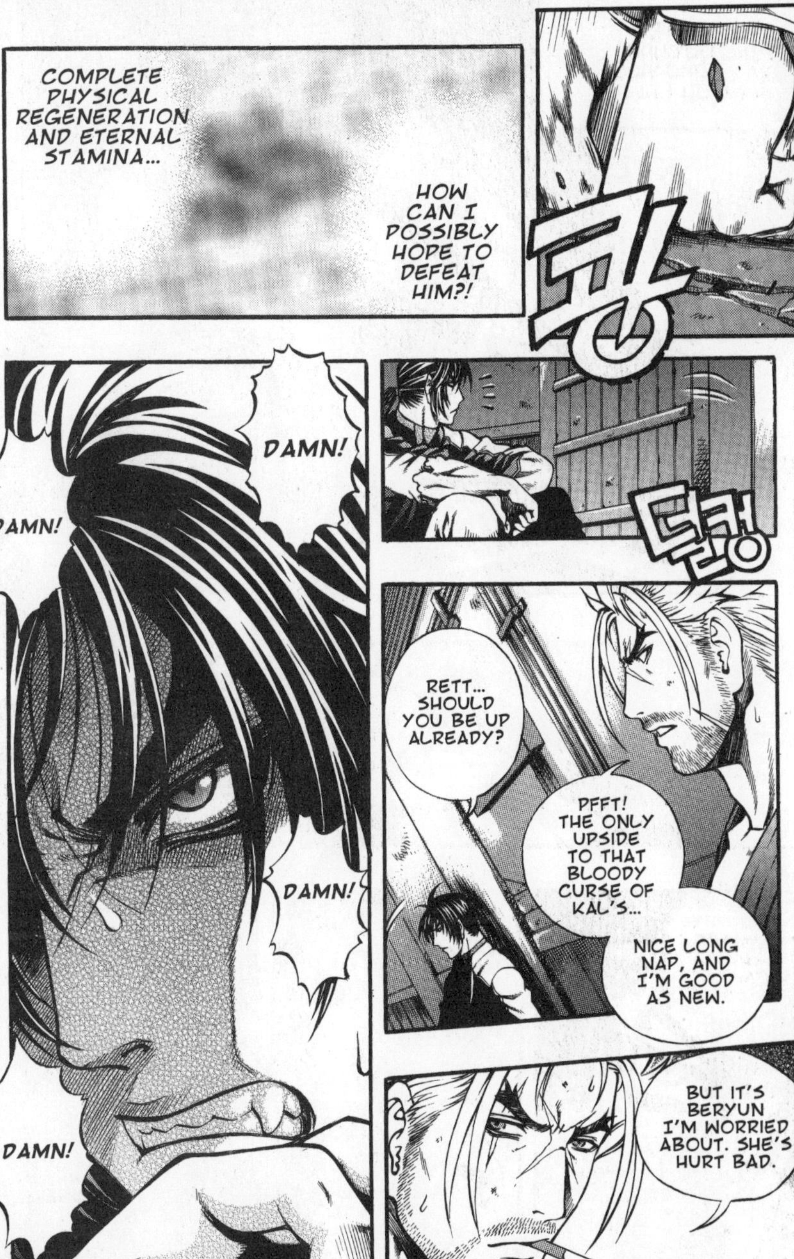
COMPLETE PHYSICAL REGENERATION AND ETERNAL STAMINA...
HOW CAN I POSSIBLY HOPE TO DEFEAT HIM?!
쾅
DAMN!
DAMN!
DAMN!
DAMN!
덜컹
RETT... SHOULD YOU BE UP ALREADY?
PFFT! THE ONLY UPSIDE TO THAT BLOODY CURSE OF KAL'S...
NICE LONG NAP, AND I'M GOOD AS NEW.
BUT IT'S BERYUN I'M WORRIED ABOUT. SHE'S HURT BAD.

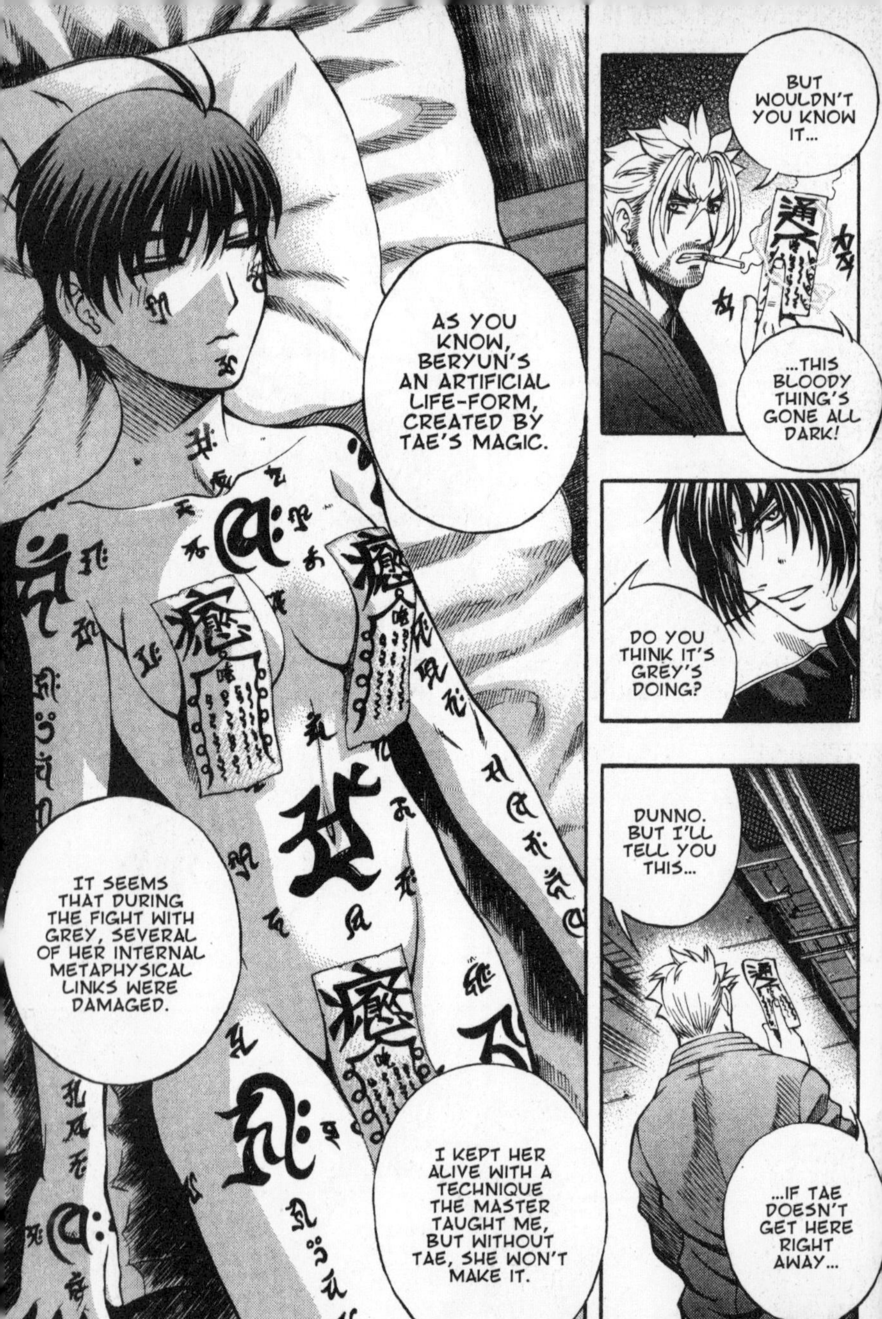
AS YOU KNOW, BERYUN'S AN ARTIFICIAL LIFE-FORM, CREATED BY TAE'S MAGIC.
IT SEEMS THAT DURING THE FIGHT WITH GREY, SEVERAL OF HER INTERNAL METAPHYSICAL LINKS WERE DAMAGED.
I KEPT HER ALIVE WITH A TECHNIQUE THE MASTER TAUGHT ME, BUT WITHOUT TAE, SHE WON'T MAKE IT.
BUT WOULDN'T YOU KNOW IT...
...THIS BLOODY THING'S GONE ALL DARK!
DO YOU THINK IT'S GREY'S DOING?
DUNNO. BUT I'LL TELL YOU THIS...
...IF TAE DOESN'T GET HERE RIGHT AWAY...

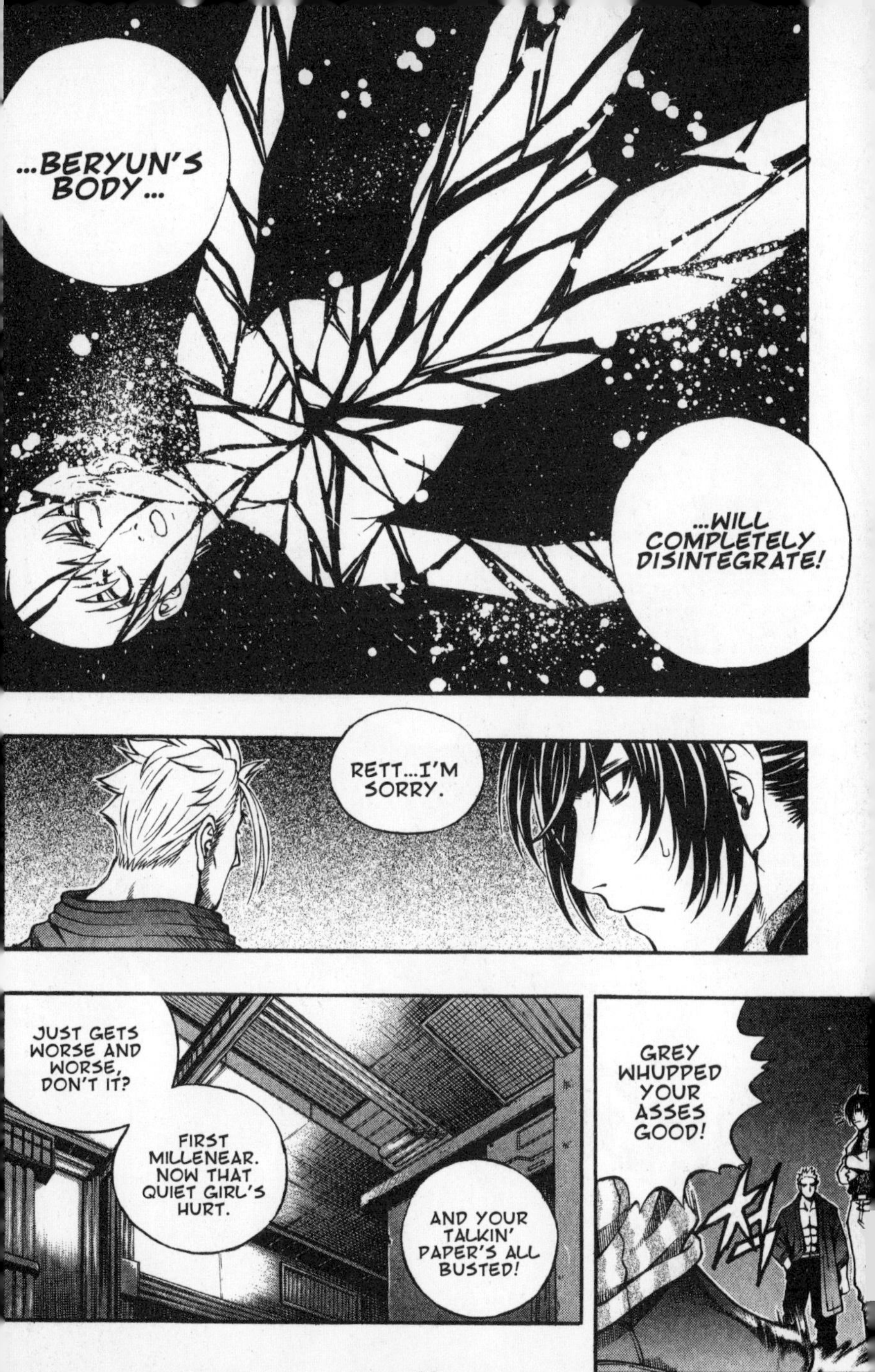
...BERYUN'S BODY...
...WILL COMPLETELY DISINTEGRATE!
RETT...I'M SORRY.
JUST GETS WORSE AND WORSE, DON'T IT?
FIRST MILLENEAR. NOW THAT QUIET GIRL'S HURT.
AND YOUR TALKIN' PAPER'S ALL BUSTED!
GREY WHUPPED YOUR ASSES GOOD!

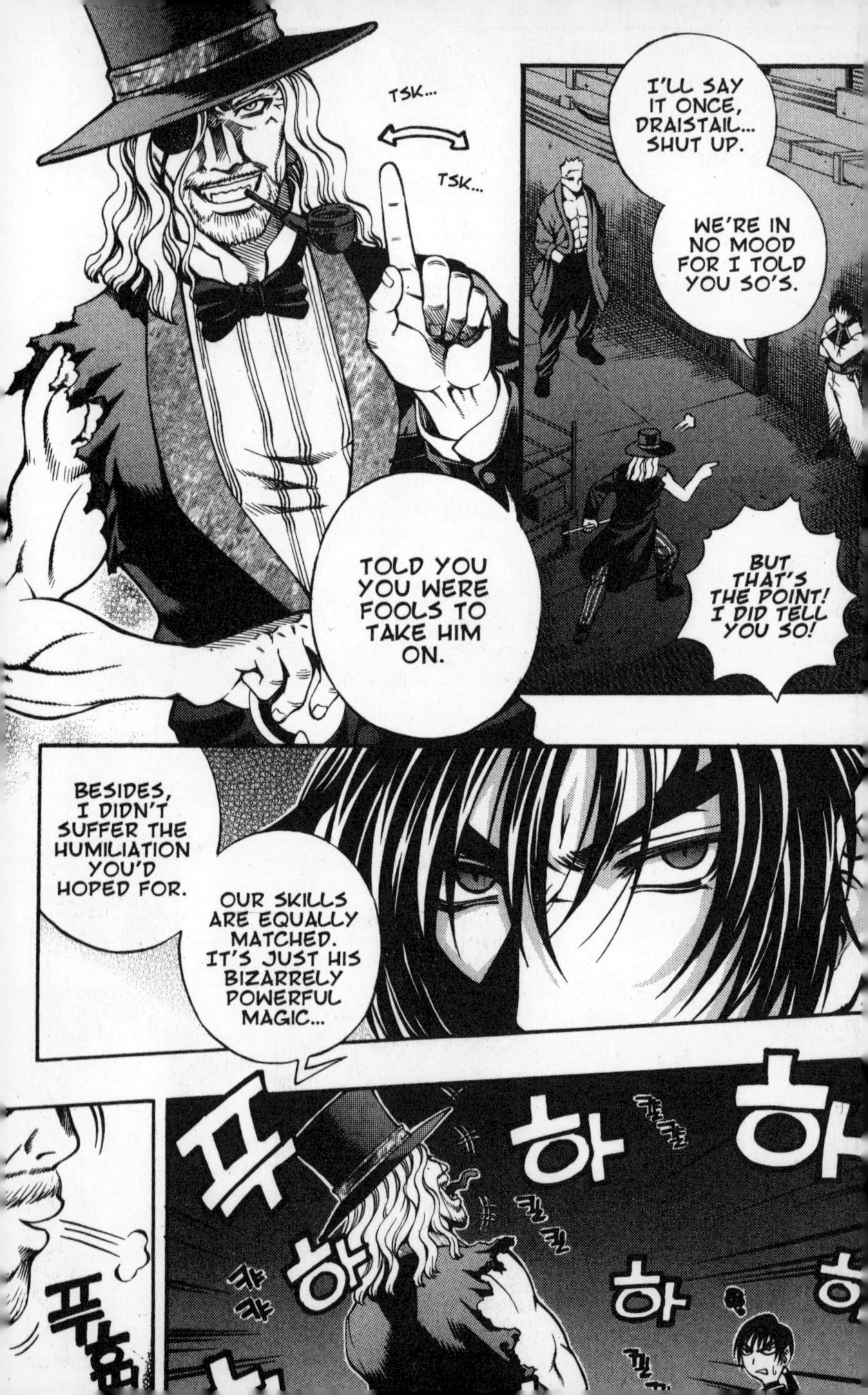
TSK...
TSK...
TOLD YOU YOU WERE FOOLS TO TAKE HIM ON.
I'LL SAY IT ONCE, DRAISTAIL... SHUT UP.
WE'RE IN NO MOOD FOR I TOLD YOU SO'S.
BUT THAT'S THE POINT! I DID TELL YOU SO!
BESIDES, I DIDN'T SUFFER THE HUMILIATION YOU'D HOPED FOR.
OUR SKILLS ARE EQUALLY MATCHED. IT'S JUST HIS BIZARRELY POWERFUL MAGIC...
푸 하 하
하 하 하

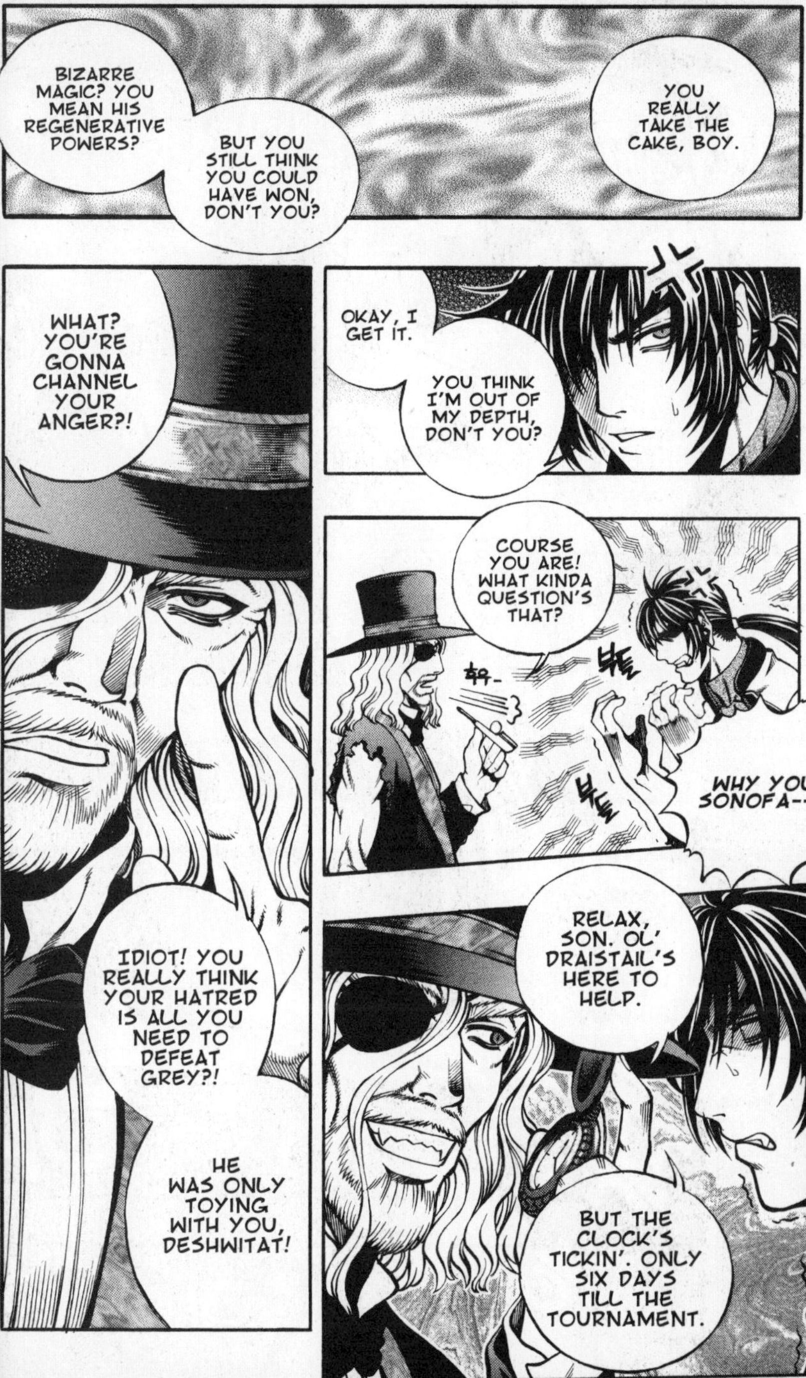
BIZARRE MAGIC? YOU MEAN HIS REGENERATIVE POWERS?
BUT YOU STILL THINK YOU COULD HAVE WON, DON'T YOU?
YOU REALLY TAKE THE CAKE, BOY.
WHAT? YOU'RE GONNA CHANNEL YOUR ANGER?!
OKAY, I GET IT.
YOU THINK I'M OUT OF MY DEPTH, DON'T YOU?
COURSE YOU ARE! WHAT KINDA QUESTION'S THAT?
WHY YOU SONOFA--!!
IDIOT! YOU REALLY THINK YOUR HATRED IS ALL YOU NEED TO DEFEAT GREY?!
HE WAS ONLY TOYING WITH YOU, DESHWITAT!
RELAX, SON. OL' DRAISTAIL'S HERE TO HELP.
BUT THE CLOCK'S TICKIN'. ONLY SIX DAYS TILL THE TOURNAMENT.

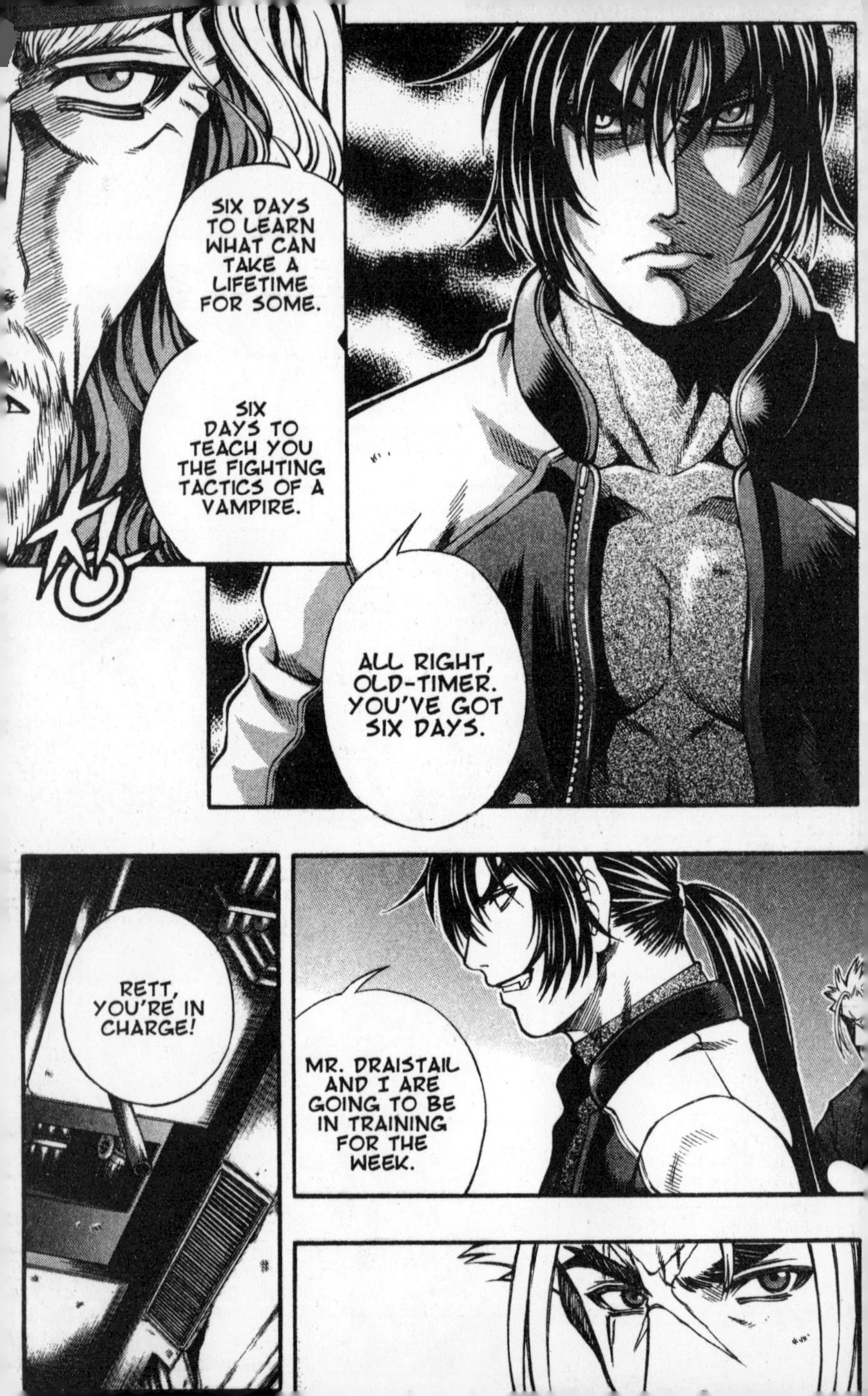
SIX DAYS TO LEARN WHAT CAN TAKE A LIFETIME FOR SOME.
SIX DAYS TO TEACH YOU THE FIGHTING TACTICS OF A VAMPIRE.
ALL RIGHT, OLD-TIMER. YOU'VE GOT SIX DAYS.
MR. DRAISTAIL AND I ARE GOING TO BE IN TRAINING FOR THE WEEK.
RETT, YOU'RE IN CHARGE!

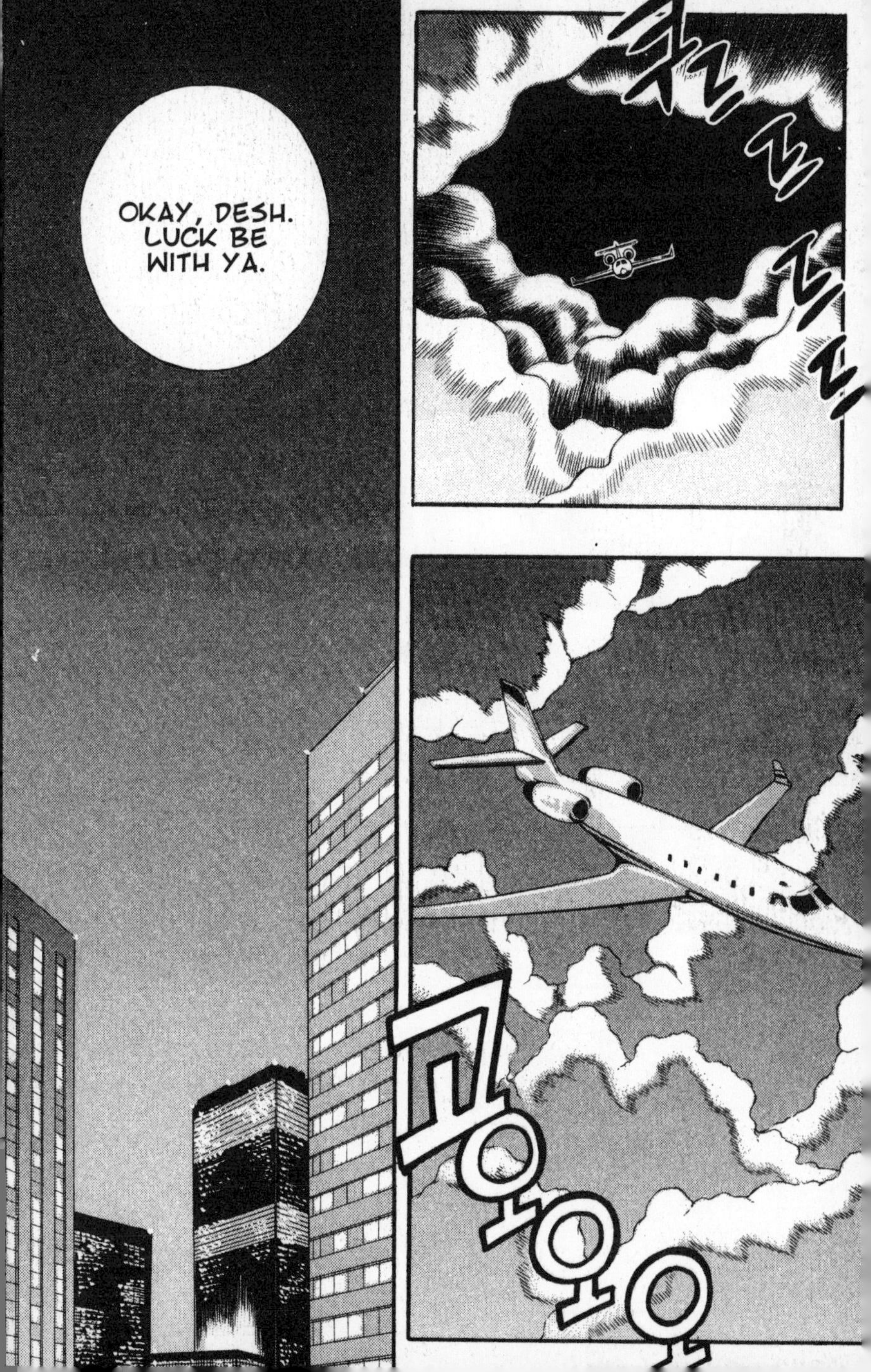
OKAY, DESH. LUCK BE WITH YA.

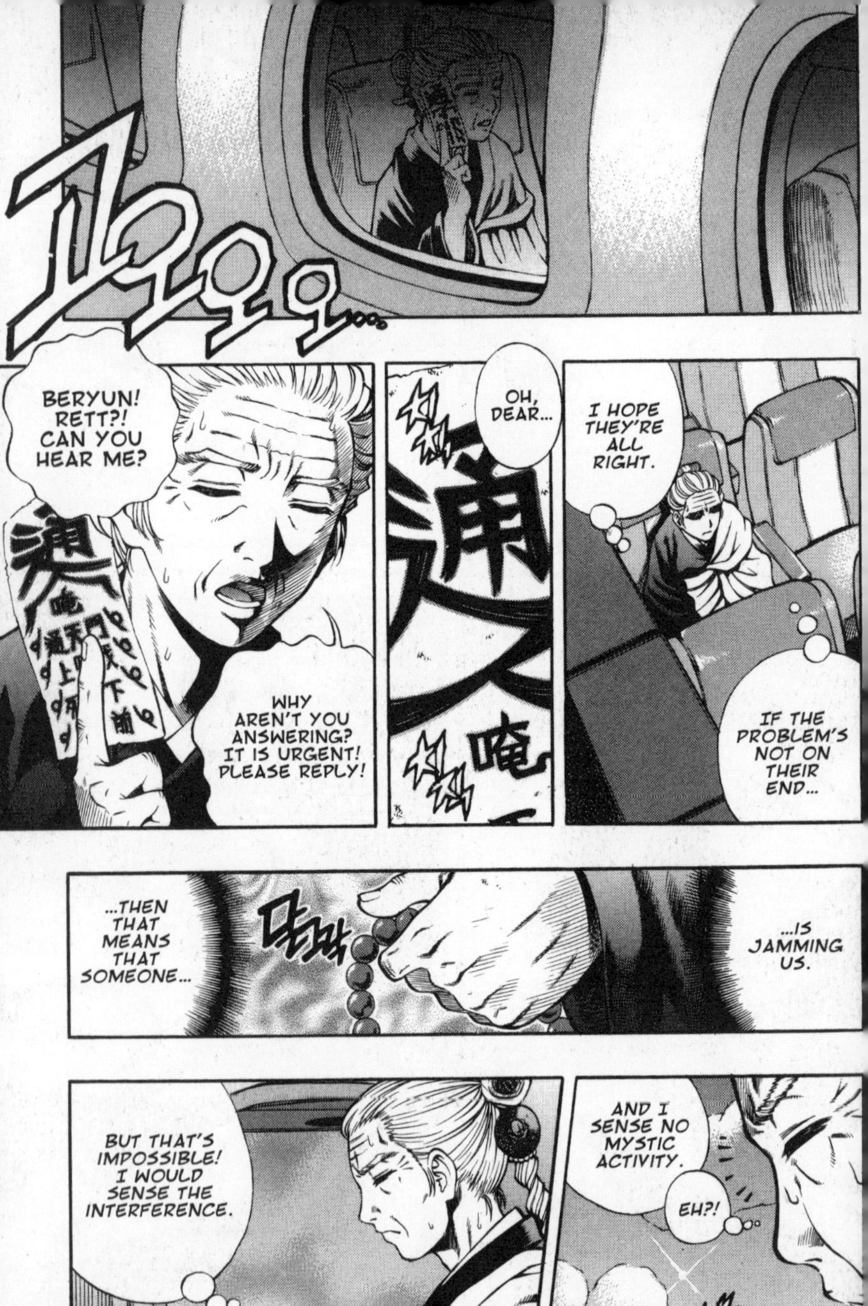
BERYUN! RETT?! CAN YOU HEAR ME?
WHY AREN'T YOU ANSWERING? IT IS URGENT! PLEASE REPLY!
OH, DEAR...
I HOPE THEY'RE ALL RIGHT.
IF THE PROBLEM'S NOT ON THEIR END...
...THEN THAT MEANS THAT SOMEONE...
...IS JAMMING US.
BUT THAT'S IMPOSSIBLE! I WOULD SENSE THE INTERFERENCE.
AND I SENSE NO MYSTIC ACTIVITY.
EH?!

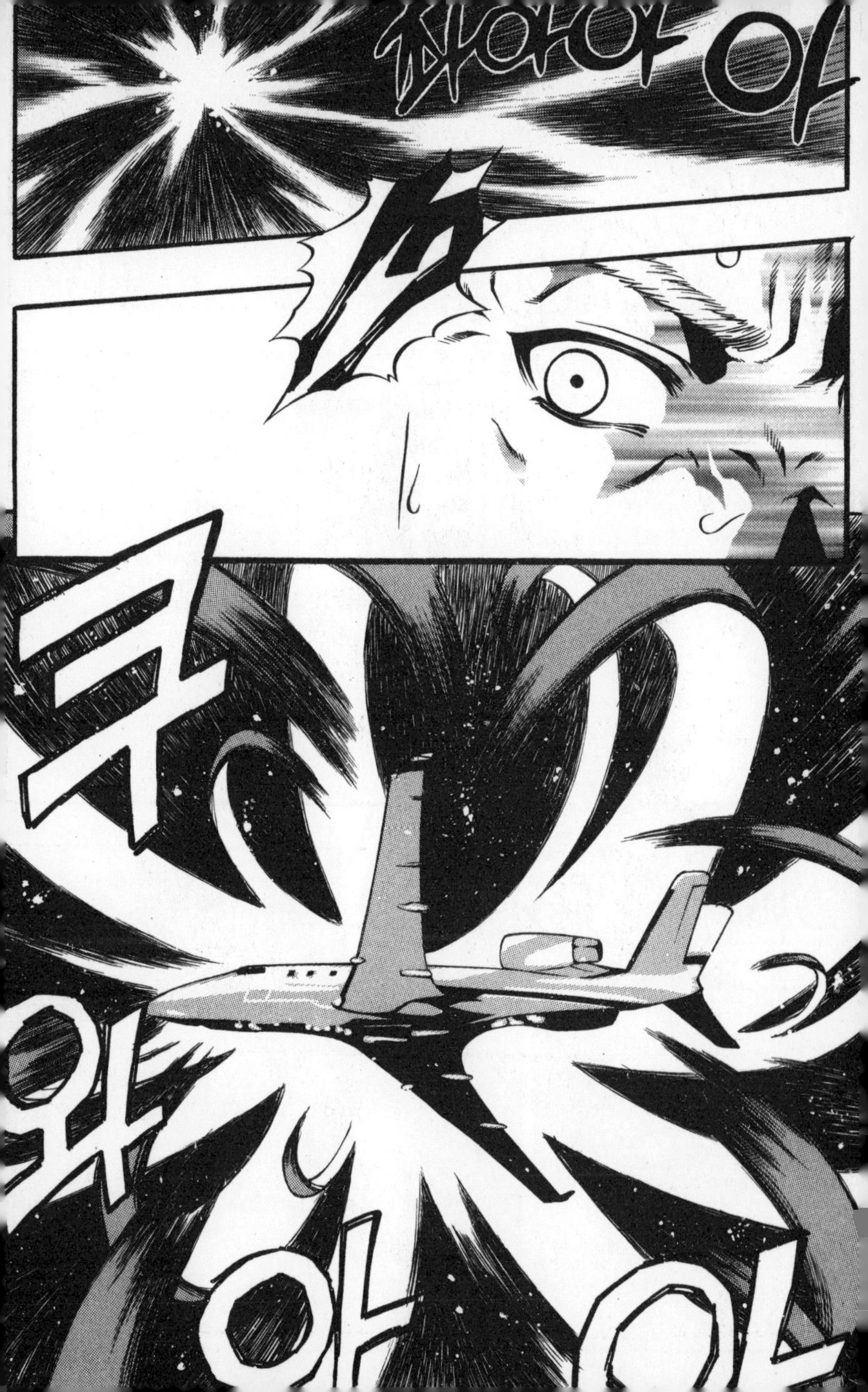
쫘아아 아
콰아아

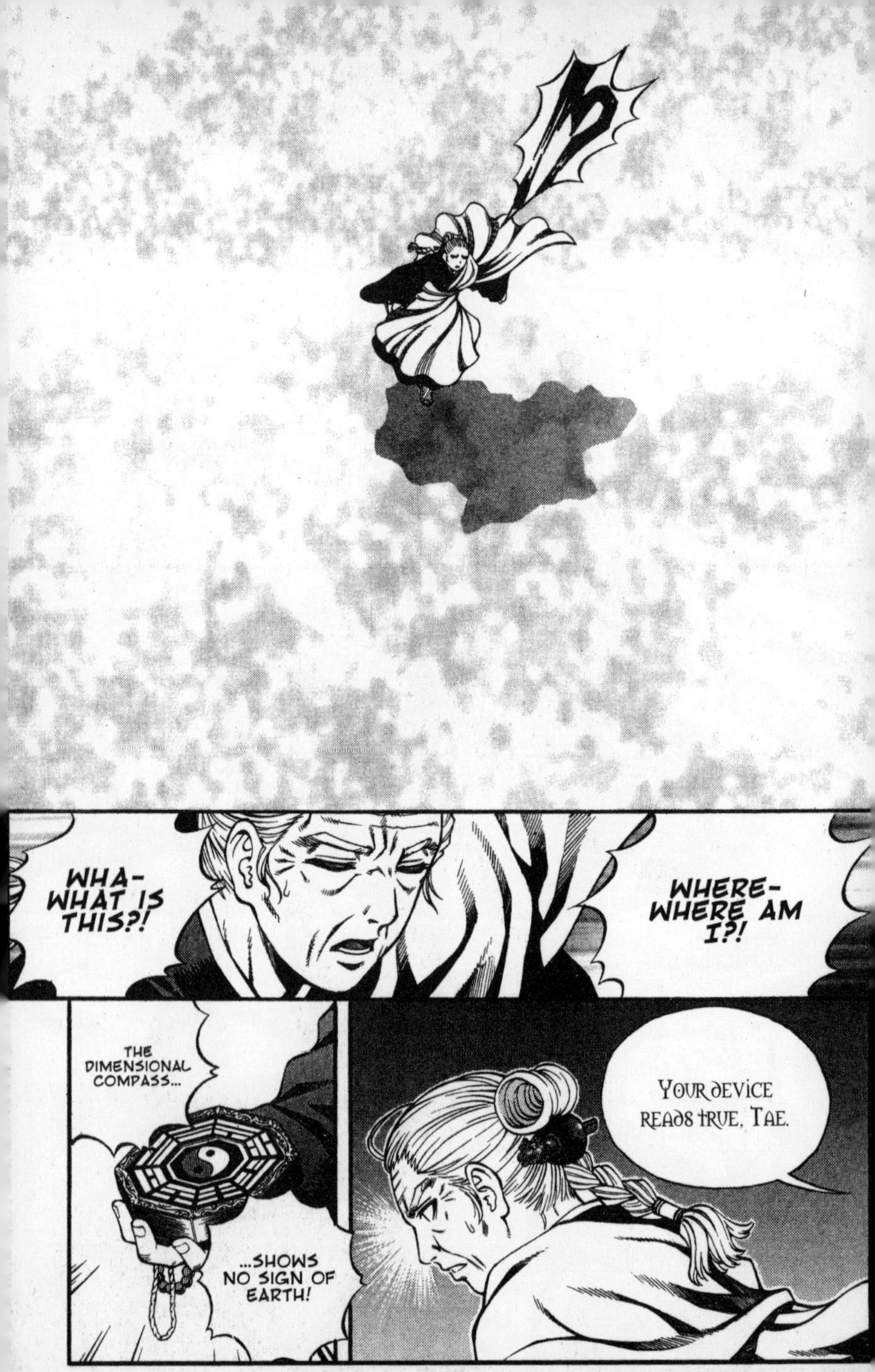
WHA-WHAT IS THIS?!
WHERE-WHERE AM I?!
THE DIMENSIONAL COMPASS...
...SHOWS NO SIGN OF EARTH!
YOUR DEVICE READS TRUE, TAE.

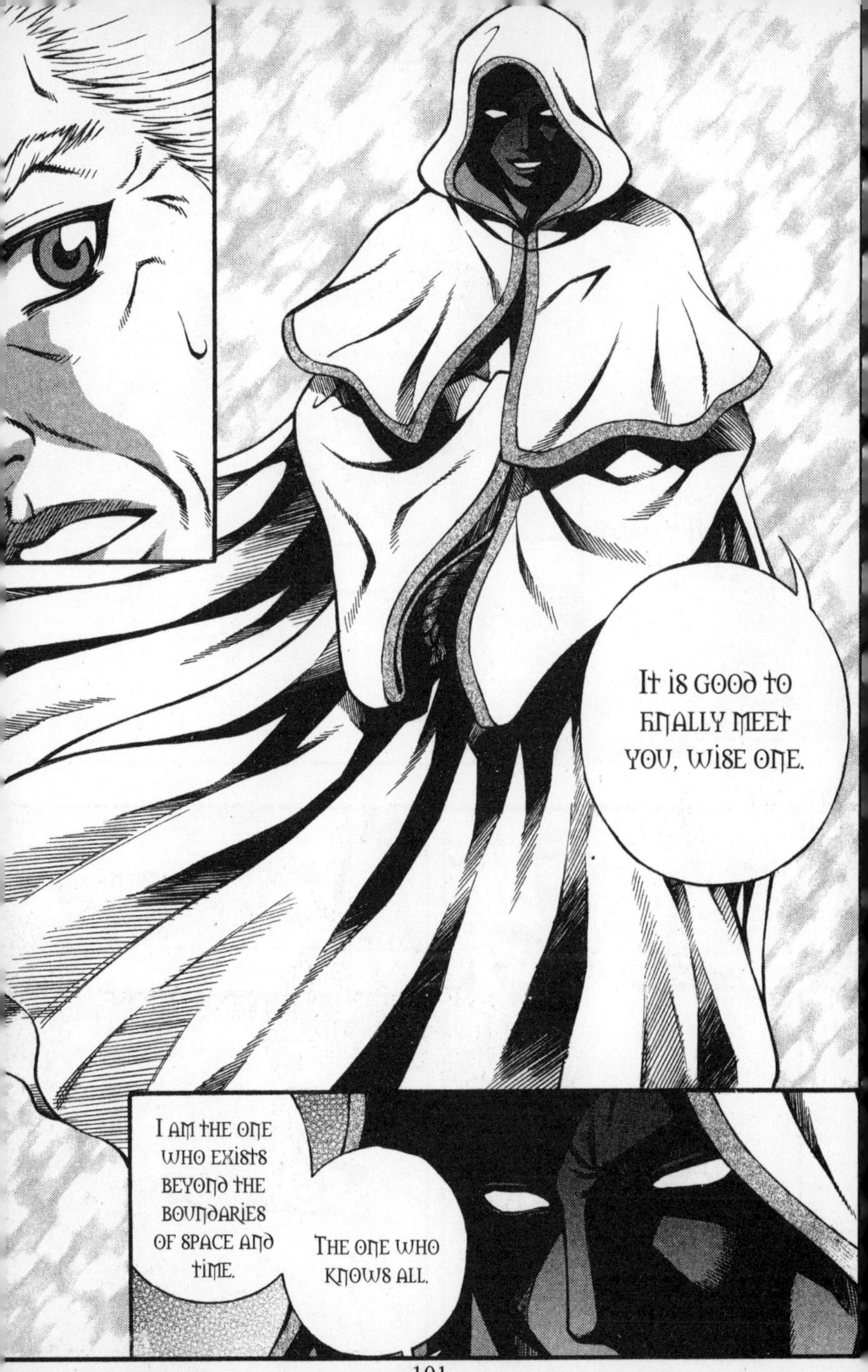

It is GOOD to FINALLY MEET YOU, WISE ONE.
I AM THE ONE WHO EXISTS BEYOND THE BOUNDARIES OF SPACE AND TIME.
THE ONE WHO KNOWS ALL.

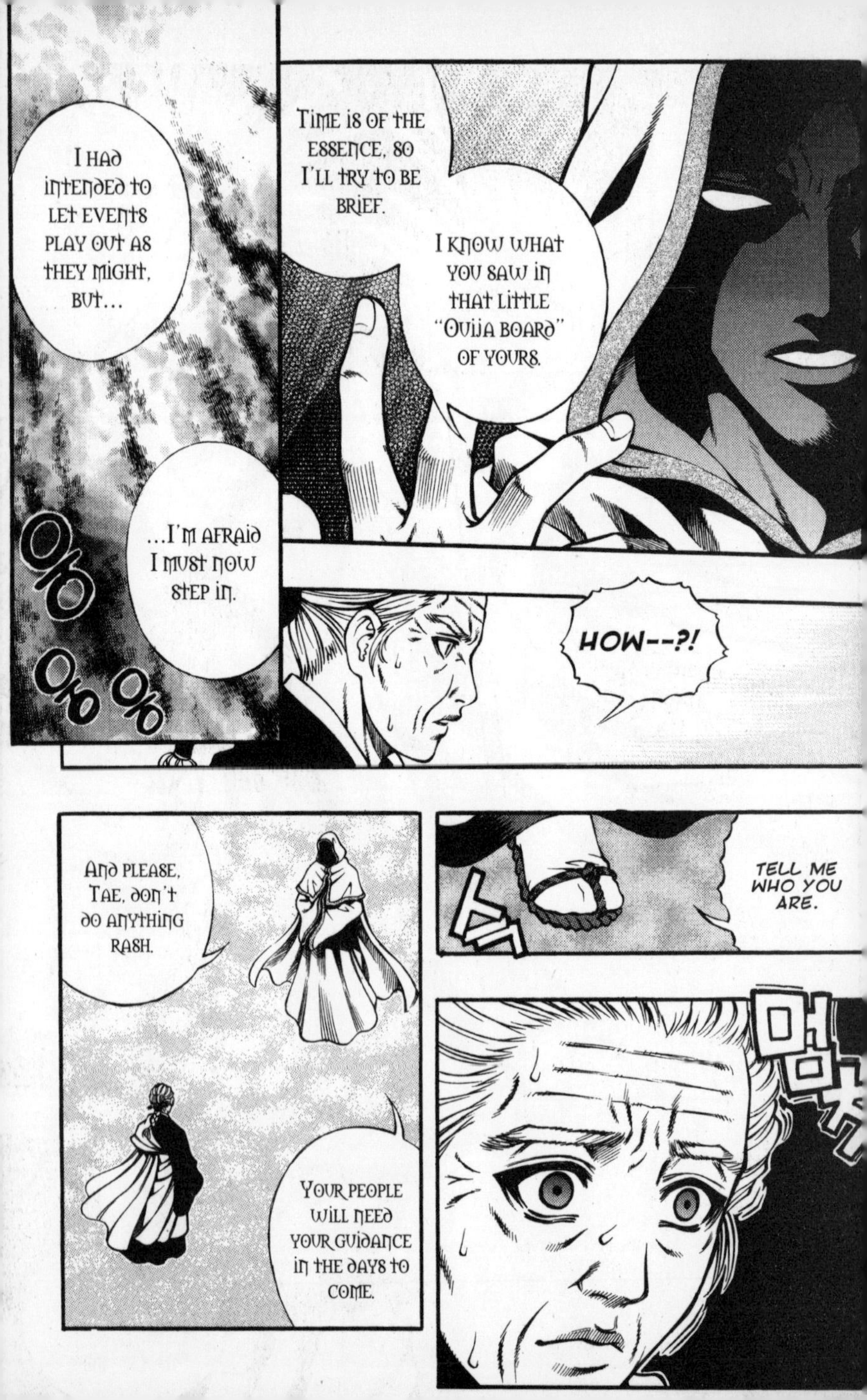
I HAD INTENDED TO LET EVENTS PLAY OUT AS THEY MIGHT, BUT…
…I'M AFRAID I MUST NOW STEP IN.
TIME IS OF THE ESSENCE, SO I'LL TRY TO BE BRIEF.
I KNOW WHAT YOU SAW IN THAT LITTLE "OUIJA BOARD" OF YOURS.
HOW--?!
TELL ME WHO YOU ARE.
AND PLEASE, TAE, DON'T DO ANYTHING RASH.
YOUR PEOPLE WILL NEED YOUR GUIDANCE IN THE DAYS TO COME.

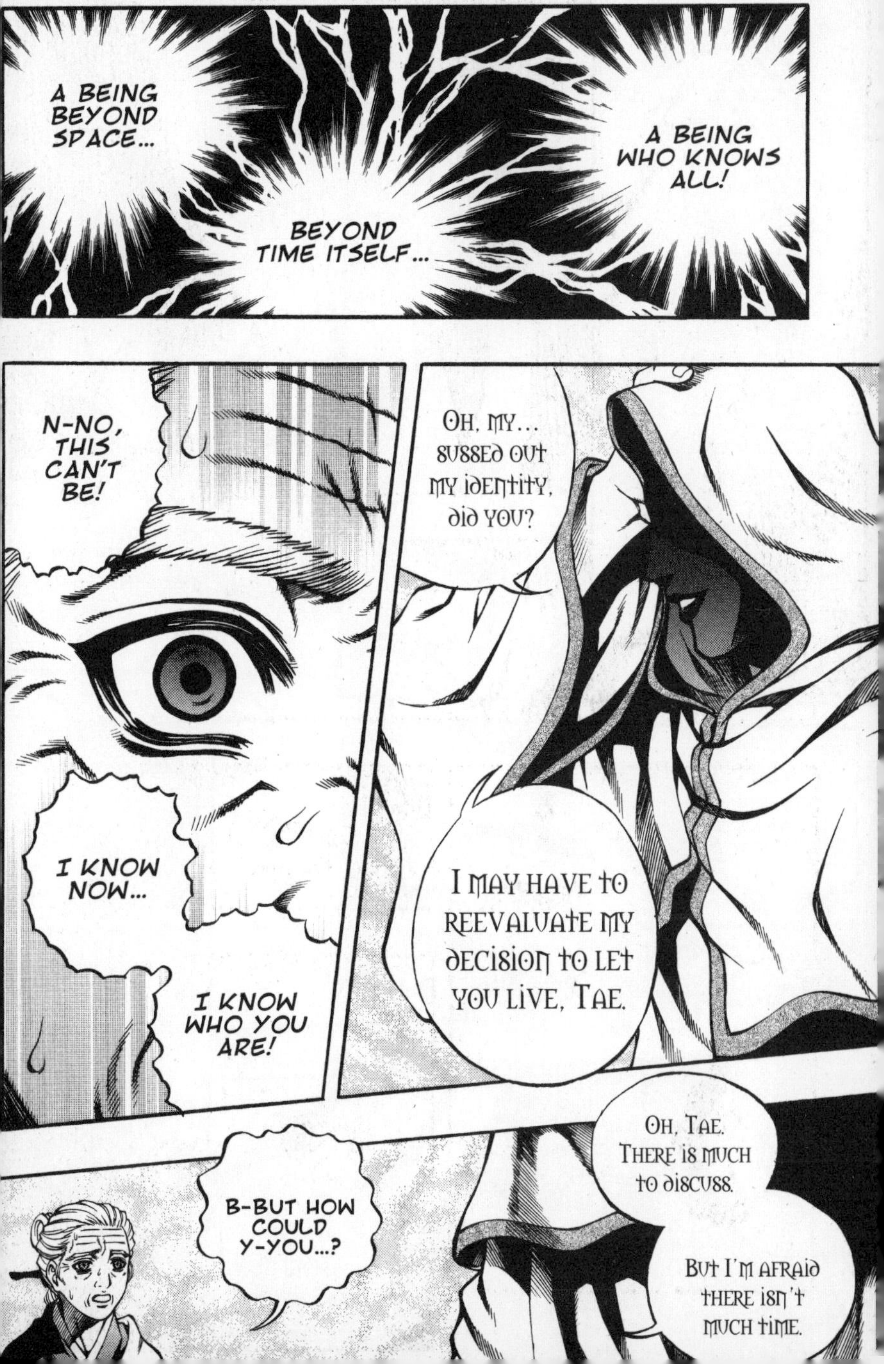
A BEING BEYOND SPACE...
BEYOND TIME ITSELF...
A BEING WHO KNOWS ALL!
N-NO, THIS CAN'T BE!
I KNOW NOW...
I KNOW WHO YOU ARE!
OH, MY... SUSSED OUT MY IDENTITY, DID YOU?
I MAY HAVE TO REEVALUATE MY DECISION TO LET YOU LIVE, TAE.
B-BUT HOW COULD Y-YOU...?
OH, TAE. THERE IS MUCH TO DISCUSS.
BUT I'M AFRAID THERE ISN'T MUCH TIME.

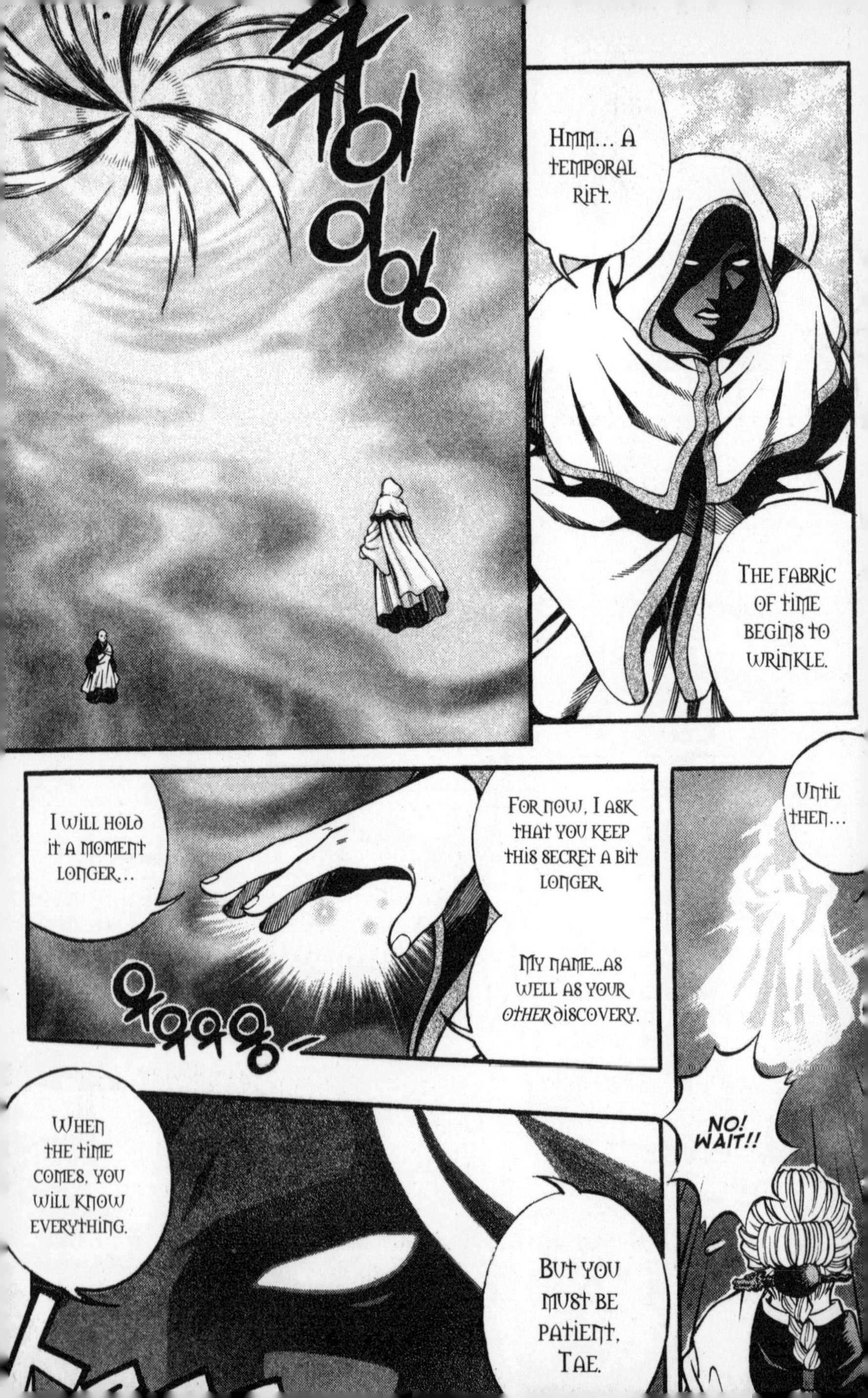
Hmm... A temporal rift.
The fabric of time begins to wrinkle.
I will hold it a moment longer...
For now, I ask that you keep this secret a bit longer.
My name...as well as your *other* discovery.
Until then...
When the time comes, you will know everything.
But you must be patient, Tae.
NO! WAIT!!

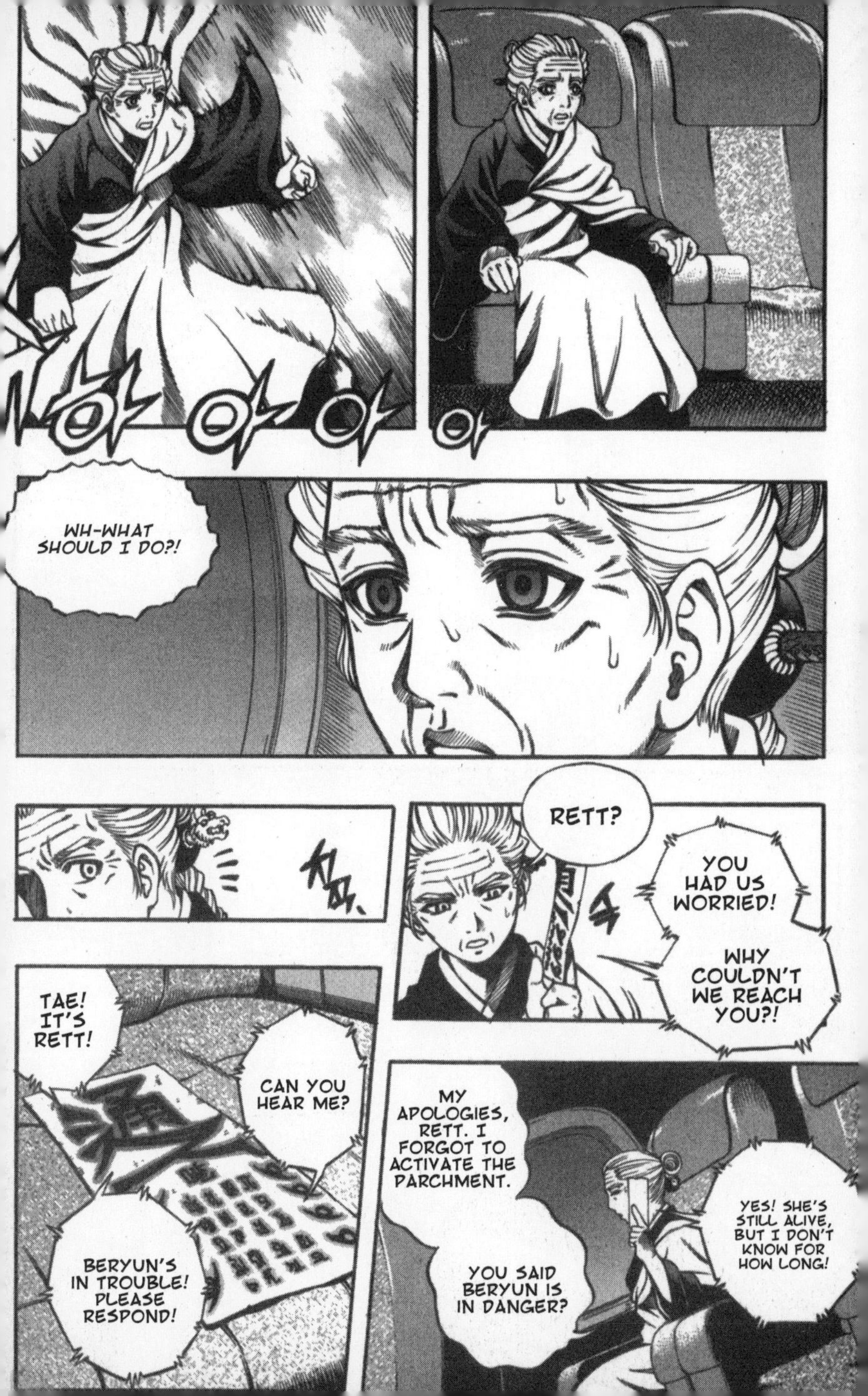
WH-WHAT SHOULD I DO?!
RETT?
YOU HAD US WORRIED!
WHY COULDN'T WE REACH YOU?!
TAE! IT'S RETT!
CAN YOU HEAR ME?
BERYUN'S IN TROUBLE! PLEASE RESPOND!
MY APOLOGIES, RETT. I FORGOT TO ACTIVATE THE PARCHMENT.
YOU SAID BERYUN IS IN DANGER?
YES! SHE'S STILL ALIVE, BUT I DON'T KNOW FOR HOW LONG!

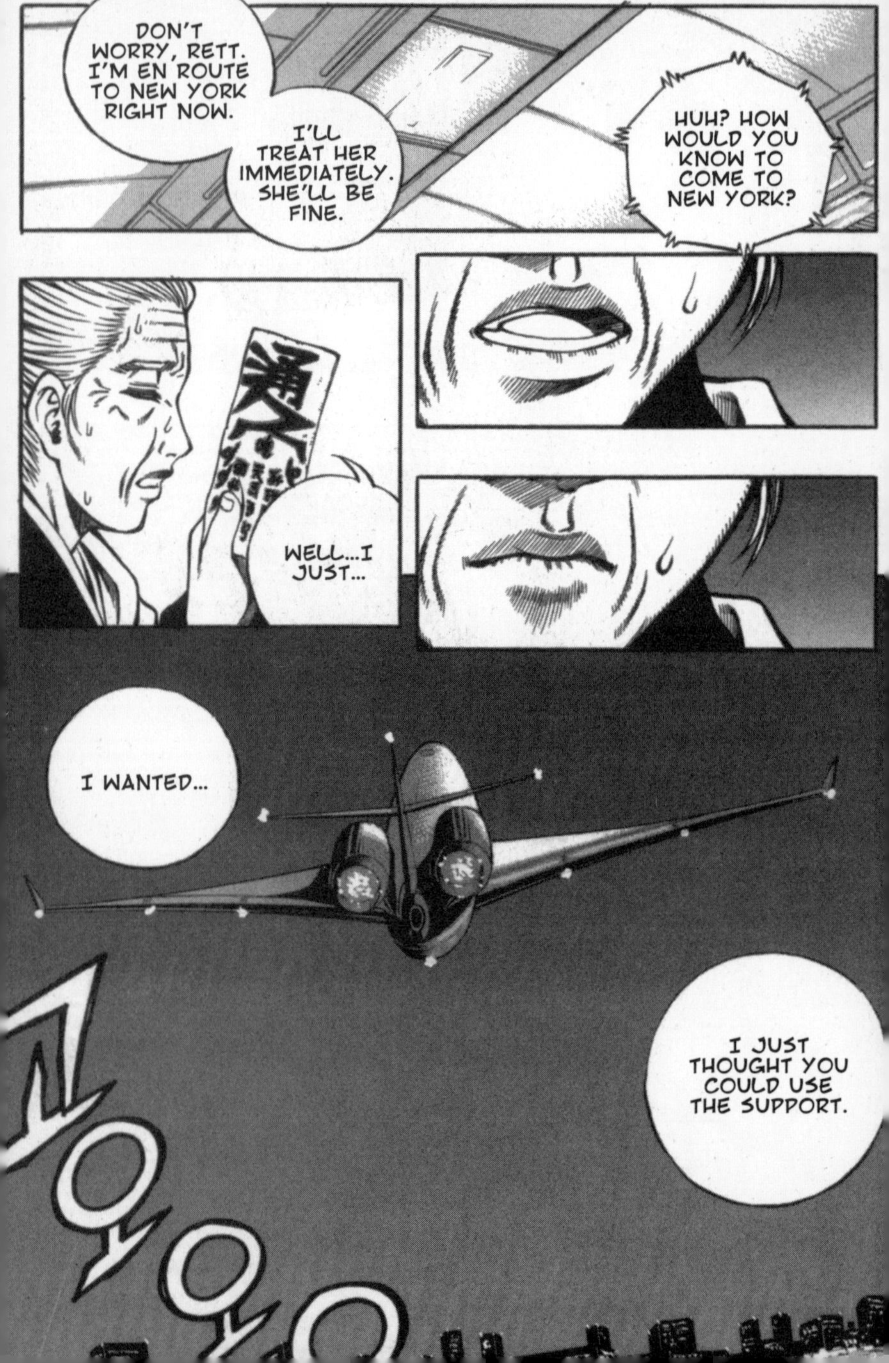
DON'T WORRY, RETT. I'M EN ROUTE TO NEW YORK RIGHT NOW.
I'LL TREAT HER IMMEDIATELY. SHE'LL BE FINE.
HUH? HOW WOULD YOU KNOW TO COME TO NEW YORK?
WELL...I JUST...
I WANTED...
I JUST THOUGHT YOU COULD USE THE SUPPORT.
ZOOOO

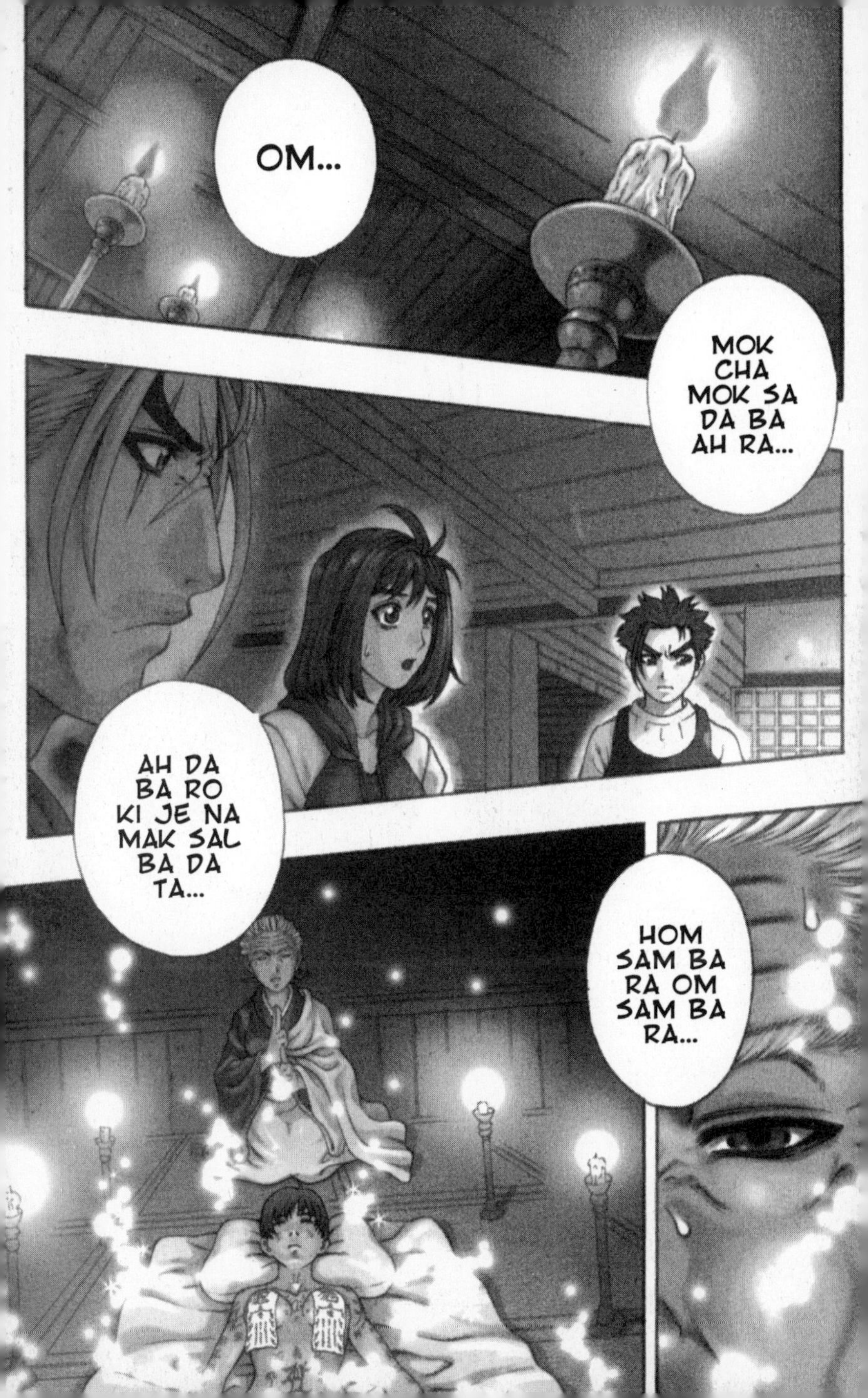
OM...
MOK CHA MOK SA DA BA AH RA...
AH DA BA RO KI JE NA MAK SAL BA DA TA...
HOM SAM BA RA OM SAM BA RA...

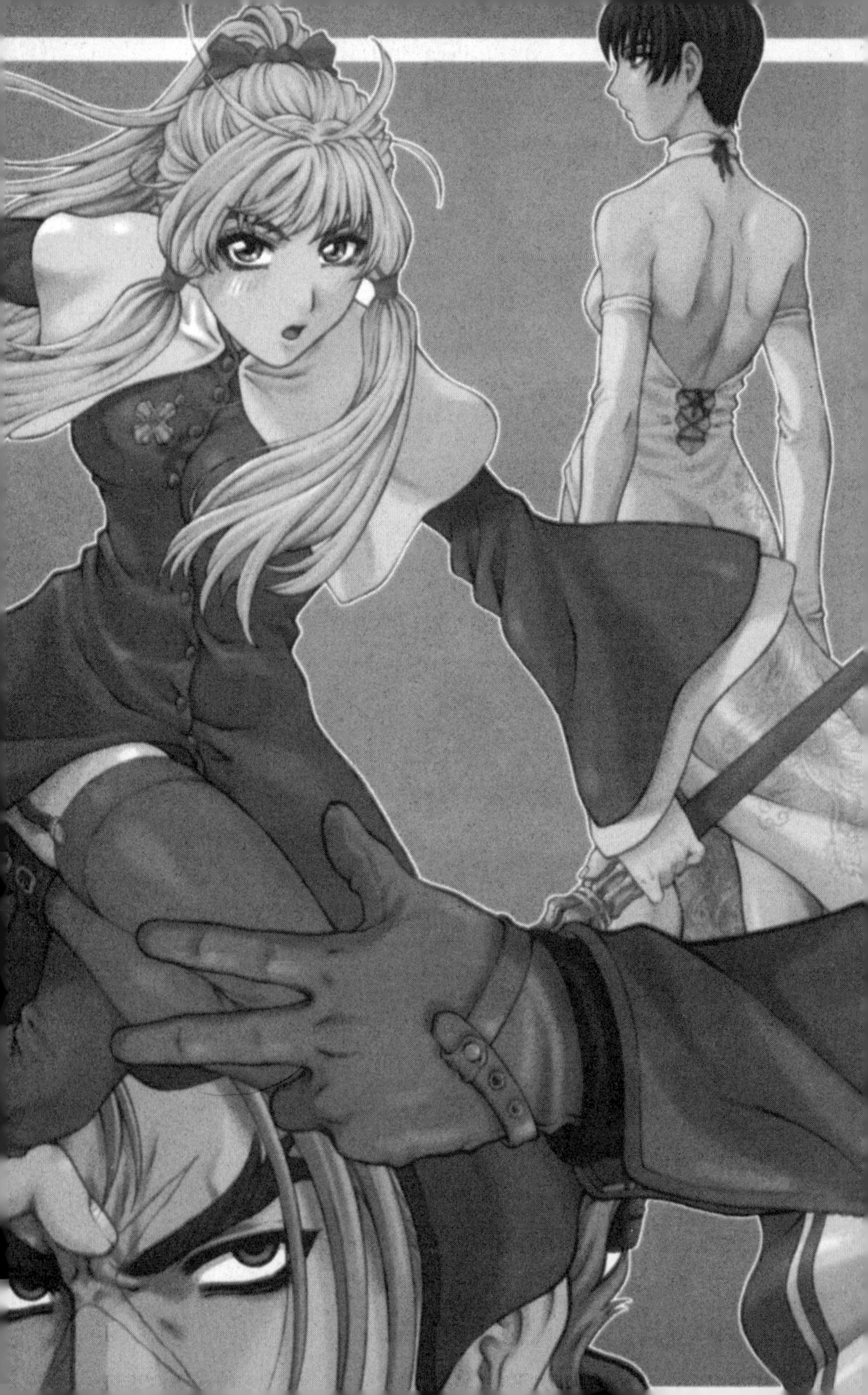

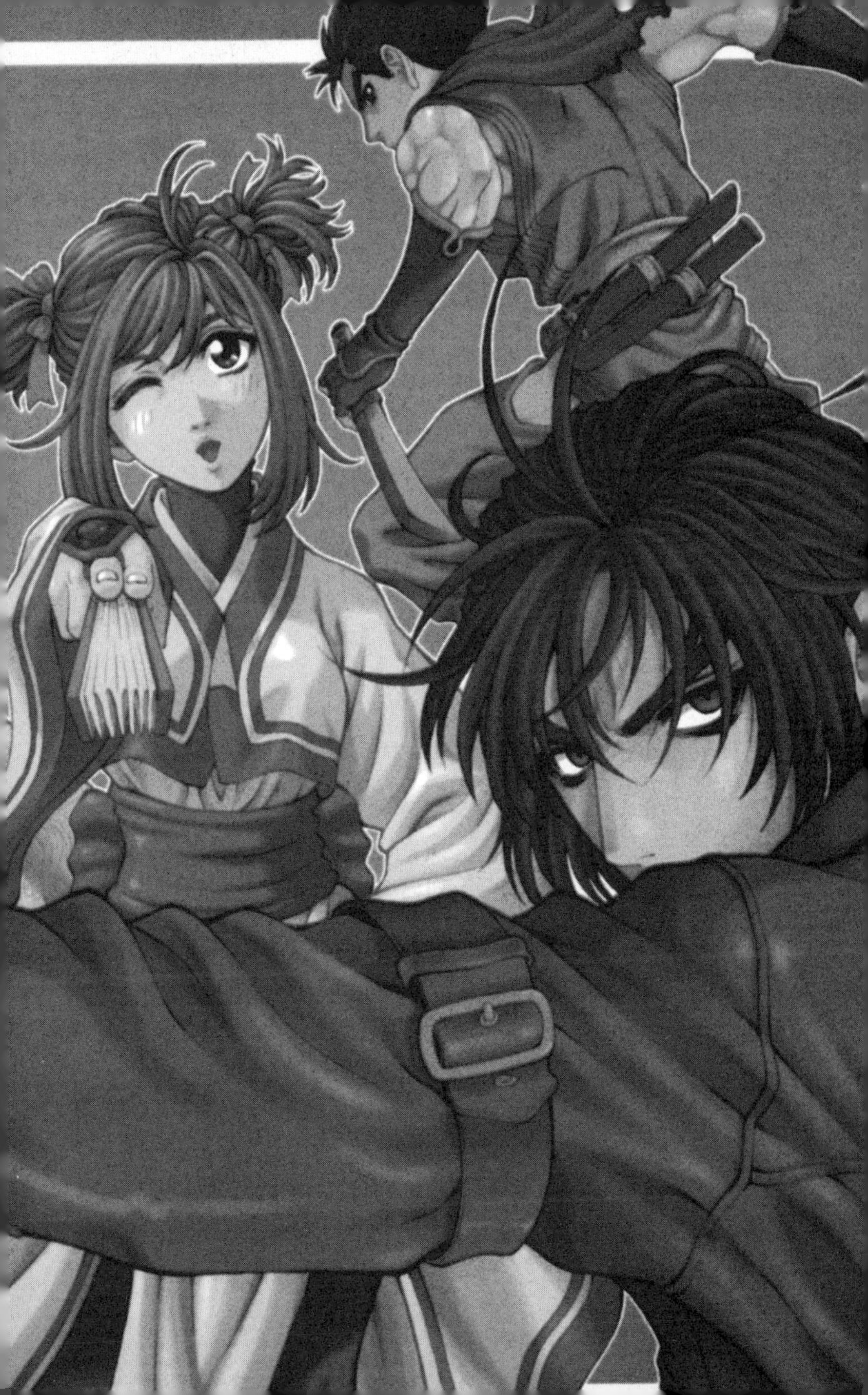

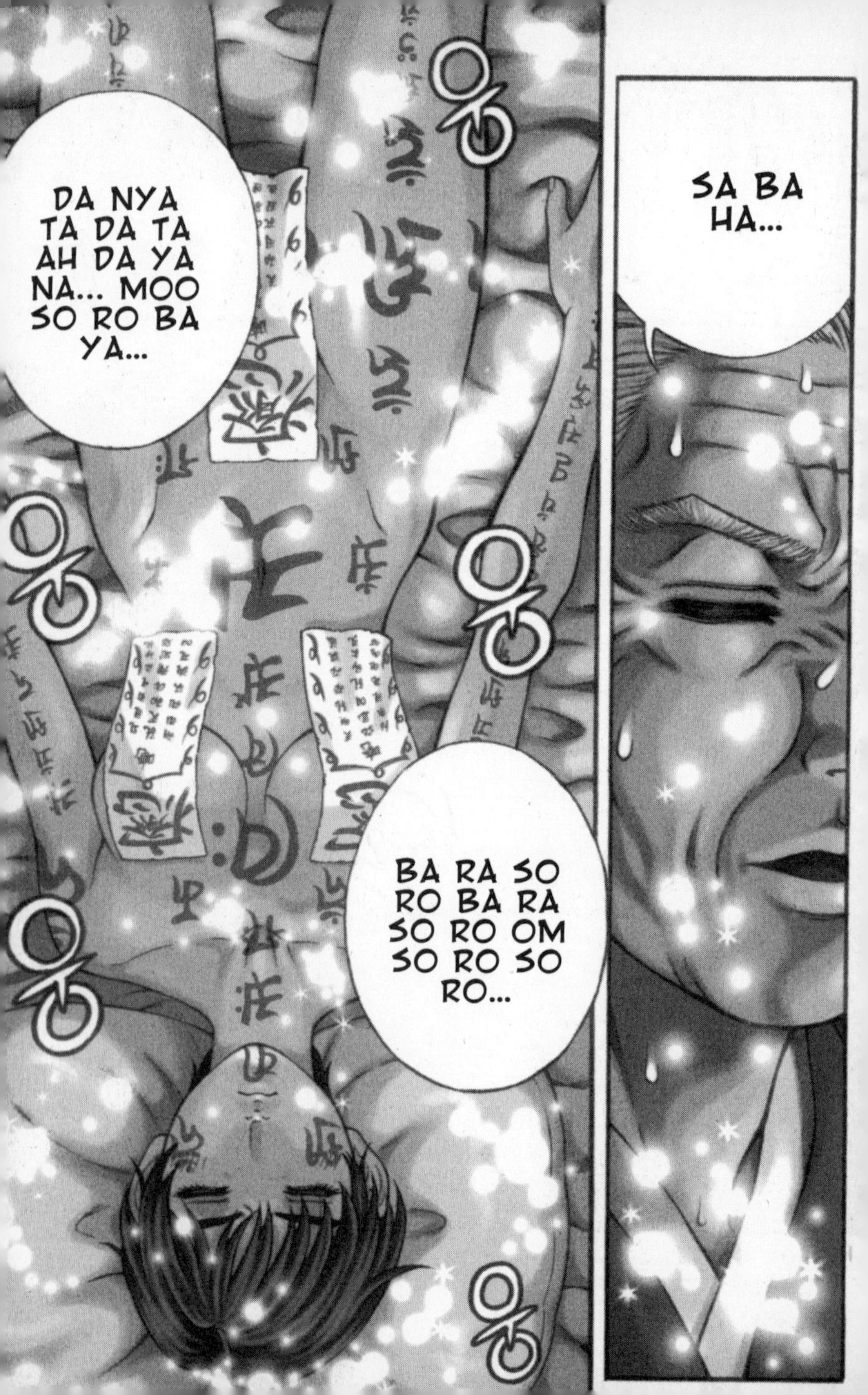
SA BA HA...
DA NYA TA DA TA AH DA YA NA... MOO SO RO BA YA...
BA RA SO RO BA RA SO RO OM SO RO SO RO...

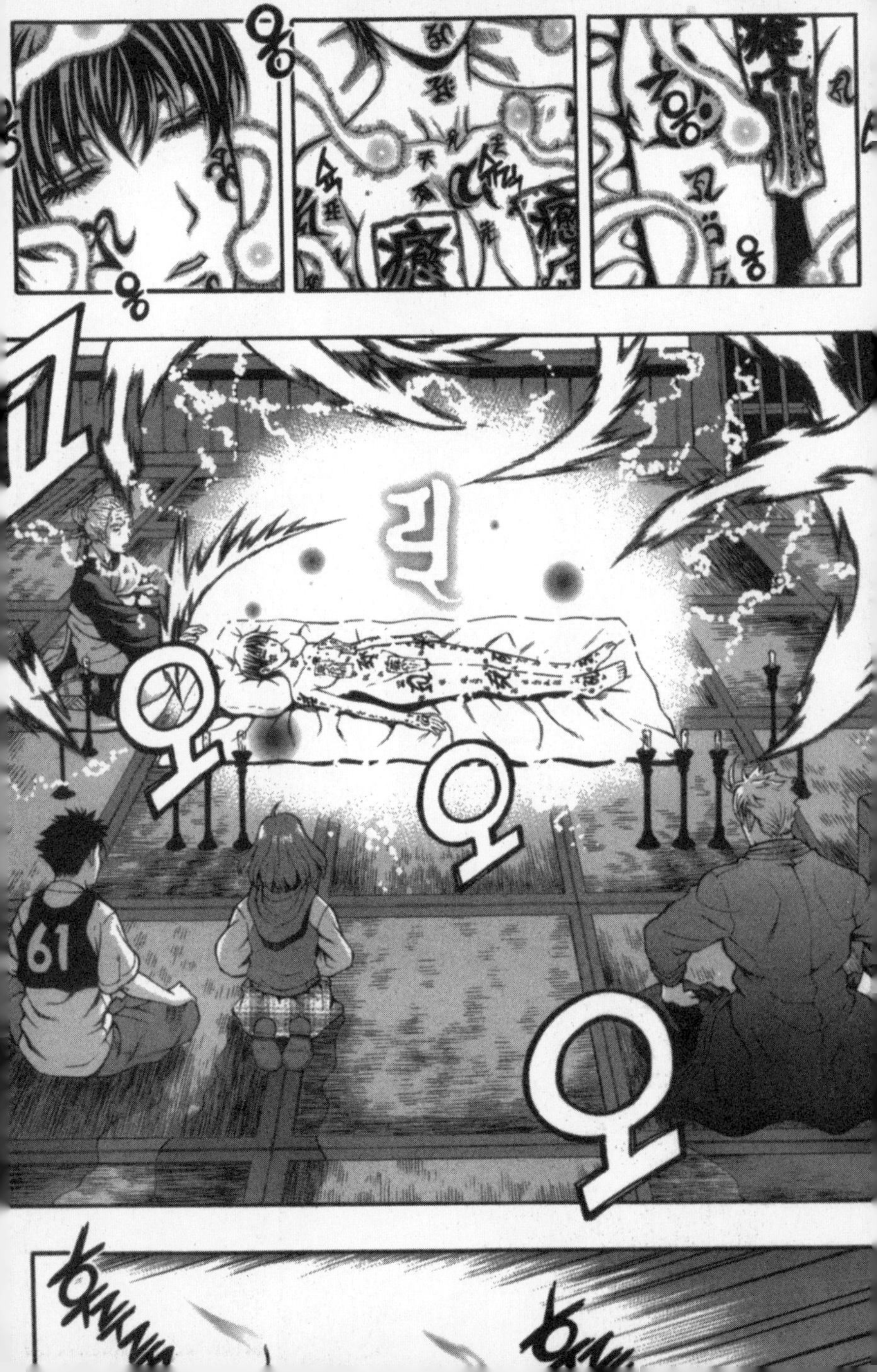

옹
옹
옹
리
오
오
오

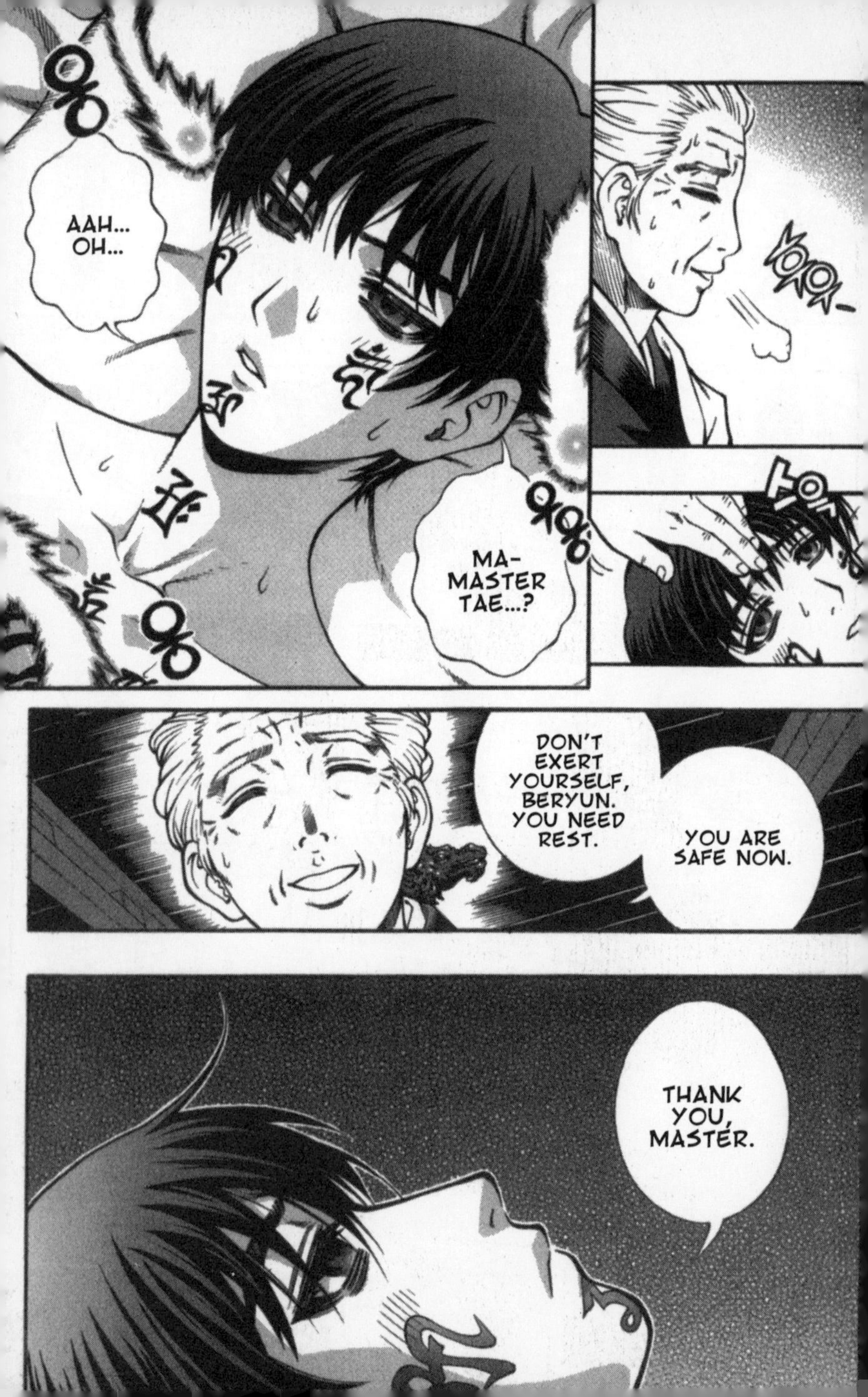
AAH... OH...
MA- MASTER TAE...?
DON'T EXERT YOURSELF, BERYUN. YOU NEED REST.
YOU ARE SAFE NOW.
THANK YOU, MASTER.

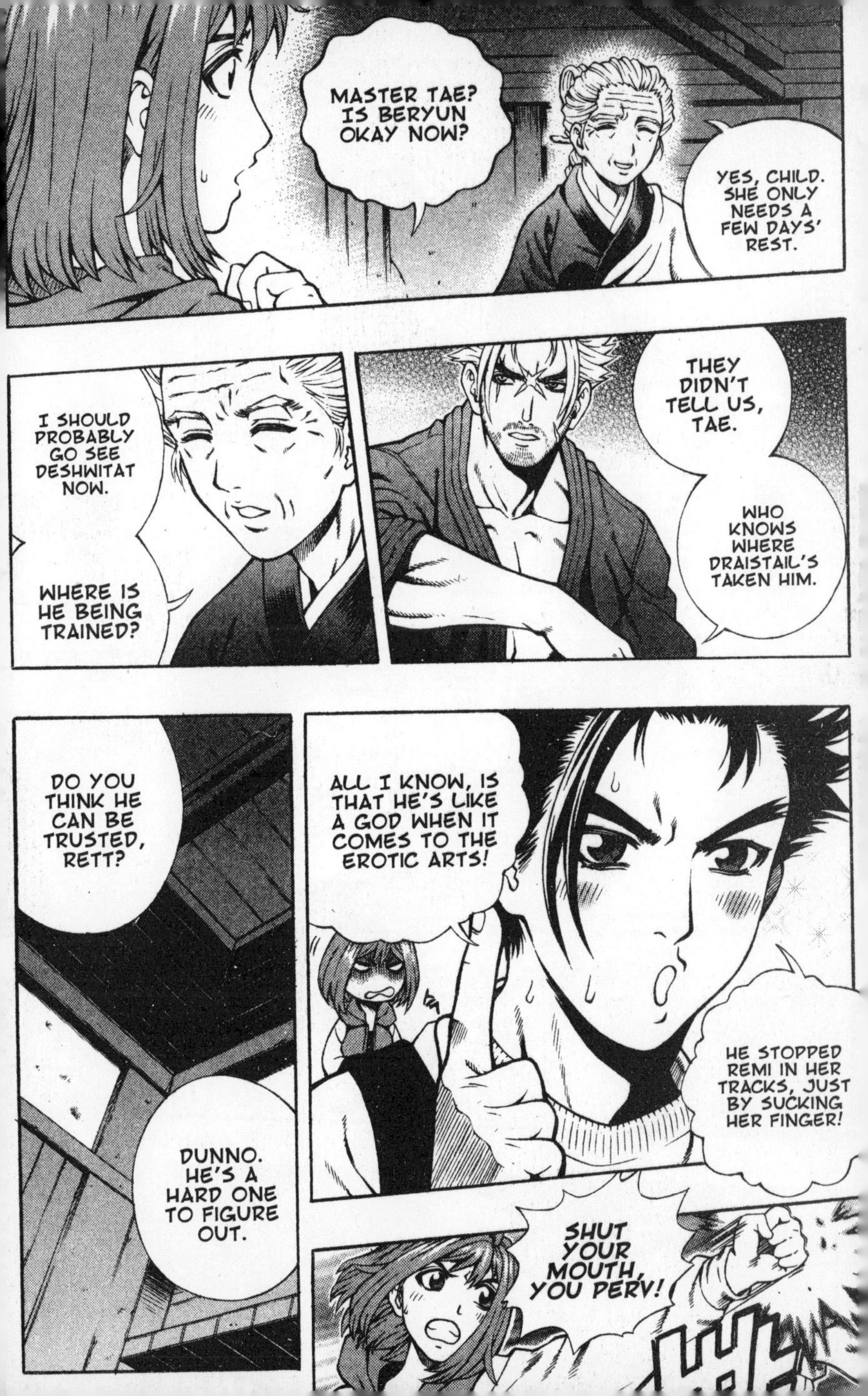
MASTER TAE? IS BERYUN OKAY NOW?
YES, CHILD. SHE ONLY NEEDS A FEW DAYS' REST.
I SHOULD PROBABLY GO SEE DESHWITAT NOW.
WHERE IS HE BEING TRAINED?
THEY DIDN'T TELL US, TAE.
WHO KNOWS WHERE DRAISTAIL'S TAKEN HIM.
DO YOU THINK HE CAN BE TRUSTED, RETT?
DUNNO. HE'S A HARD ONE TO FIGURE OUT.
ALL I KNOW, IS THAT HE'S LIKE A GOD WHEN IT COMES TO THE EROTIC ARTS!
HE STOPPED REMI IN HER TRACKS, JUST BY SUCKING HER FINGER!
SHUT YOUR MOUTH, YOU PERV!

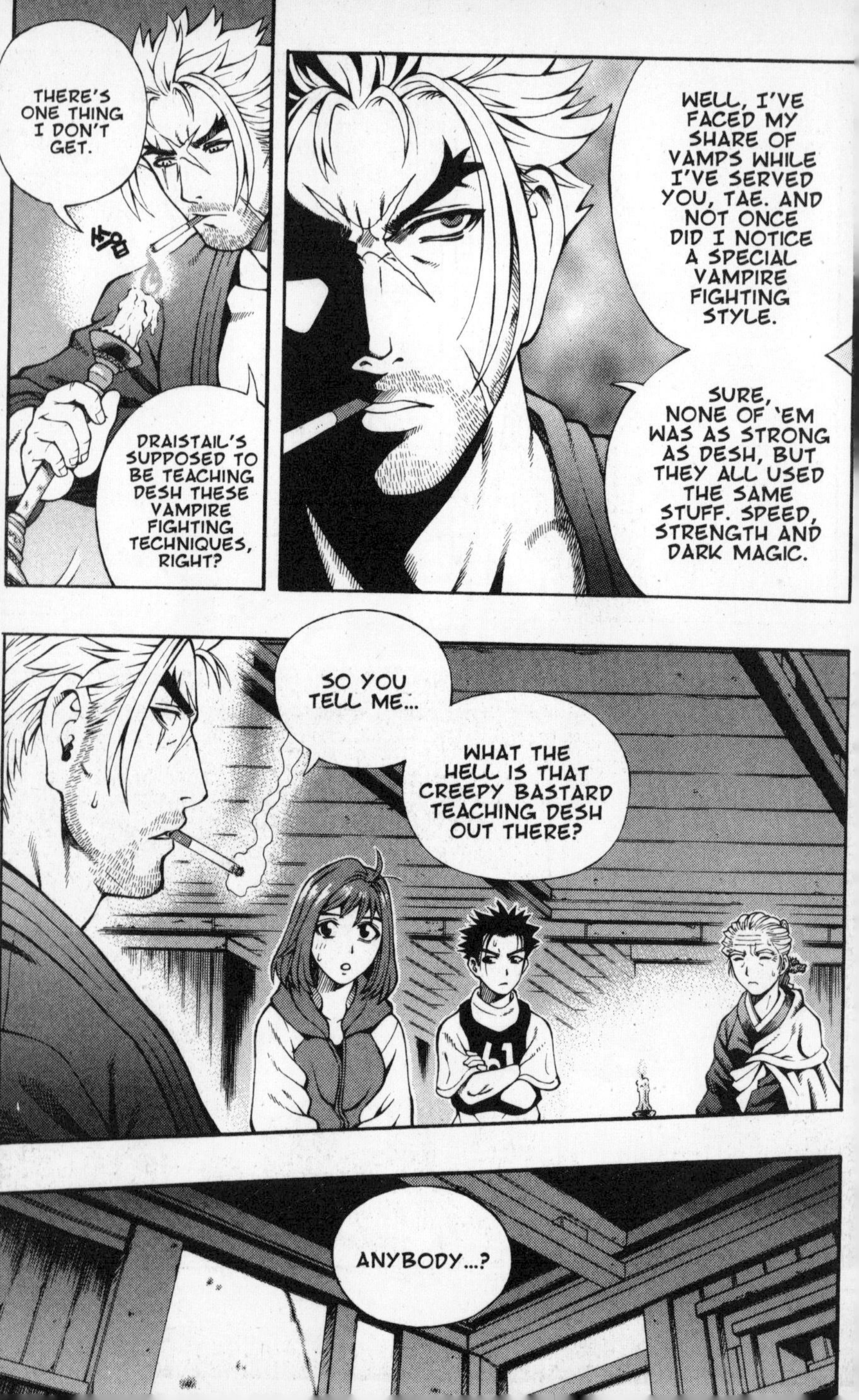
THERE'S ONE THING I DON'T GET.
DRAISTAIL'S SUPPOSED TO BE TEACHING DESH THESE VAMPIRE FIGHTING TECHNIQUES, RIGHT?
WELL, I'VE FACED MY SHARE OF VAMPS WHILE I'VE SERVED YOU, TAE. AND NOT ONCE DID I NOTICE A SPECIAL VAMPIRE FIGHTING STYLE.
SURE, NONE OF 'EM WAS AS STRONG AS DESH, BUT THEY ALL USED THE SAME STUFF. SPEED, STRENGTH AND DARK MAGIC.
SO YOU TELL ME...
WHAT THE HELL IS THAT CREEPY BASTARD TEACHING DESH OUT THERE?
ANYBODY...?

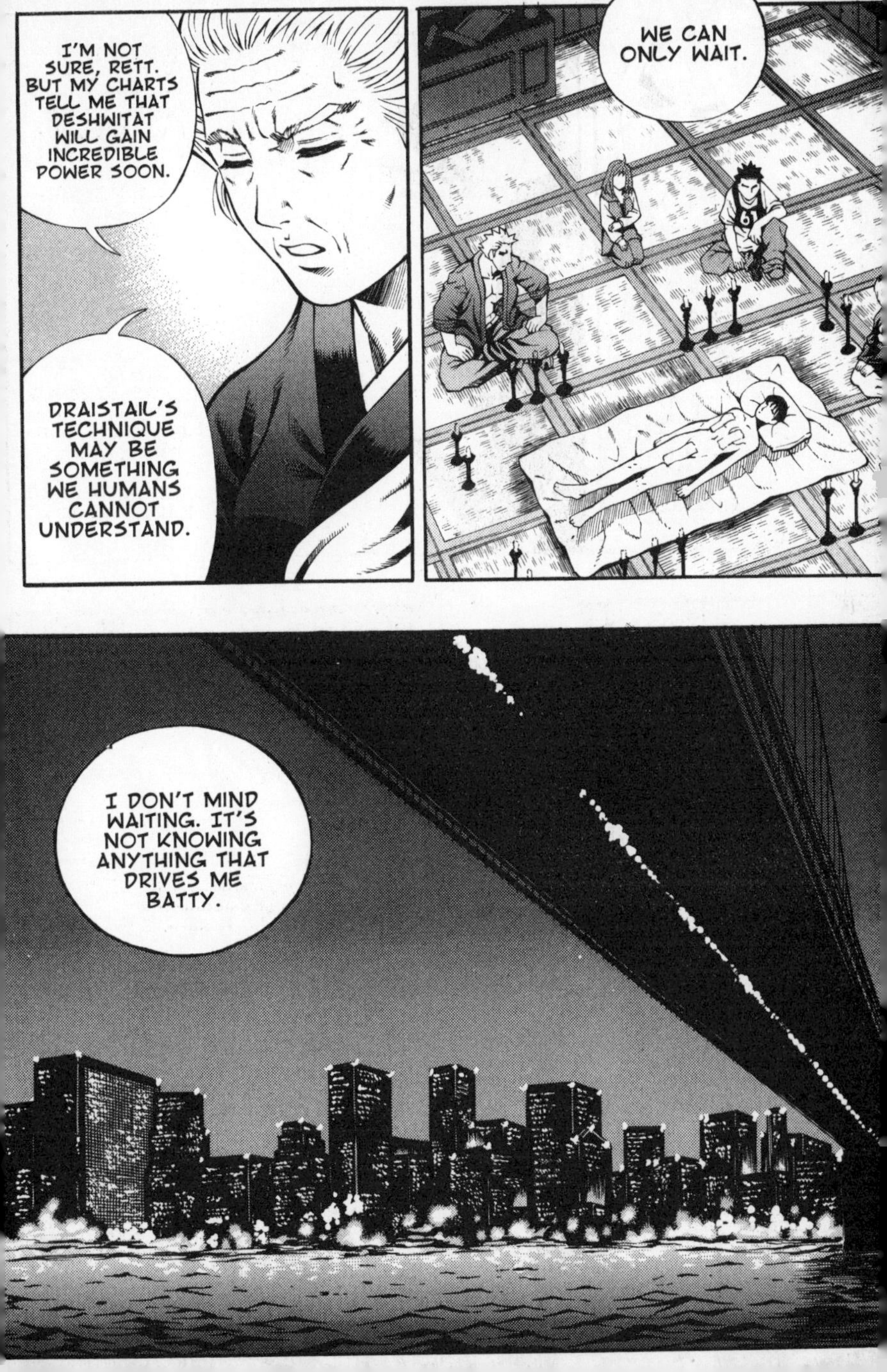
I'M NOT SURE, RETT. BUT MY CHARTS TELL ME THAT DESHWITAT WILL GAIN INCREDIBLE POWER SOON.
WE CAN ONLY WAIT.
DRAISTAIL'S TECHNIQUE MAY BE SOMETHING WE HUMANS CANNOT UNDERSTAND.
I DON'T MIND WAITING. IT'S NOT KNOWING ANYTHING THAT DRIVES ME BATTY.

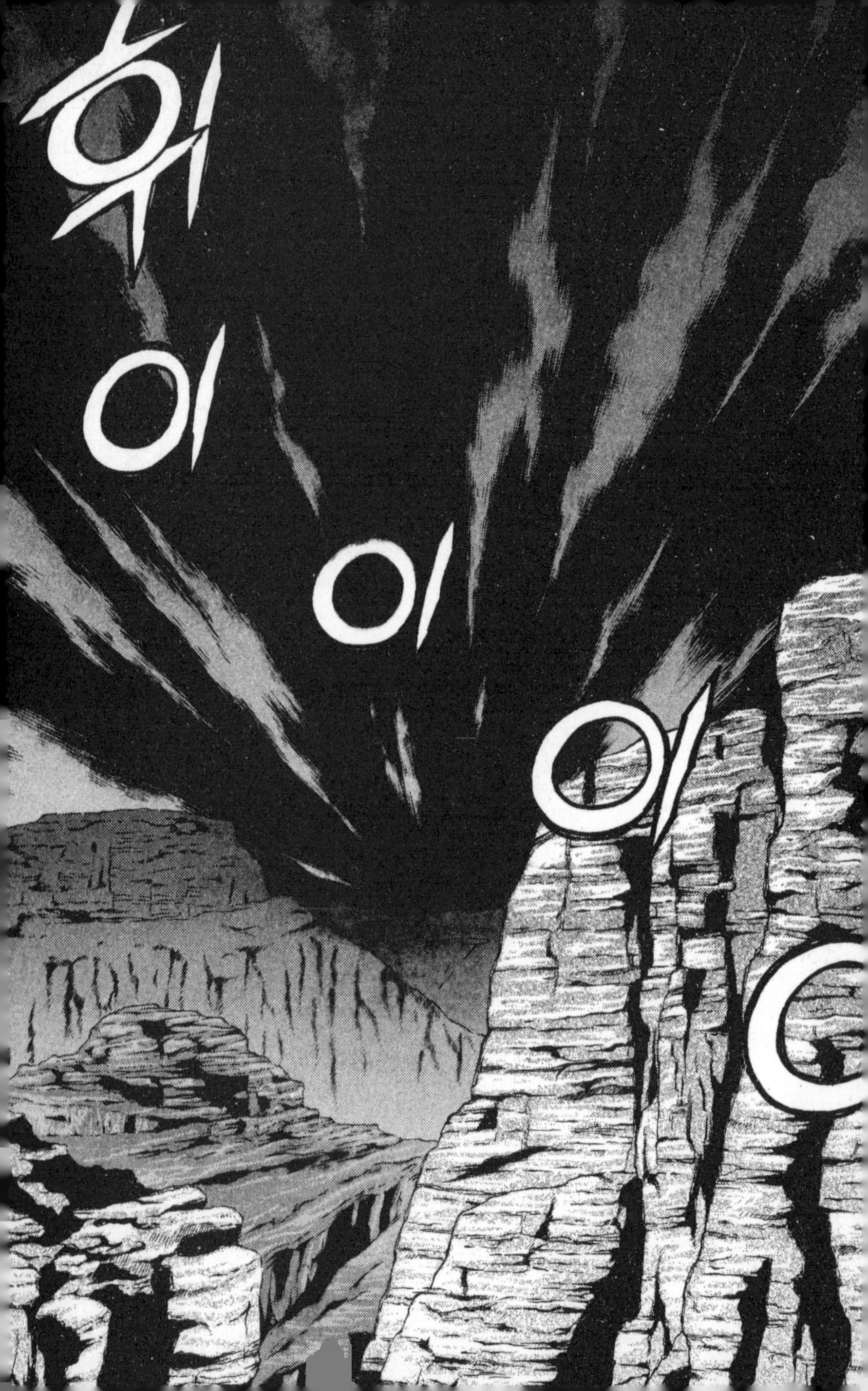
와아아아

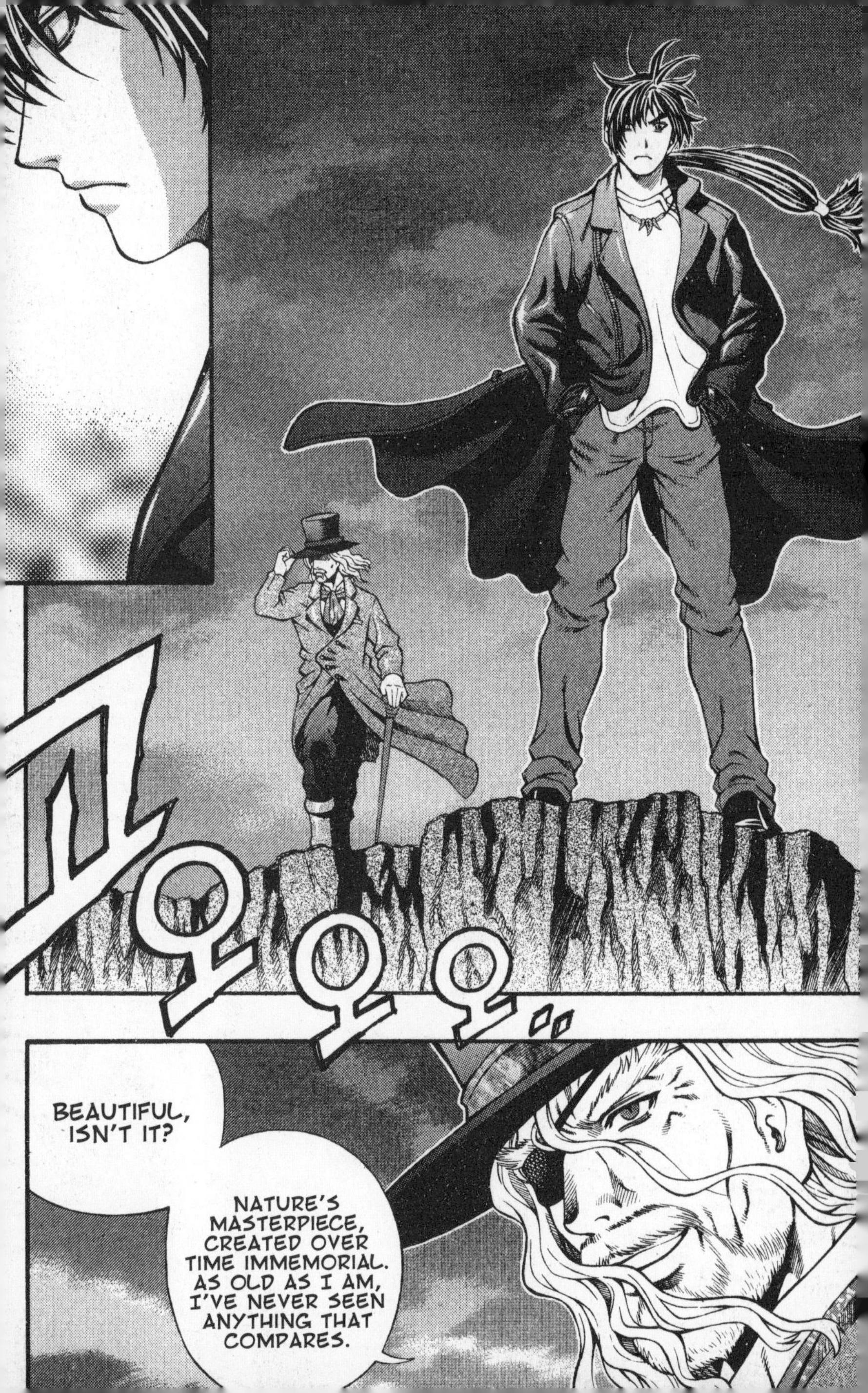
BEAUTIFUL, ISN'T IT?
NATURE'S MASTERPIECE, CREATED OVER TIME IMMEMORIAL. AS OLD AS I AM, I'VE NEVER SEEN ANYTHING THAT COMPARES.

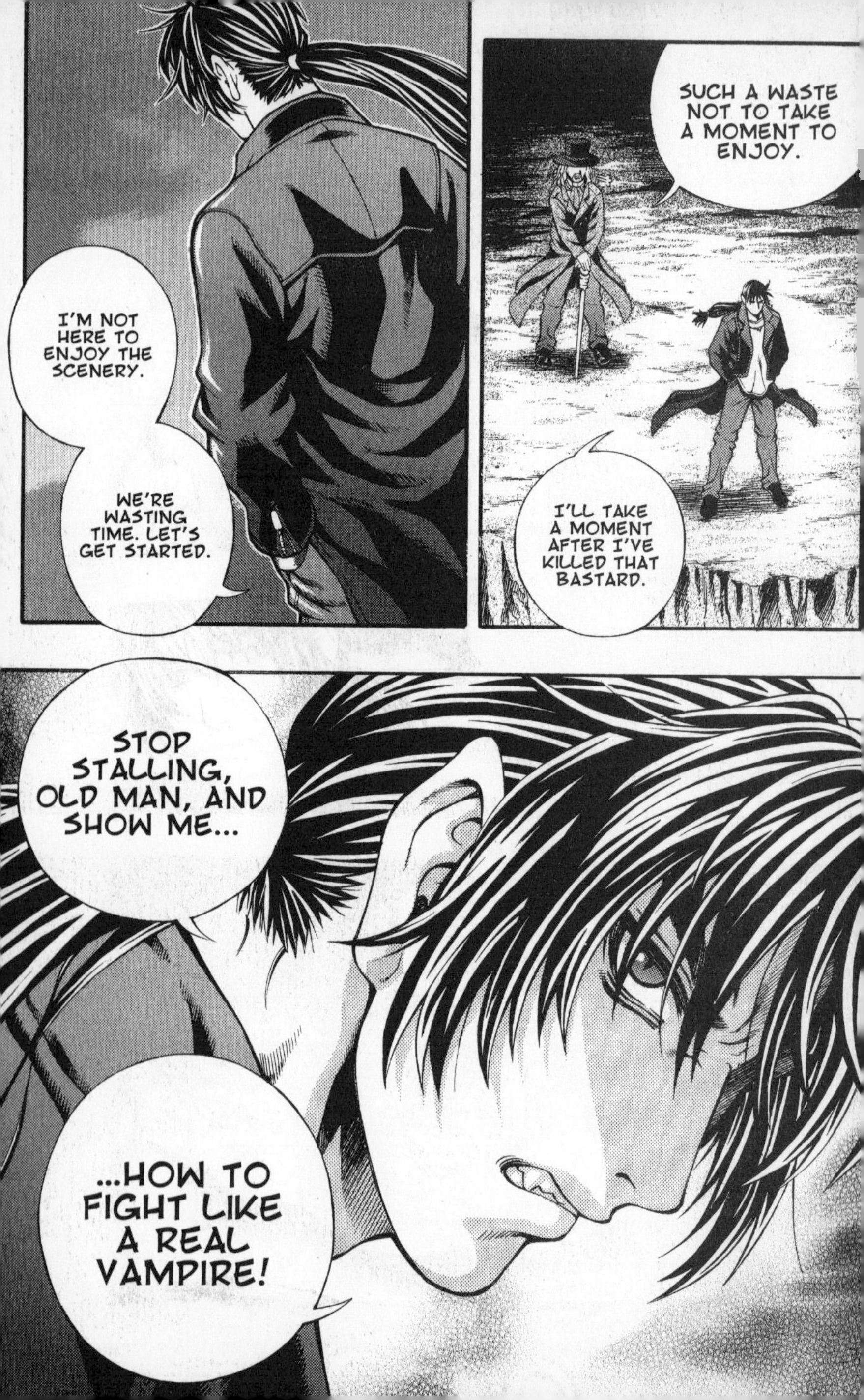
SUCH A WASTE NOT TO TAKE A MOMENT TO ENJOY.
I'LL TAKE A MOMENT AFTER I'VE KILLED THAT BASTARD.
I'M NOT HERE TO ENJOY THE SCENERY.
WE'RE WASTING TIME. LET'S GET STARTED.
STOP STALLING, OLD MAN, AND SHOW ME...
...HOW TO FIGHT LIKE A REAL VAMPIRE!

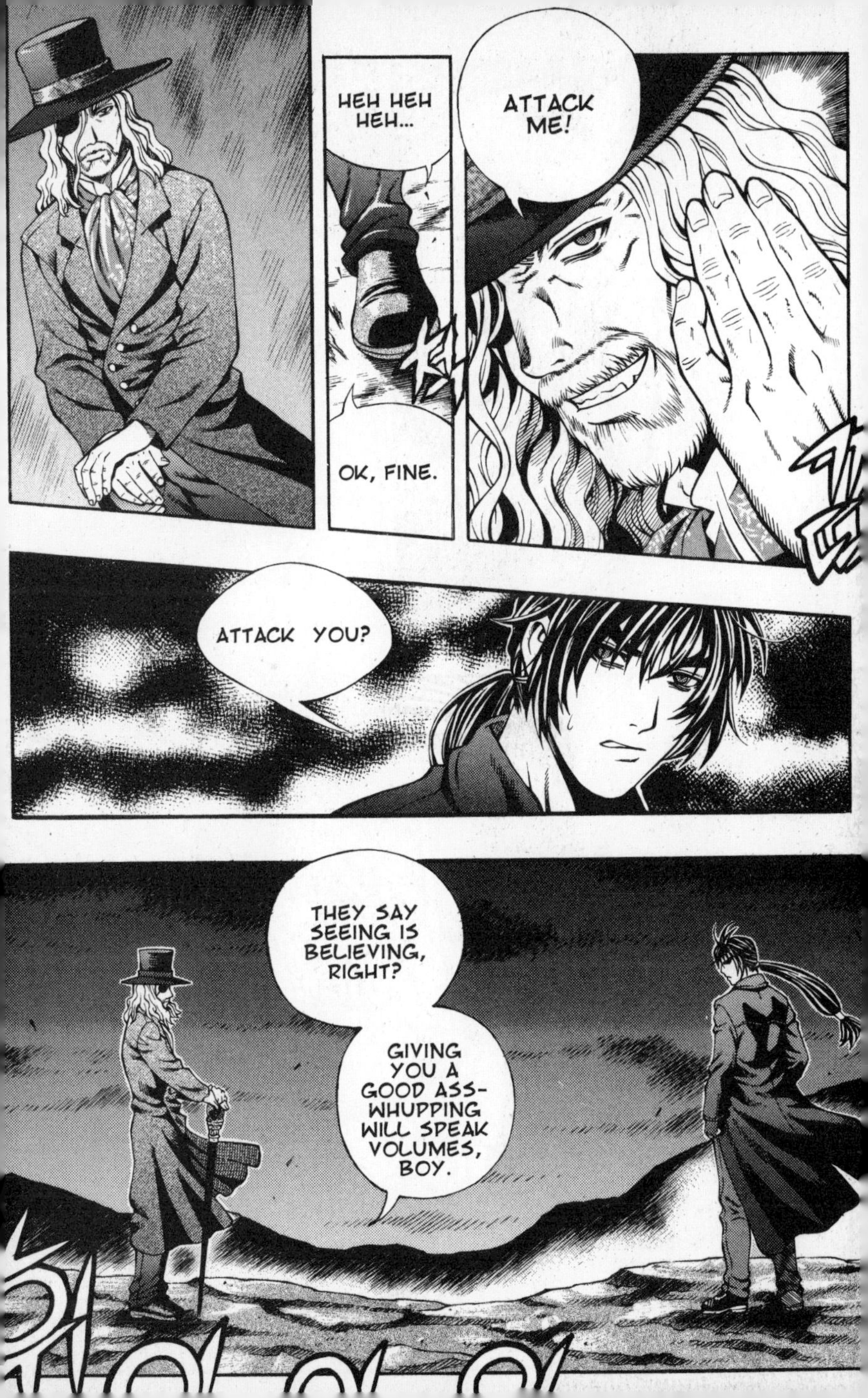
HEH HEH HEH...
ATTACK ME!
OK, FINE.
ATTACK YOU?
THEY SAY SEEING IS BELIEVING, RIGHT?
GIVING YOU A GOOD ASS-WHUPPING WILL SPEAK VOLUMES, BOY.

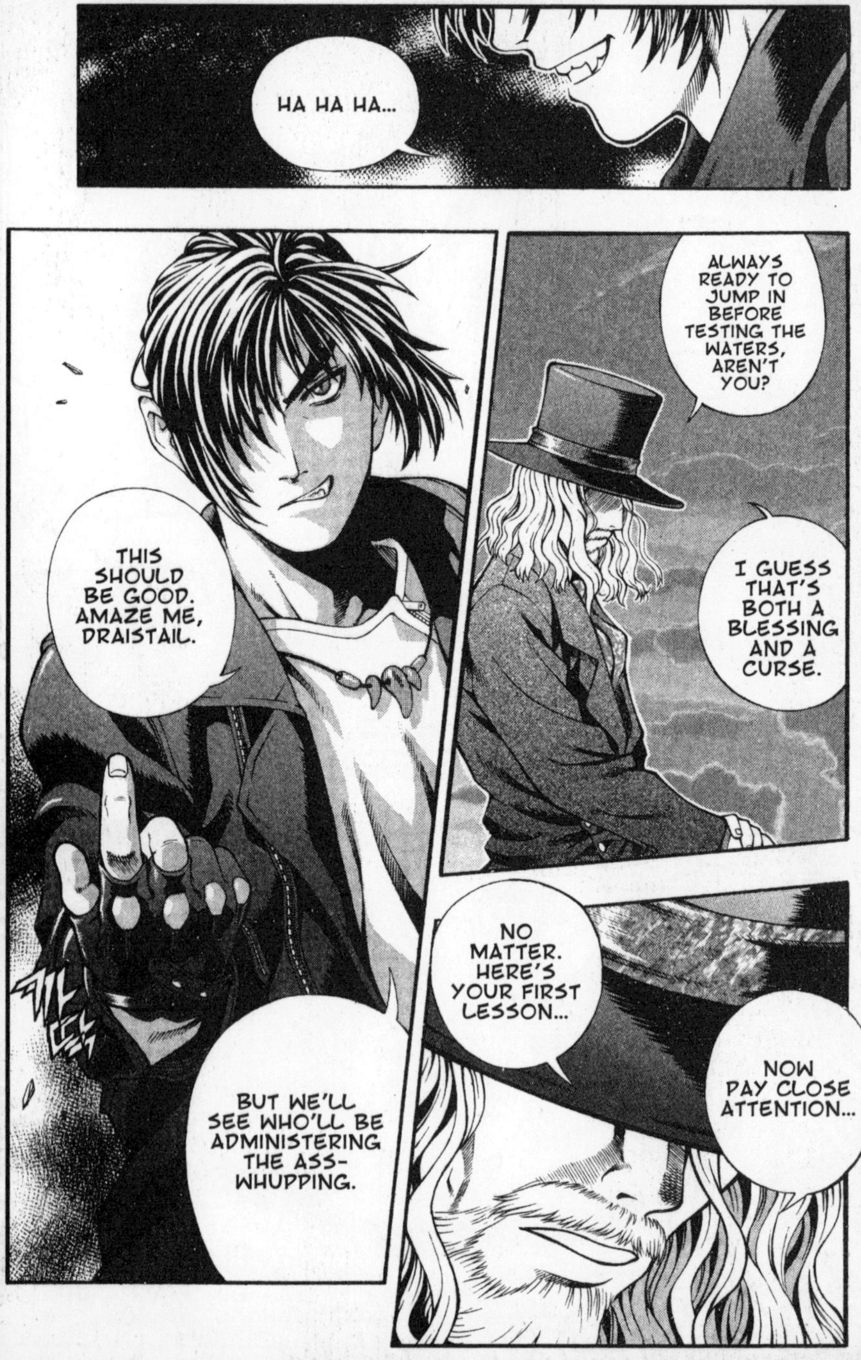
HA HA HA...
ALWAYS READY TO JUMP IN BEFORE TESTING THE WATERS, AREN'T YOU?
I GUESS THAT'S BOTH A BLESSING AND A CURSE.
NO MATTER. HERE'S YOUR FIRST LESSON...
NOW PAY CLOSE ATTENTION...
THIS SHOULD BE GOOD. AMAZE ME, DRAISTAIL.
BUT WE'LL SEE WHO'LL BE ADMINISTERING THE ASS-WHUPPING.

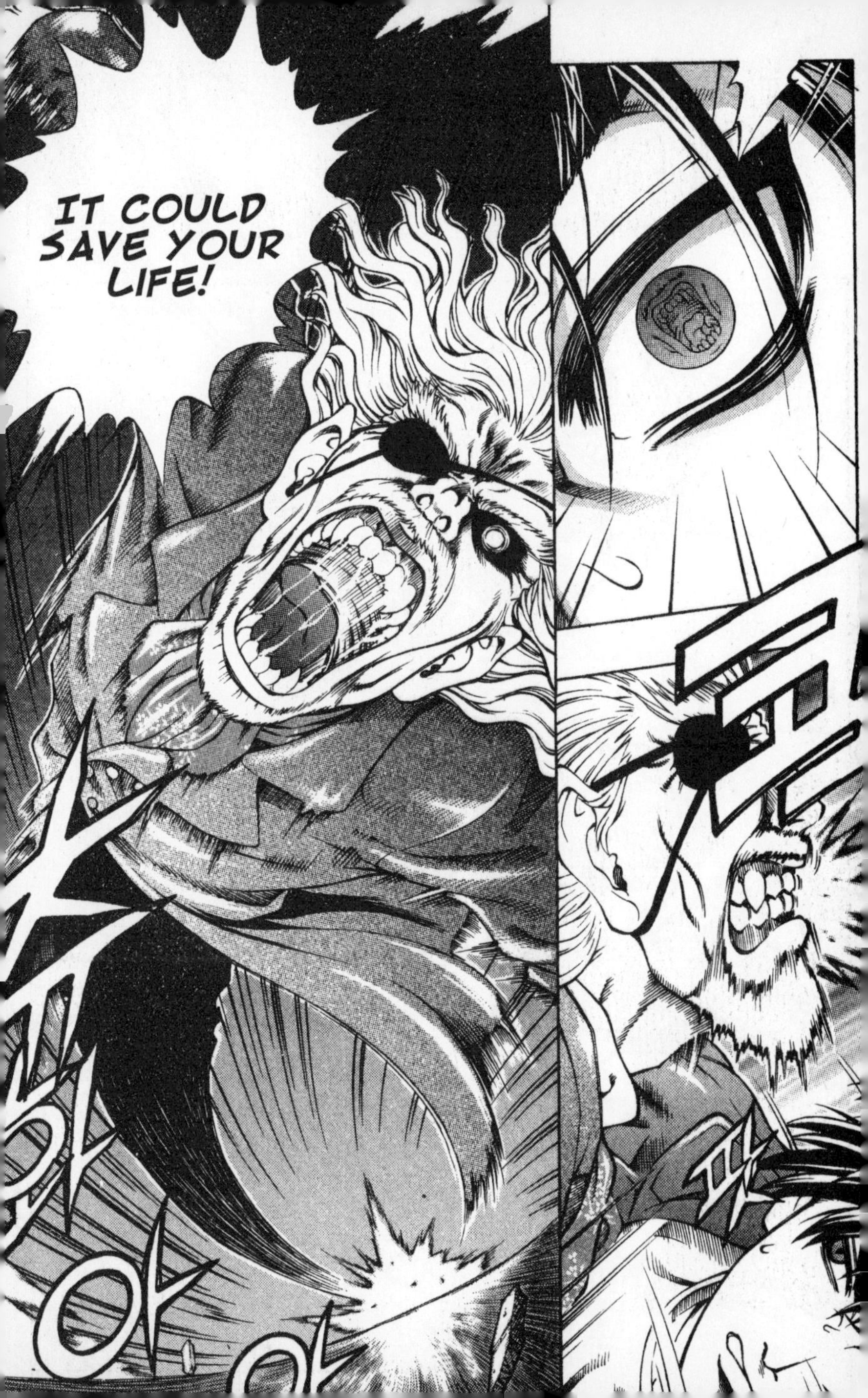
IT COULD SAVE YOUR LIFE!

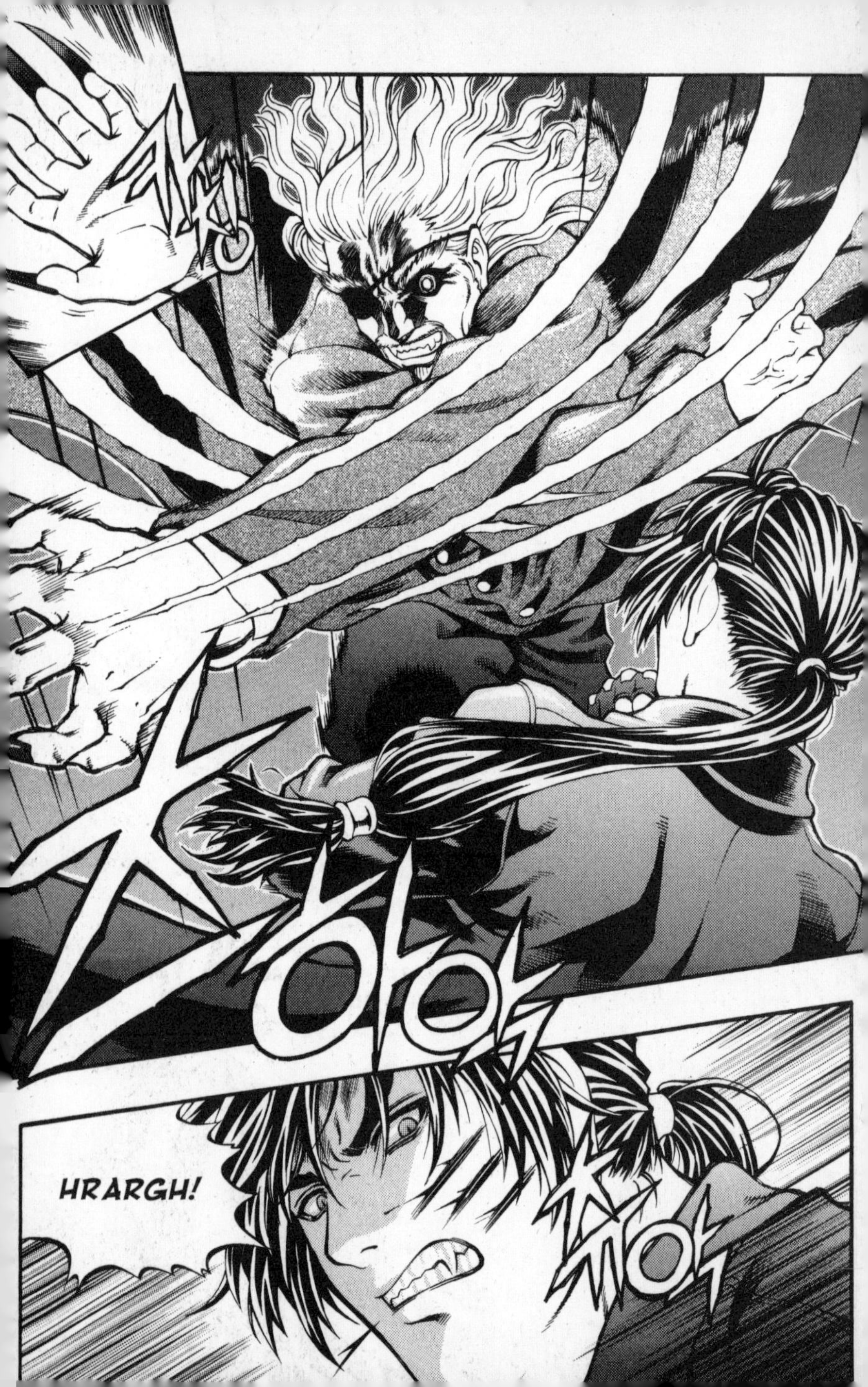
HRARGH!

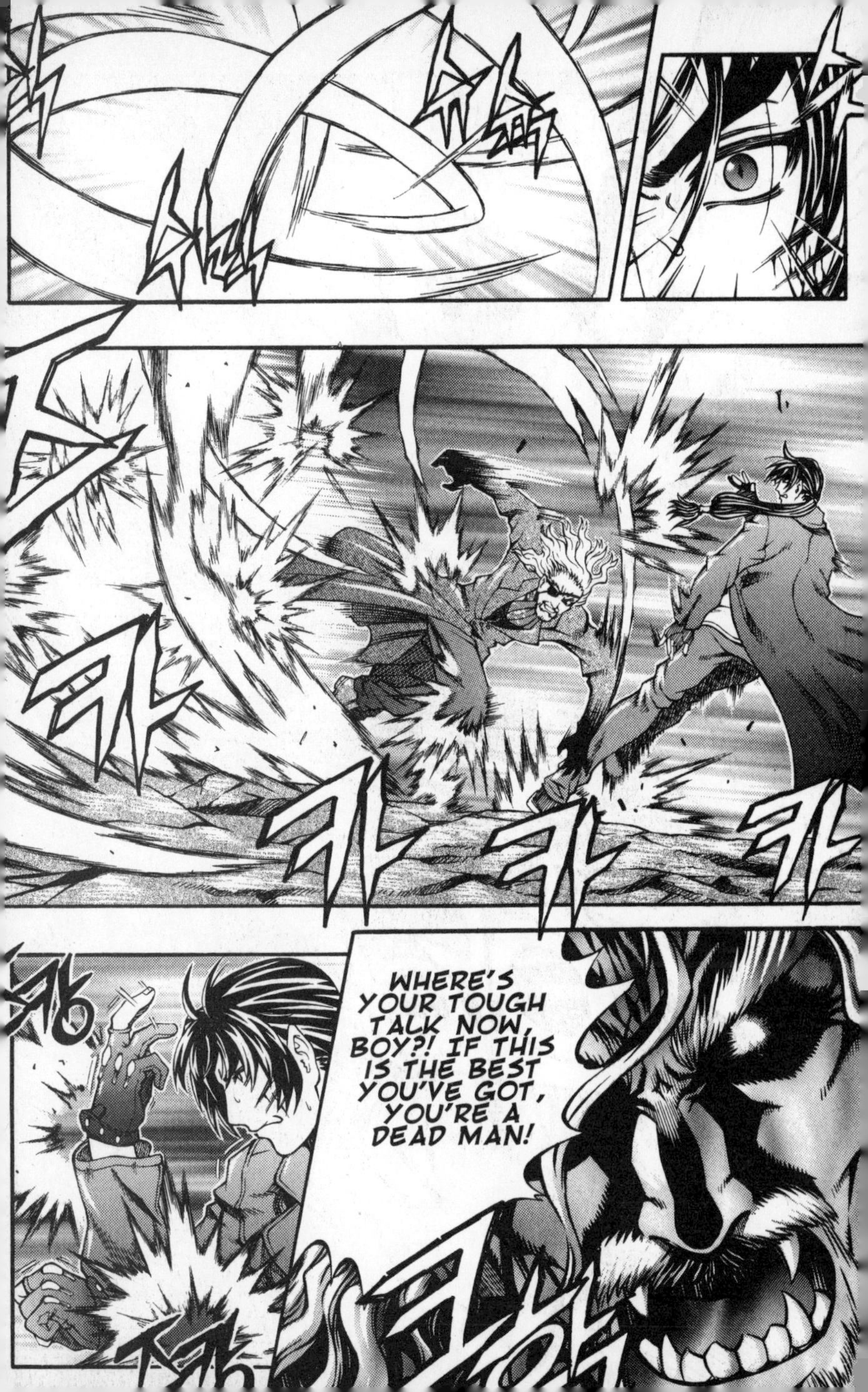
WHERE'S YOUR TOUGH TALK NOW, BOY?! IF THIS IS THE BEST YOU'VE GOT, YOU'RE A DEAD MAN!

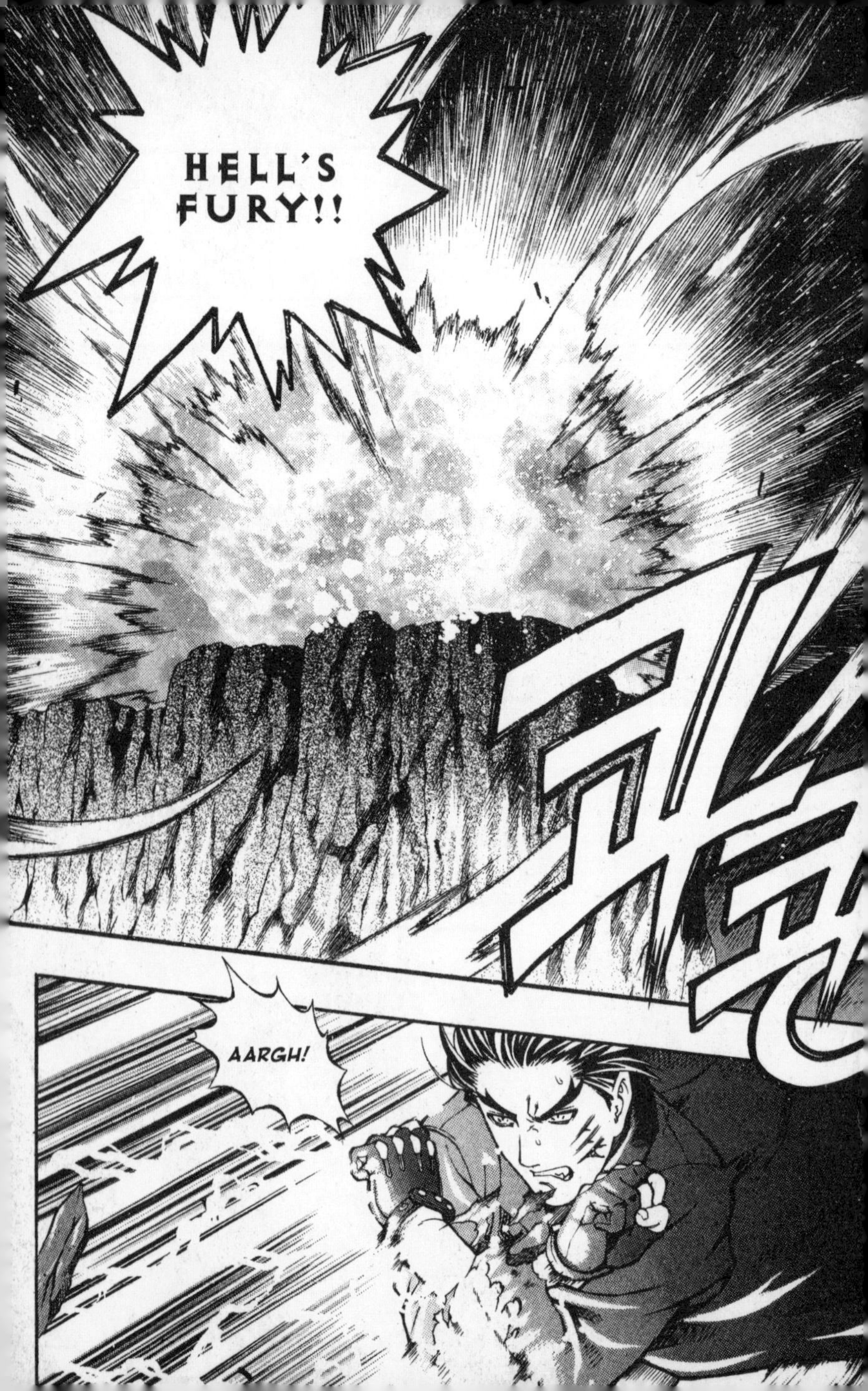
HELL'S FURY!!
AARGH!

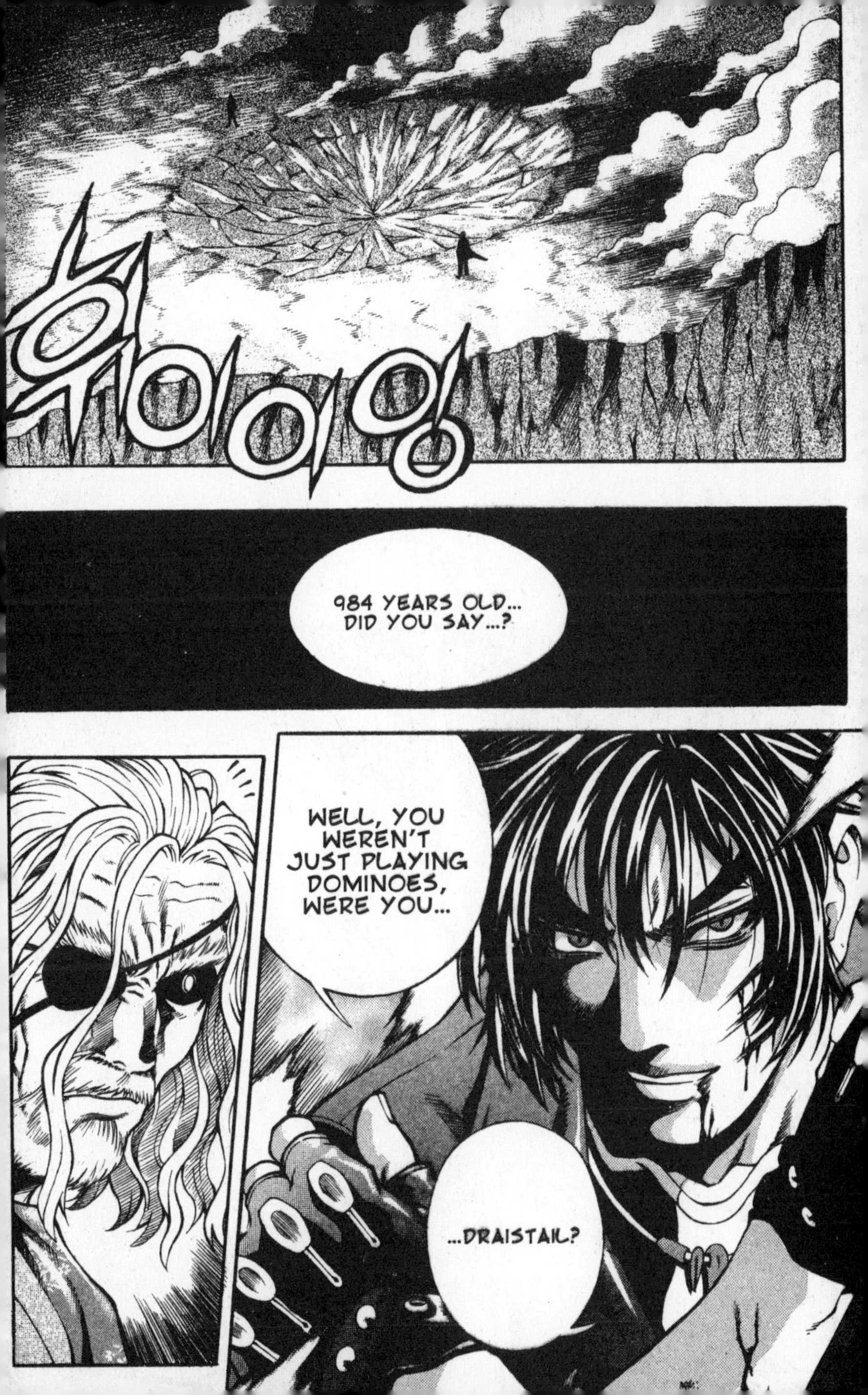
우아아앙!
984 YEARS OLD... DID YOU SAY...?
WELL, YOU WEREN'T JUST PLAYING DOMINOES, WERE YOU...
...DRAISTAIL?

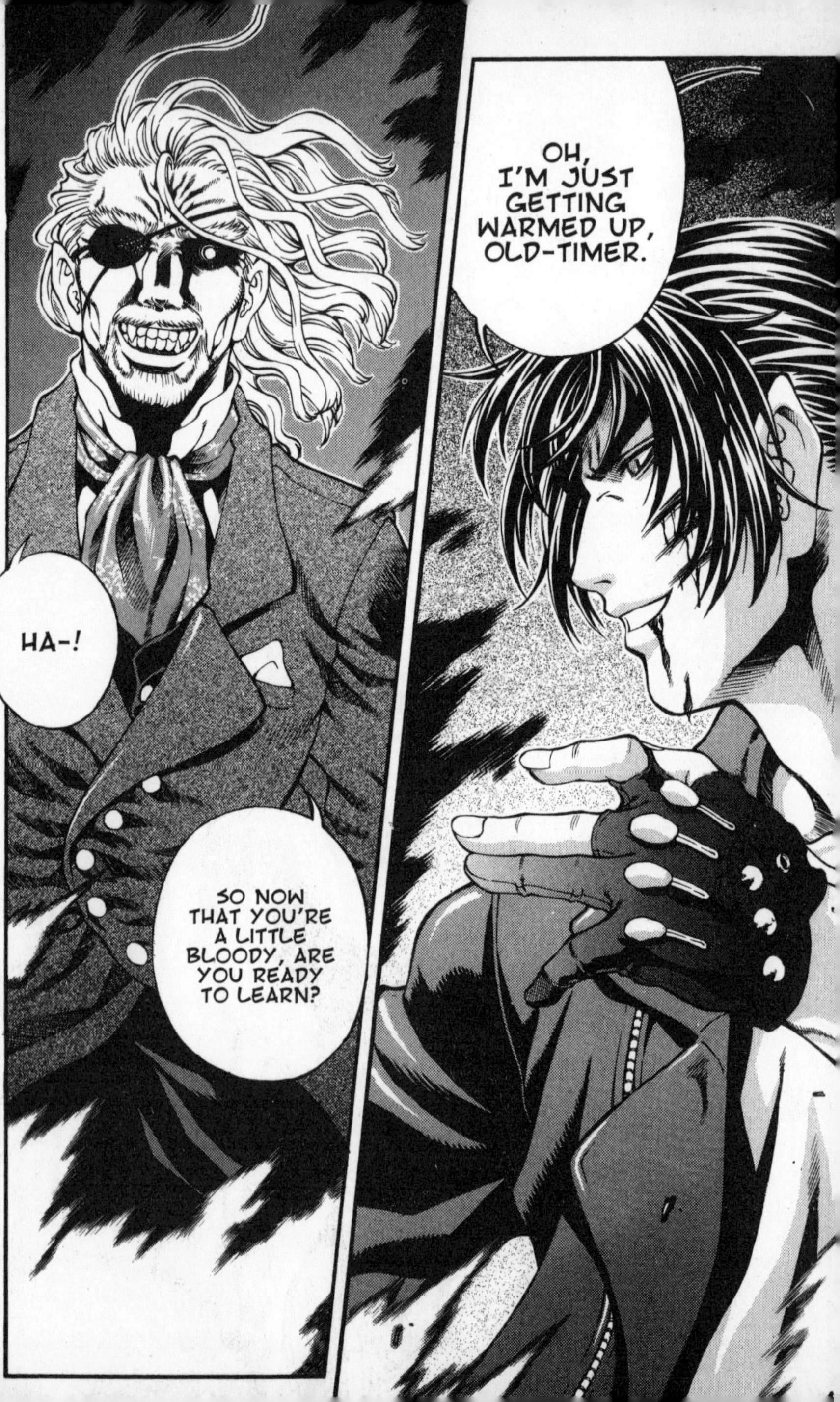
HA-!
SO NOW THAT YOU'RE A LITTLE BLOODY, ARE YOU READY TO LEARN?
OH, I'M JUST GETTING WARMED UP, OLD-TIMER.

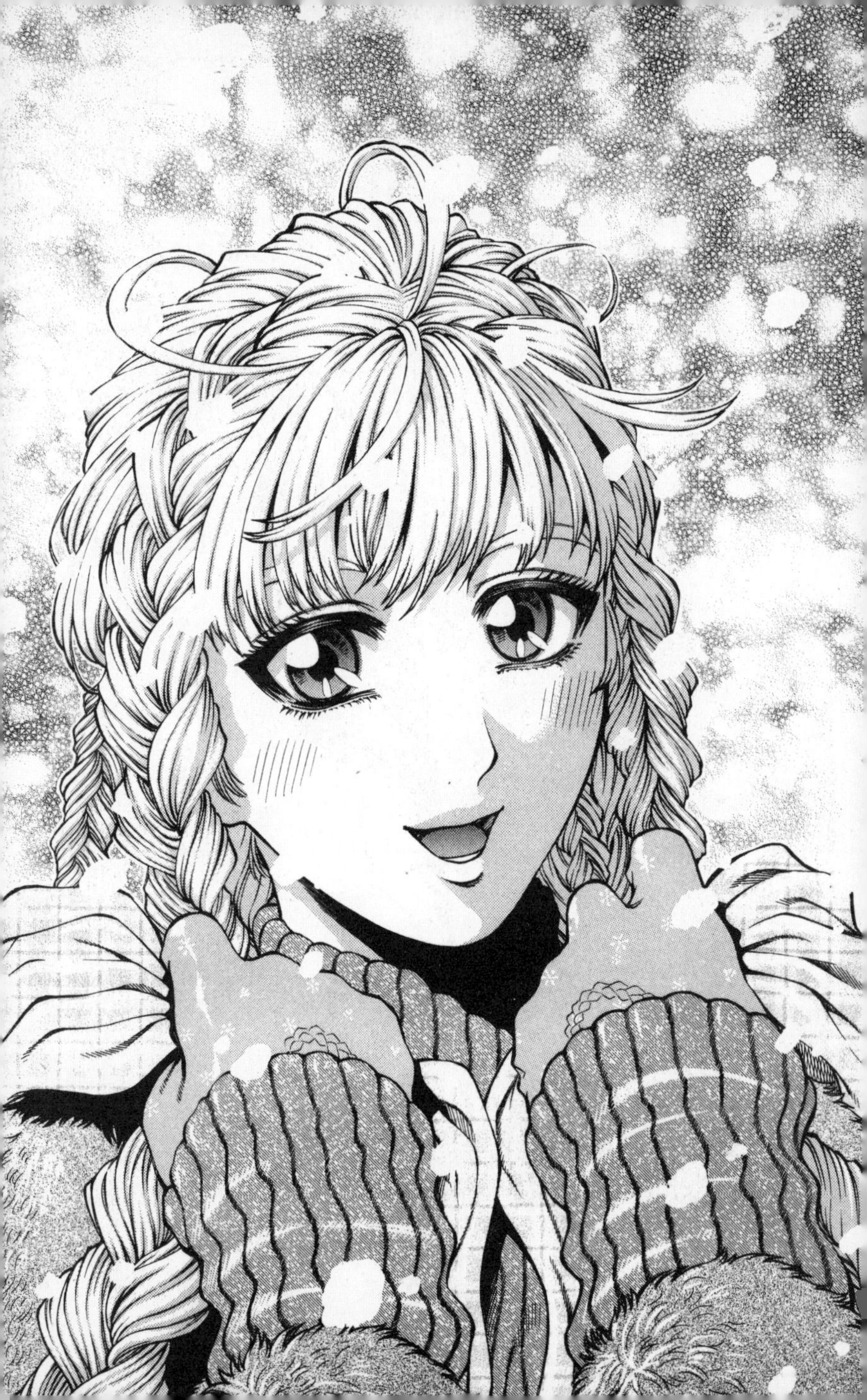

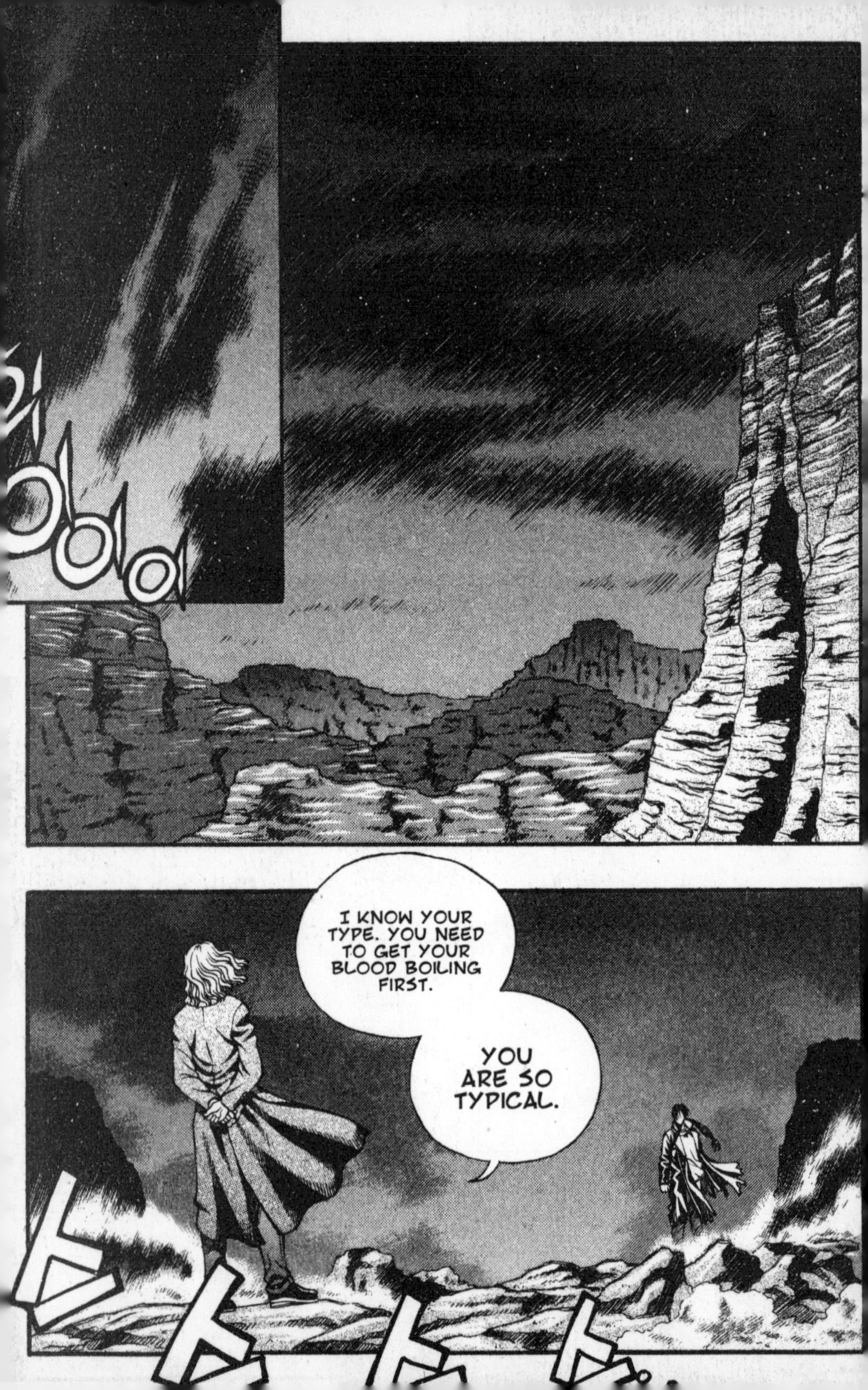
I KNOW YOUR TYPE. YOU NEED TO GET YOUR BLOOD BOILING FIRST.
YOU ARE SO TYPICAL.

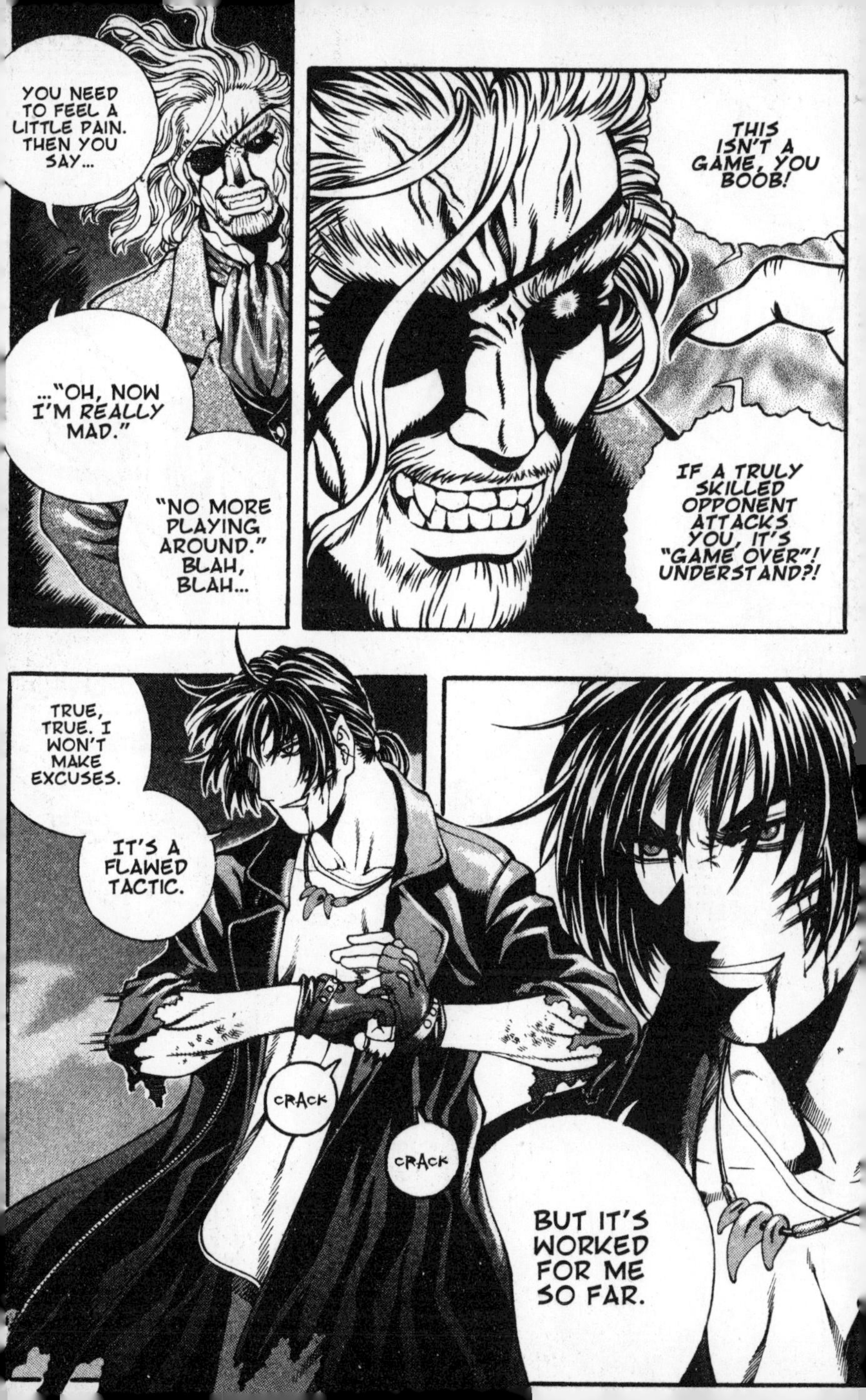
YOU NEED TO FEEL A LITTLE PAIN. THEN YOU SAY...
..."OH, NOW I'M REALLY MAD."
"NO MORE PLAYING AROUND." BLAH, BLAH...
THIS ISN'T A GAME, YOU BOOB!
IF A TRULY SKILLED OPPONENT ATTACKS YOU, IT'S "GAME OVER"! UNDERSTAND?!
TRUE, TRUE. I WON'T MAKE EXCUSES.
IT'S A FLAWED TACTIC.
CRACK
CRACK
BUT IT'S WORKED FOR ME SO FAR.

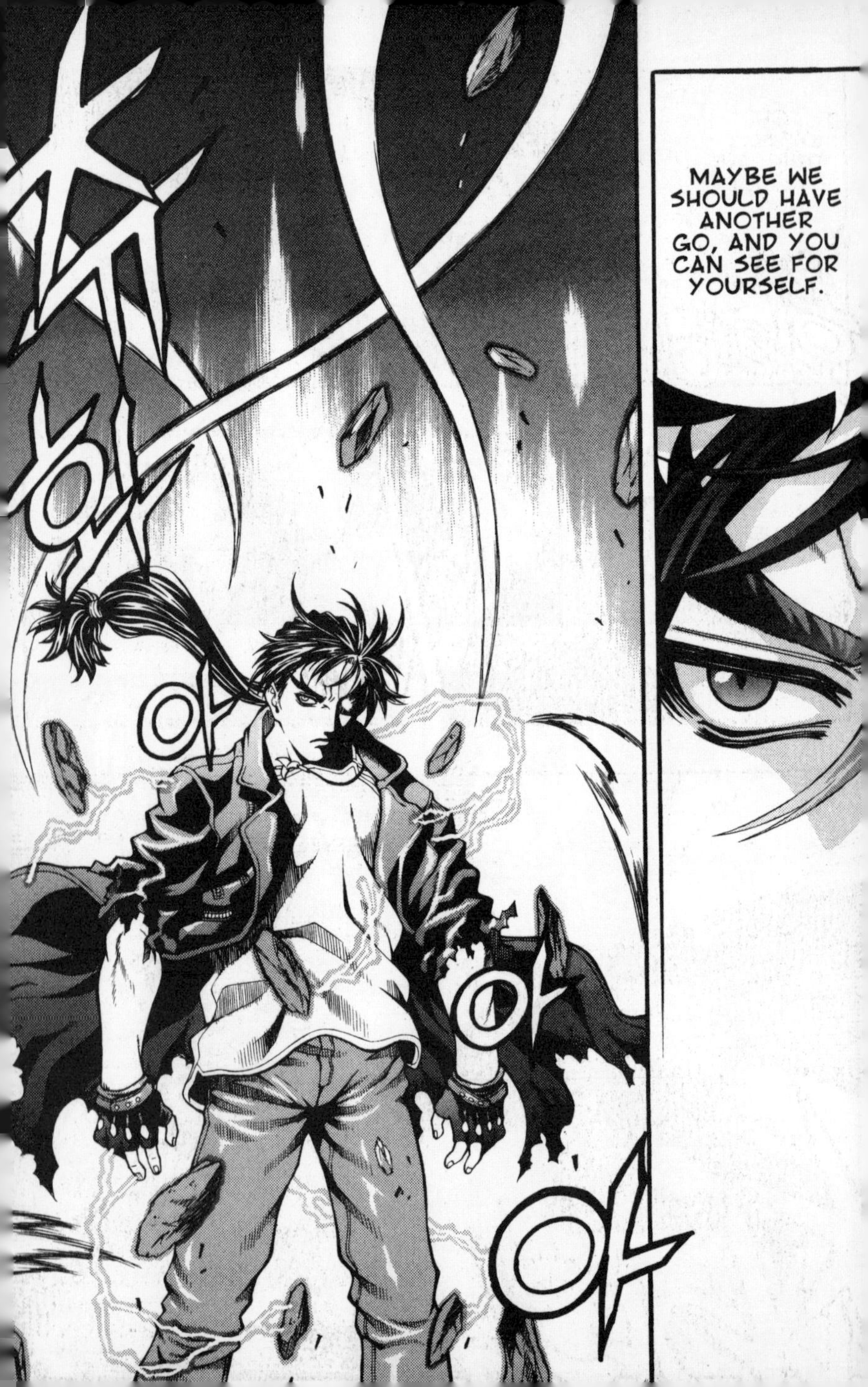
MAYBE WE SHOULD HAVE ANOTHER GO, AND YOU CAN SEE FOR YOURSELF.

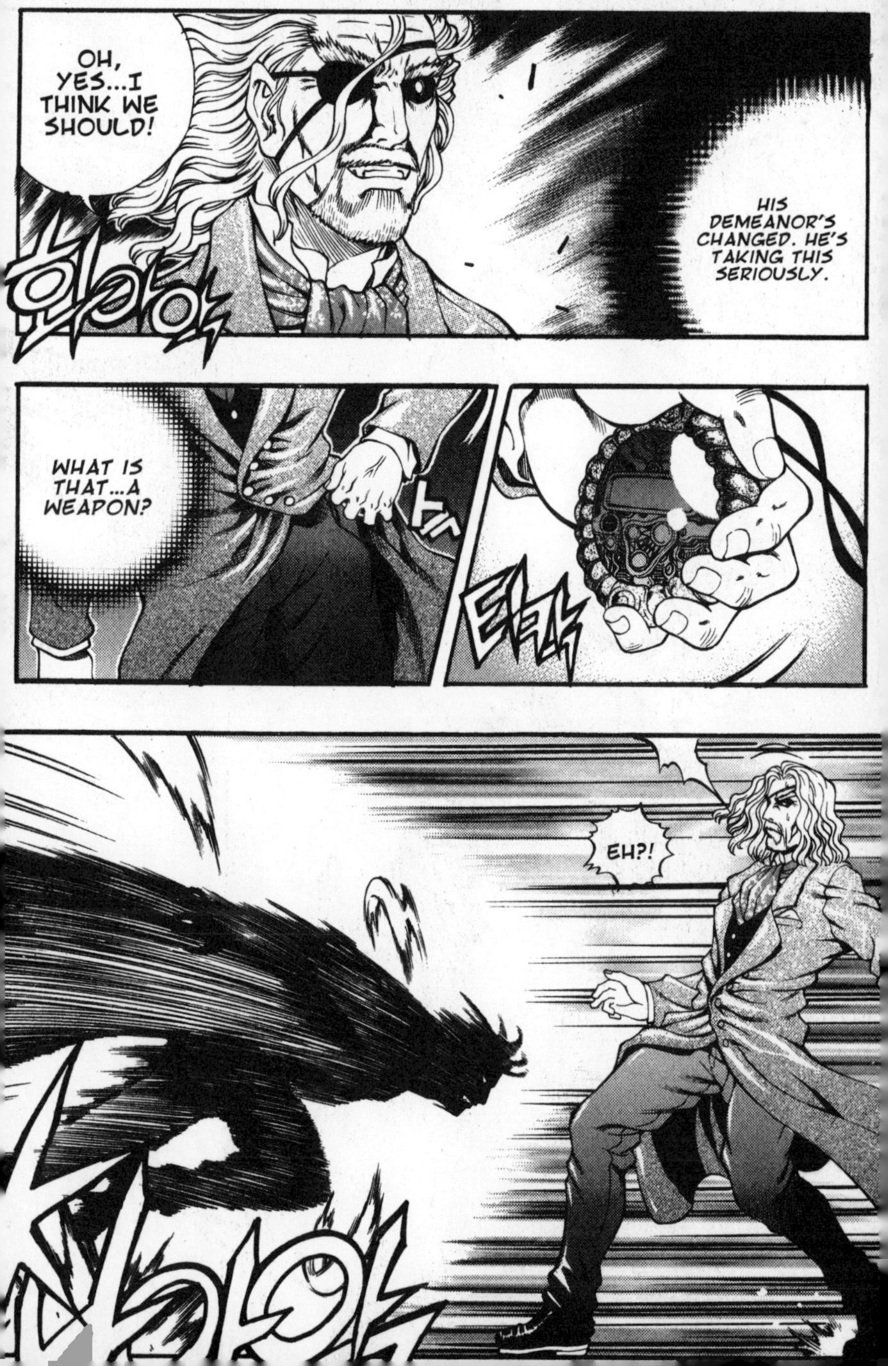
OH, YES...I THINK WE SHOULD!
HIS DEMEANOR'S CHANGED. HE'S TAKING THIS SERIOUSLY.
WHAT IS THAT...A WEAPON?
EH?!

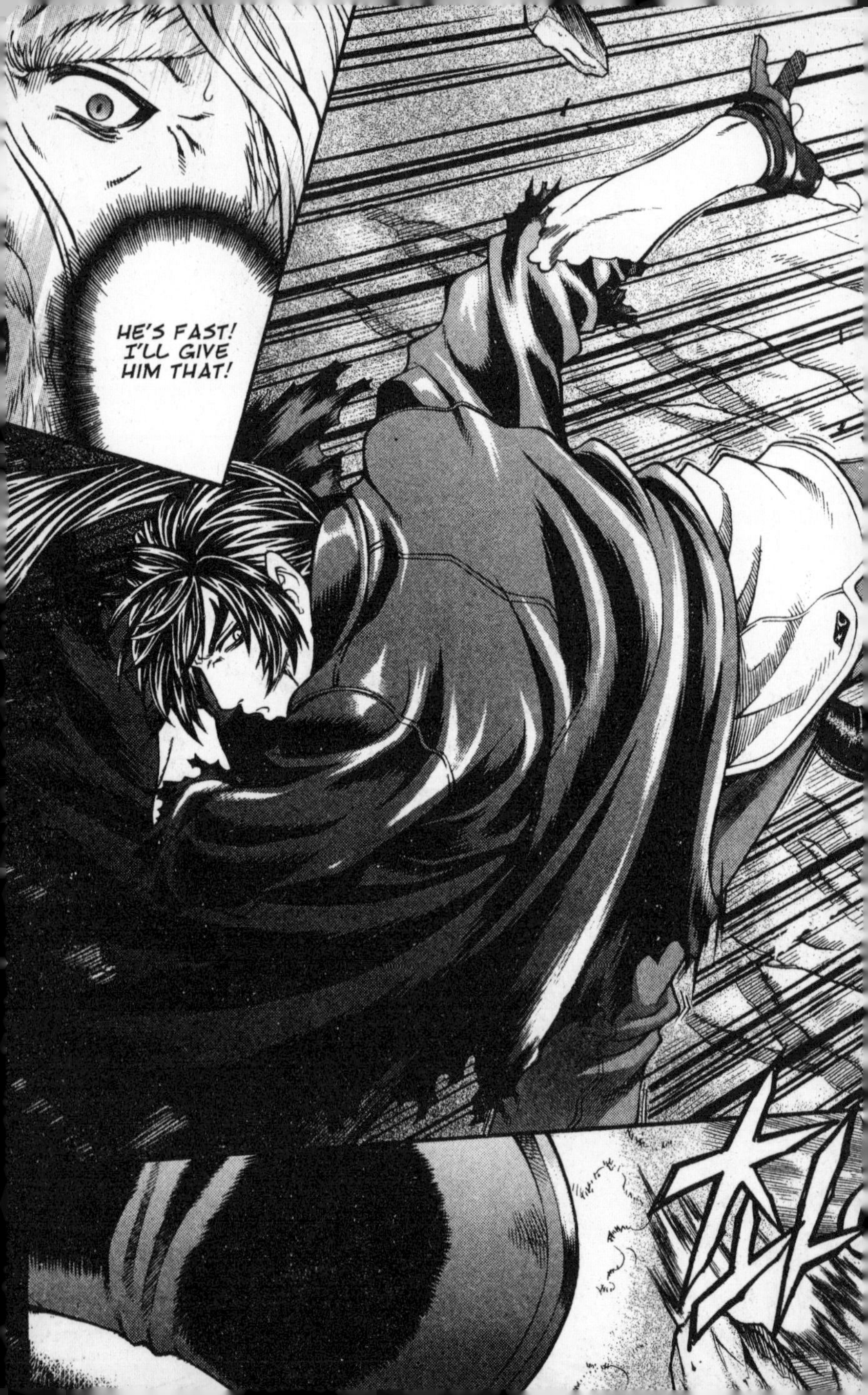
HE'S FAST! I'LL GIVE HIM THAT!

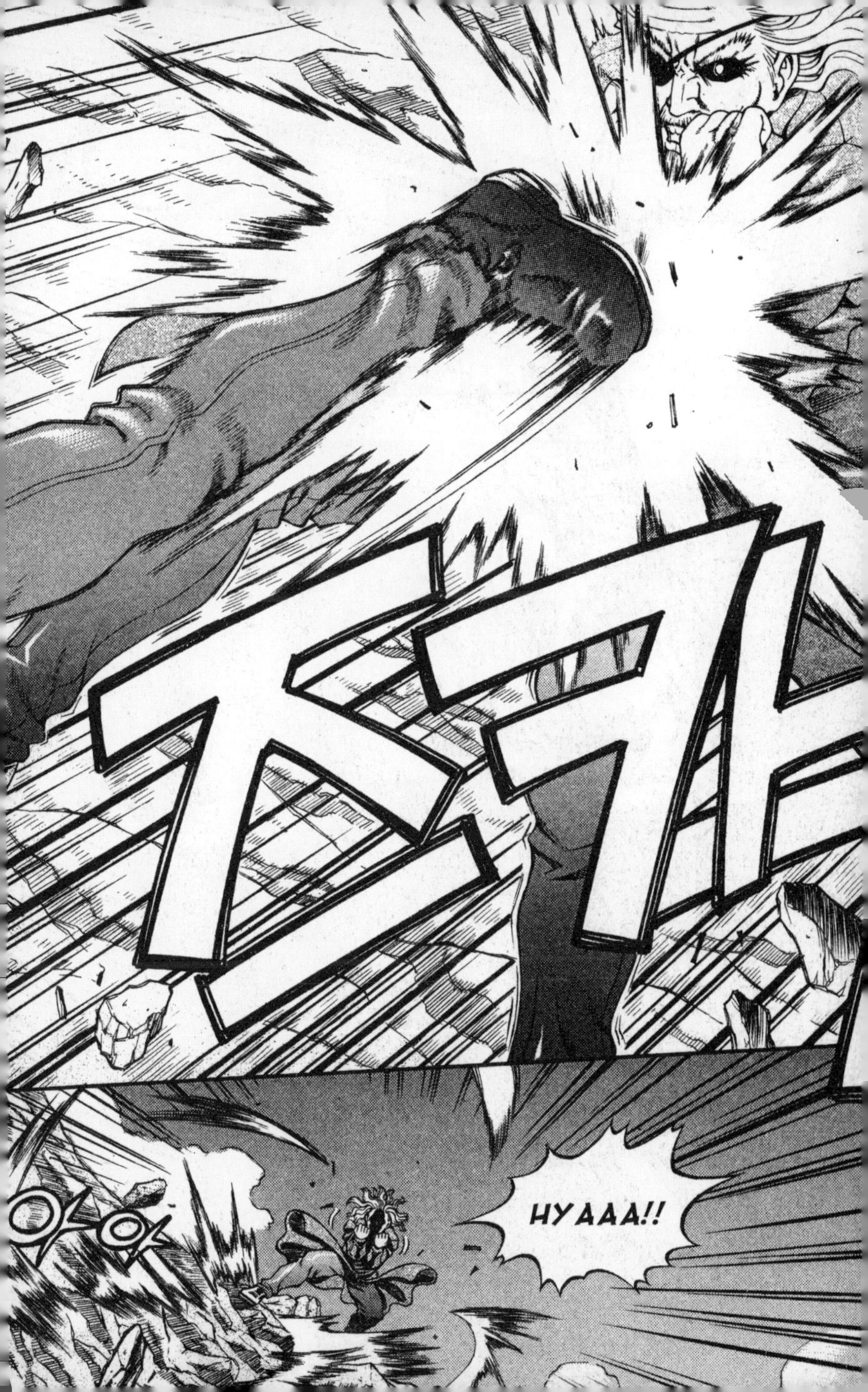
HYAAA!!

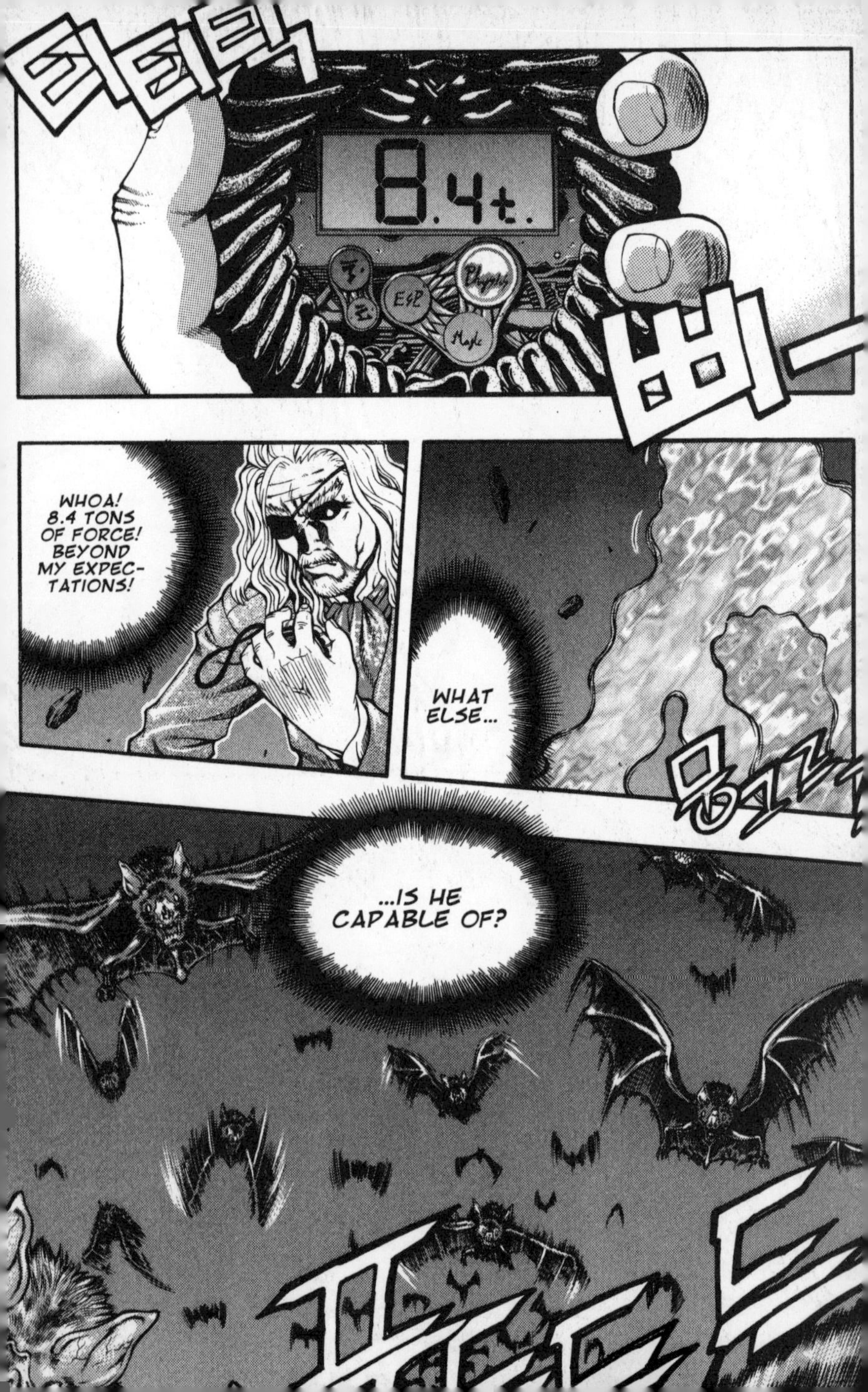
8.4t.
WHOA! 8.4 TONS OF FORCE! BEYOND MY EXPECTATIONS!
WHAT ELSE...
...IS HE CAPABLE OF?

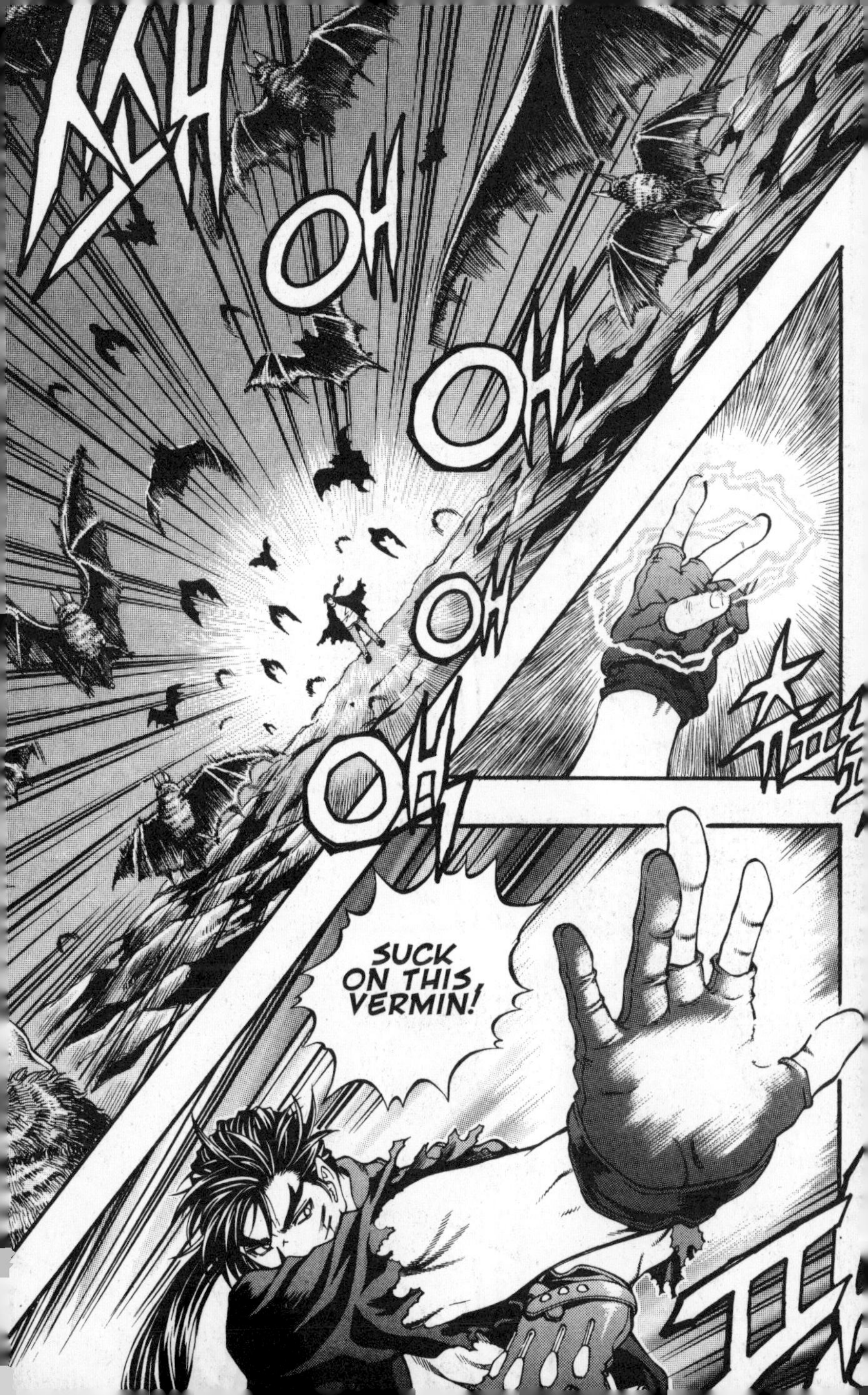
OH
OH
OH
OH
SUCK ON THIS VERMIN!

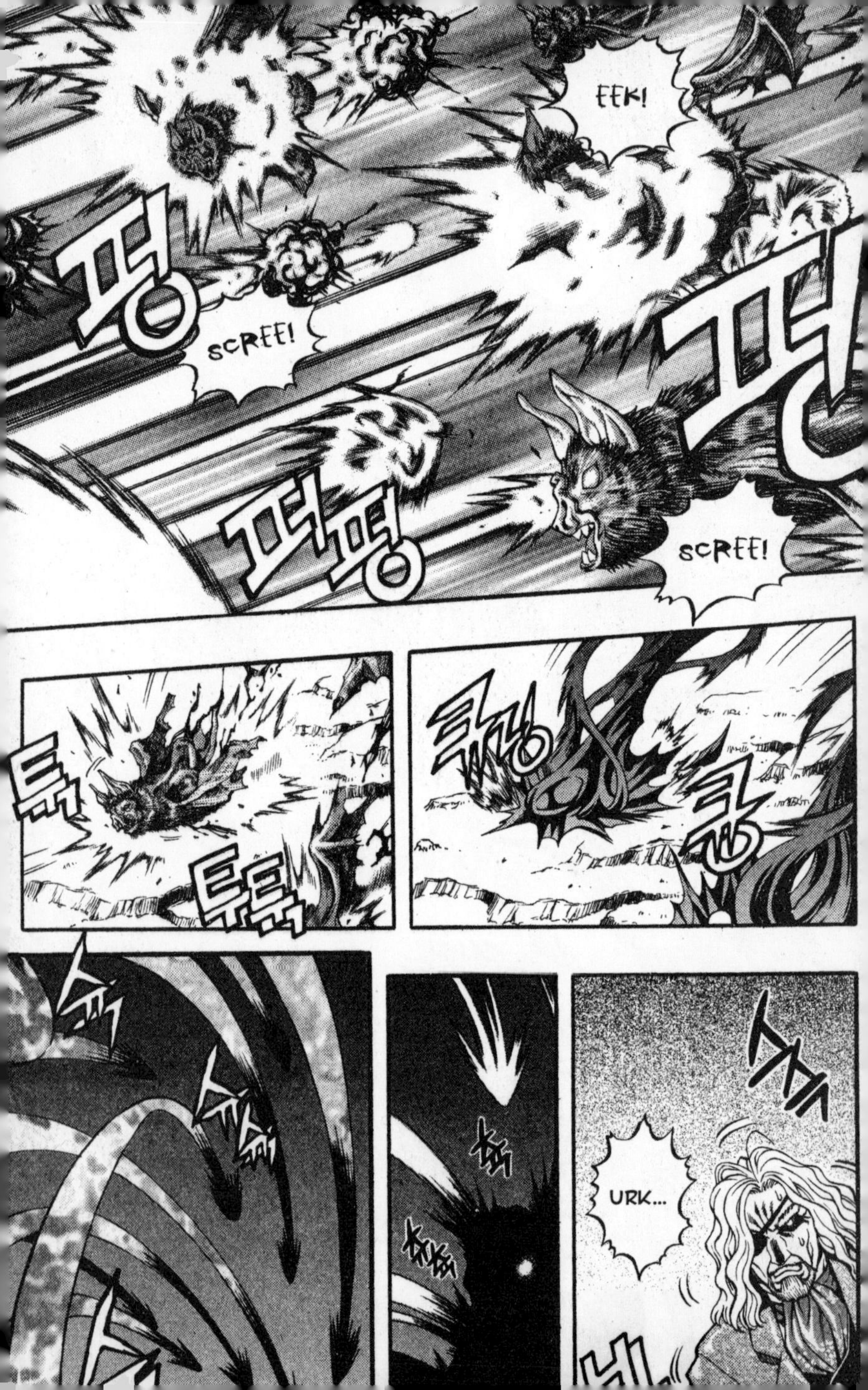

EEK!
펑
SCREE!
펑
퍽
펑
SCREE!
투
투투
크
크
URK...

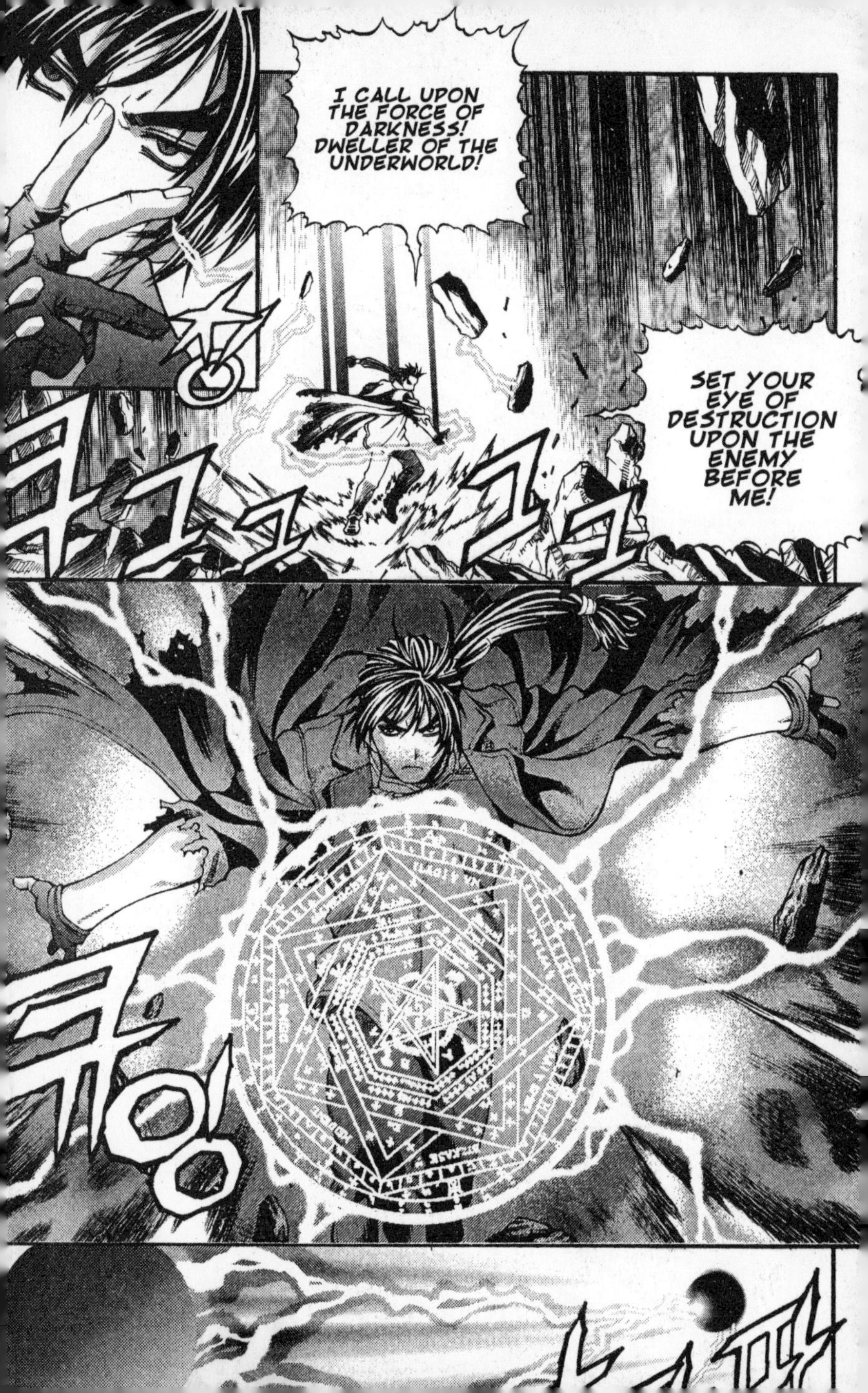
I CALL UPON THE FORCE OF DARKNESS! DWELLER OF THE UNDERWORLD!
SET YOUR EYE OF DESTRUCTION UPON THE ENEMY BEFORE ME!

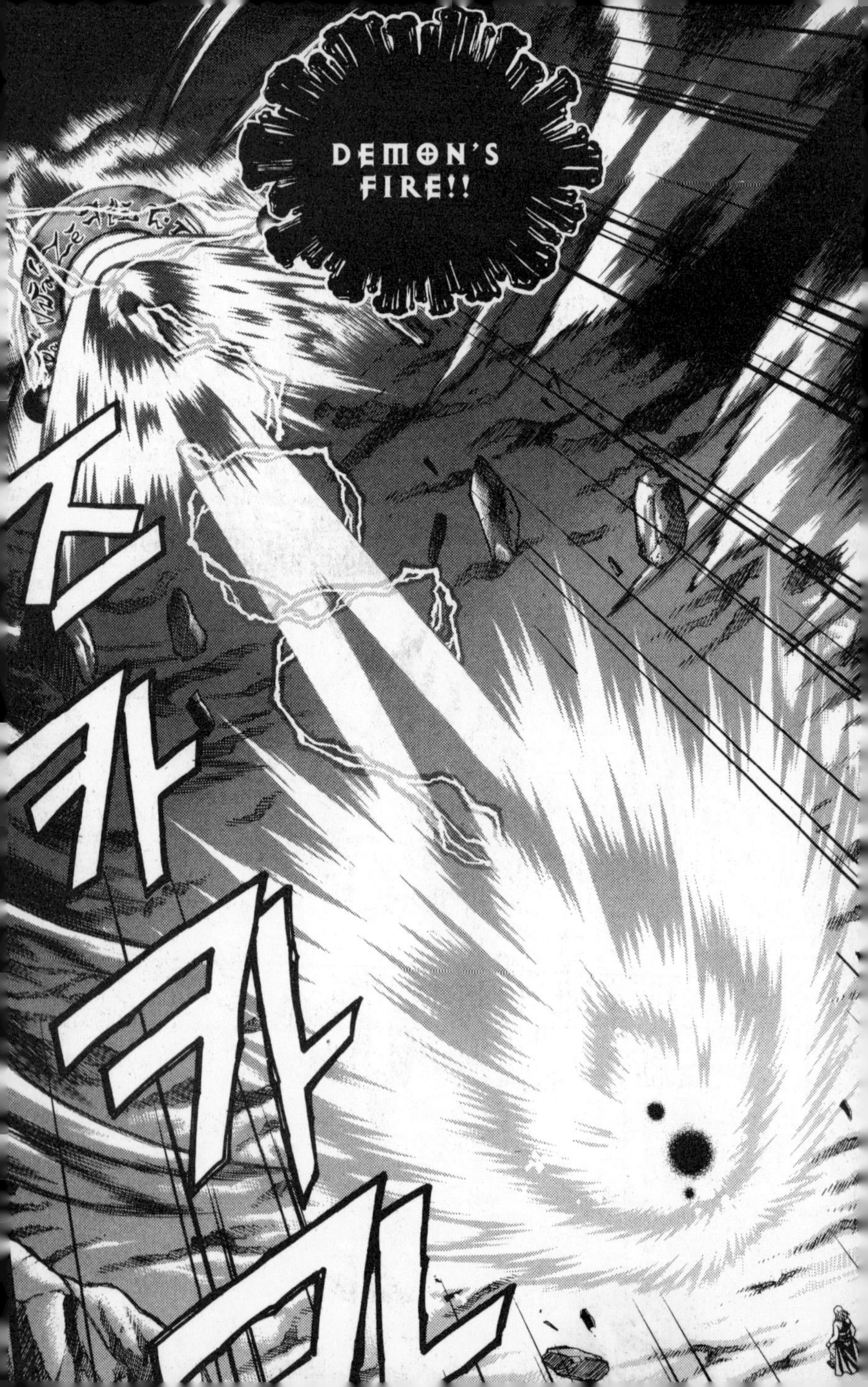
DEMON'S FIRE!!

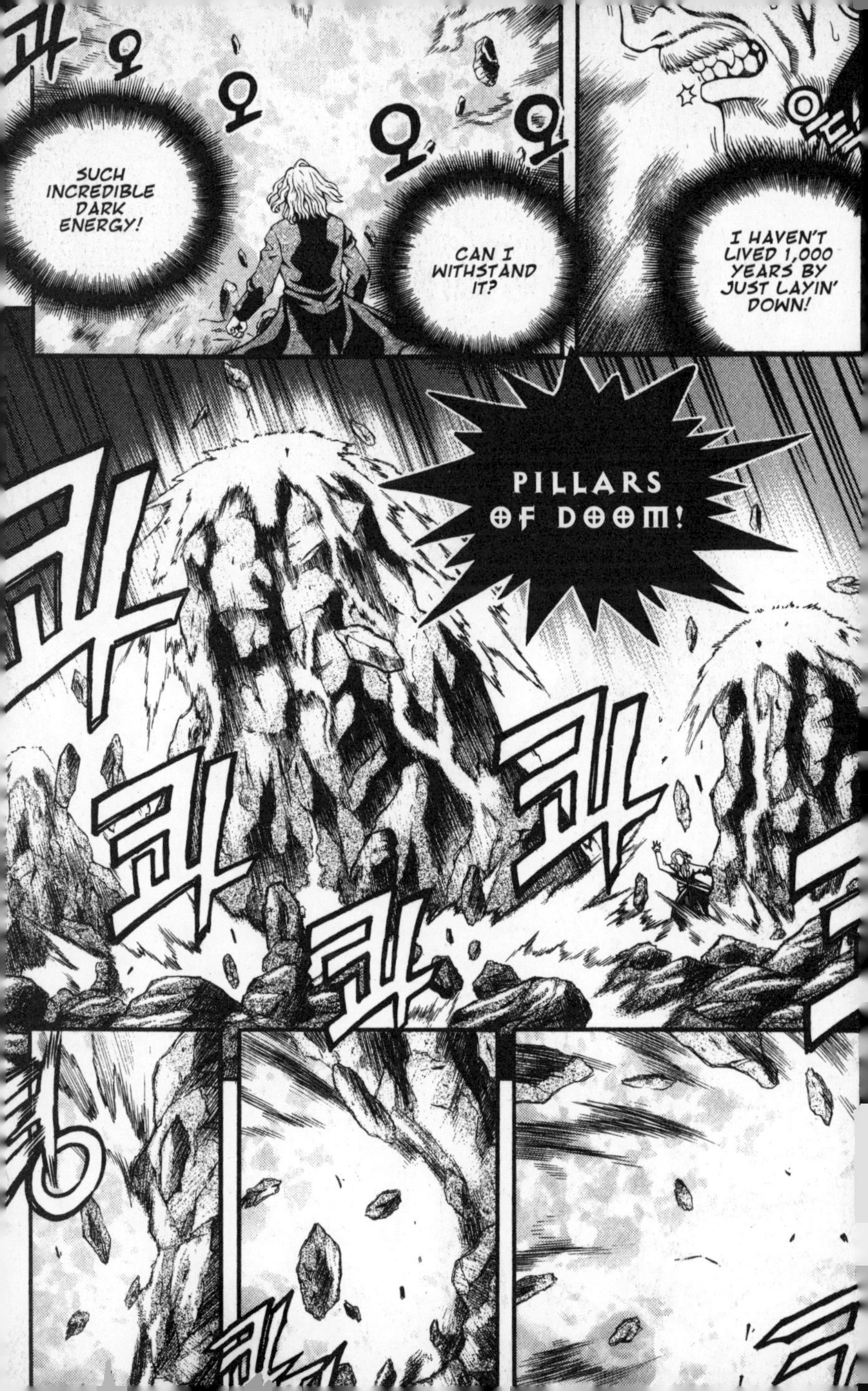
과오오오오
SUCH INCREDIBLE DARK ENERGY!
CAN I WITHSTAND IT?
I HAVEN'T LIVED 1,000 YEARS BY JUST LAYIN' DOWN!
PILLARS OF DOOM!
콰콰콰콰

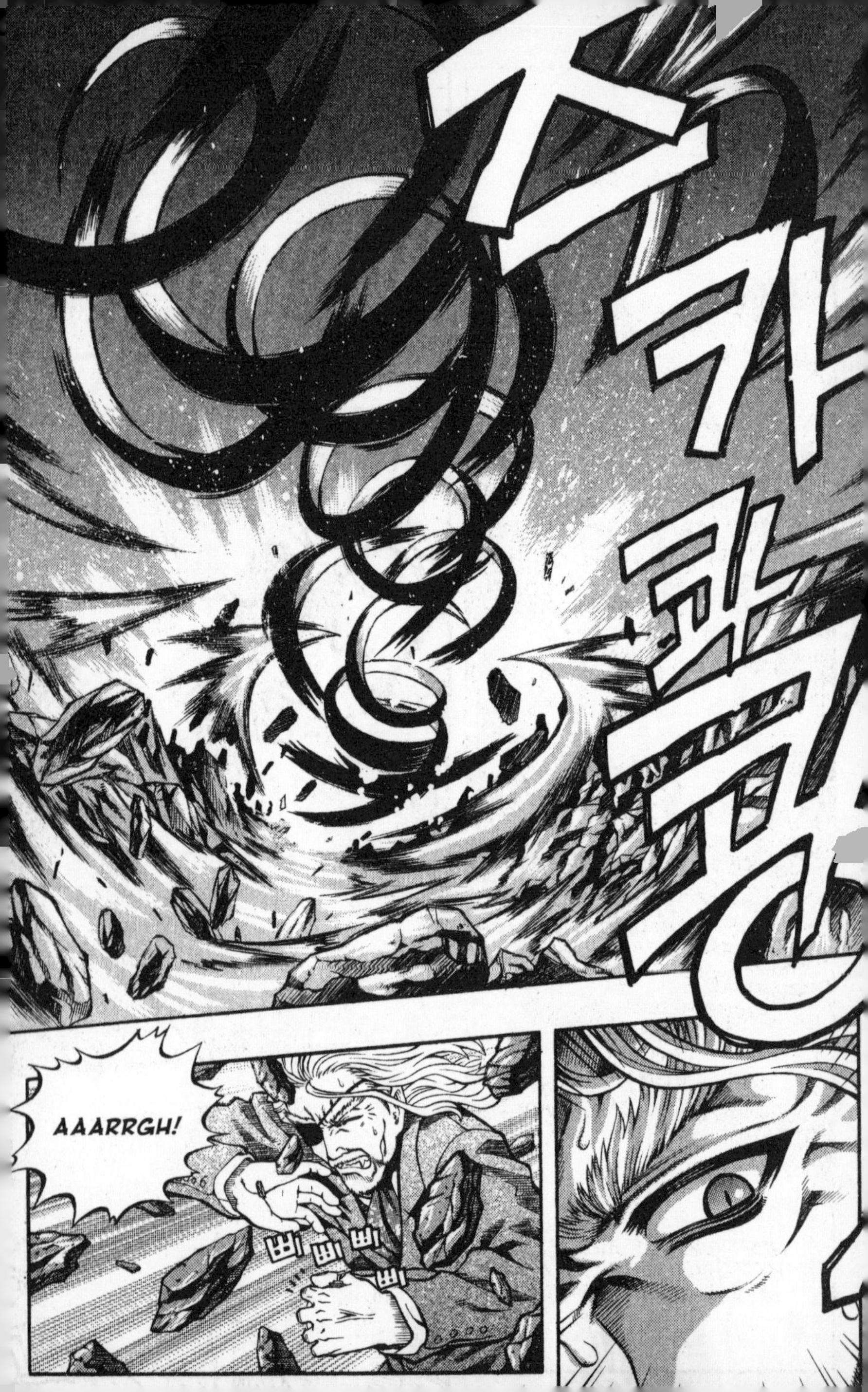
AAARRGH!

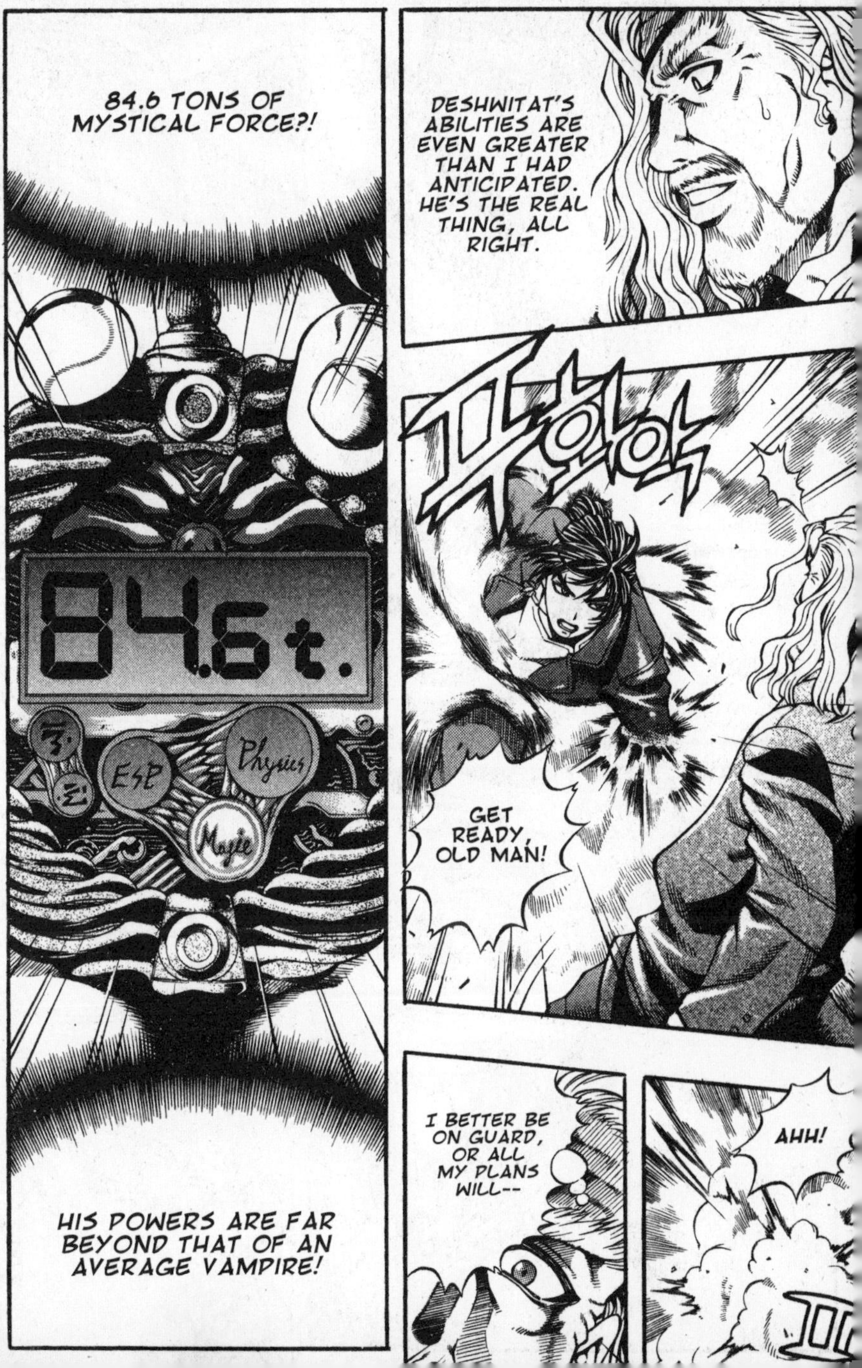
84.6 TONS OF MYSTICAL FORCE?!
84.6t.
ESP
Physics
Magic
HIS POWERS ARE FAR BEYOND THAT OF AN AVERAGE VAMPIRE!
DESHWITAT'S ABILITIES ARE EVEN GREATER THAN I HAD ANTICIPATED. HE'S THE REAL THING, ALL RIGHT.
GET READY, OLD MAN!
I BETTER BE ON GUARD, OR ALL MY PLANS WILL--
AHH!

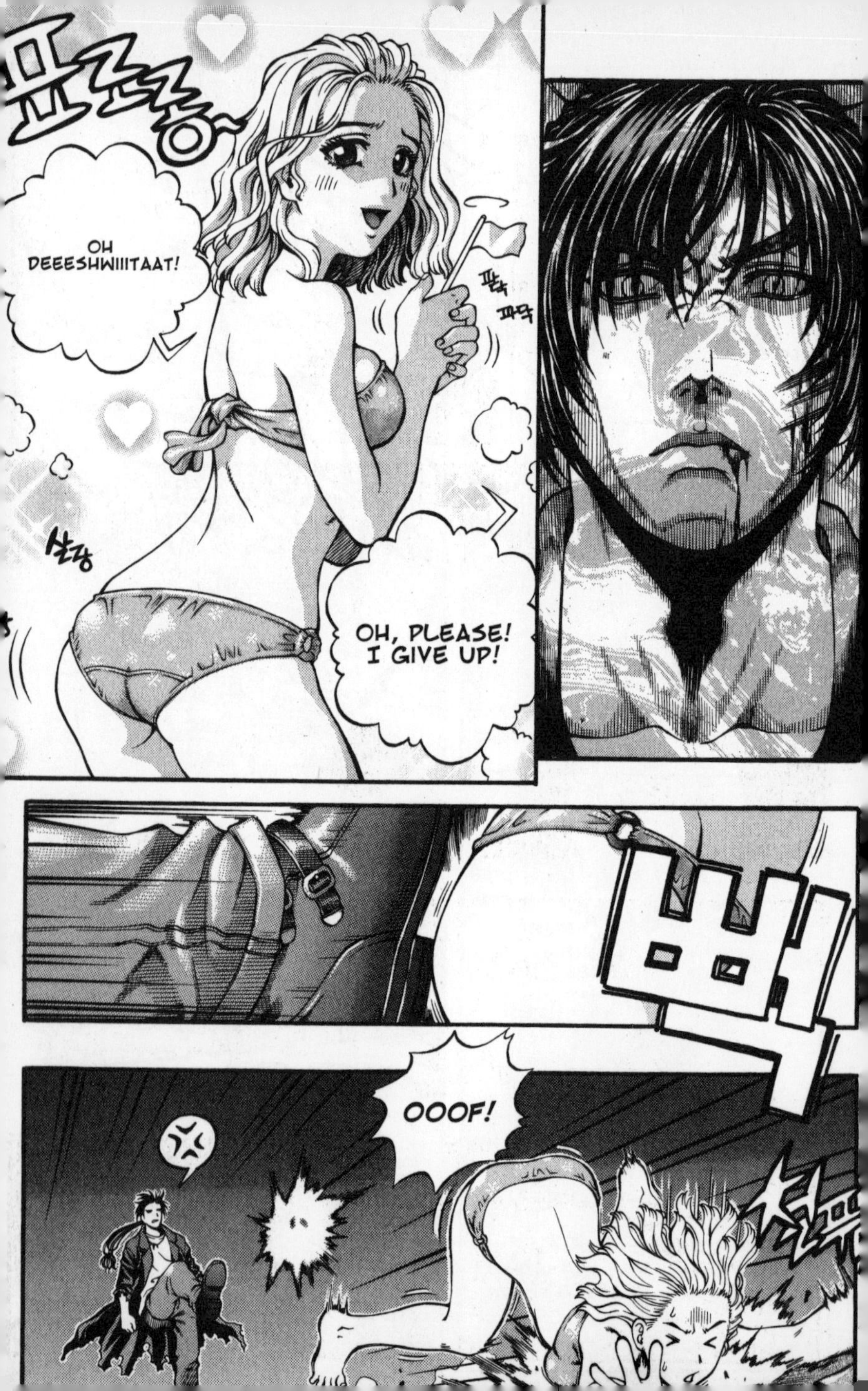
OH DEEESHWIIITAAT!
OH, PLEASE! I GIVE UP!
OOOF!

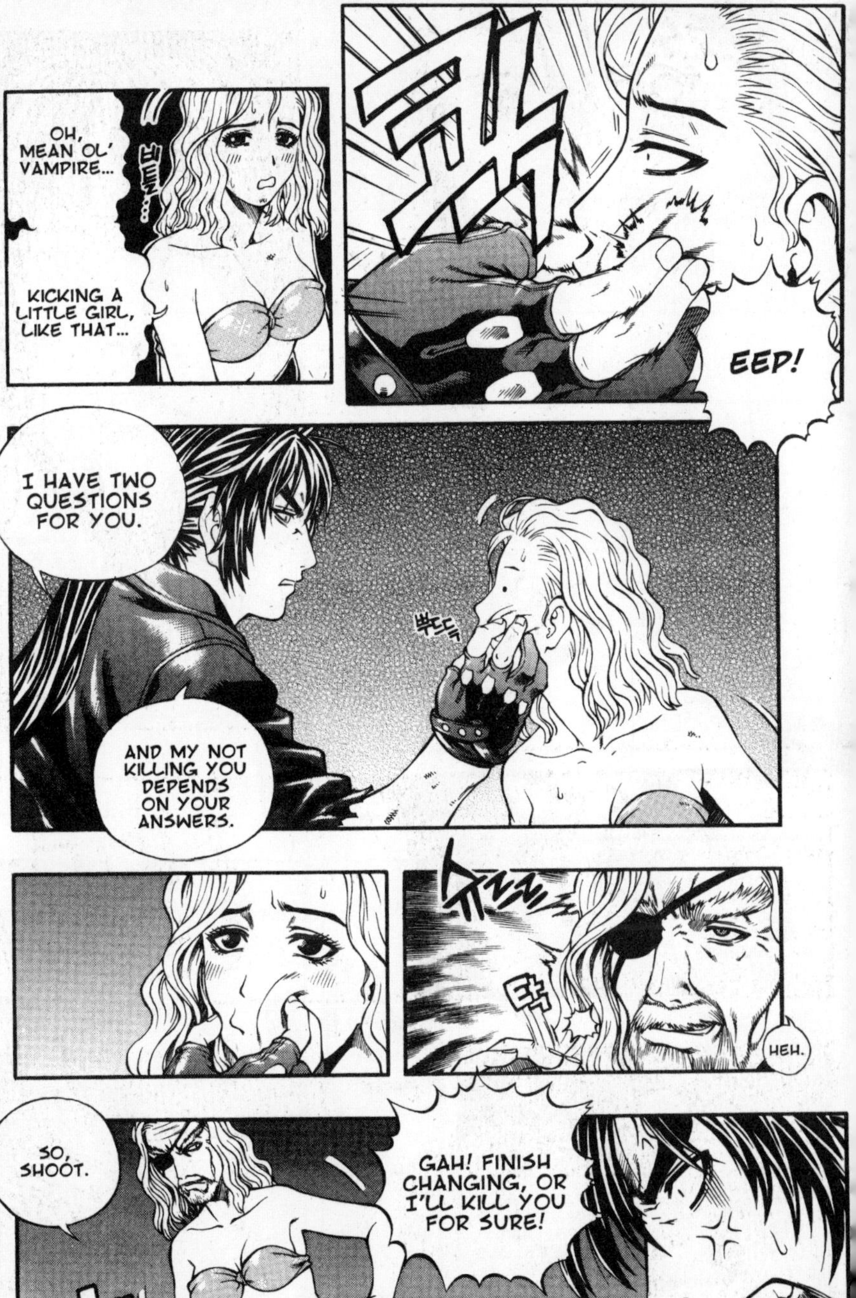
OH, MEAN OL' VAMPIRE...
KICKING A LITTLE GIRL, LIKE THAT...
EEP!
I HAVE TWO QUESTIONS FOR YOU.
AND MY NOT KILLING YOU DEPENDS ON YOUR ANSWERS.
HEH.
SO, SHOOT.
GAH! FINISH CHANGING, OR I'LL KILL YOU FOR SURE!

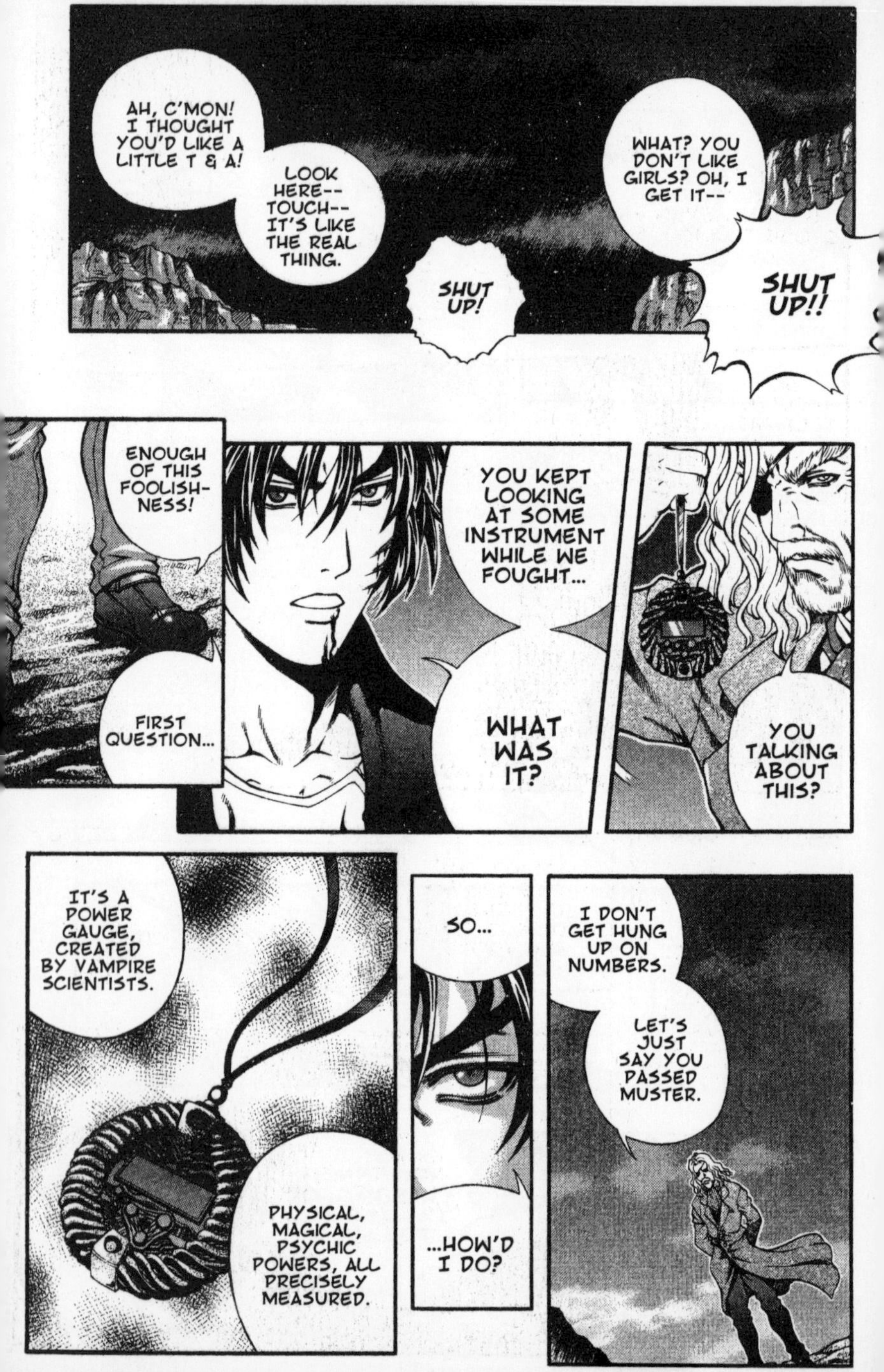
AH, C'MON! I THOUGHT YOU'D LIKE A LITTLE T & A!
LOOK HERE-- TOUCH-- IT'S LIKE THE REAL THING.
WHAT? YOU DON'T LIKE GIRLS? OH, I GET IT--
SHUT UP!
SHUT UP!!
ENOUGH OF THIS FOOLISH-NESS!
FIRST QUESTION...
YOU KEPT LOOKING AT SOME INSTRUMENT WHILE WE FOUGHT...
WHAT WAS IT?
YOU TALKING ABOUT THIS?
IT'S A POWER GAUGE, CREATED BY VAMPIRE SCIENTISTS.
PHYSICAL, MAGICAL, PSYCHIC POWERS, ALL PRECISELY MEASURED.
SO...
...HOW'D I DO?
I DON'T GET HUNG UP ON NUMBERS.
LET'S JUST SAY YOU PASSED MUSTER.

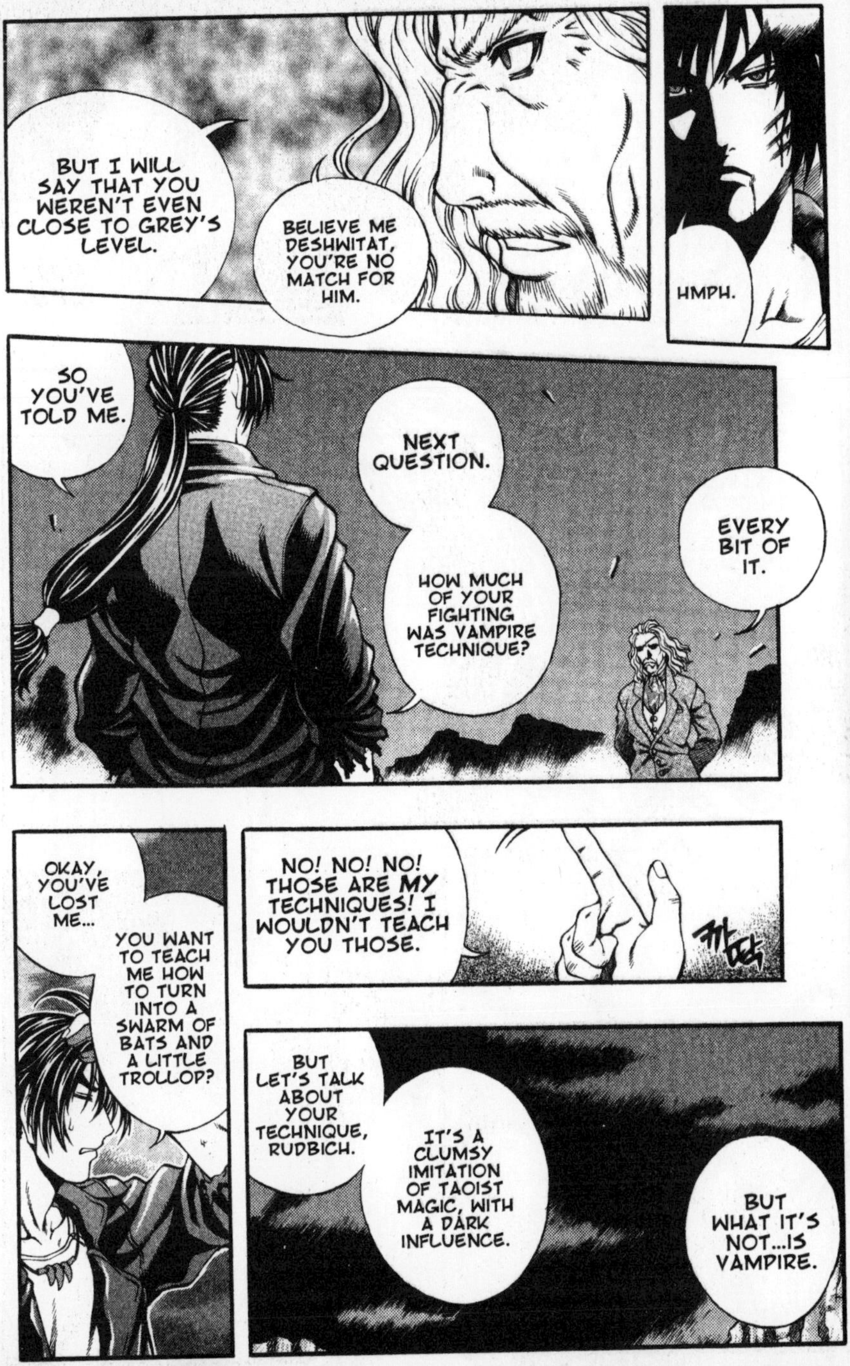
HMPH.
BELIEVE ME DESHWITAT, YOU'RE NO MATCH FOR HIM.
BUT I WILL SAY THAT YOU WEREN'T EVEN CLOSE TO GREY'S LEVEL.
SO YOU'VE TOLD ME.
NEXT QUESTION.
HOW MUCH OF YOUR FIGHTING WAS VAMPIRE TECHNIQUE?
EVERY BIT OF IT.
NO! NO! NO! THOSE ARE MY TECHNIQUES! I WOULDN'T TEACH YOU THOSE.
OKAY, YOU'VE LOST ME...
YOU WANT TO TEACH ME HOW TO TURN INTO A SWARM OF BATS AND A LITTLE TROLLOP?
BUT LET'S TALK ABOUT YOUR TECHNIQUE, RUDBICH.
IT'S A CLUMSY IMITATION OF TAOIST MAGIC, WITH A DARK INFLUENCE.
BUT WHAT IT'S NOT...IS VAMPIRE.

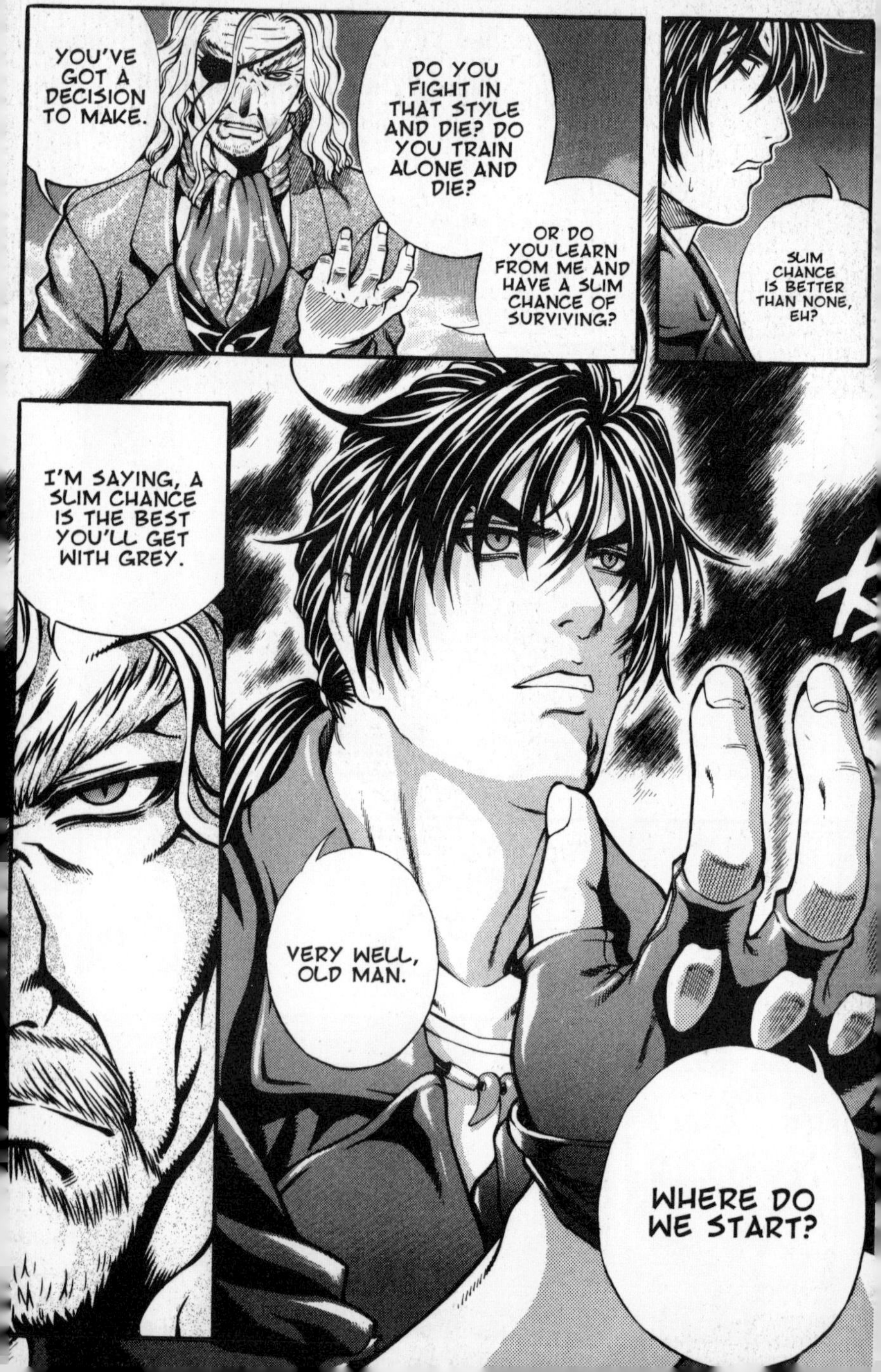

YOU'VE GOT A DECISION TO MAKE.
DO YOU FIGHT IN THAT STYLE AND DIE? DO YOU TRAIN ALONE AND DIE?
OR DO YOU LEARN FROM ME AND HAVE A SLIM CHANCE OF SURVIVING?
SLIM CHANCE IS BETTER THAN NONE, EH?
I'M SAYING, A SLIM CHANCE IS THE BEST YOU'LL GET WITH GREY.
VERY WELL, OLD MAN.
WHERE DO WE START?

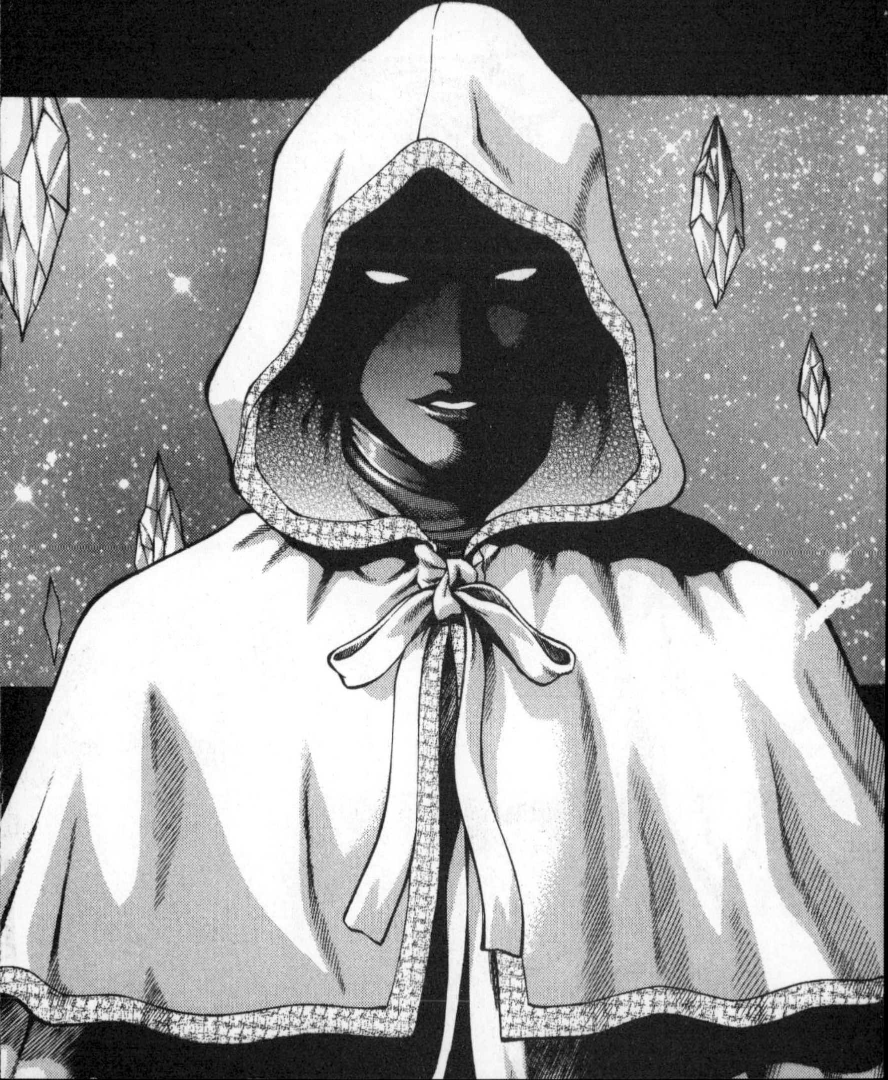

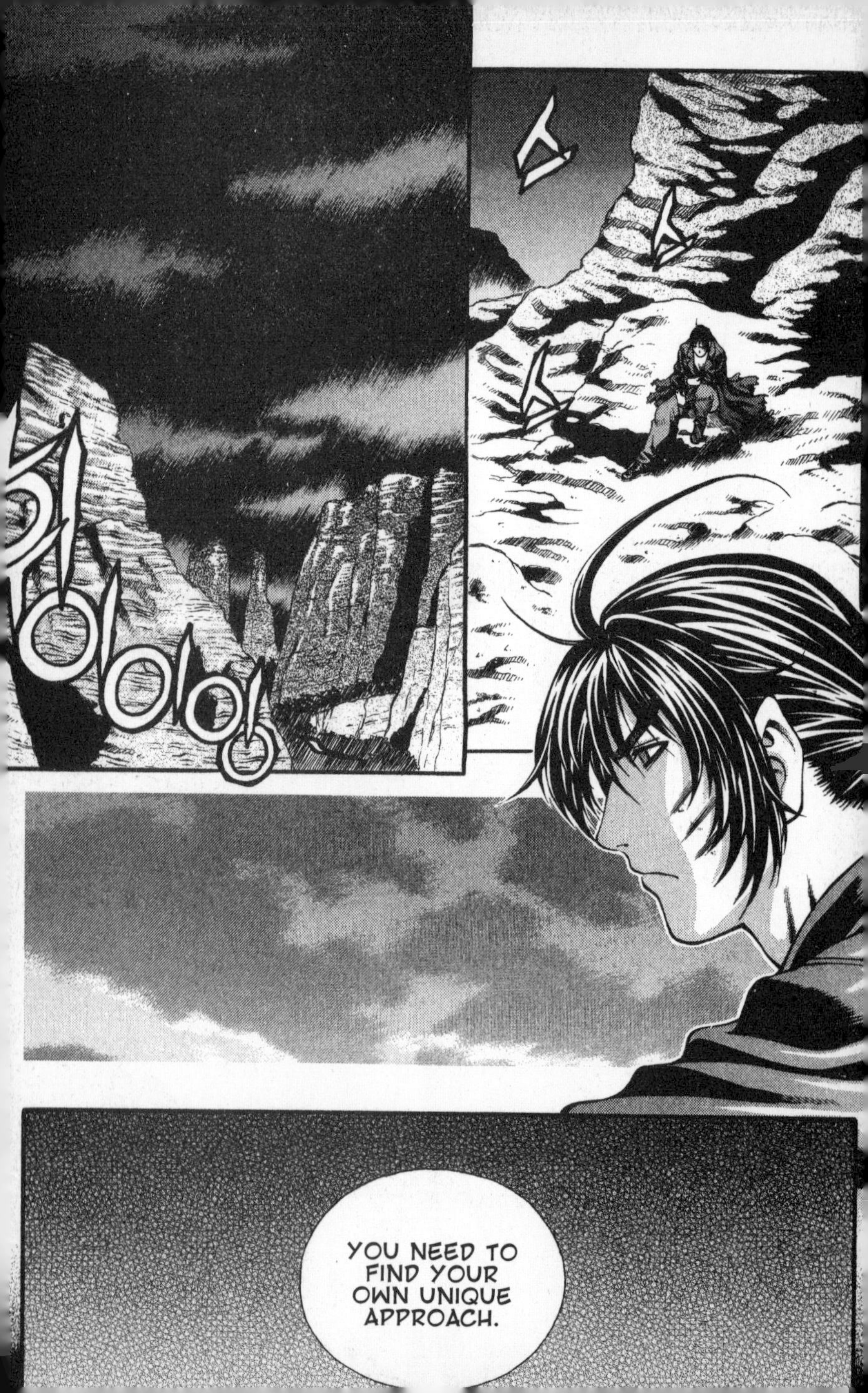
YOU NEED TO FIND YOUR OWN UNIQUE APPROACH.

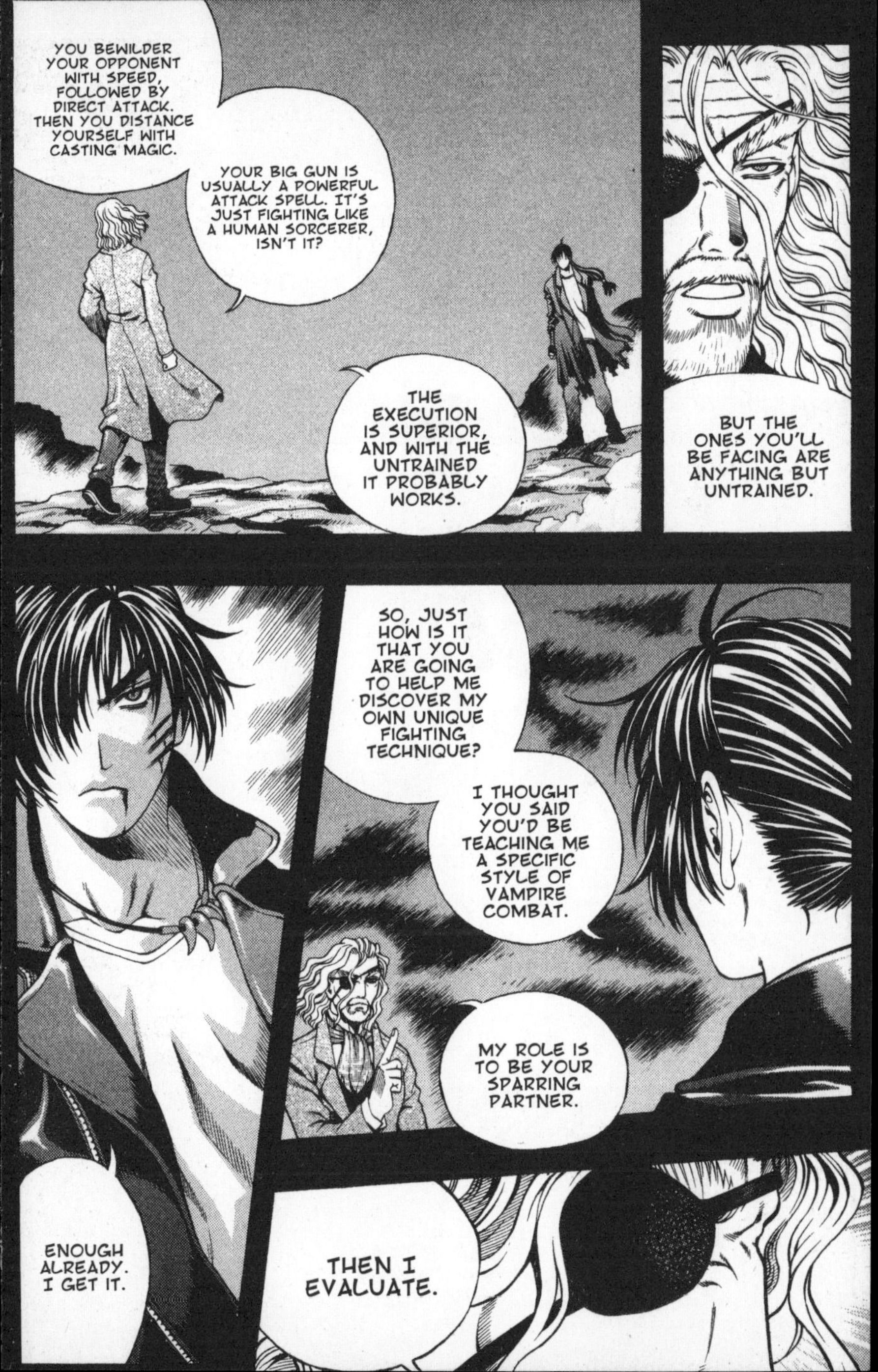

YOU BEWILDER YOUR OPPONENT WITH SPEED, FOLLOWED BY DIRECT ATTACK. THEN YOU DISTANCE YOURSELF WITH CASTING MAGIC.
YOUR BIG GUN IS USUALLY A POWERFUL ATTACK SPELL. IT'S JUST FIGHTING LIKE A HUMAN SORCERER, ISN'T IT?
THE EXECUTION IS SUPERIOR, AND WITH THE UNTRAINED IT PROBABLY WORKS.
BUT THE ONES YOU'LL BE FACING ARE ANYTHING BUT UNTRAINED.
SO, JUST HOW IS IT THAT YOU ARE GOING TO HELP ME DISCOVER MY OWN UNIQUE FIGHTING TECHNIQUE?
I THOUGHT YOU SAID YOU'D BE TEACHING ME A SPECIFIC STYLE OF VAMPIRE COMBAT.
MY ROLE IS TO BE YOUR SPARRING PARTNER.
THEN I EVALUATE.
ENOUGH ALREADY. I GET IT.

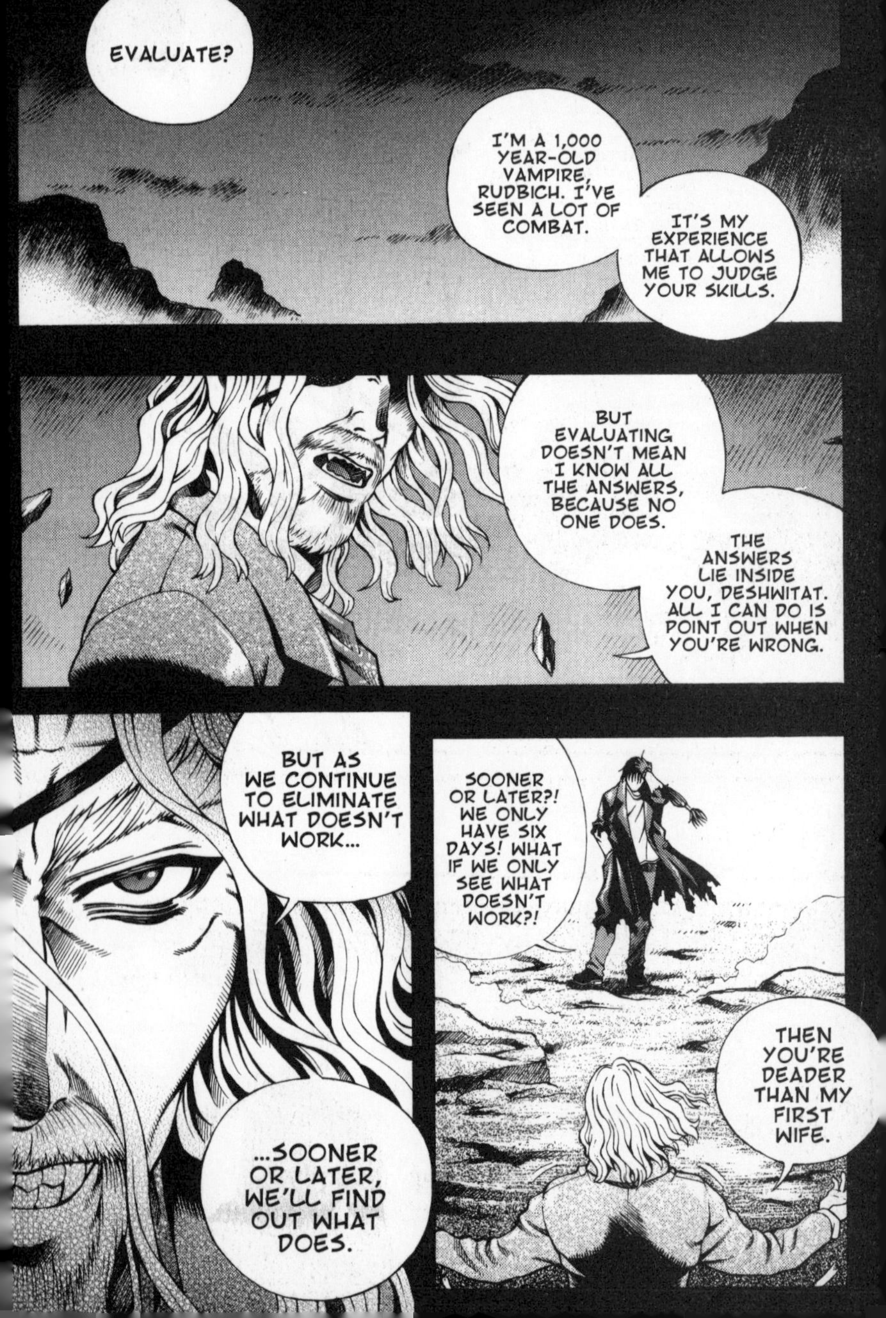
EVALUATE?
I'M A 1,000 YEAR-OLD VAMPIRE, RUDBICH. I'VE SEEN A LOT OF COMBAT.
IT'S MY EXPERIENCE THAT ALLOWS ME TO JUDGE YOUR SKILLS.
BUT EVALUATING DOESN'T MEAN I KNOW ALL THE ANSWERS, BECAUSE NO ONE DOES.
THE ANSWERS LIE INSIDE YOU, DESHWITAT. ALL I CAN DO IS POINT OUT WHEN YOU'RE WRONG.
BUT AS WE CONTINUE TO ELIMINATE WHAT DOESN'T WORK...
...SOONER OR LATER, WE'LL FIND OUT WHAT DOES.
SOONER OR LATER?! WE ONLY HAVE SIX DAYS! WHAT IF WE ONLY SEE WHAT DOESN'T WORK?!
THEN YOU'RE DEADER THAN MY FIRST WIFE.

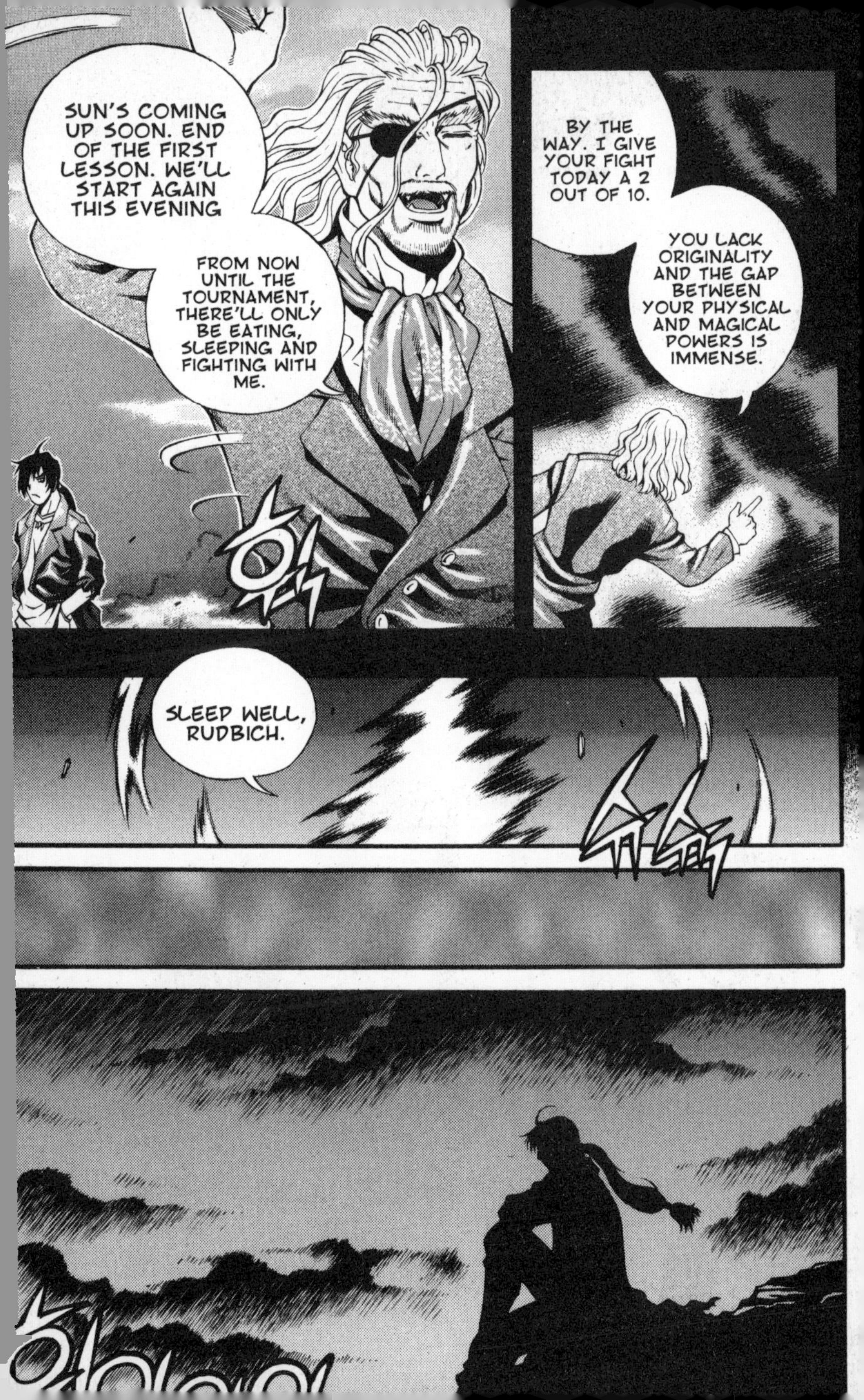

SUN'S COMING UP SOON. END OF THE FIRST LESSON. WE'LL START AGAIN THIS EVENING
FROM NOW UNTIL THE TOURNAMENT, THERE'LL ONLY BE EATING, SLEEPING AND FIGHTING WITH ME.
BY THE WAY. I GIVE YOUR FIGHT TODAY A 2 OUT OF 10.
YOU LACK ORIGINALITY AND THE GAP BETWEEN YOUR PHYSICAL AND MAGICAL POWERS IS IMMENSE.
SLEEP WELL, RUDBICH.

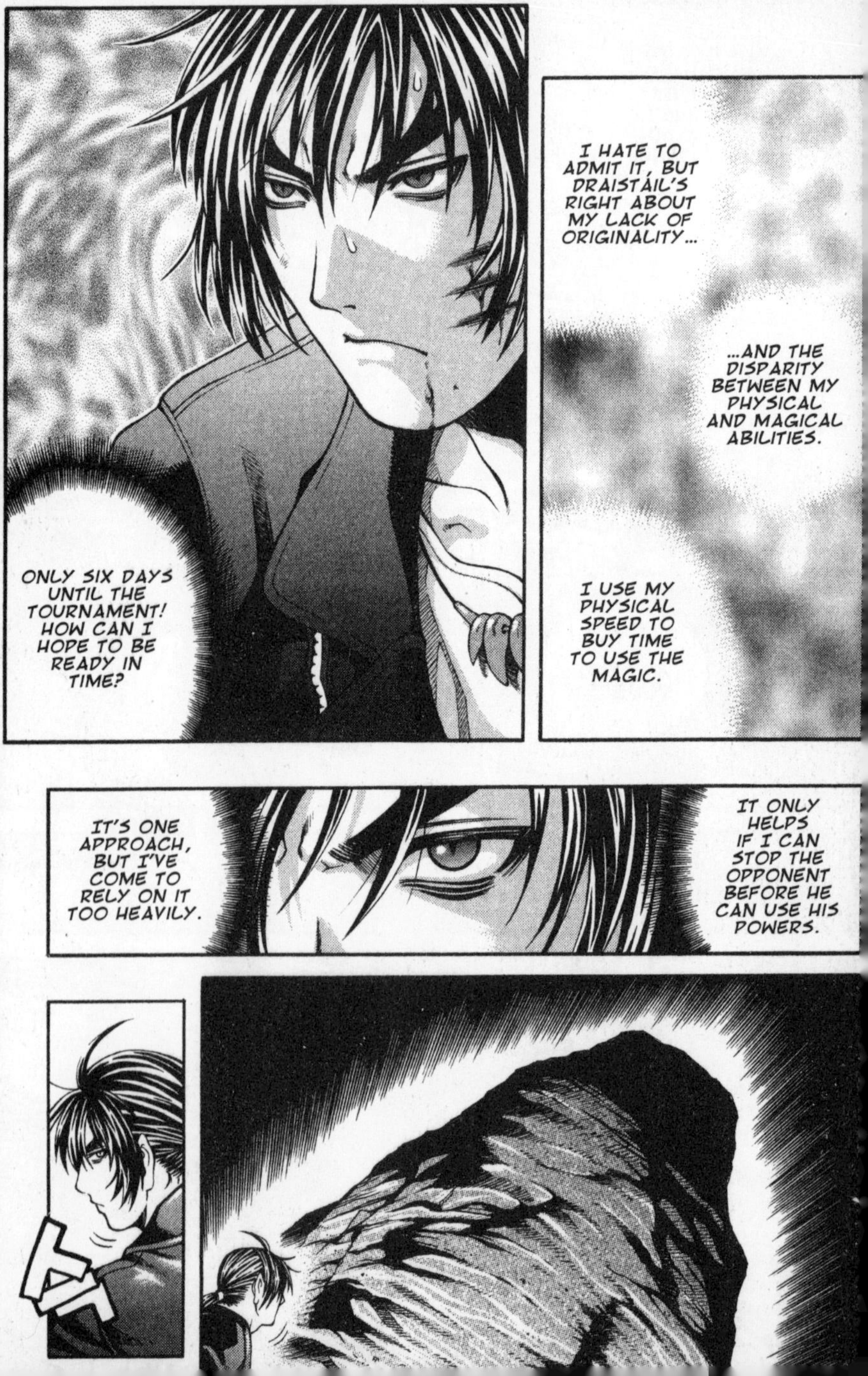
I HATE TO ADMIT IT, BUT DRAISTAIL'S RIGHT ABOUT MY LACK OF ORIGINALITY...
...AND THE DISPARITY BETWEEN MY PHYSICAL AND MAGICAL ABILITIES.
I USE MY PHYSICAL SPEED TO BUY TIME TO USE THE MAGIC.
ONLY SIX DAYS UNTIL THE TOURNAMENT! HOW CAN I HOPE TO BE READY IN TIME?
IT ONLY HELPS IF I CAN STOP THE OPPONENT BEFORE HE CAN USE HIS POWERS.
IT'S ONE APPROACH, BUT I'VE COME TO RELY ON IT TOO HEAVILY.

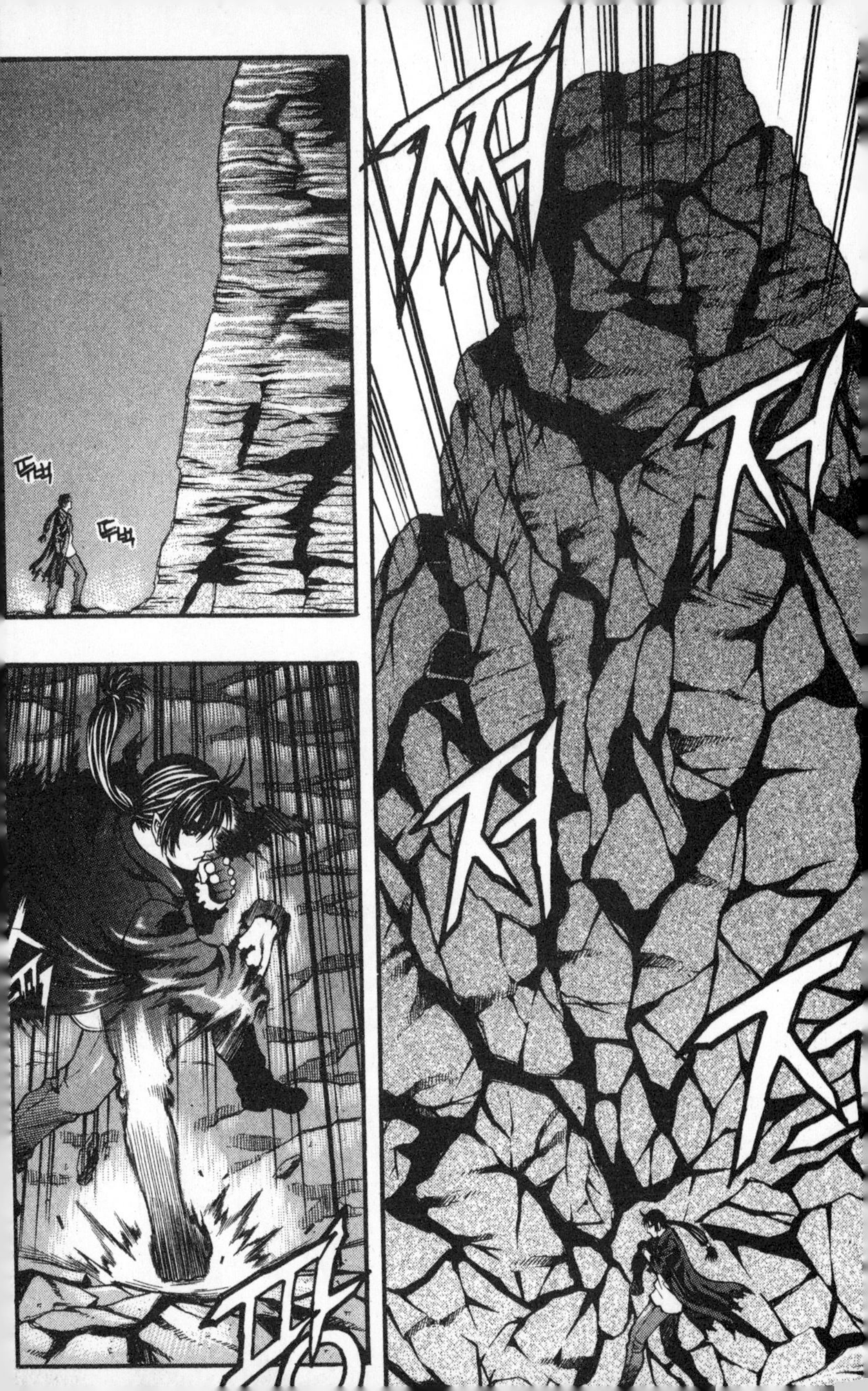
뚜벅
뚜벅

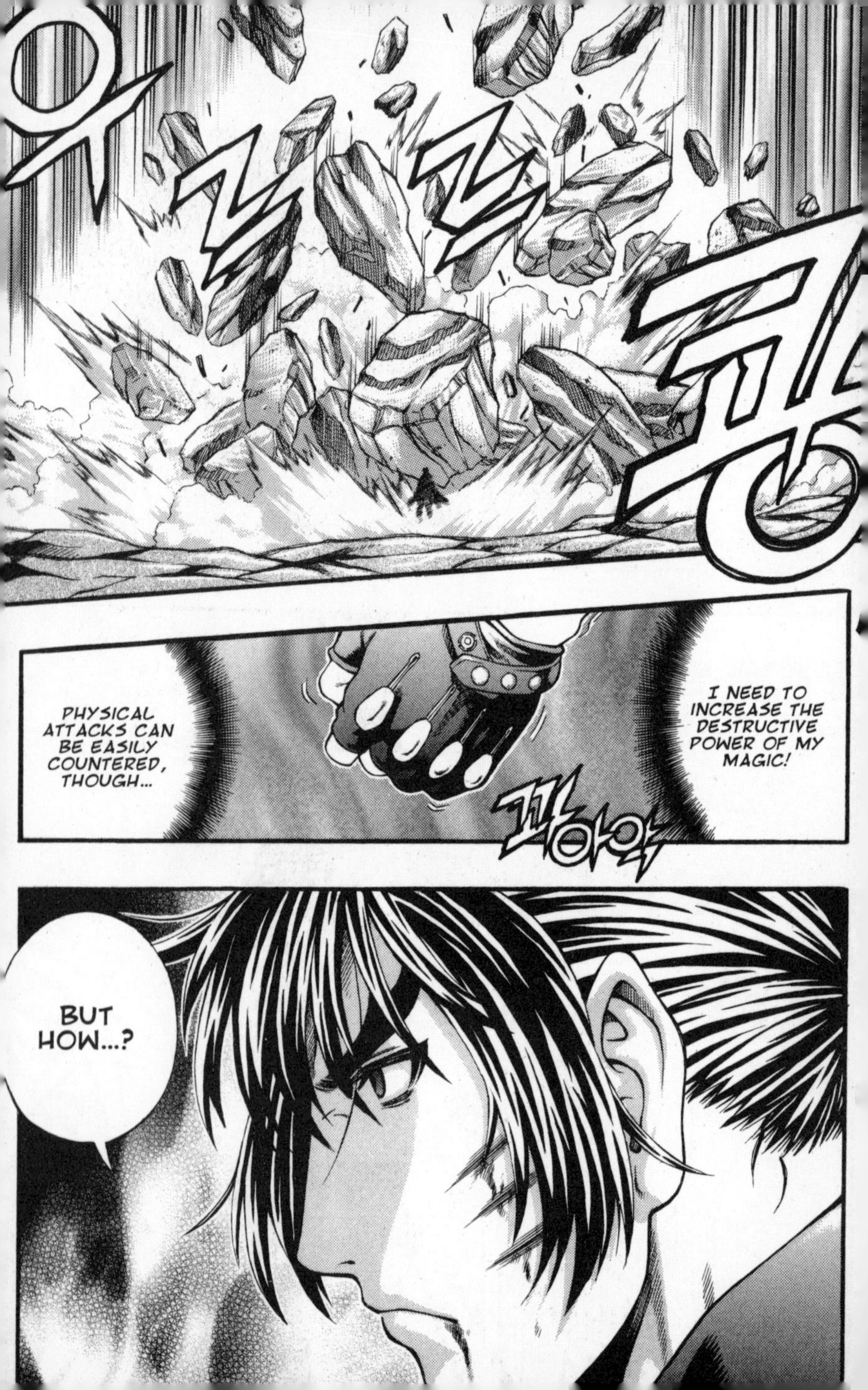
I NEED TO INCREASE THE DESTRUCTIVE POWER OF MY MAGIC!
PHYSICAL ATTACKS CAN BE EASILY COUNTERED, THOUGH...
BUT HOW...?

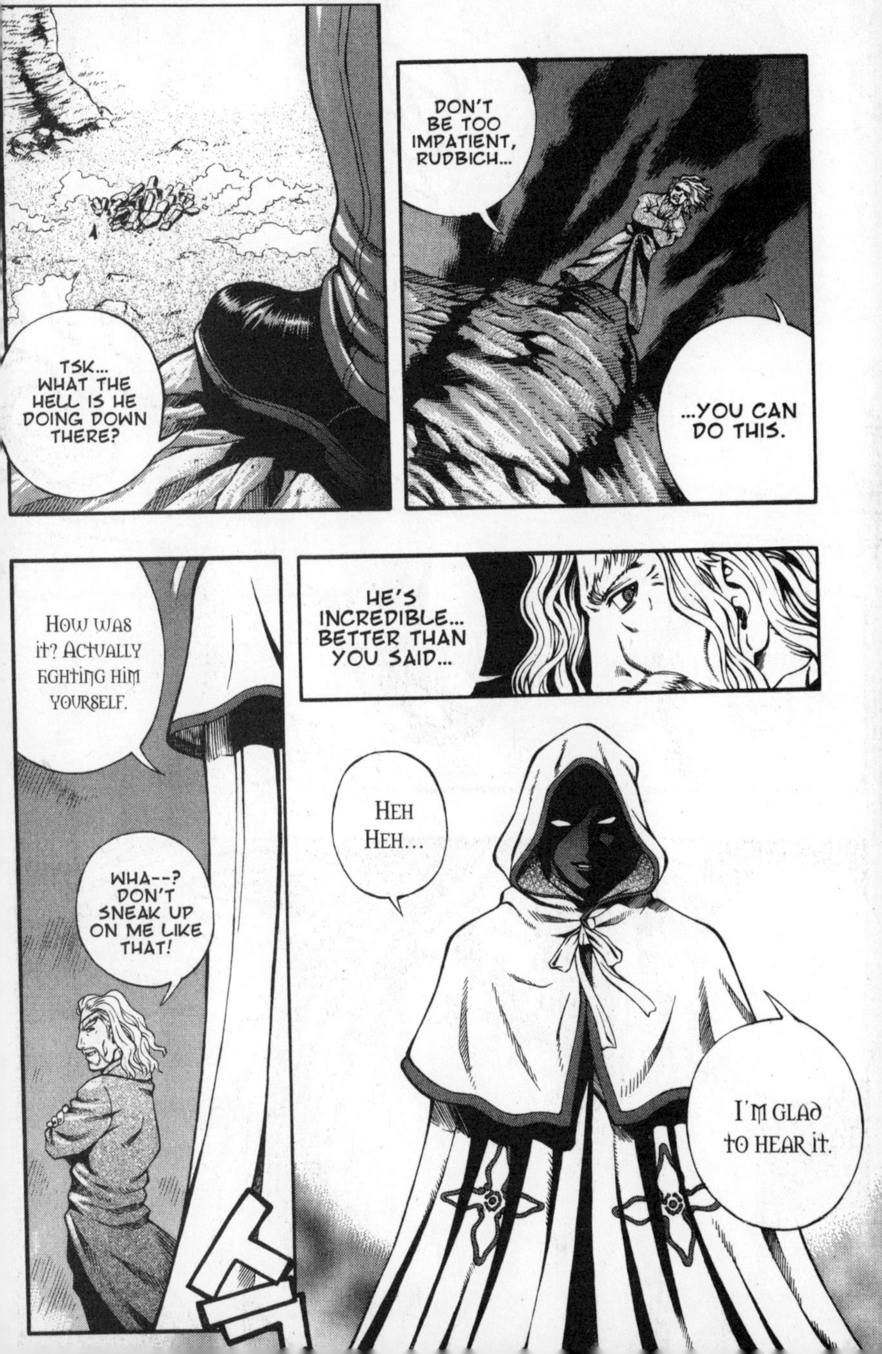
TSK... WHAT THE HELL IS HE DOING DOWN THERE?
DON'T BE TOO IMPATIENT, RUDBICH...
...YOU CAN DO THIS.
HOW WAS IT? ACTUALLY FIGHTING HIM YOURSELF.
WHA--? DON'T SNEAK UP ON ME LIKE THAT!
HE'S INCREDIBLE... BETTER THAN YOU SAID...
HEH HEH...
I'M GLAD TO HEAR IT.

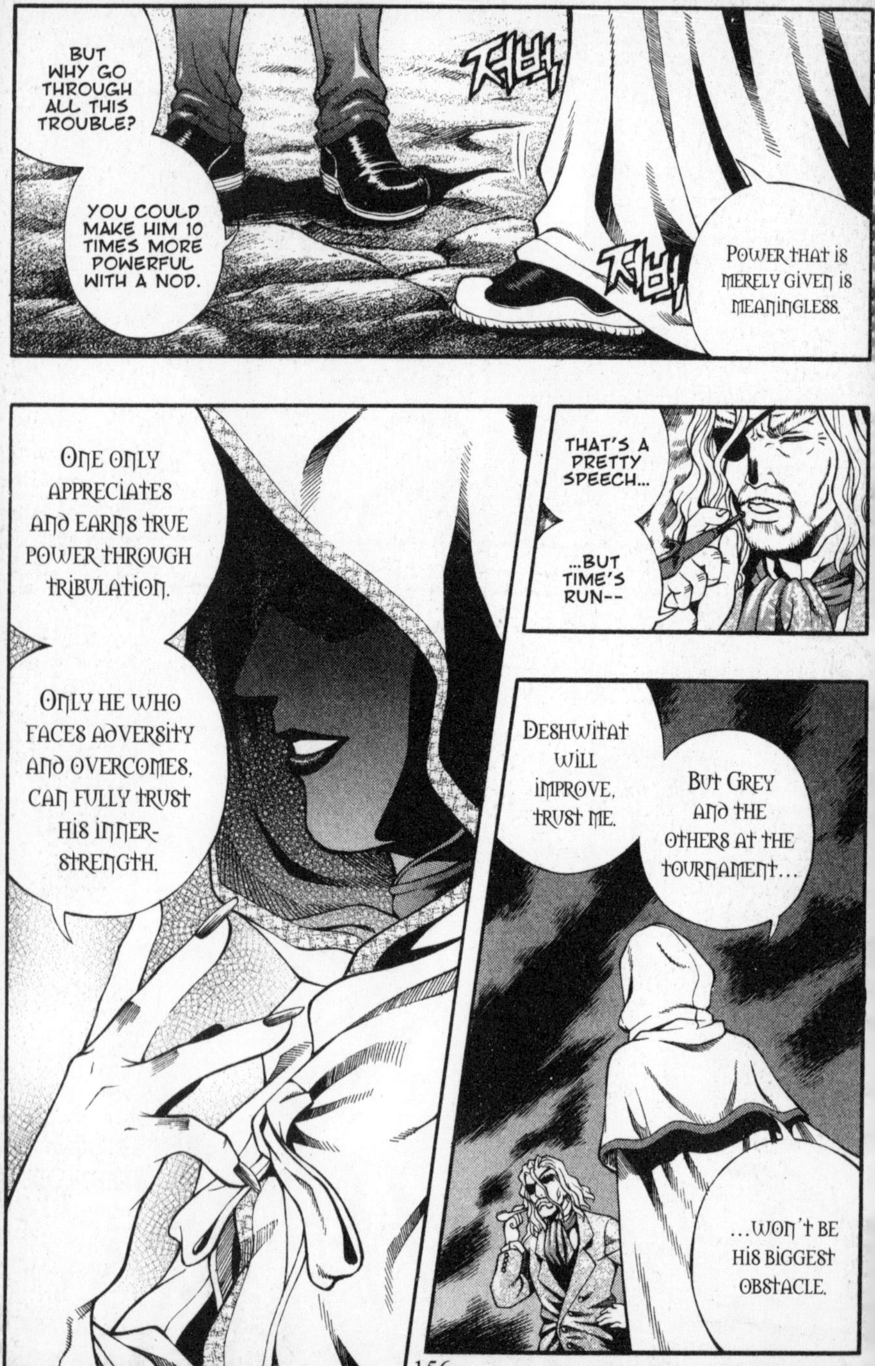
BUT WHY GO THROUGH ALL THIS TROUBLE?
YOU COULD MAKE HIM 10 TIMES MORE POWERFUL WITH A NOD.
저벅
저벅
POWER THAT IS MERELY GIVEN IS MEANINGLESS.
ONE ONLY APPRECIATES AND EARNS TRUE POWER THROUGH TRIBULATION.
ONLY HE WHO FACES ADVERSITY AND OVERCOMES, CAN FULLY TRUST HIS INNER-STRENGTH.
THAT'S A PRETTY SPEECH...
...BUT TIME'S RUN--
DESHWITAT WILL IMPROVE, TRUST ME.
BUT GREY AND THE OTHERS AT THE TOURNAMENT...
...WON'T BE HIS BIGGEST OBSTACLE.

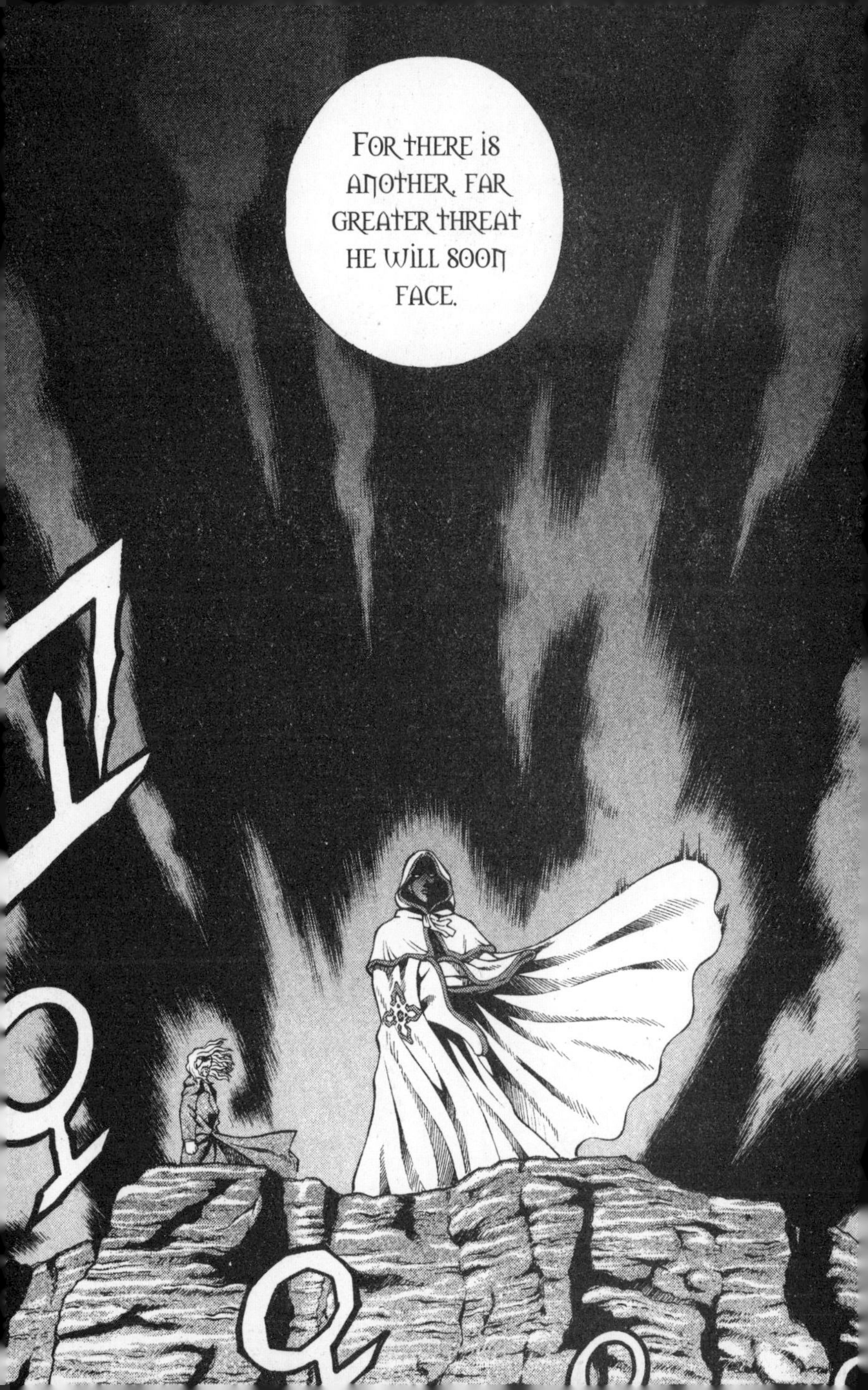
FOR THERE IS ANOTHER, FAR GREATER THREAT HE WILL SOON FACE.

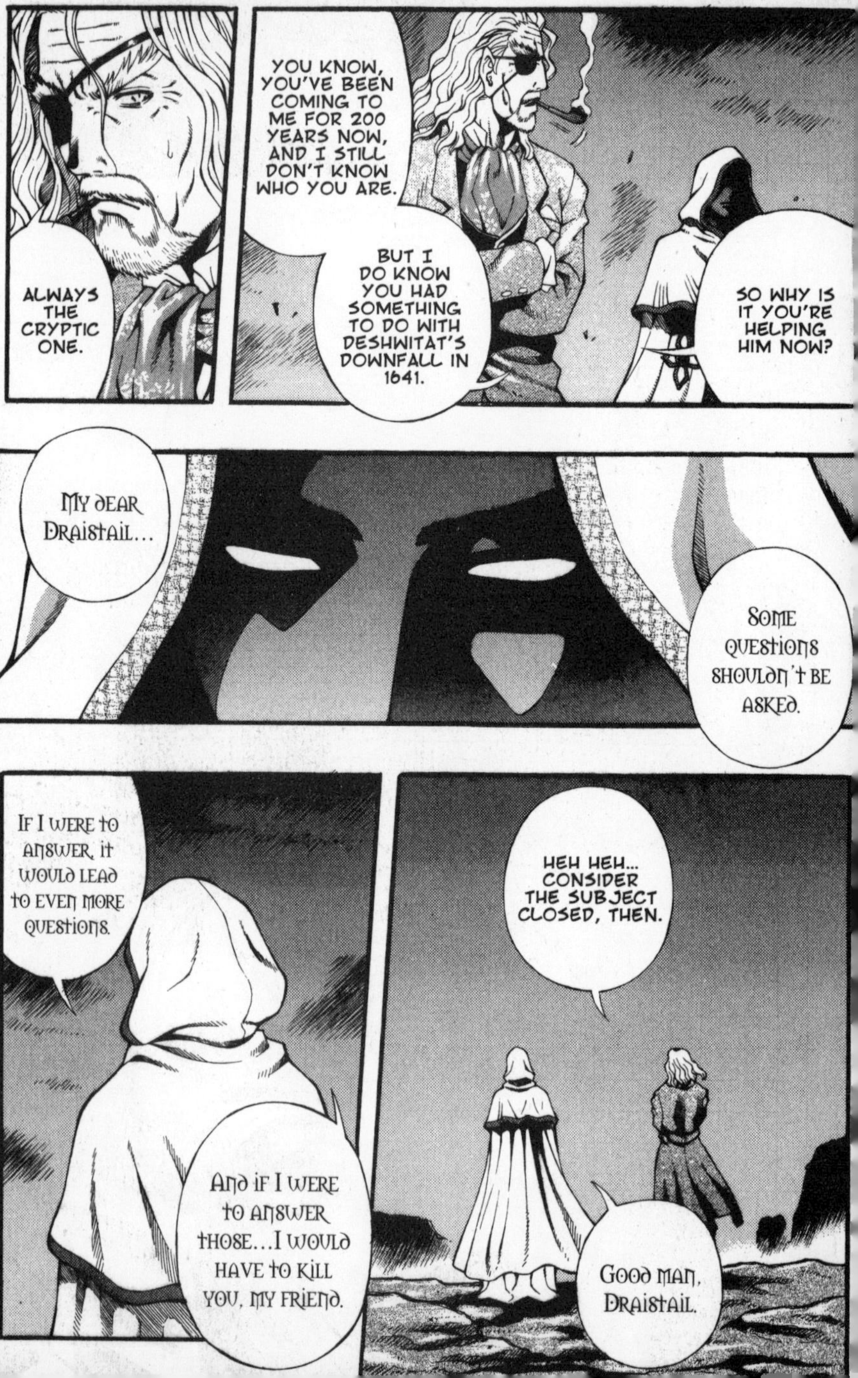
ALWAYS THE CRYPTIC ONE.
YOU KNOW, YOU'VE BEEN COMING TO ME FOR 200 YEARS NOW, AND I STILL DON'T KNOW WHO YOU ARE.
BUT I DO KNOW YOU HAD SOMETHING TO DO WITH DESHWITAT'S DOWNFALL IN 1641.
SO WHY IS IT YOU'RE HELPING HIM NOW?
My dear Draistail...
Some questions shouldn't be asked.
If I were to answer, it would lead to even more questions.
And if I were to answer those...I would have to kill you, my friend.
HEH HEH... CONSIDER THE SUBJECT CLOSED, THEN.
Good man, Draistail.

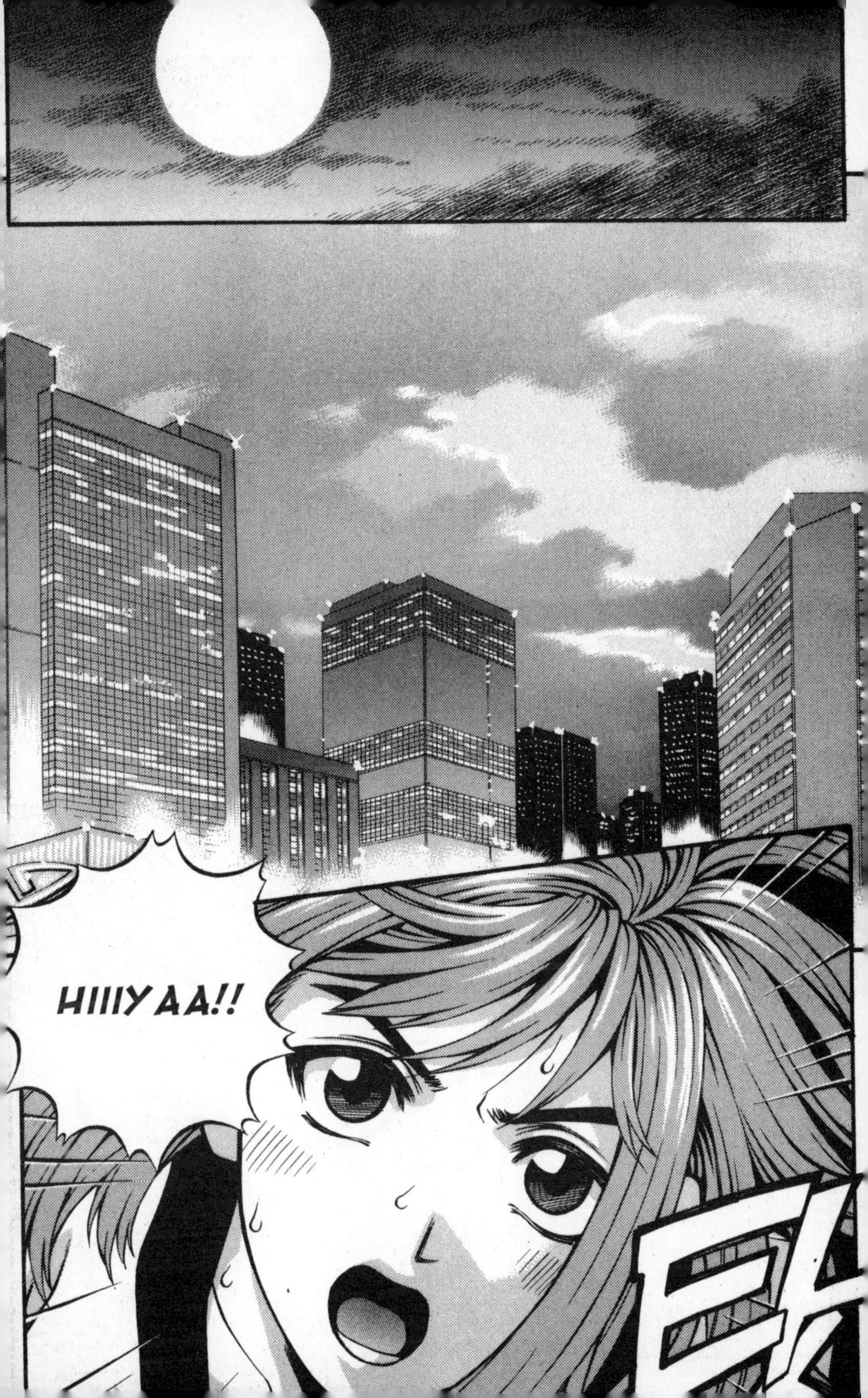
HIIIYAA!!

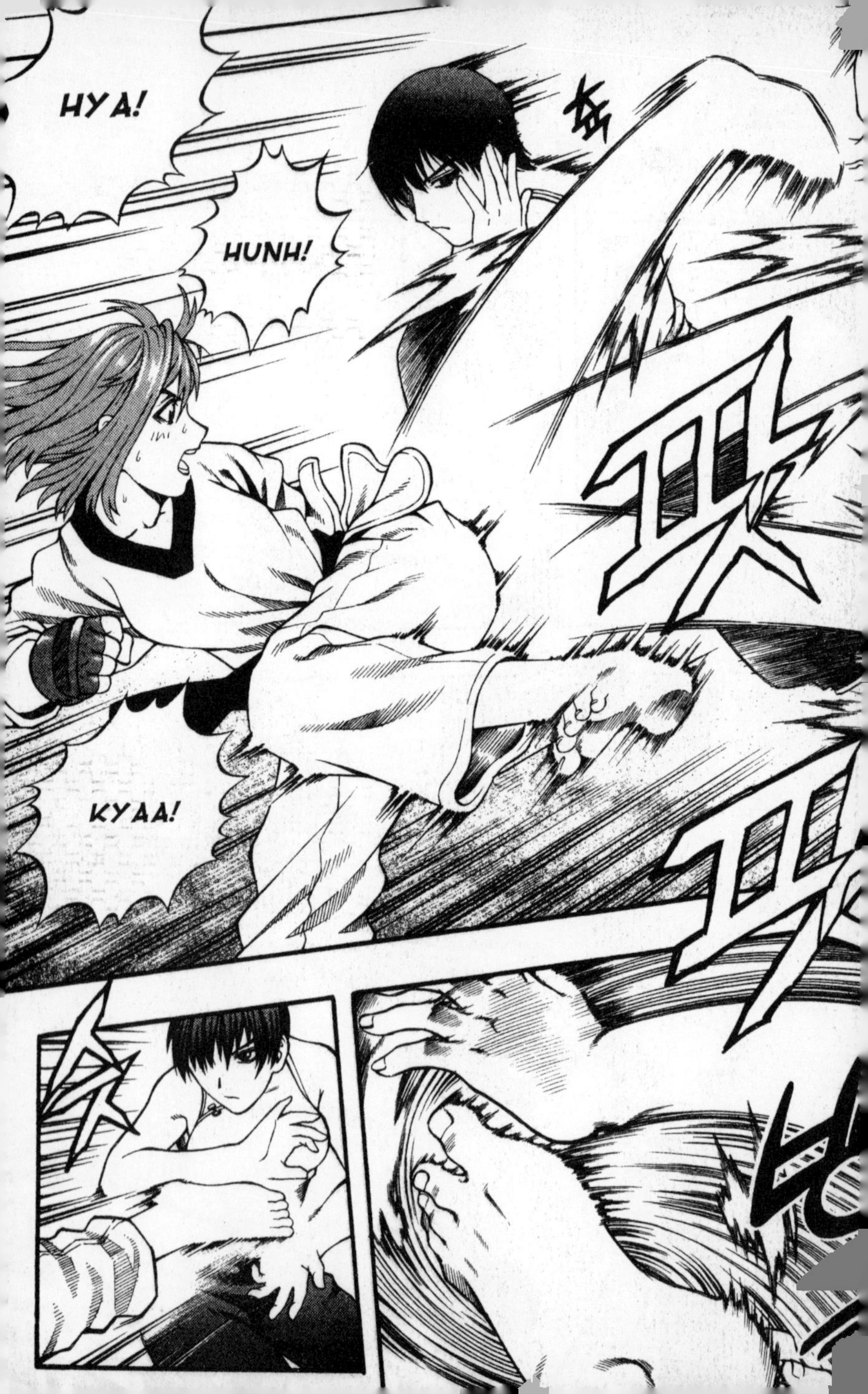
HYA!
HUNH!
KYAA!

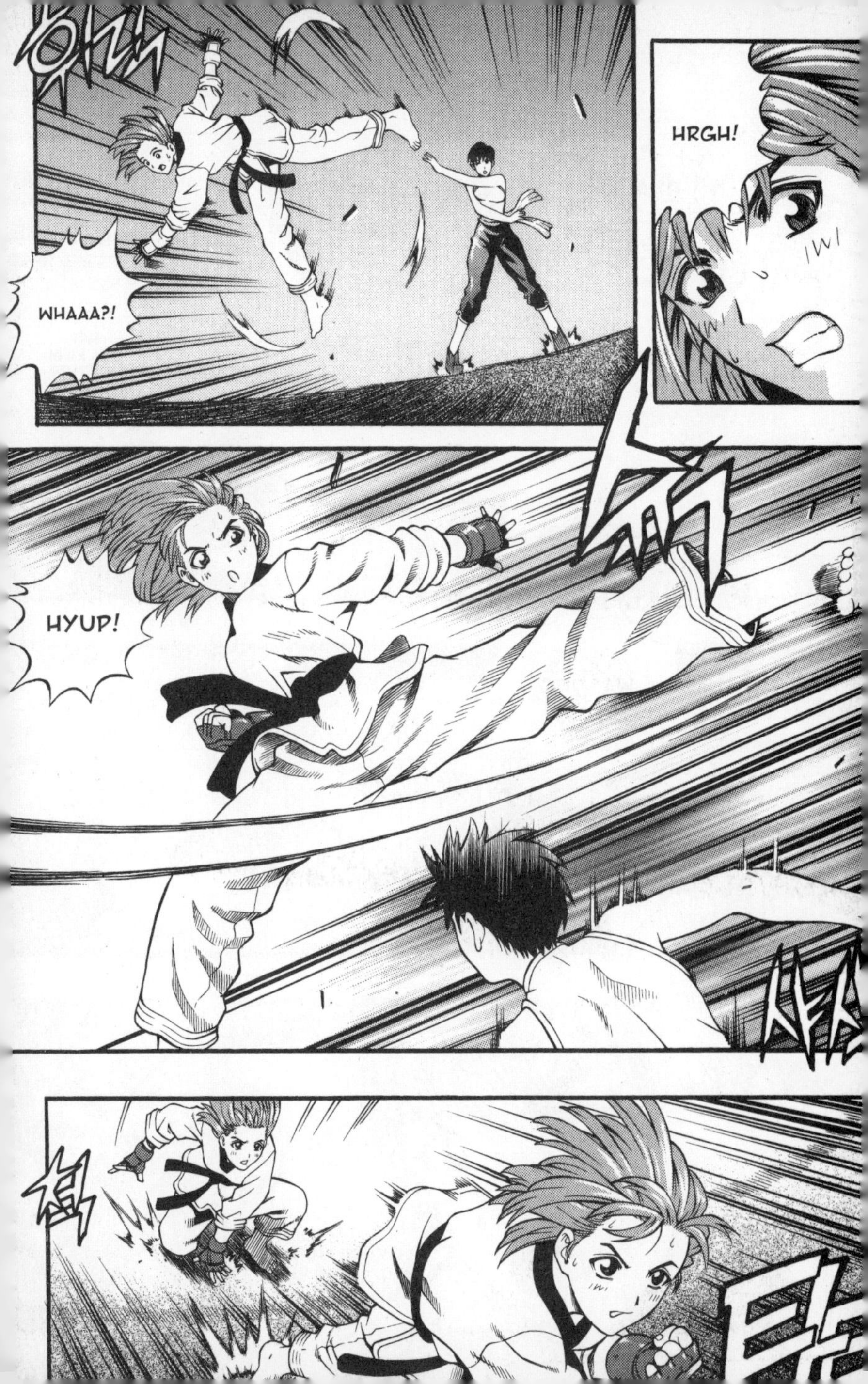
HRGH!
WHAAA?!
HYUP!

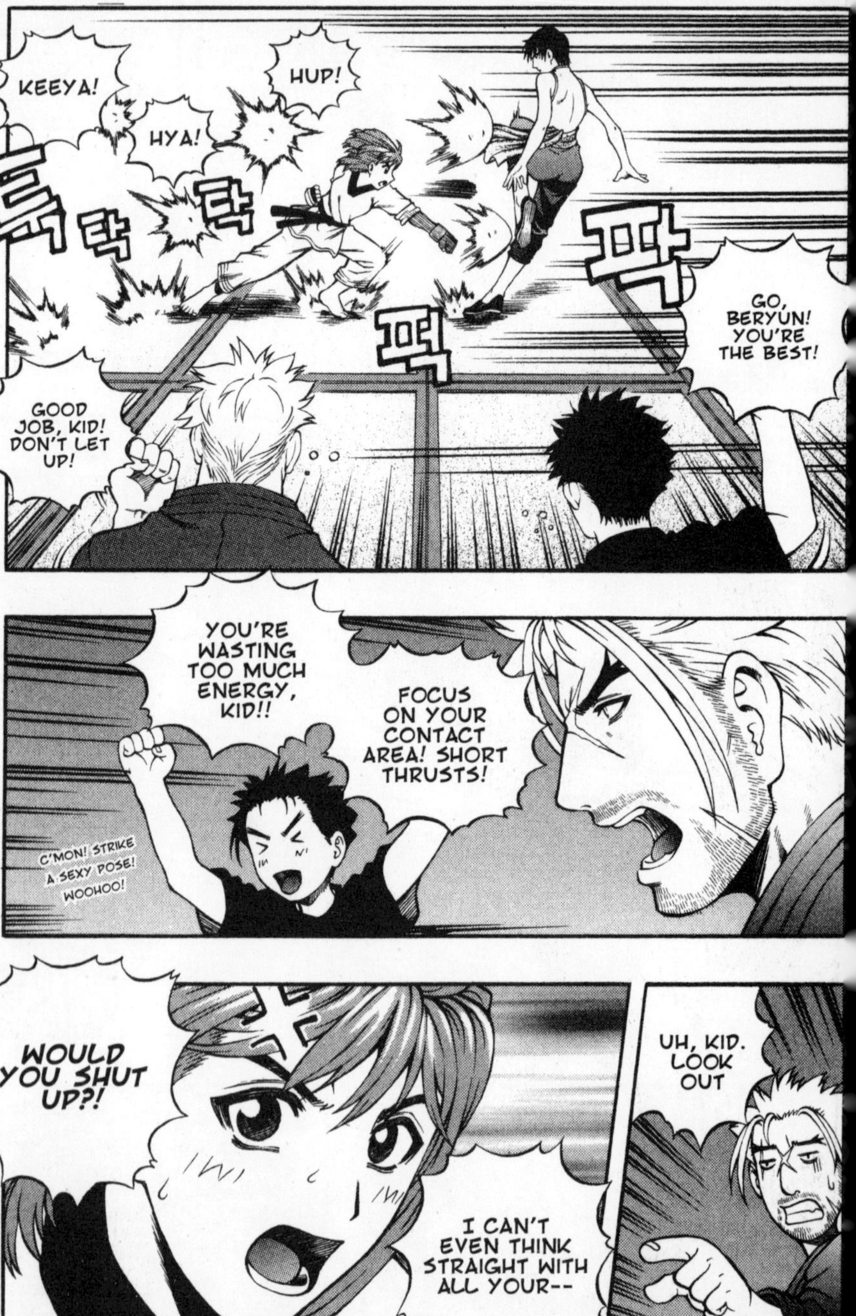
KEEYA!
HYA!
HUP!
툭
탁
탁
퍽
퍽
GO, BERYUN! YOU'RE THE BEST!
GOOD JOB, KID! DON'T LET UP!
YOU'RE WASTING TOO MUCH ENERGY, KID!!
FOCUS ON YOUR CONTACT AREA! SHORT THRUSTS!
C'MON! STRIKE A SEXY POSE! WOOHOO!
WOULD YOU SHUT UP?!
I CAN'T EVEN THINK STRAIGHT WITH ALL YOUR--
UH, KID. LOOK OUT

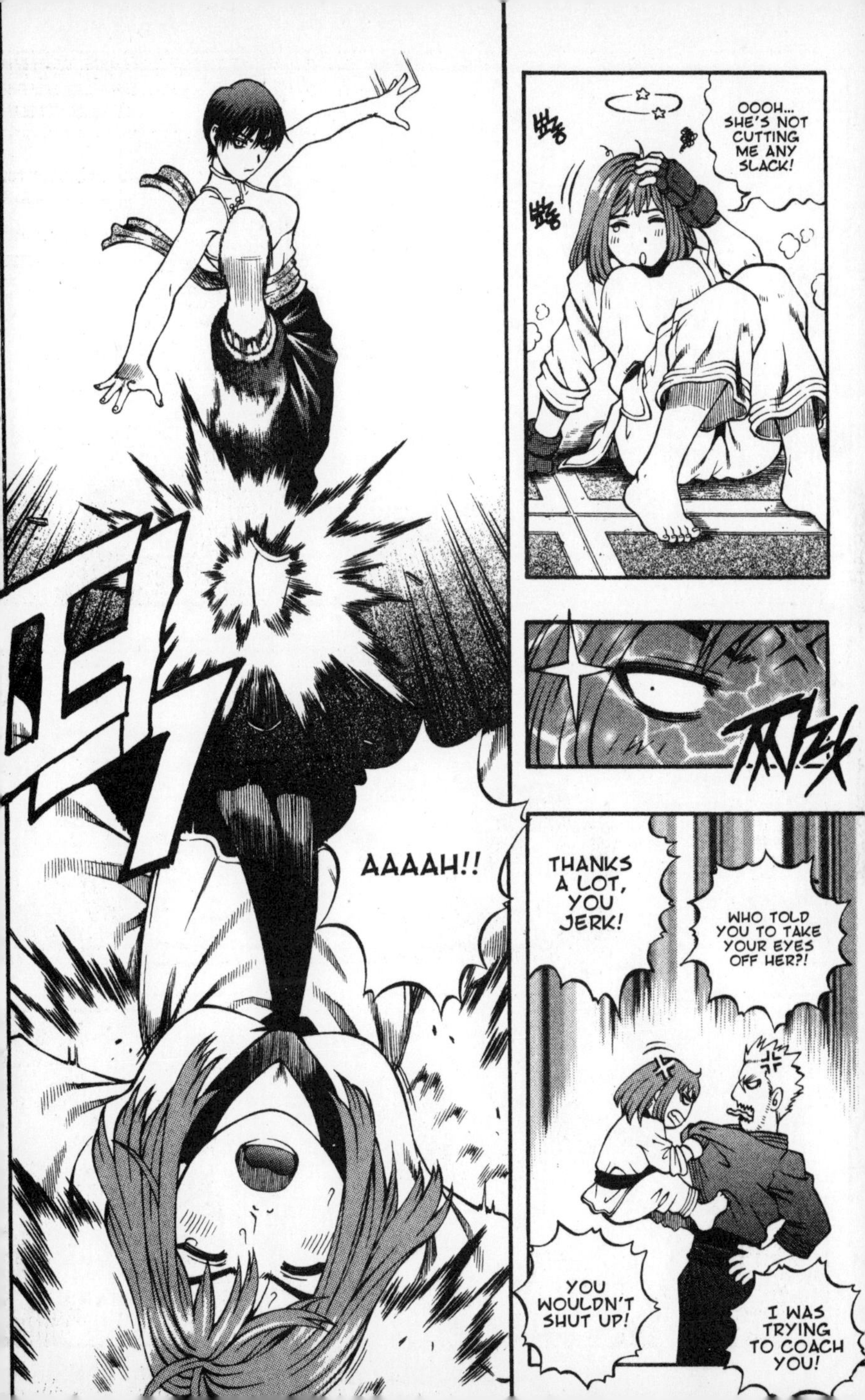
AAAAH!!
OOOH... SHE'S NOT CUTTING ME ANY SLACK!
THANKS A LOT, YOU JERK!
WHO TOLD YOU TO TAKE YOUR EYES OFF HER?!
YOU WOULDN'T SHUT UP!
I WAS TRYING TO COACH YOU!

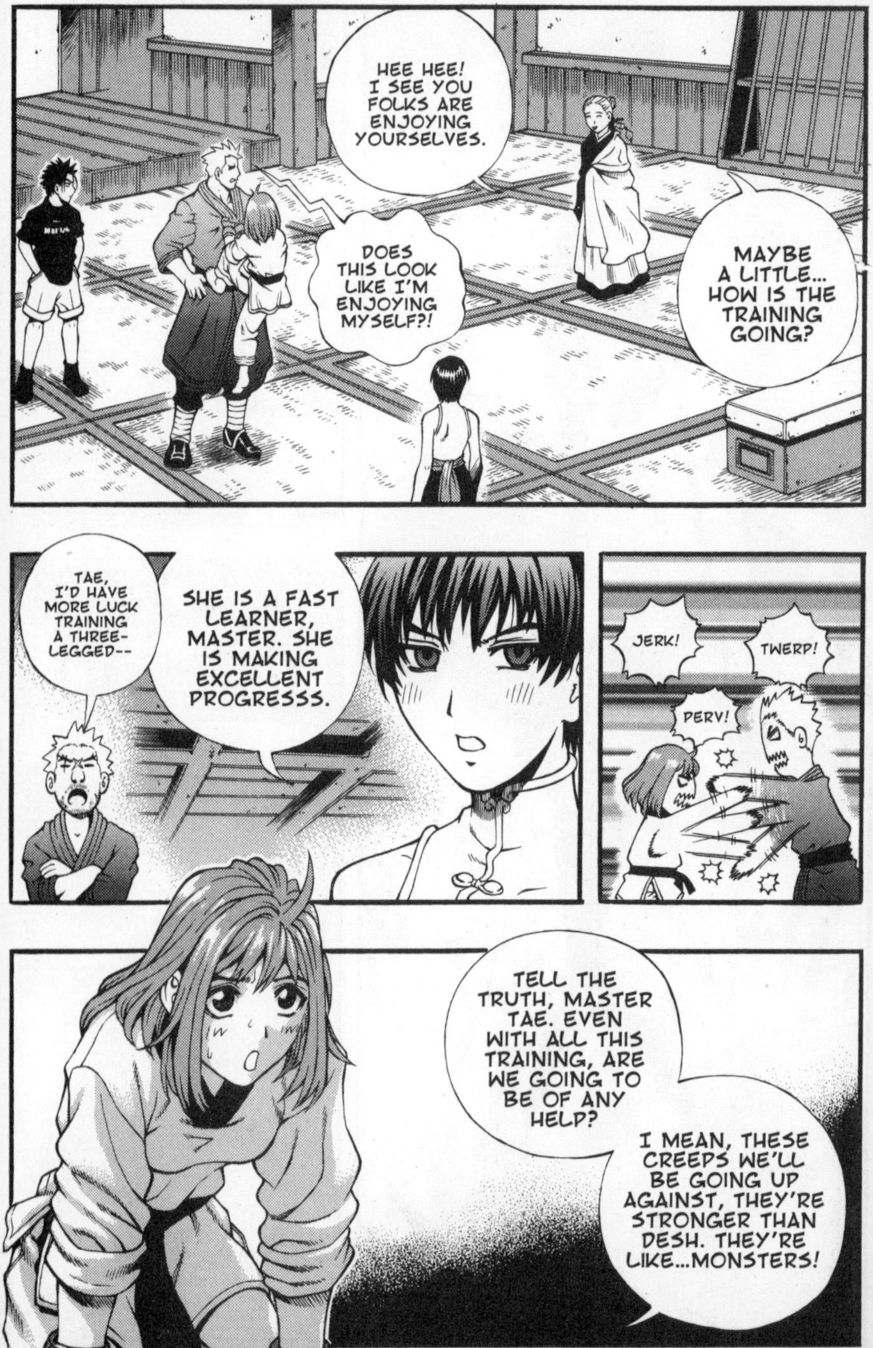
HEE HEE! I SEE YOU FOLKS ARE ENJOYING YOURSELVES.
DOES THIS LOOK LIKE I'M ENJOYING MYSELF?!
MAYBE A LITTLE... HOW IS THE TRAINING GOING?
SHE IS A FAST LEARNER, MASTER. SHE IS MAKING EXCELLENT PROGRESSS.
TAE, I'D HAVE MORE LUCK TRAINING A THREE-LEGGED--
JERK!
TWERP!
PERV!
TELL THE TRUTH, MASTER TAE. EVEN WITH ALL THIS TRAINING, ARE WE GOING TO BE OF ANY HELP?
I MEAN, THESE CREEPS WE'LL BE GOING UP AGAINST, THEY'RE STRONGER THAN DESH. THEY'RE LIKE...MONSTERS!

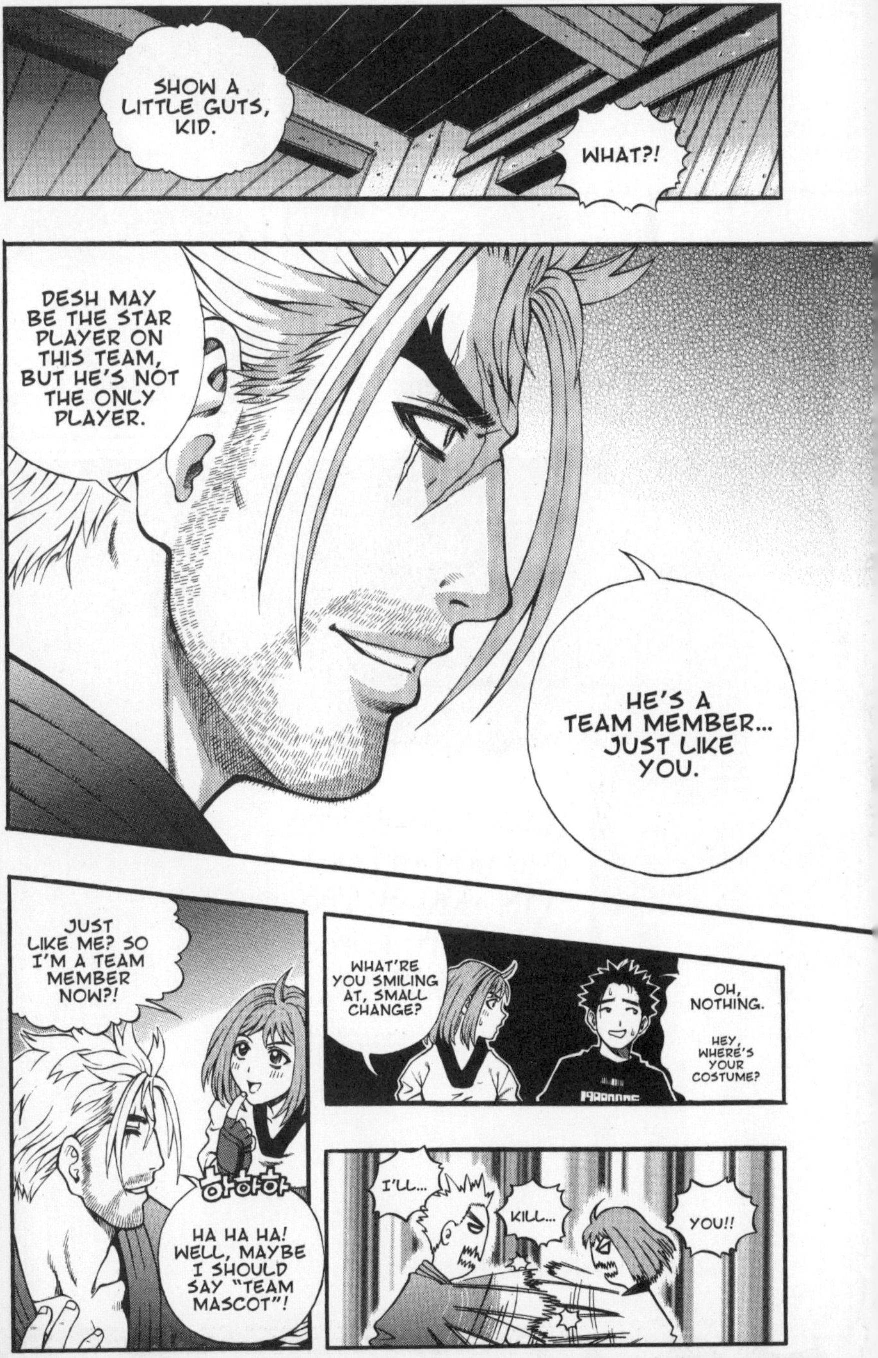
SHOW A LITTLE GUTS, KID.
WHAT?!
DESH MAY BE THE STAR PLAYER ON THIS TEAM, BUT HE'S NOT THE ONLY PLAYER.
HE'S A TEAM MEMBER... JUST LIKE YOU.
JUST LIKE ME? SO I'M A TEAM MEMBER NOW?!
하하하
HA HA HA! WELL, MAYBE I SHOULD SAY "TEAM MASCOT"!
WHAT'RE YOU SMILING AT, SMALL CHANGE?
OH, NOTHING.
HEY, WHERE'S YOUR COSTUME?
I'LL...
KILL...
YOU!!

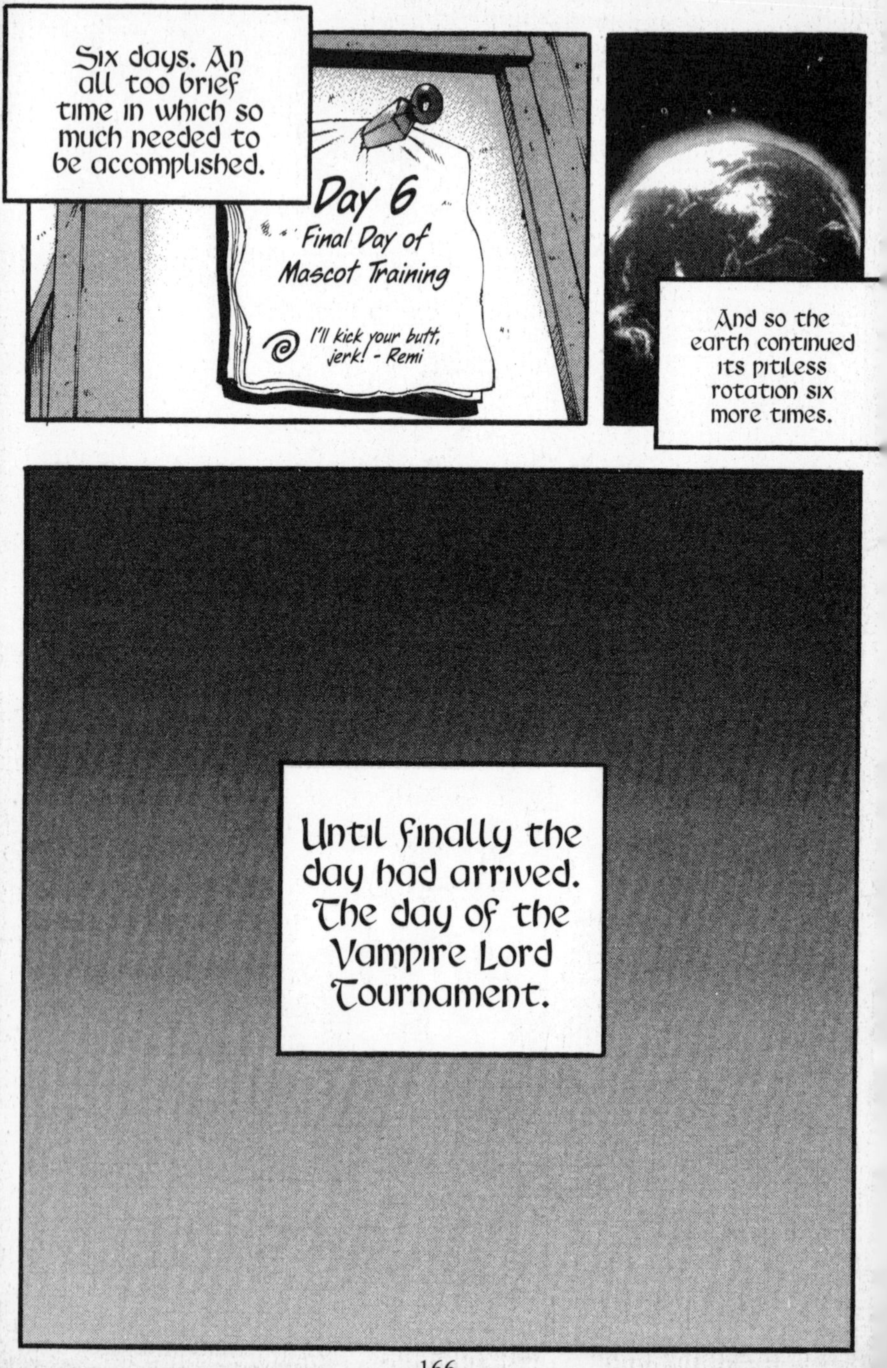
Six days. An all too brief time in which so much needed to be accomplished.
Day 6
Final Day of Mascot Training
I'll kick your butt, jerk! - Remi
And so the earth continued its pitiless rotation six more times.
Until finally the day had arrived. The day of the Vampire Lord Tournament.

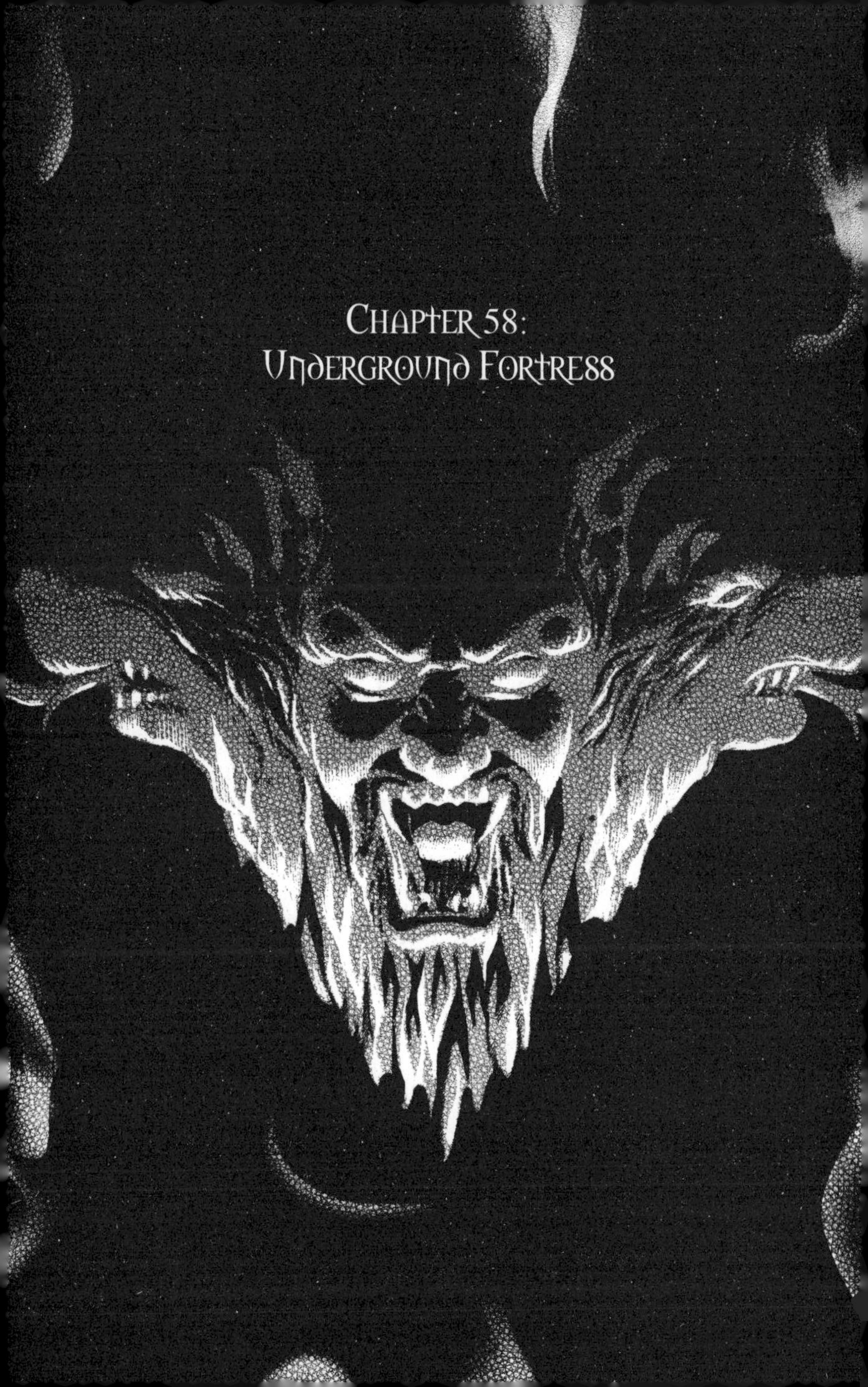
Chapter 58:
Underground Fortress

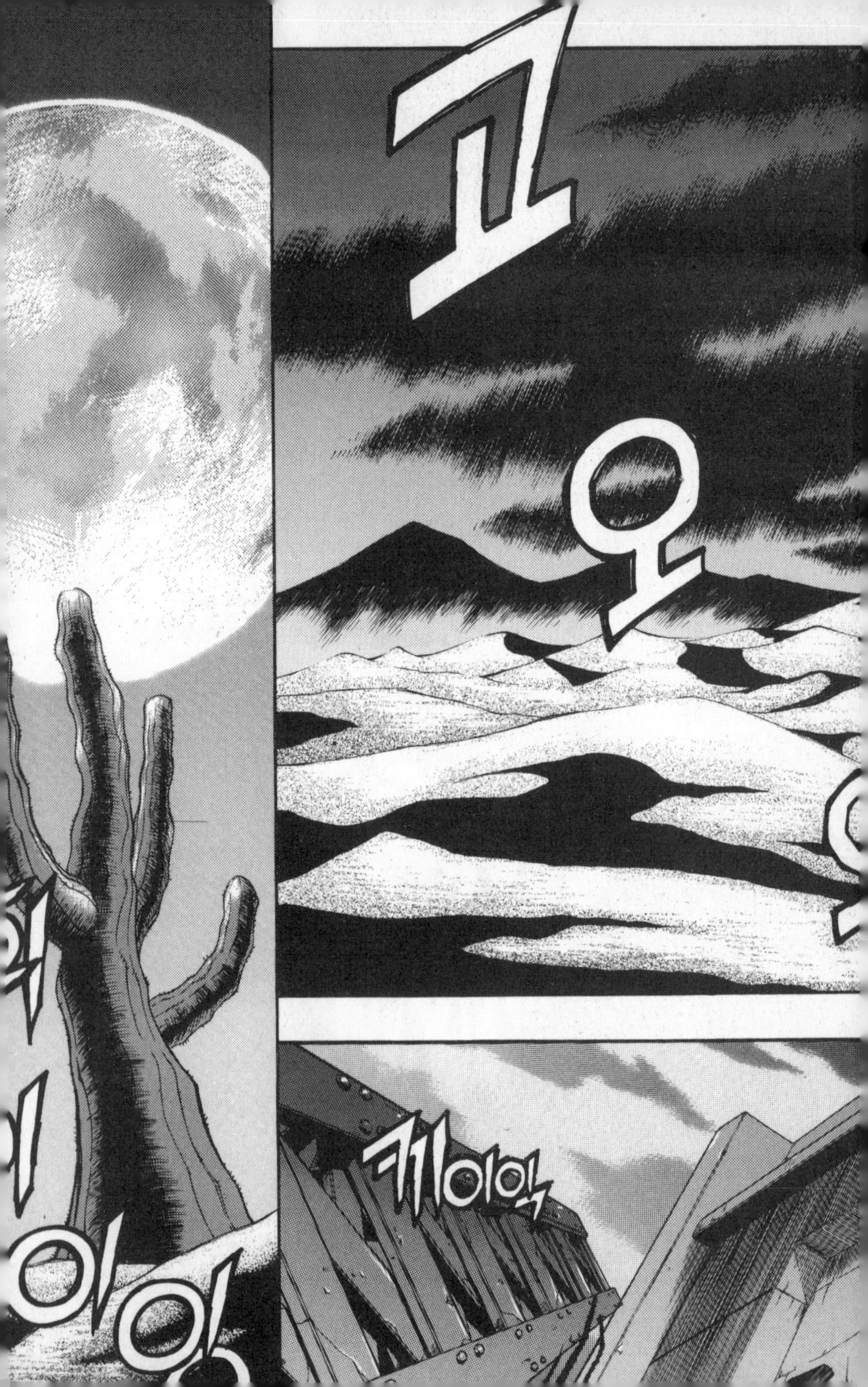
끼이이익

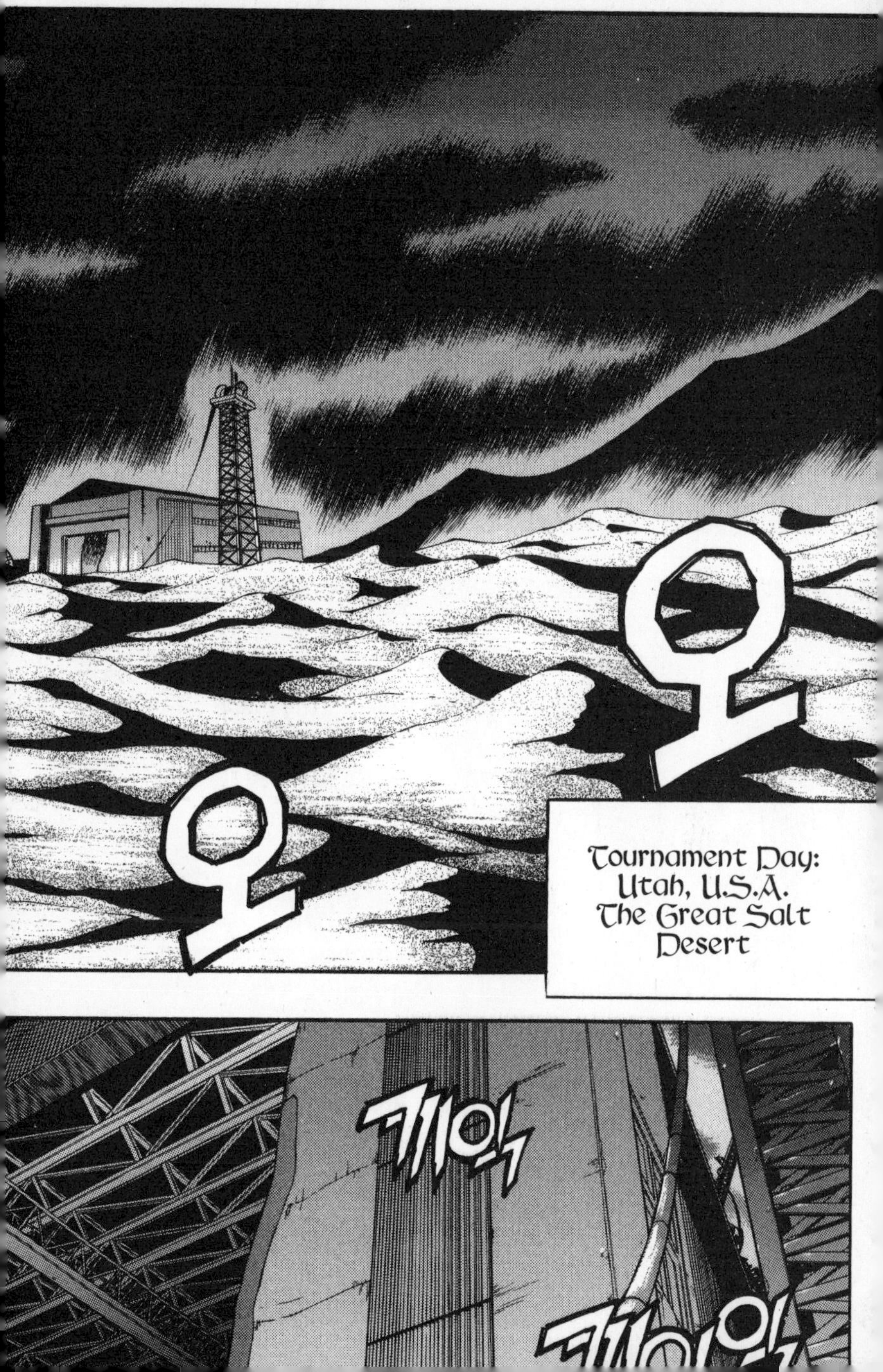
Tournament Day: Utah, U.S.A. The Great Salt Desert
끼익
끼이익

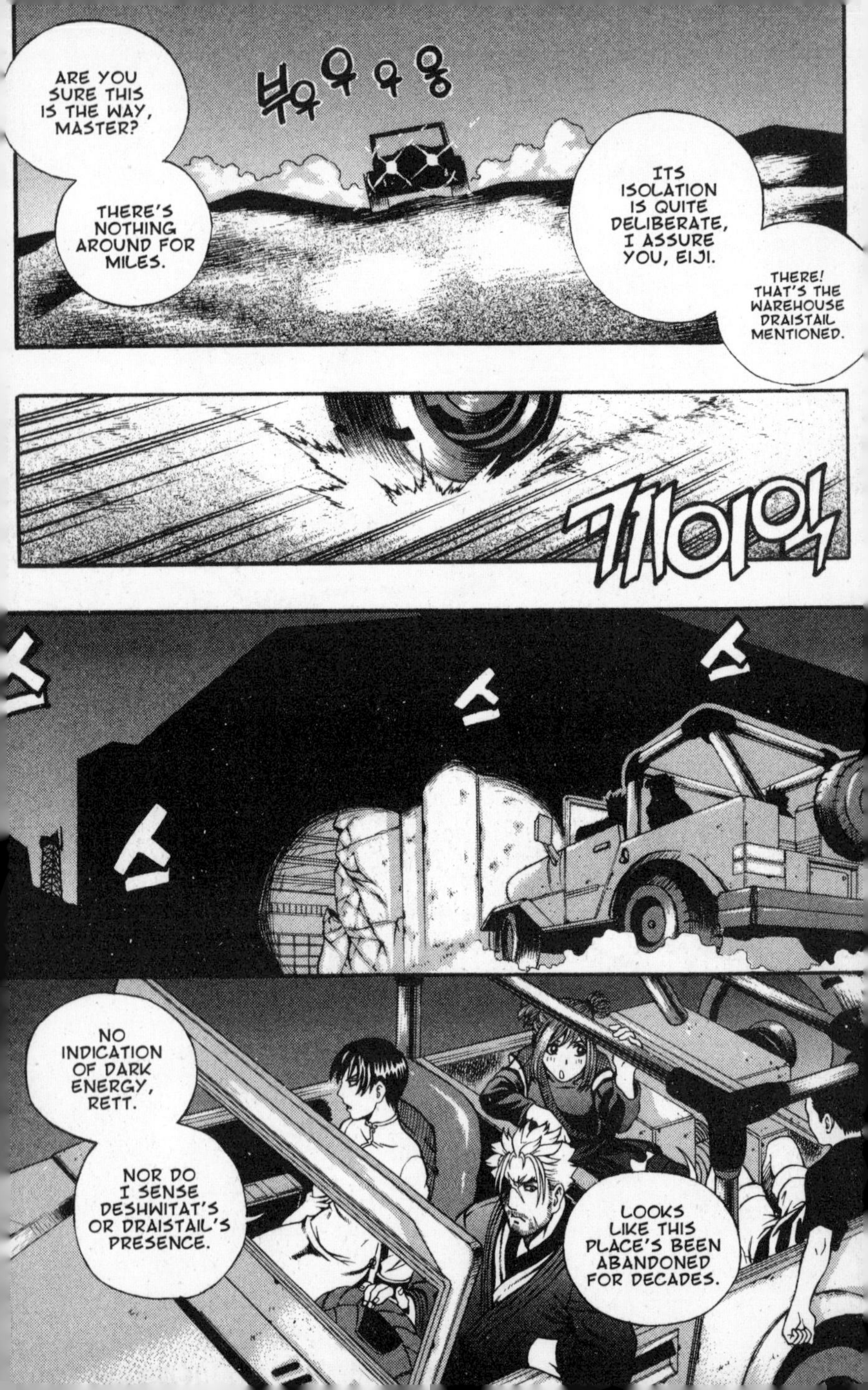

ARE YOU SURE THIS IS THE WAY, MASTER?
부우우우웅
THERE'S NOTHING AROUND FOR MILES.
ITS ISOLATION IS QUITE DELIBERATE, I ASSURE YOU, EIJI.
THERE! THAT'S THE WAREHOUSE DRAISTAIL MENTIONED.
끼이익
스
스
스
스
NO INDICATION OF DARK ENERGY, RETT.
NOR DO I SENSE DESHWITAT'S OR DRAISTAIL'S PRESENCE.
LOOKS LIKE THIS PLACE'S BEEN ABANDONED FOR DECADES.

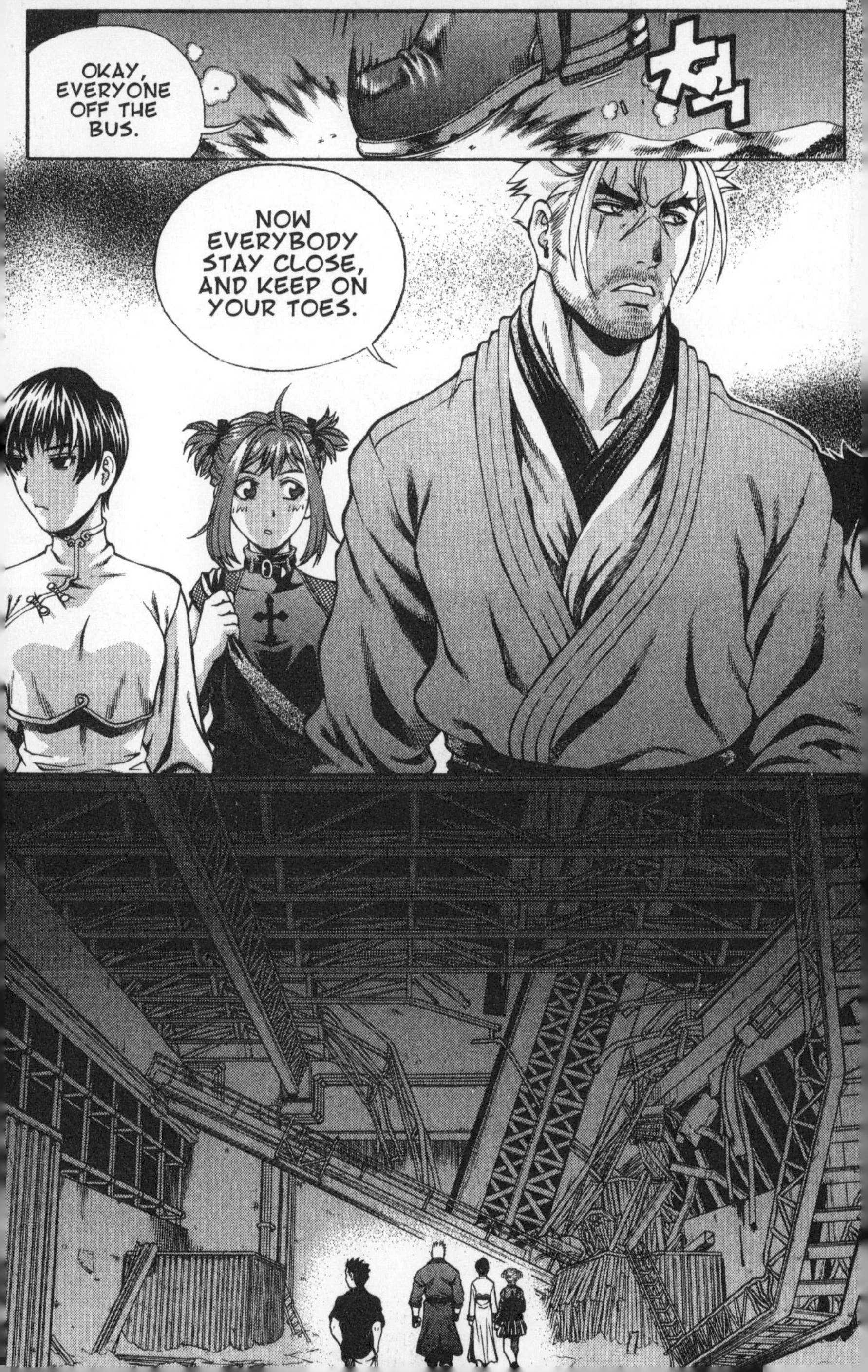
OKAY, EVERYONE OFF THE BUS.
NOW EVERYBODY STAY CLOSE, AND KEEP ON YOUR TOES.

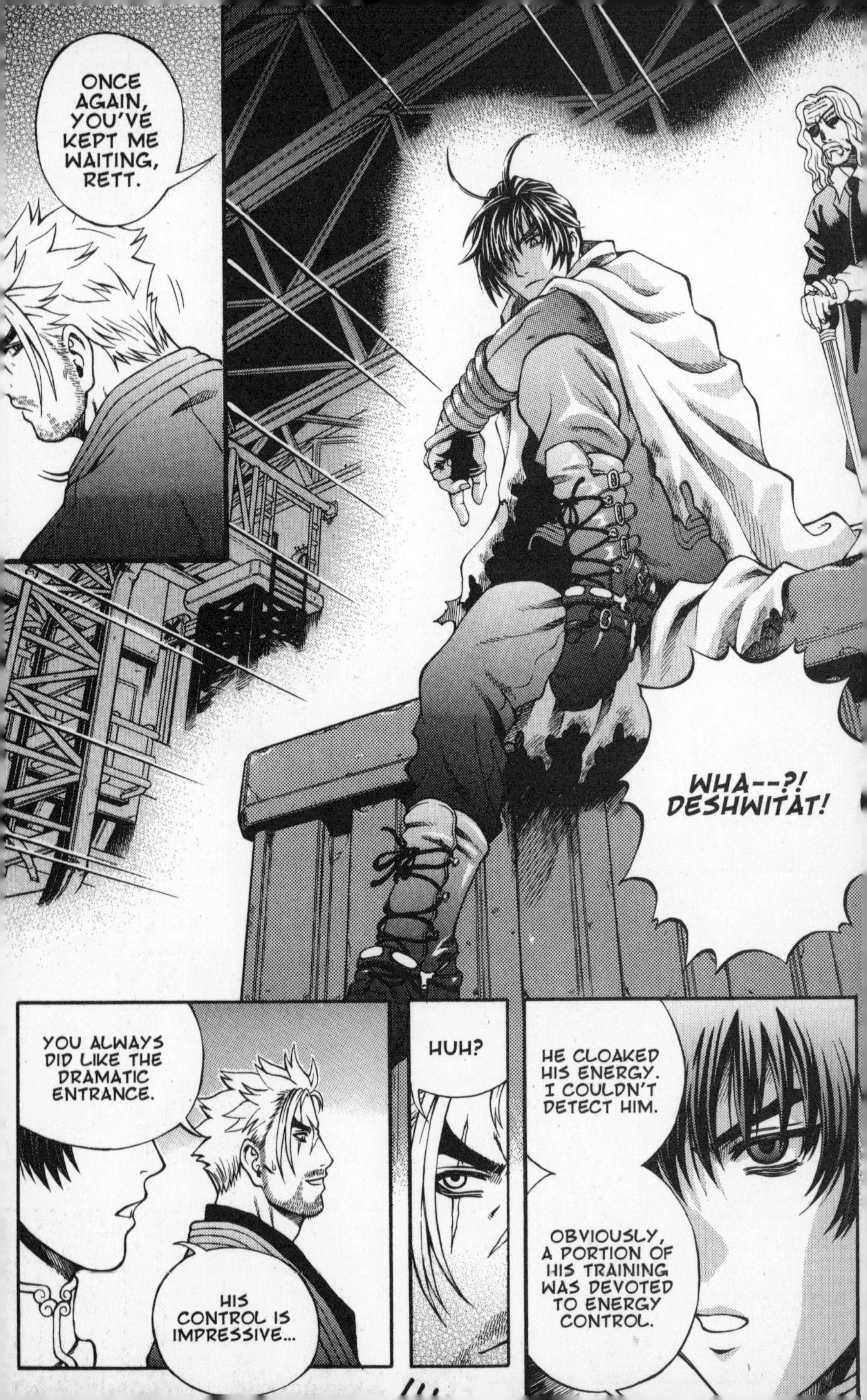
ONCE AGAIN, YOU'VE KEPT ME WAITING, RETT.
WHA--?! DESHWITAT!
YOU ALWAYS DID LIKE THE DRAMATIC ENTRANCE.
HIS CONTROL IS IMPRESSIVE...
HUH?
HE CLOAKED HIS ENERGY. I COULDN'T DETECT HIM.
OBVIOUSLY, A PORTION OF HIS TRAINING WAS DEVOTED TO ENERGY CONTROL.

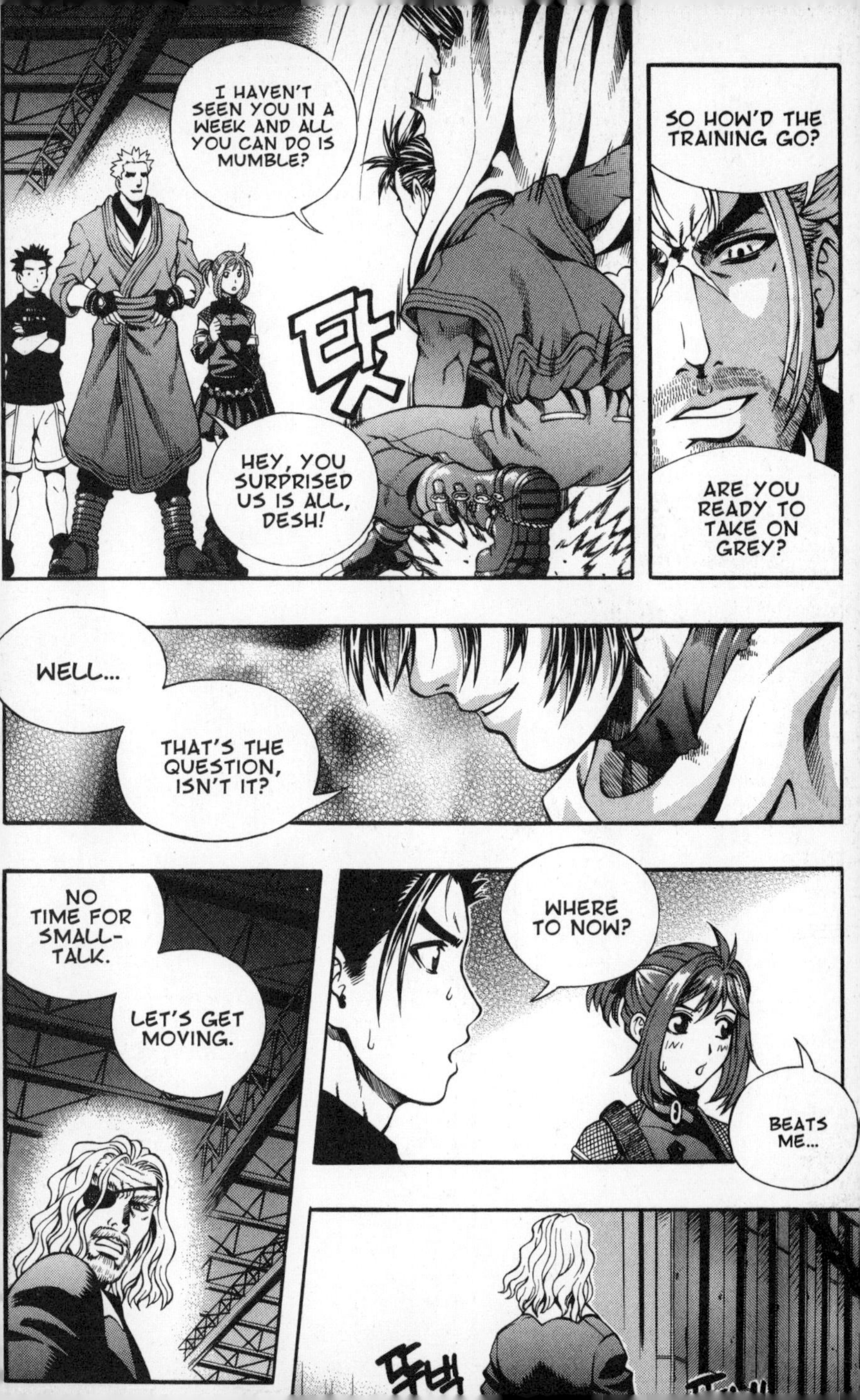
I HAVEN'T SEEN YOU IN A WEEK AND ALL YOU CAN DO IS MUMBLE?
탁
HEY, YOU SURPRISED US IS ALL, DESH!
SO HOW'D THE TRAINING GO?
ARE YOU READY TO TAKE ON GREY?
WELL...
THAT'S THE QUESTION, ISN'T IT?
NO TIME FOR SMALL-TALK.
LET'S GET MOVING.
WHERE TO NOW?
BEATS ME...

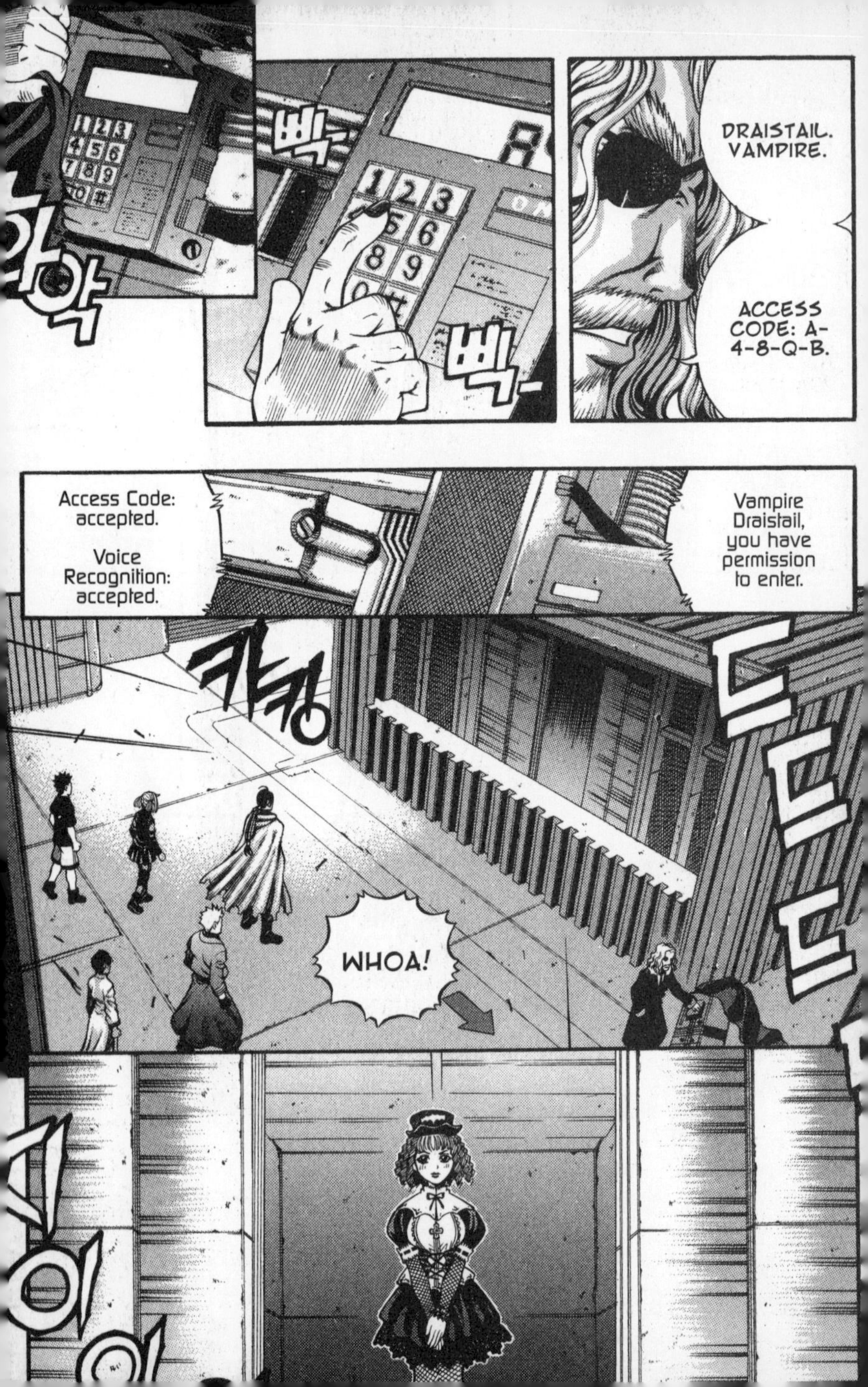

빡
빡-
DRAISTAIL. VAMPIRE.
ACCESS CODE: A-4-8-Q-B.
Access Code: accepted.
Voice Recognition: accepted.
Vampire Draistail, you have permission to enter.
WHOA!

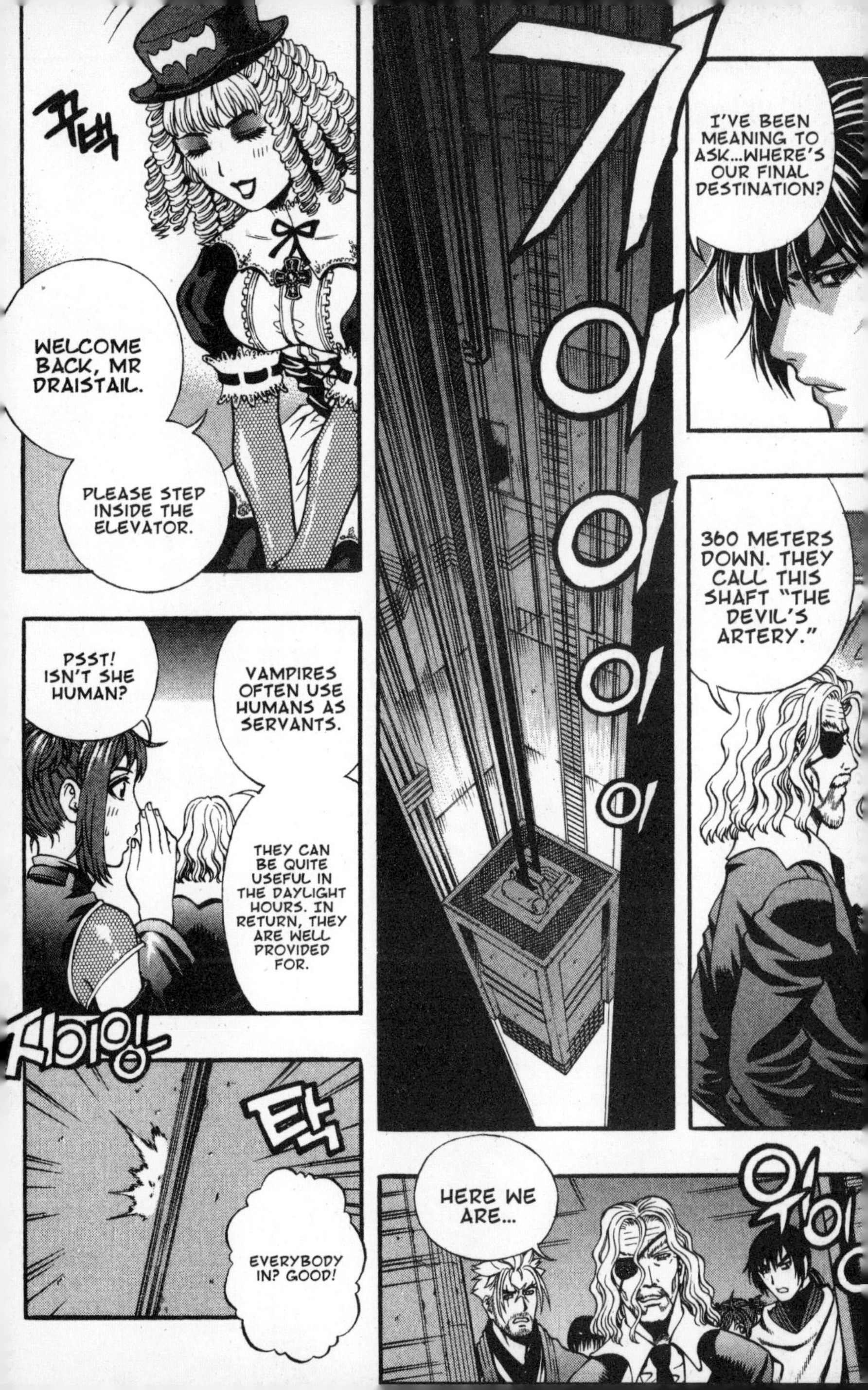

꾸벅
WELCOME BACK, MR DRAISTAIL.
PLEASE STEP INSIDE THE ELEVATOR.
PSST! ISN'T SHE HUMAN?
VAMPIRES OFTEN USE HUMANS AS SERVANTS.
THEY CAN BE QUITE USEFUL IN THE DAYLIGHT HOURS. IN RETURN, THEY ARE WELL PROVIDED FOR.
지이잉
탁
EVERYBODY IN? GOOD!
I'VE BEEN MEANING TO ASK...WHERE'S OUR FINAL DESTINATION?
360 METERS DOWN. THEY CALL THIS SHAFT "THE DEVIL'S ARTERY."
HERE WE ARE...

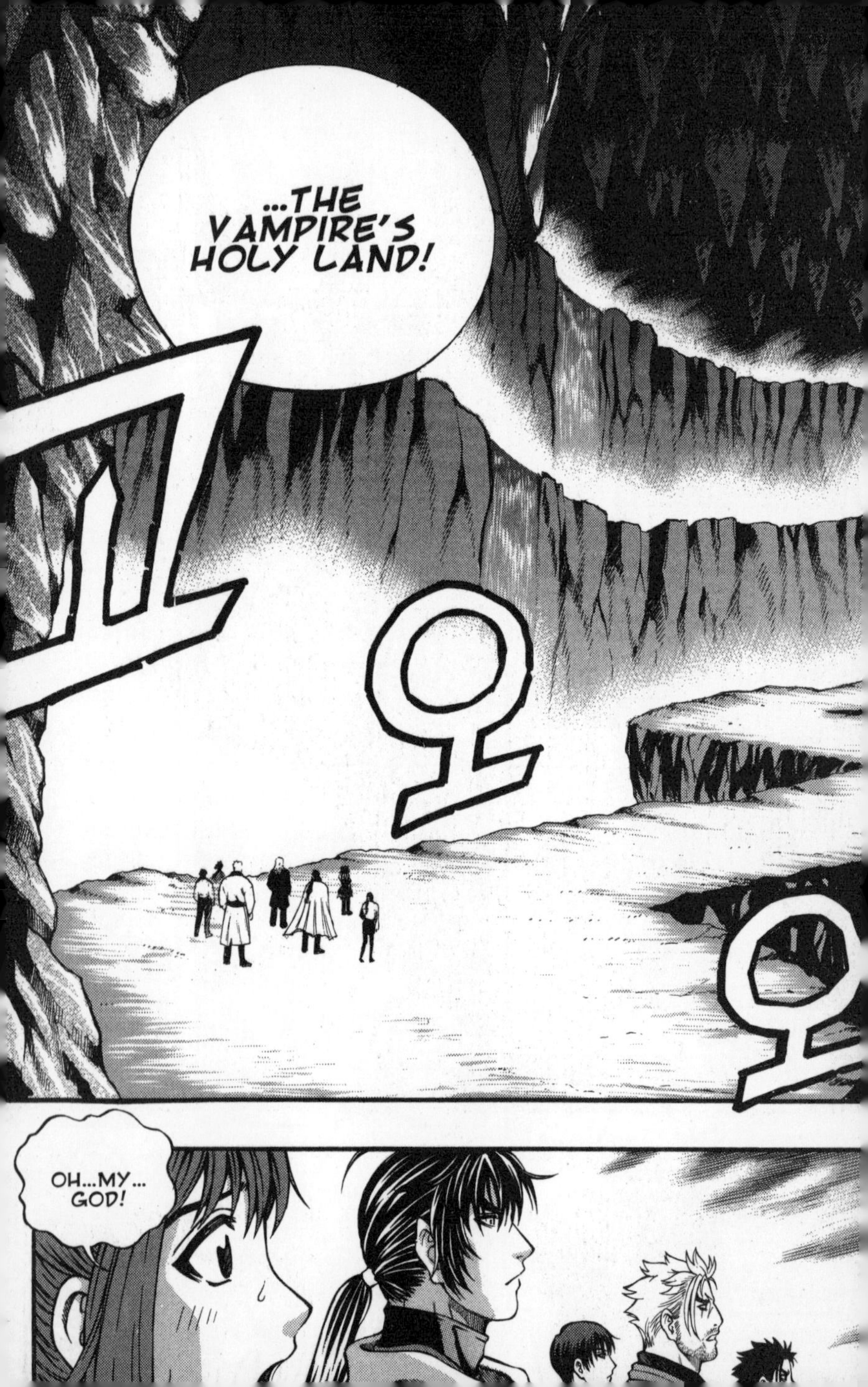
...THE VAMPIRE'S HOLY LAND!
OH...MY... GOD!

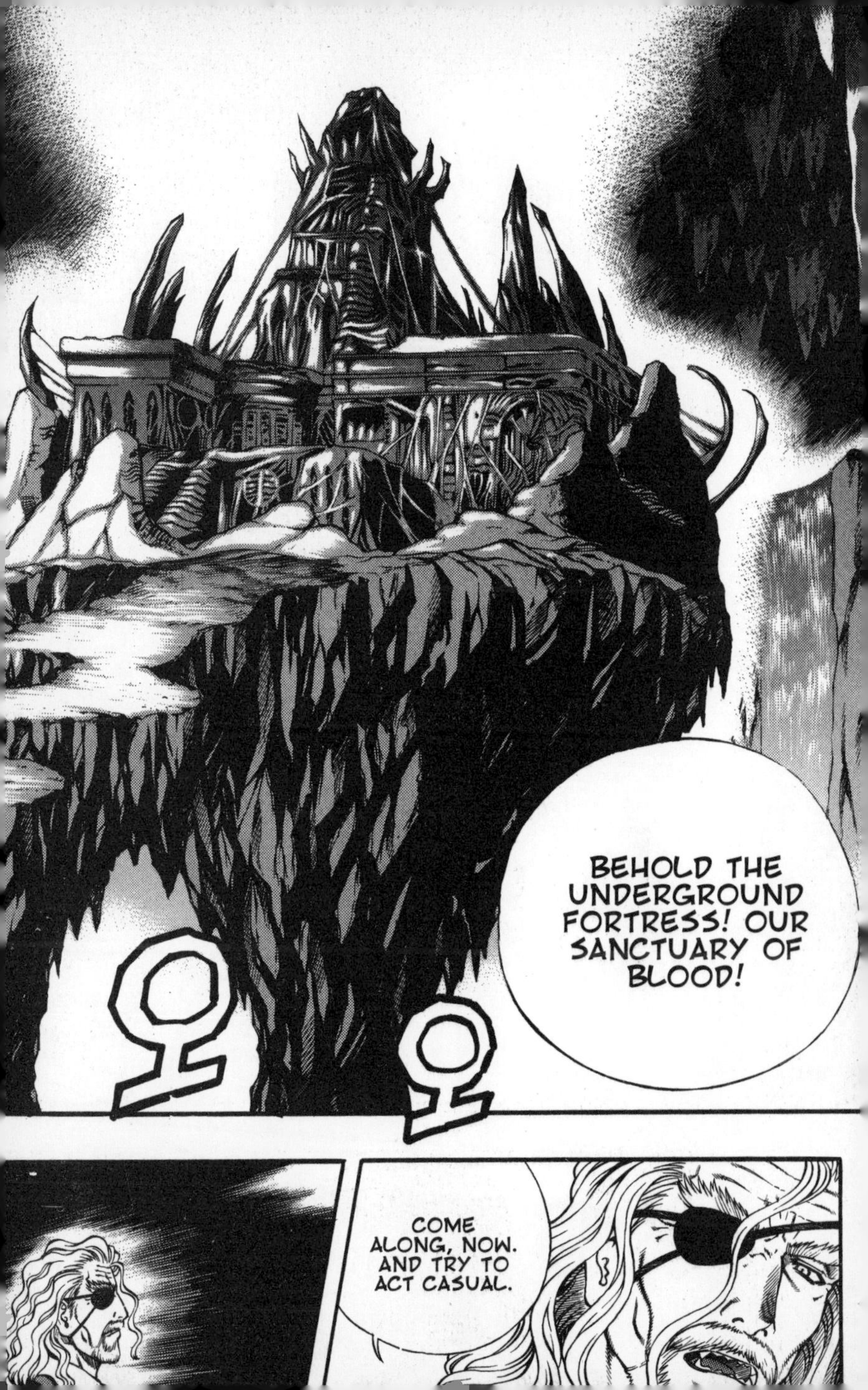
BEHOLD THE UNDERGROUND FORTRESS! OUR SANCTUARY OF BLOOD!
COME ALONG, NOW. AND TRY TO ACT CASUAL.

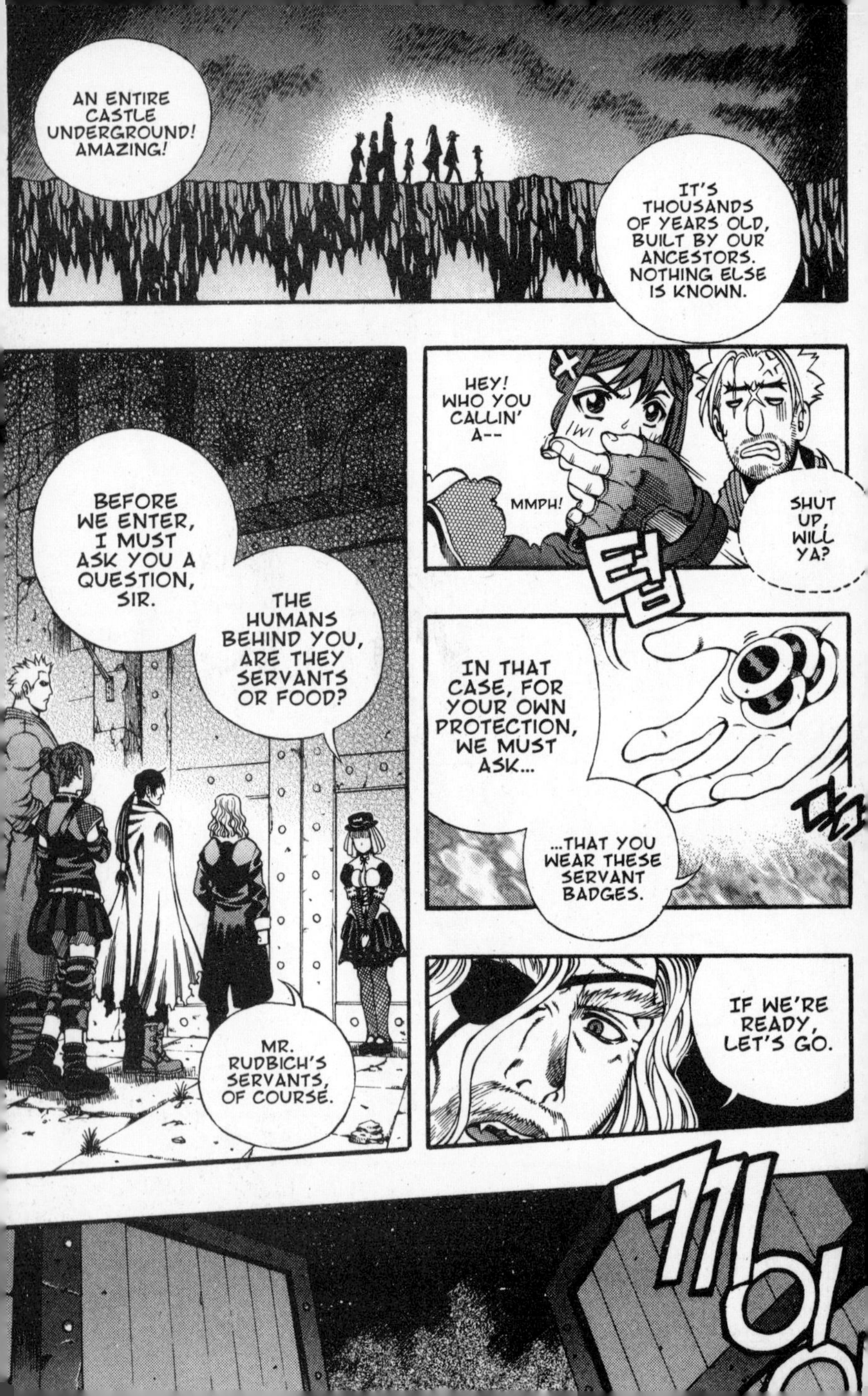
AN ENTIRE CASTLE UNDERGROUND! AMAZING!
IT'S THOUSANDS OF YEARS OLD, BUILT BY OUR ANCESTORS. NOTHING ELSE IS KNOWN.
BEFORE WE ENTER, I MUST ASK YOU A QUESTION, SIR.
THE HUMANS BEHIND YOU, ARE THEY SERVANTS OR FOOD?
MR. RUDBICH'S SERVANTS, OF COURSE.
HEY! WHO YOU CALLIN' A--
MMPH!
SHUT UP, WILL YA?
IN THAT CASE, FOR YOUR OWN PROTECTION, WE MUST ASK...
...THAT YOU WEAR THESE SERVANT BADGES.
IF WE'RE READY, LET'S GO.

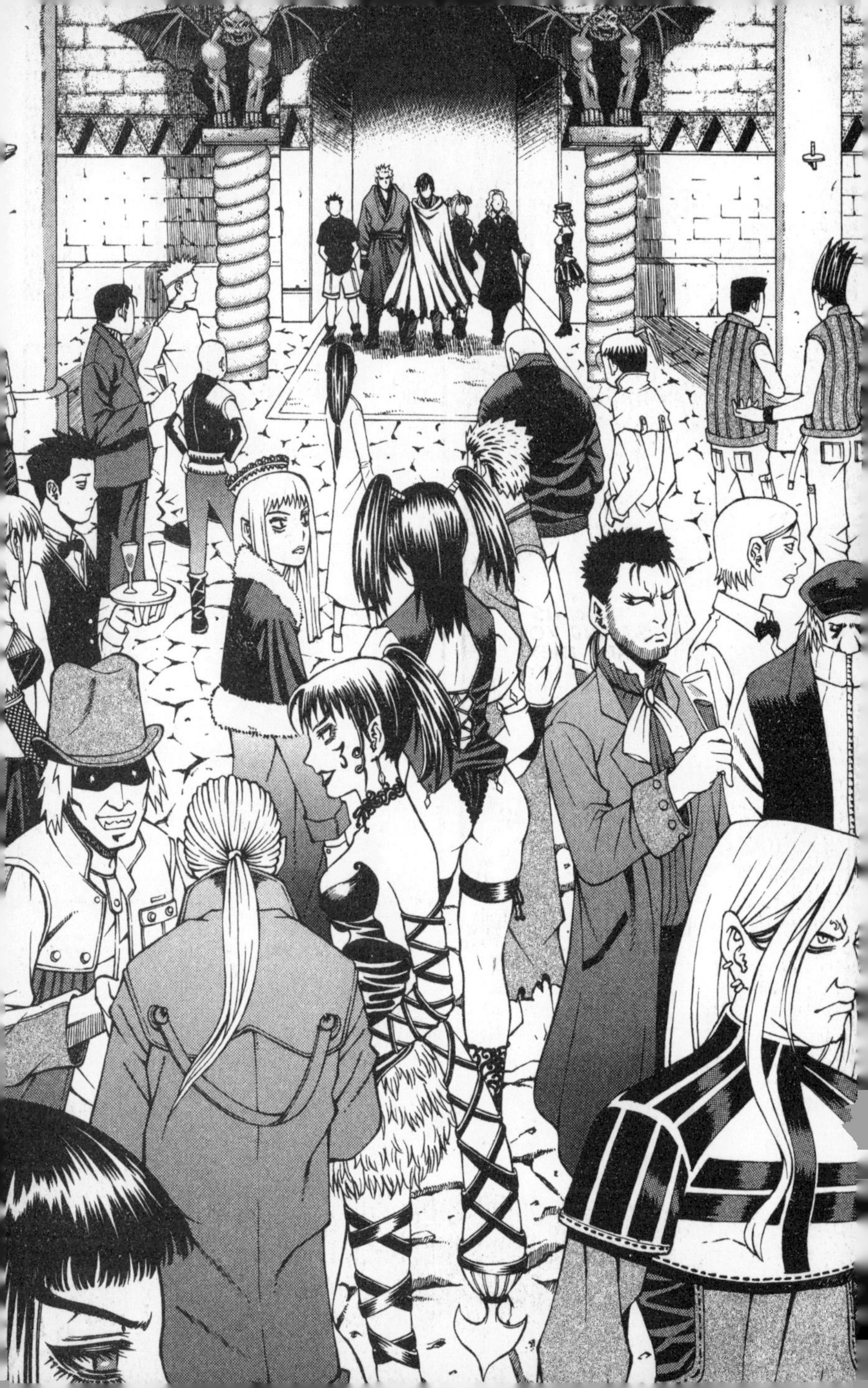

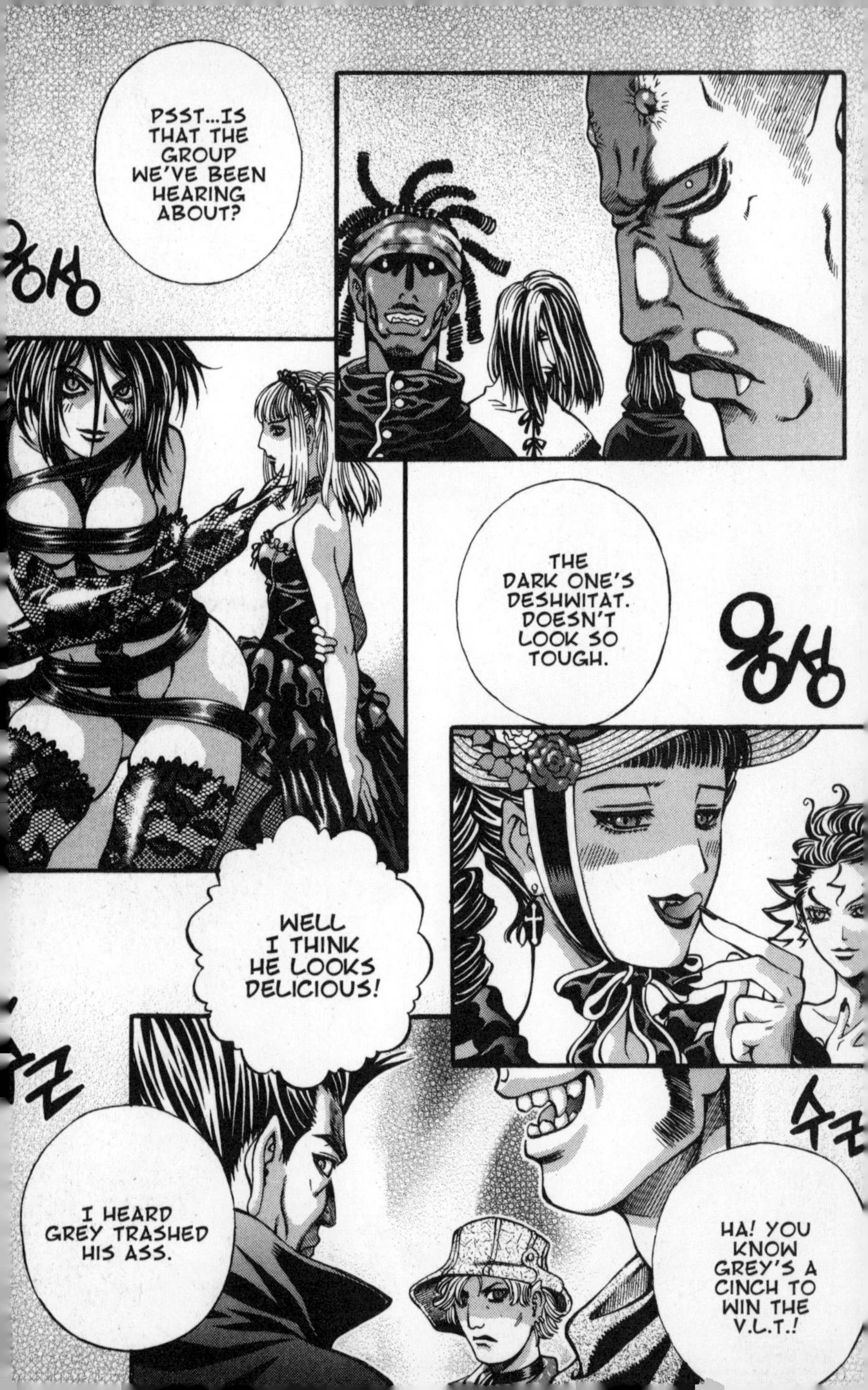
PSST...IS THAT THE GROUP WE'VE BEEN HEARING ABOUT?
THE DARK ONE'S DESHWITAT. DOESN'T LOOK SO TOUGH.
웅성
WELL I THINK HE LOOKS DELICIOUS!
I HEARD GREY TRASHED HIS ASS.
HA! YOU KNOW GREY'S A CINCH TO WIN THE V.L.T.!

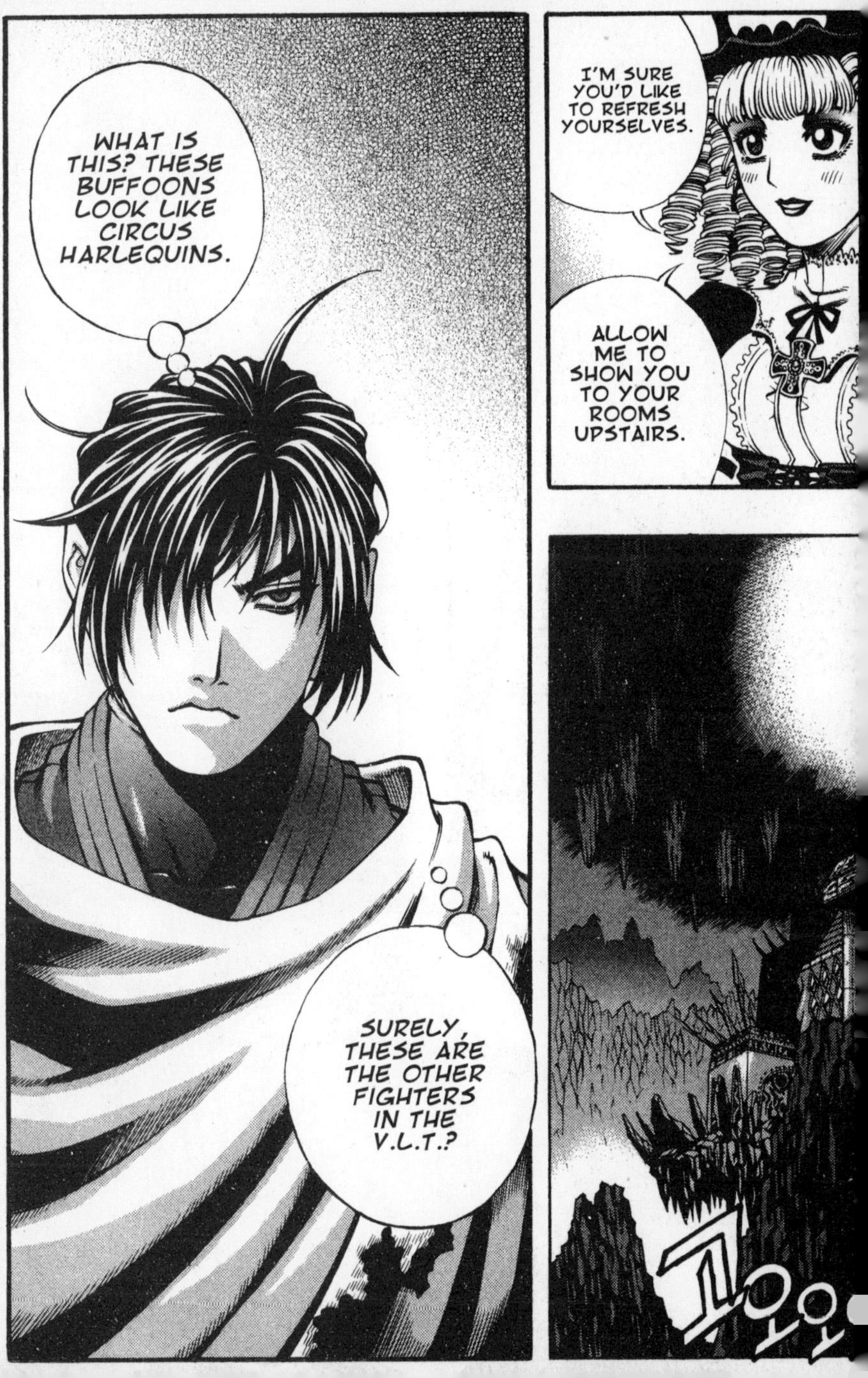
WHAT IS THIS? THESE BUFFOONS LOOK LIKE CIRCUS HARLEQUINS.
SURELY, THESE ARE THE OTHER FIGHTERS IN THE V.L.T.?
I'M SURE YOU'D LIKE TO REFRESH YOURSELVES.
ALLOW ME TO SHOW YOU TO YOUR ROOMS UPSTAIRS.

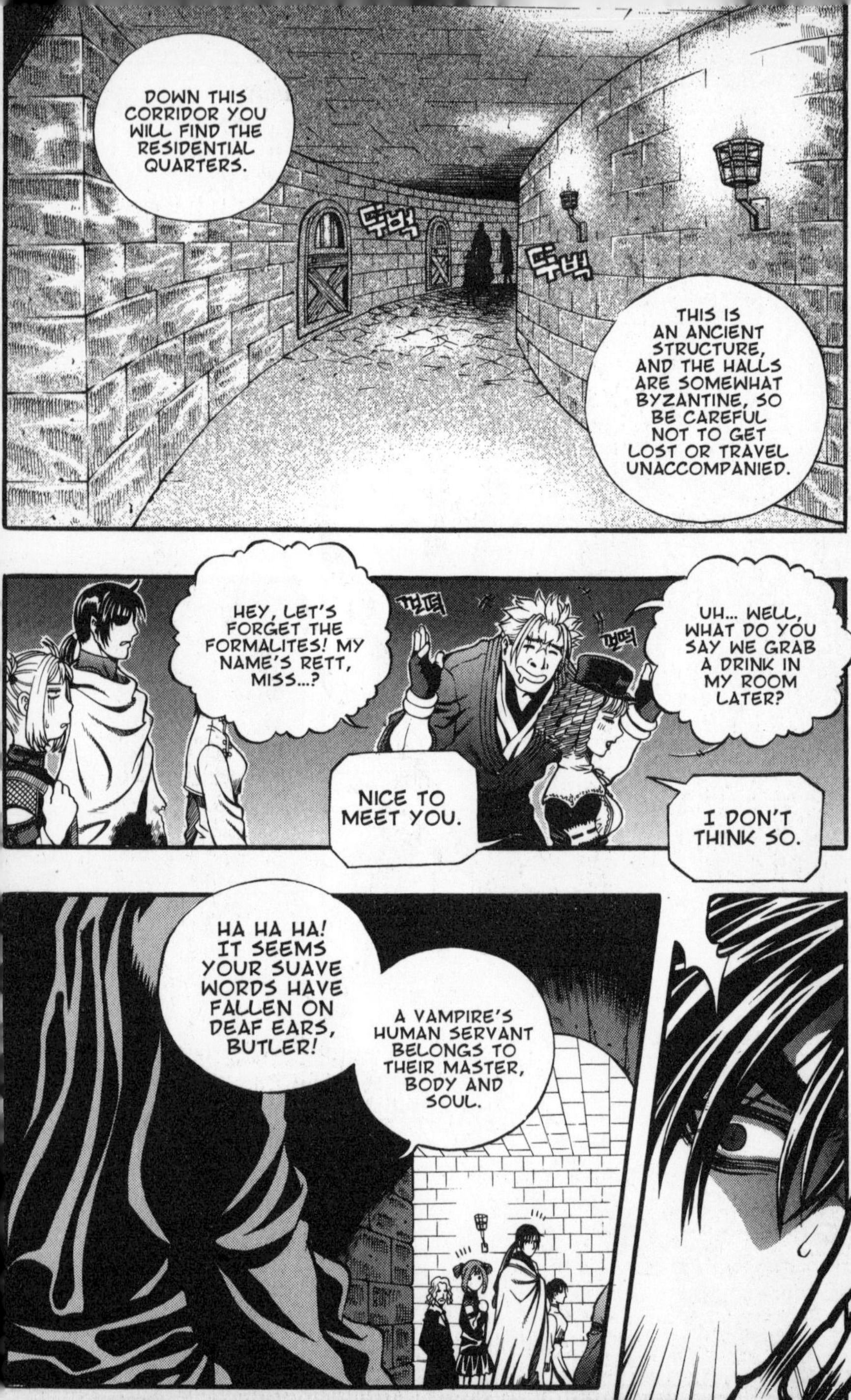
DOWN THIS CORRIDOR YOU WILL FIND THE RESIDENTIAL QUARTERS.
뚜벅
뚜벅
THIS IS AN ANCIENT STRUCTURE, AND THE HALLS ARE SOMEWHAT BYZANTINE, SO BE CAREFUL NOT TO GET LOST OR TRAVEL UNACCOMPANIED.
HEY, LET'S FORGET THE FORMALITES! MY NAME'S RETT, MISS...?
NICE TO MEET YOU.
UH... WELL, WHAT DO YOU SAY WE GRAB A DRINK IN MY ROOM LATER?
I DON'T THINK SO.
HA HA HA! IT SEEMS YOUR SUAVE WORDS HAVE FALLEN ON DEAF EARS, BUTLER!
A VAMPIRE'S HUMAN SERVANT BELONGS TO THEIR MASTER, BODY AND SOUL.

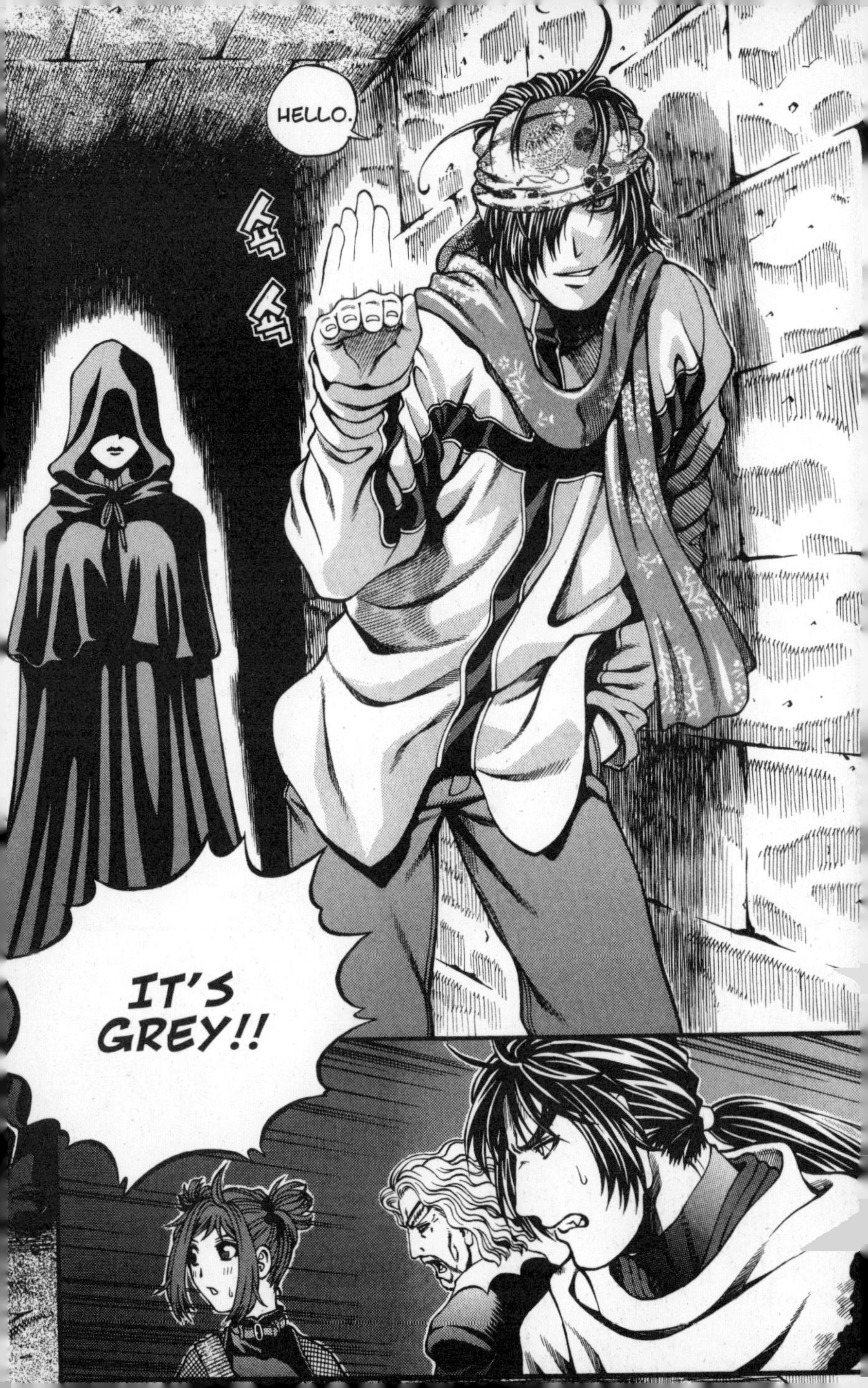
HELLO.
IT'S GREY!!

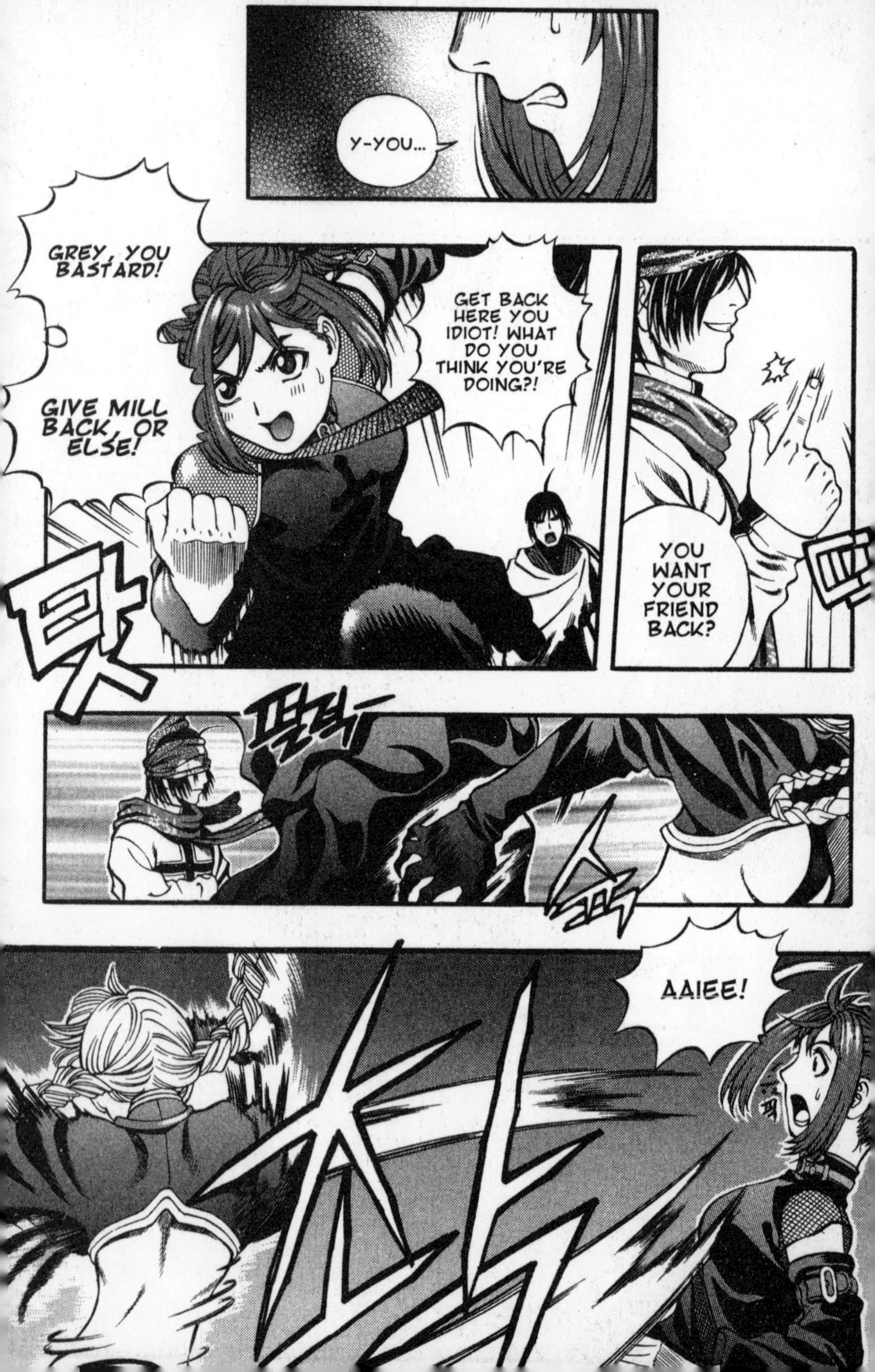
Y-YOU...
GREY, YOU BASTARD!
GIVE MILL BACK, OR ELSE!
GET BACK HERE YOU IDIOT! WHAT DO YOU THINK YOU'RE DOING?!
YOU WANT YOUR FRIEND BACK?
AAIEE!

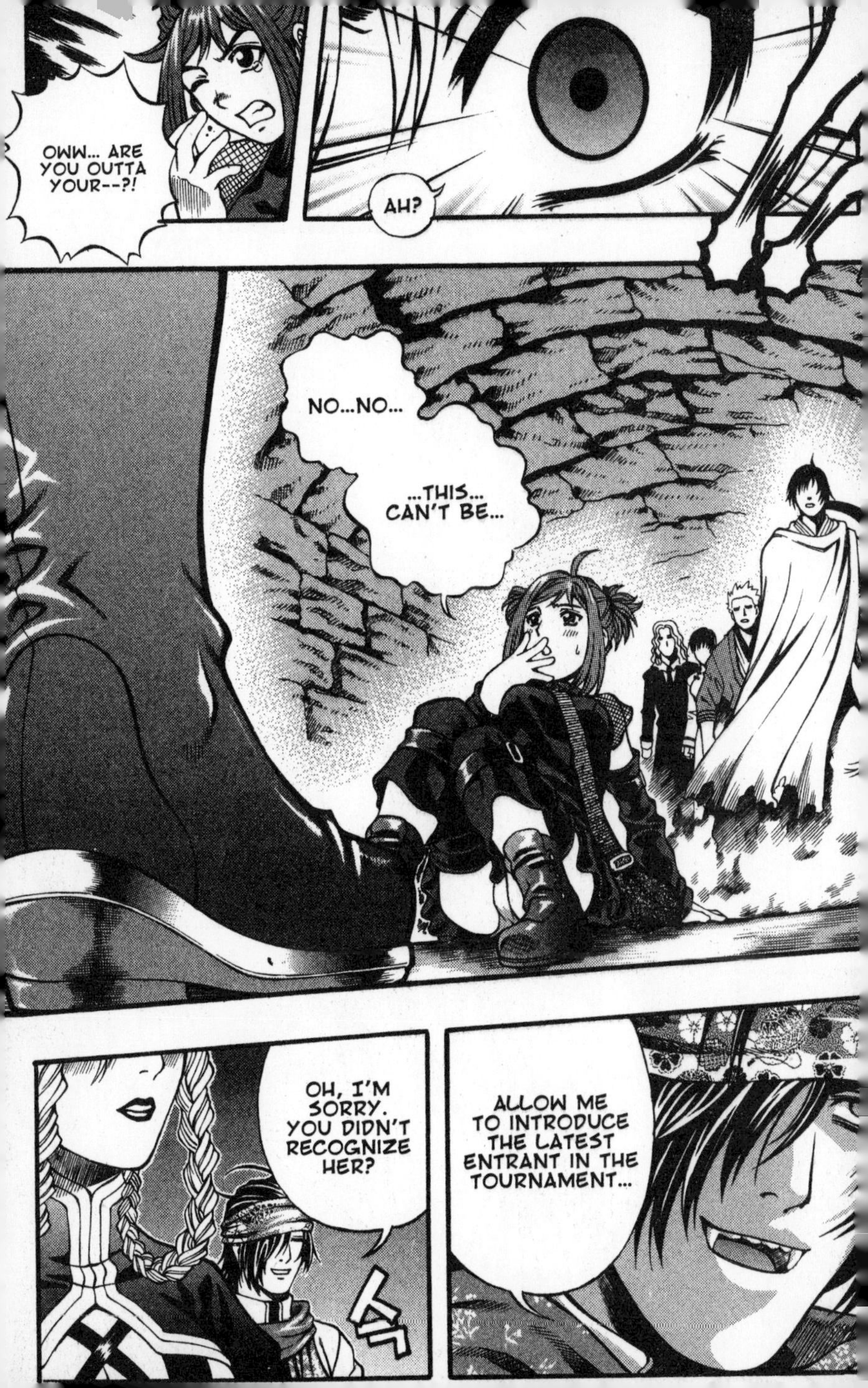
OWW... ARE YOU OUTTA YOUR--?!
AH?
NO...NO...
...THIS... CAN'T BE...
OH, I'M SORRY. YOU DIDN'T RECOGNIZE HER?
ALLOW ME TO INTRODUCE THE LATEST ENTRANT IN THE TOURNAMENT...

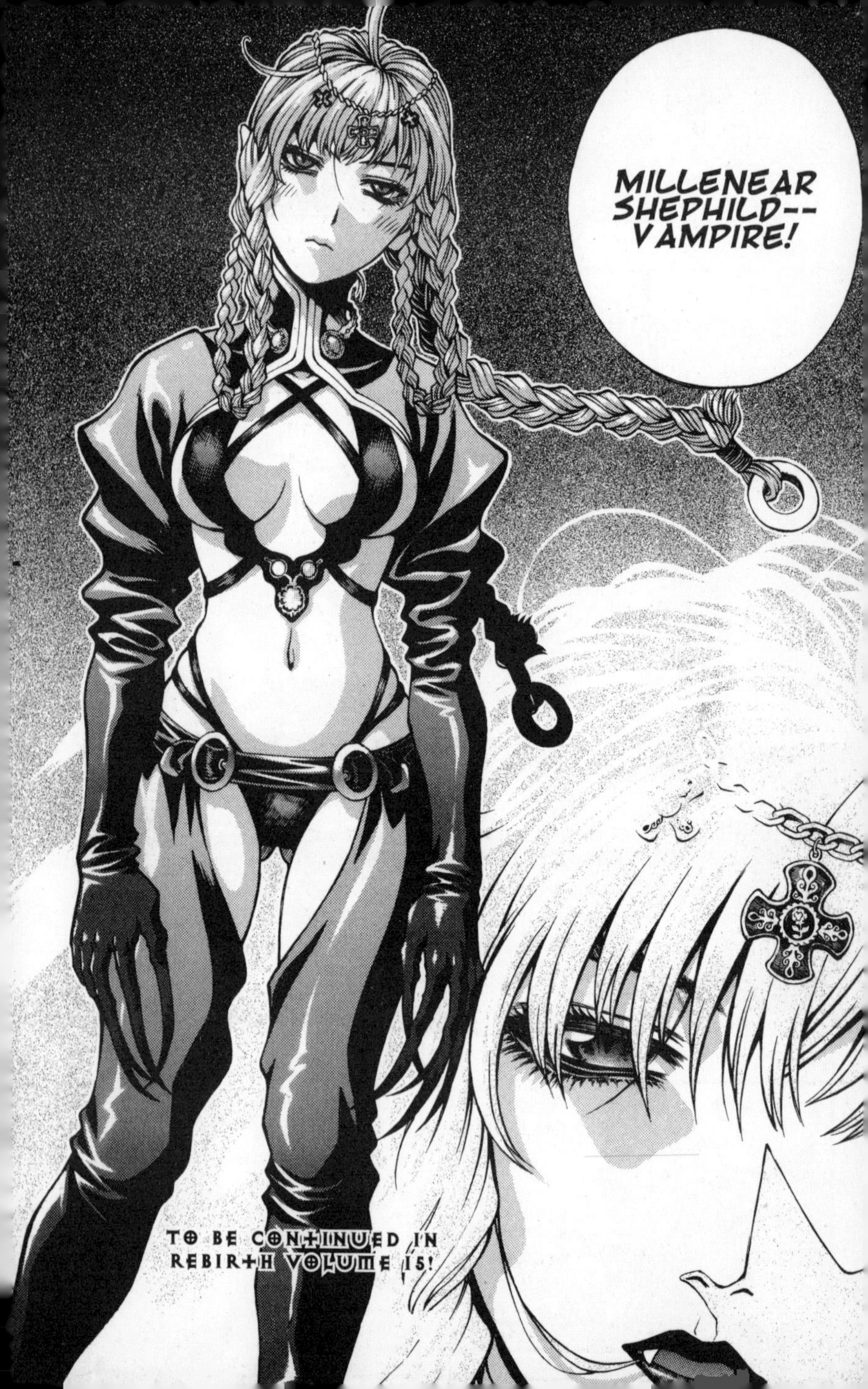
MILLENEAR SHEPHILD-- VAMPIRE!
TO BE CONTINUED IN REBIRTH VOLUME 15!

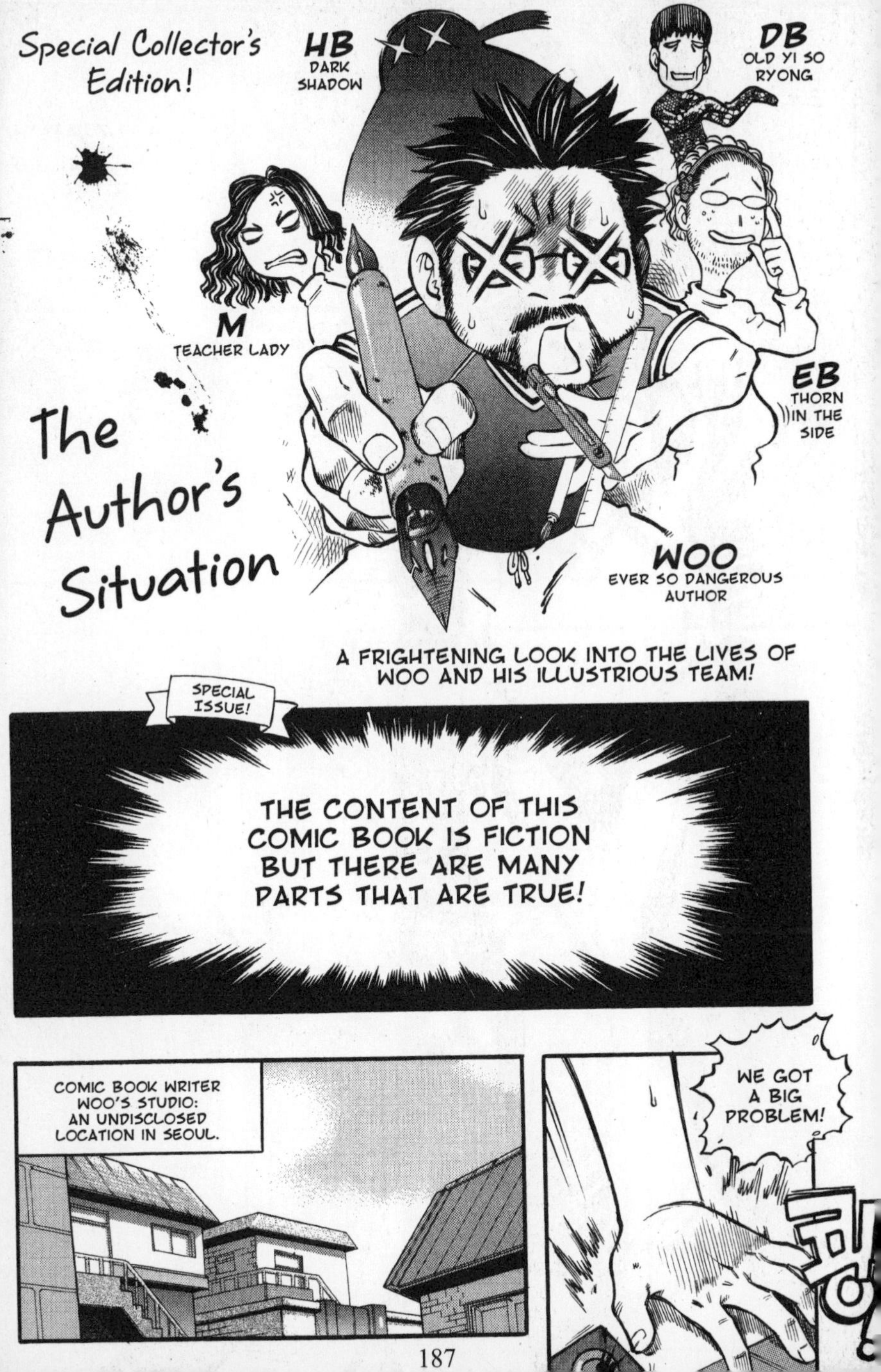
Special Collector's Edition!
HB
DARK SHADOW
DB
OLD YI SO RYONG
M
TEACHER LADY
EB
THORN IN THE SIDE
The Author's Situation
WOO
EVER SO DANGEROUS AUTHOR
A FRIGHTENING LOOK INTO THE LIVES OF WOO AND HIS ILLUSTRIOUS TEAM!
SPECIAL ISSUE!
THE CONTENT OF THIS COMIC BOOK IS FICTION BUT THERE ARE MANY PARTS THAT ARE TRUE!
COMIC BOOK WRITER WOO'S STUDIO: AN UNDISCLOSED LOCATION IN SEOUL.
WE GOT A BIG PROBLEM!

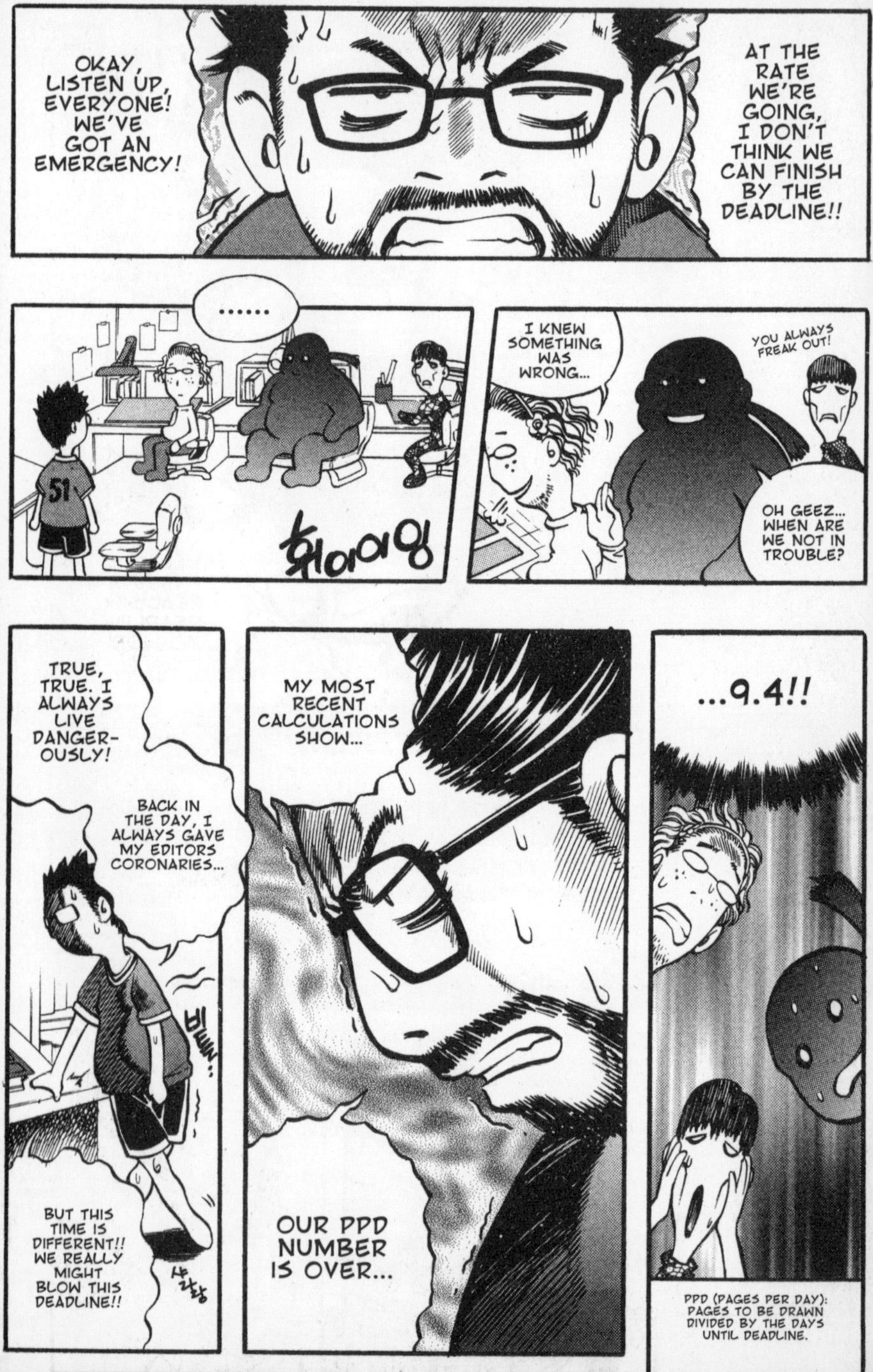

OKAY, LISTEN UP, EVERYONE! WE'VE GOT AN EMERGENCY!
AT THE RATE WE'RE GOING, I DON'T THINK WE CAN FINISH BY THE DEADLINE!!
......
I KNEW SOMETHING WAS WRONG...
YOU ALWAYS FREAK OUT!
OH GEEZ... WHEN ARE WE NOT IN TROUBLE?
TRUE, TRUE. I ALWAYS LIVE DANGER-OUSLY!
BACK IN THE DAY, I ALWAYS GAVE MY EDITORS CORONARIES...
BUT THIS TIME IS DIFFERENT!! WE REALLY MIGHT BLOW THIS DEADLINE!!
MY MOST RECENT CALCULATIONS SHOW...
OUR PPD NUMBER IS OVER...
...9.4!!
PPD (PAGES PER DAY): PAGES TO BE DRAWN DIVIDED BY THE DAYS UNTIL DEADLINE.

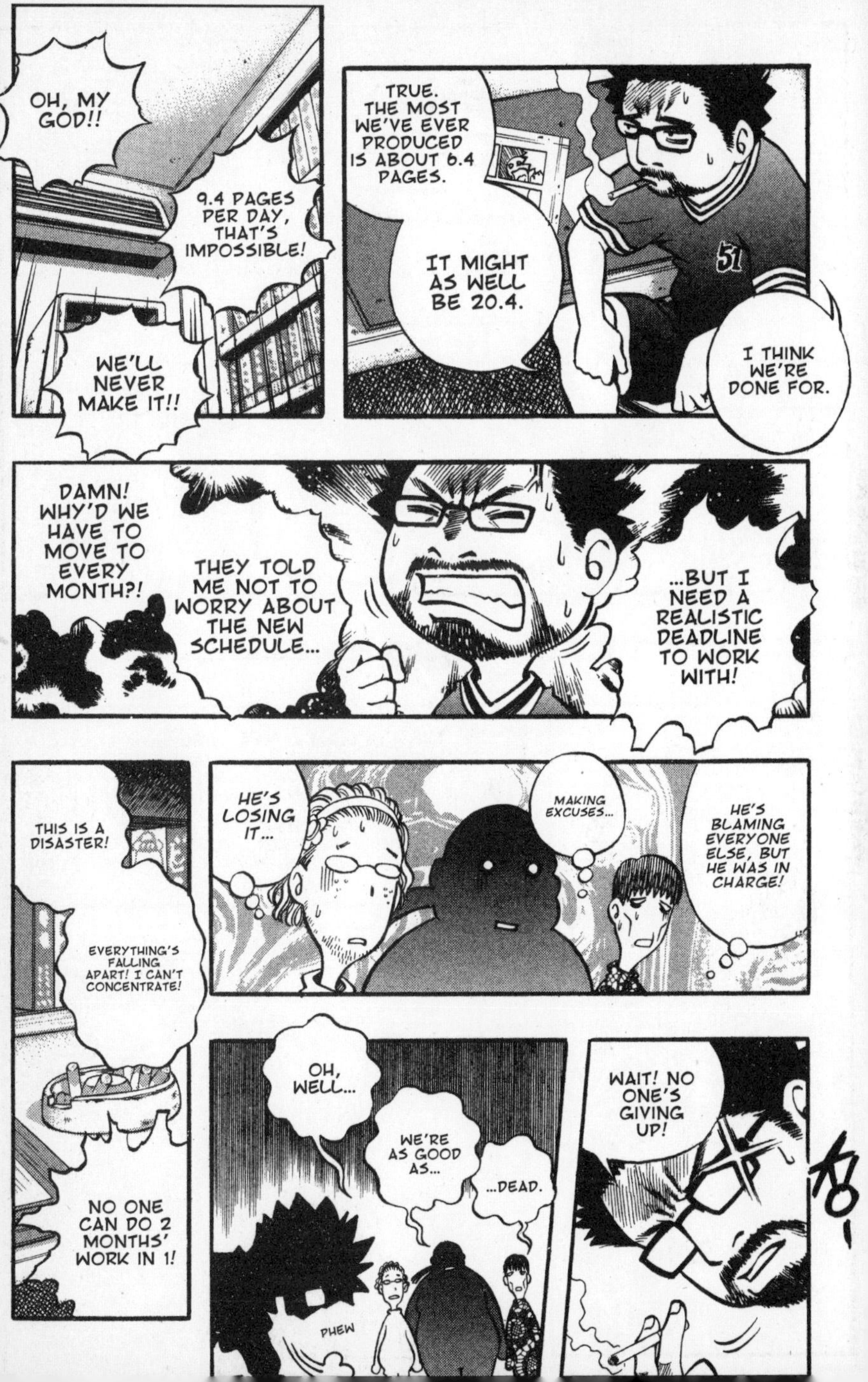
OH, MY GOD!!
9.4 PAGES PER DAY, THAT'S IMPOSSIBLE!
WE'LL NEVER MAKE IT!!
TRUE. THE MOST WE'VE EVER PRODUCED IS ABOUT 6.4 PAGES.
IT MIGHT AS WELL BE 20.4.
I THINK WE'RE DONE FOR.
DAMN! WHY'D WE HAVE TO MOVE TO EVERY MONTH?!
THEY TOLD ME NOT TO WORRY ABOUT THE NEW SCHEDULE...
...BUT I NEED A REALISTIC DEADLINE TO WORK WITH!
THIS IS A DISASTER!
EVERYTHING'S FALLING APART! I CAN'T CONCENTRATE!
NO ONE CAN DO 2 MONTHS' WORK IN 1!
HE'S LOSING IT...
MAKING EXCUSES...
HE'S BLAMING EVERYONE ELSE, BUT HE WAS IN CHARGE!
OH, WELL...
WE'RE AS GOOD AS...
...DEAD.
PHEW
WAIT! NO ONE'S GIVING UP!

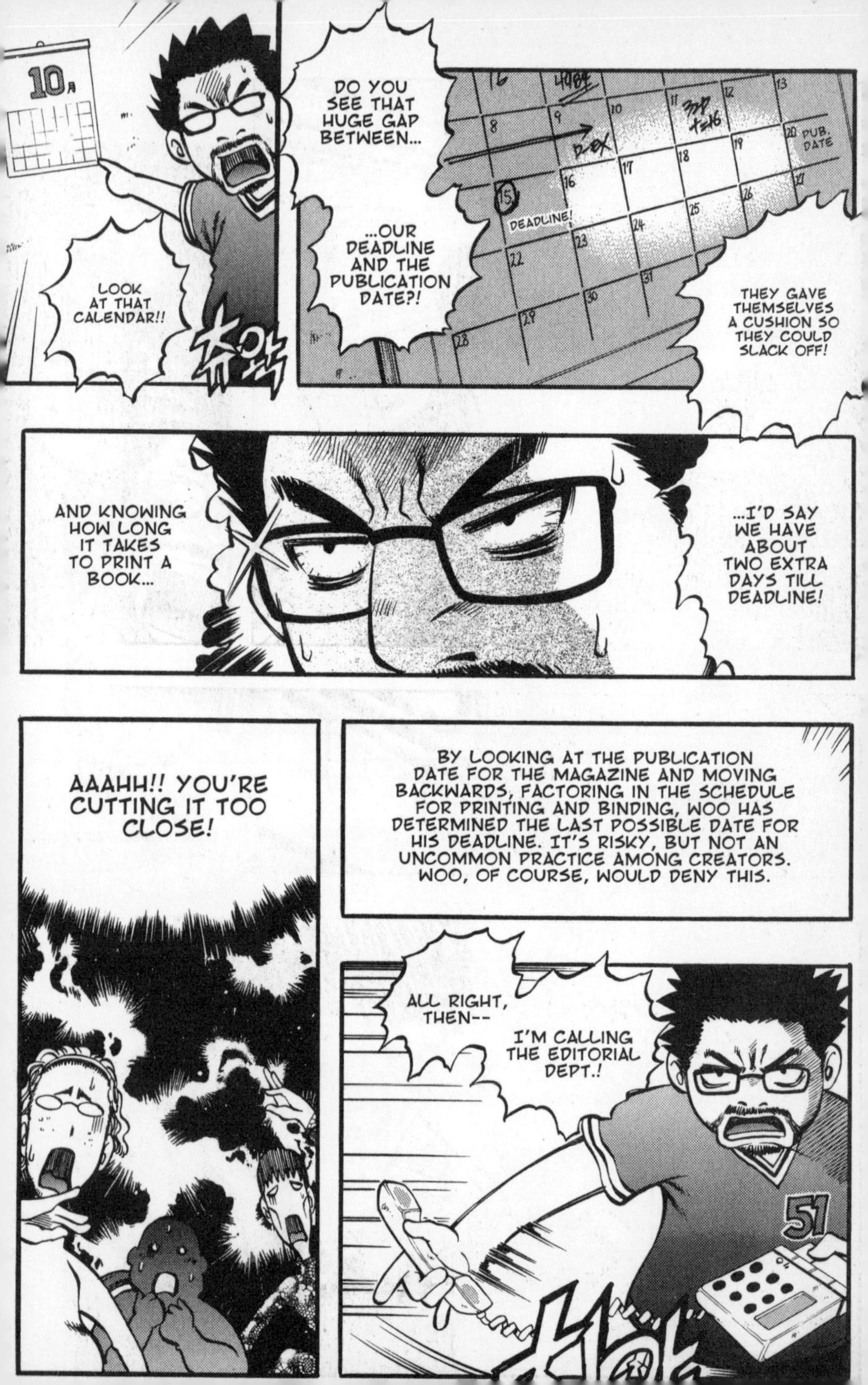
LOOK AT THAT CALENDAR!!
DO YOU SEE THAT HUGE GAP BETWEEN...
...OUR DEADLINE AND THE PUBLICATION DATE?!
DEADLINE!
PUB. DATE
THEY GAVE THEMSELVES A CUSHION SO THEY COULD SLACK OFF!
AND KNOWING HOW LONG IT TAKES TO PRINT A BOOK...
...I'D SAY WE HAVE ABOUT TWO EXTRA DAYS TILL DEADLINE!
BY LOOKING AT THE PUBLICATION DATE FOR THE MAGAZINE AND MOVING BACKWARDS, FACTORING IN THE SCHEDULE FOR PRINTING AND BINDING, WOO HAS DETERMINED THE LAST POSSIBLE DATE FOR HIS DEADLINE. IT'S RISKY, BUT NOT AN UNCOMMON PRACTICE AMONG CREATORS. WOO, OF COURSE, WOULD DENY THIS.
AAAHH!! YOU'RE CUTTING IT TOO CLOSE!
ALL RIGHT, THEN--
I'M CALLING THE EDITORIAL DEPT.!

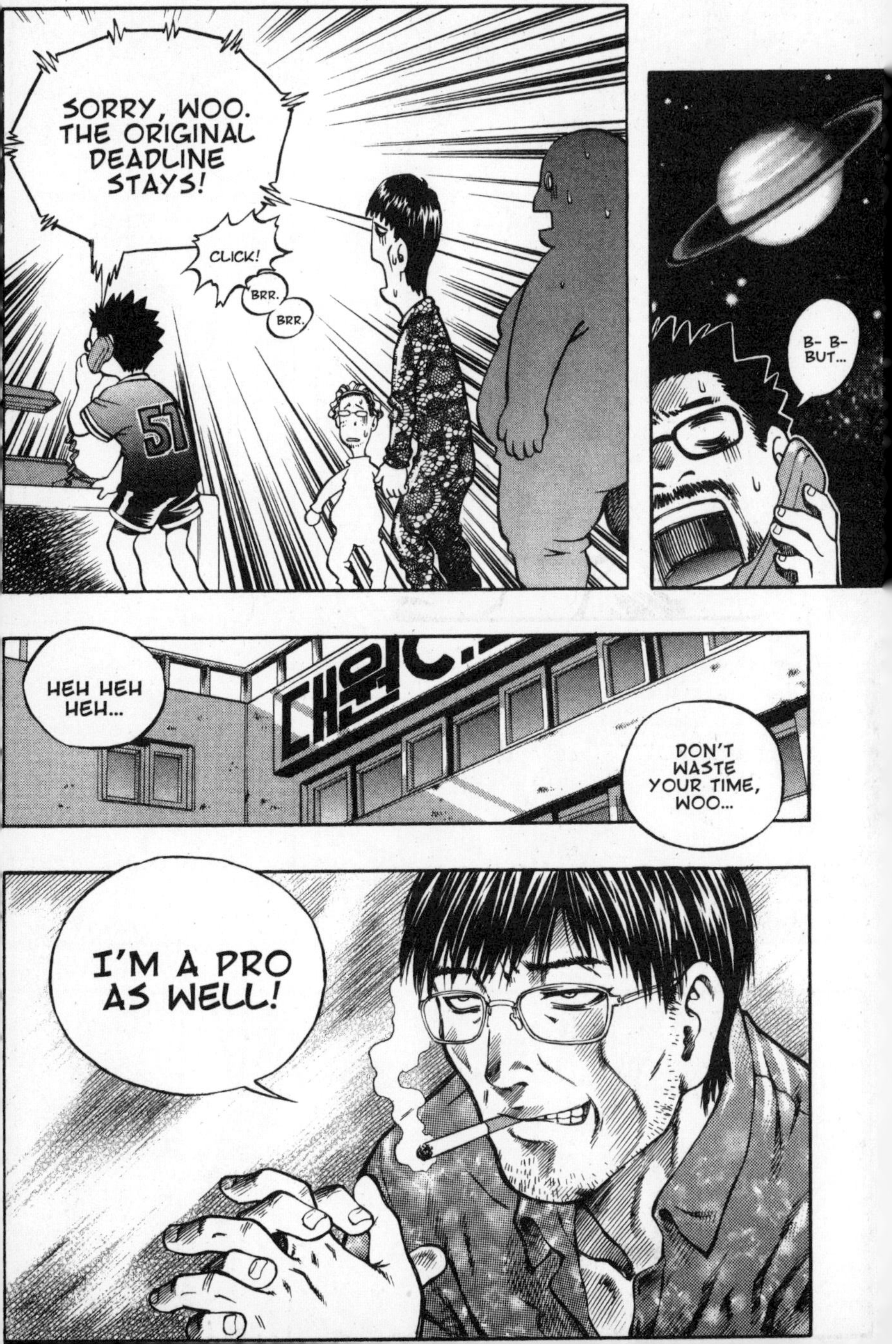
SORRY, WOO. THE ORIGINAL DEADLINE STAYS!
CLICK!
BRR.
BRR.
B- B- BUT...
HEH HEH HEH...
DON'T WASTE YOUR TIME, WOO...
I'M A PRO AS WELL!

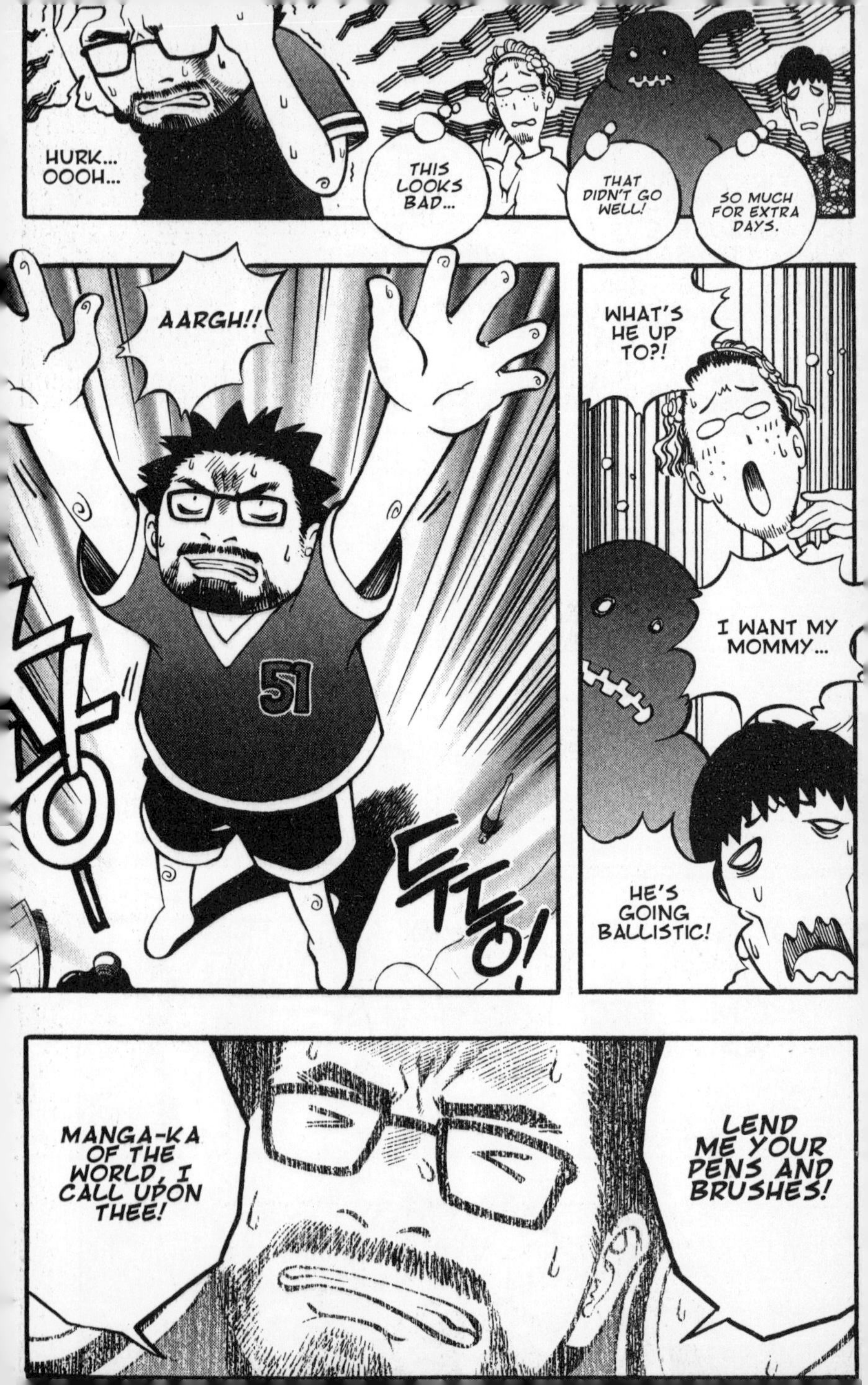
HURK... OOOH...
THIS LOOKS BAD...
THAT DIDN'T GO WELL!
SO MUCH FOR EXTRA DAYS.
AARGH!!
WHAT'S HE UP TO?!
I WANT MY MOMMY...
HE'S GOING BALLISTIC!
MANGA-KA OF THE WORLD, I CALL UPON THEE!
LEND ME YOUR PENS AND BRUSHES!

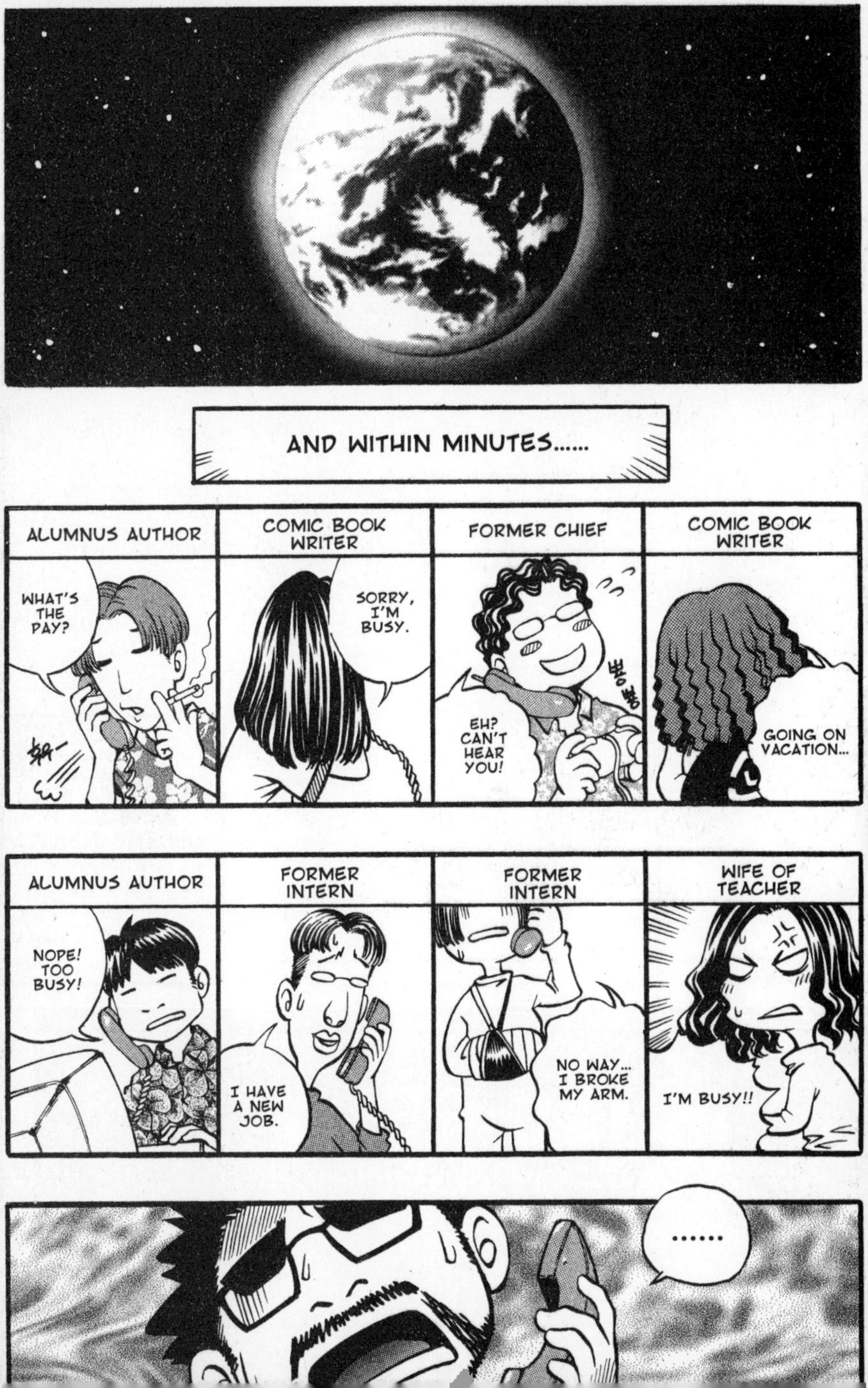
AND WITHIN MINUTES......
ALUMNUS AUTHOR
WHAT'S THE PAY?
COMIC BOOK WRITER
SORRY, I'M BUSY.
FORMER CHIEF
EH? CAN'T HEAR YOU!
COMIC BOOK WRITER
GOING ON VACATION...
ALUMNUS AUTHOR
NOPE! TOO BUSY!
FORMER INTERN
I HAVE A NEW JOB.
FORMER INTERN
NO WAY... I BROKE MY ARM.
WIFE OF TEACHER
I'M BUSY!!
......

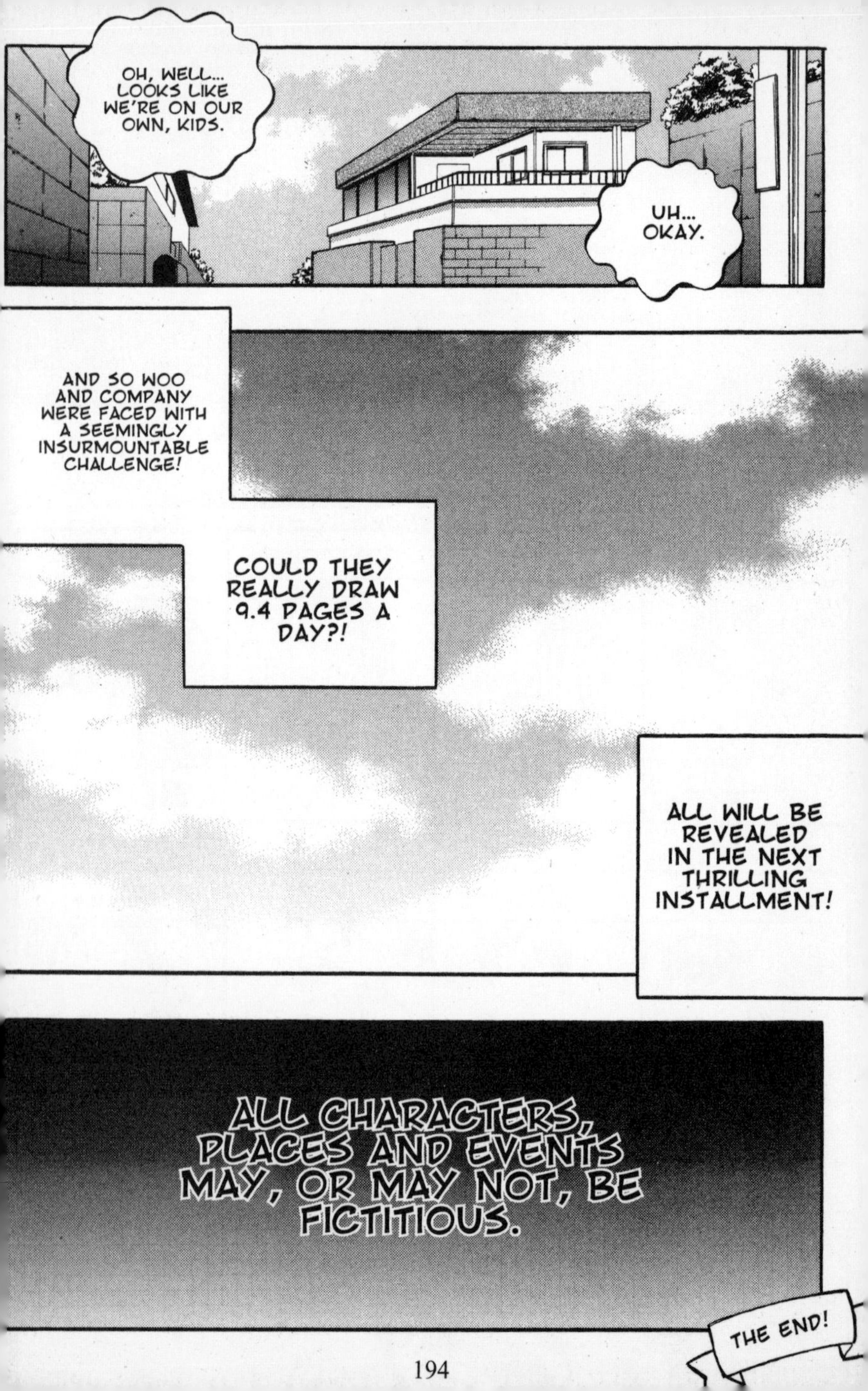
OH, WELL... LOOKS LIKE WE'RE ON OUR OWN, KIDS.
UH... OKAY.
AND SO WOO AND COMPANY WERE FACED WITH A SEEMINGLY INSURMOUNTABLE CHALLENGE!
COULD THEY REALLY DRAW 9.4 PAGES A DAY?!
ALL WILL BE REVEALED IN THE NEXT THRILLING INSTALLMENT!
ALL CHARACTERS, PLACES AND EVENTS MAY, OR MAY NOT, BE FICTITIOUS.
THE END!

Preview: Vol. 15

Far below the surface of the Great Salt Desert, the Vampire Lord Tournament begins! As Deshwitat and the team are instructed in the rules of the brutal contest, they struggle to come to terms with a horrible truth. Their valued comrade, Millenear, has fallen prey to the soul-draining power of Mr. Grey! But Deshwitat has little time to dwell on these dire events as he faces his first opponent—the vicious vampire warrior, Santana! Will our dark hero survive the deadly tournament's first round?!

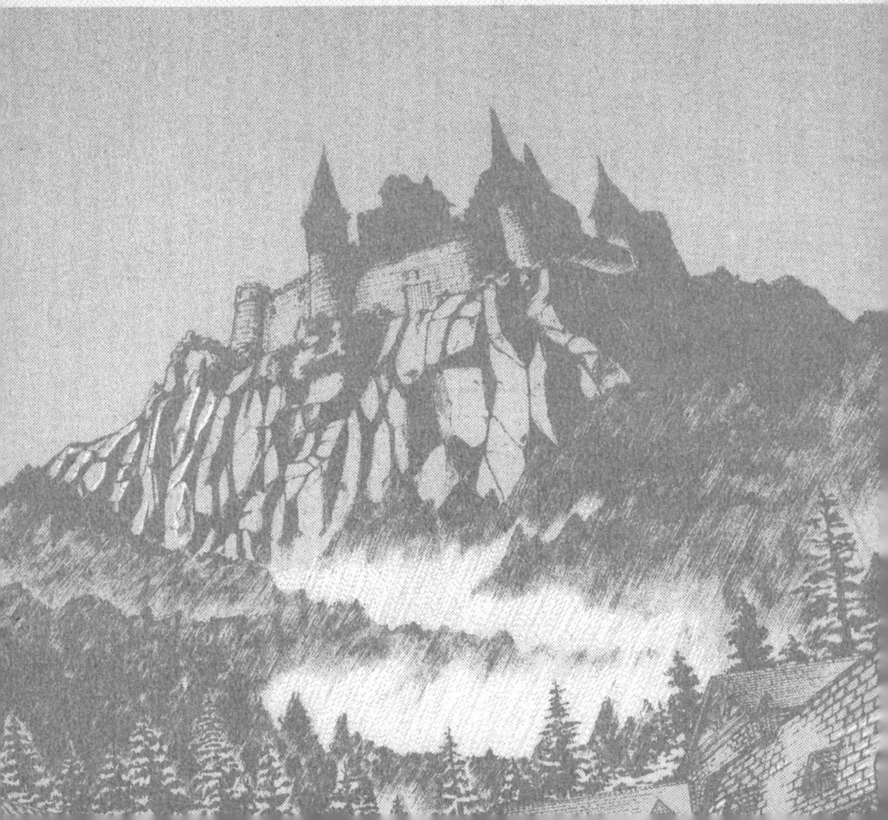

TOKYOPOP SHOP

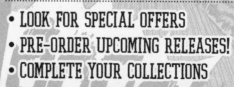

SPOTLIGHT **TOKYOPOP MANGA SUPPLEMENT**

BECK: MONGOLIAN CHOP SQUAD

OT
OLDER TEEN
AGE 16+

ROCK IN MANGA!

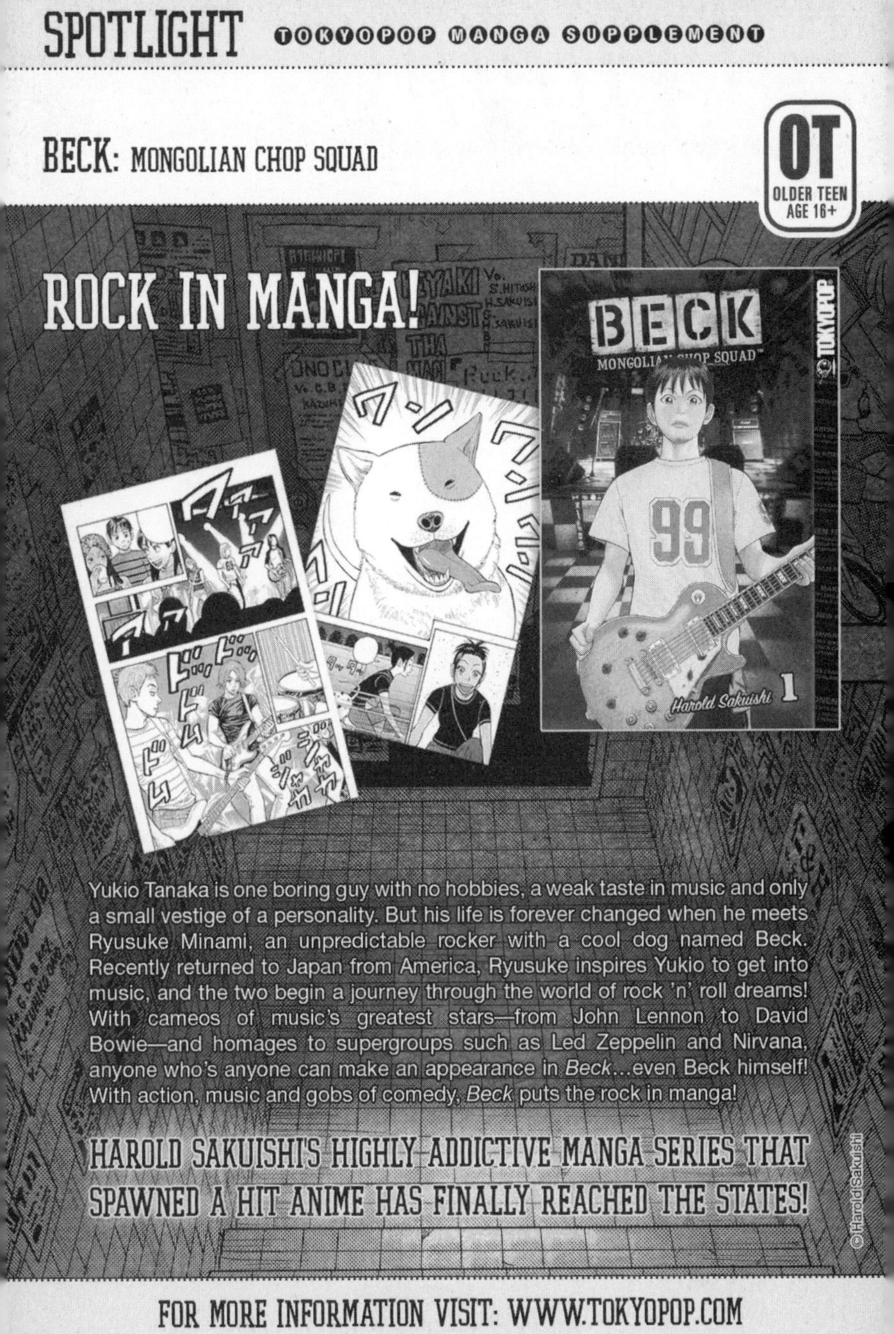
BECK
MONGOLIAN CHOP SQUAD™
TOKYOPOP
Harold Sakuishi
1

Yukio Tanaka is one boring guy with no hobbies, a weak taste in music and only a small vestige of a personality. But his life is forever changed when he meets Ryusuke Minami, an unpredictable rocker with a cool dog named Beck. Recently returned to Japan from America, Ryusuke inspires Yukio to get into music, and the two begin a journey through the world of rock 'n' roll dreams! With cameos of music's greatest stars—from John Lennon to David Bowie—and homages to supergroups such as Led Zeppelin and Nirvana, anyone who's anyone can make an appearance in *Beck*...even Beck himself! With action, music and gobs of comedy, *Beck* puts the rock in manga!

HAROLD SAKUISHI'S HIGHLY ADDICTIVE MANGA SERIES THAT SPAWNED A HIT ANIME HAS FINALLY REACHED THE STATES!

FOR MORE INFORMATION VISIT: WWW.TOKYOPOP.COM

A Diva Torn from Chaos
A Savior Doomed to Love

Volume 2

Lumination

Ai continues to search for her place in our world on the streets of Tokyo. Using her talent to support herself, Ai signs a contract with a top record label and begins her rise to stardom. But fame is unpredictable—as her talent blooms, all eyes are on Ai. When scandal surfaces, will she burn out in the spotlight of celebrity?

T
TEEN
AGE 13+

Preview the manga at:
www.TOKYOPOP.com/princessai

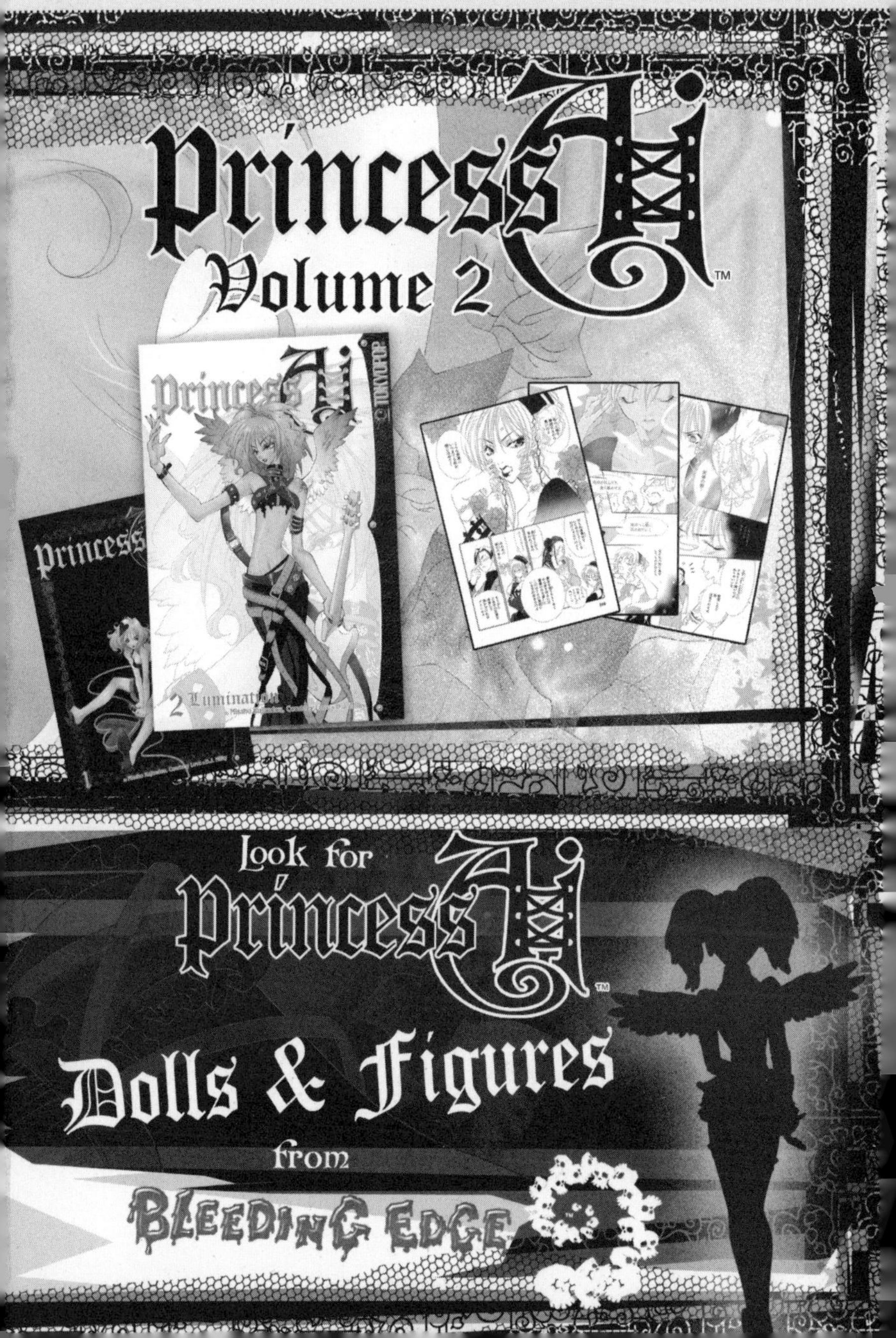
Princess Ai™
Volume 2
Look for
Princess Ai™
Dolls & Figures
from
BLEEDING EDGE

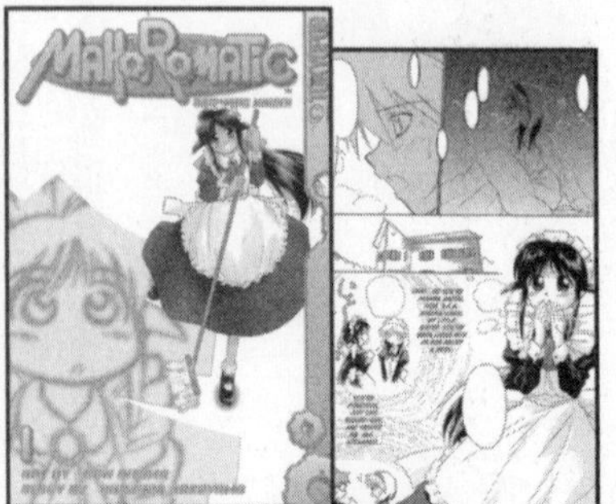

BY BUNJURO NAKAYAMA AND BOW DITAMA

MAHOROMATIC: AUTOMATIC MAIDEN

Mahoro is a sweet, cute, female battle android who decides to go from mopping up alien invaders to mopping up after Suguru Misato, a teenaged orphan boy... and hilarity most definitely ensues. This series has great art and a slick story that easily switches from truly funny to downright heartwarming...but always with a large shadow looming over it. You see, only Mahoro knows that her days are quite literally numbered, and the end of each chapter lets you know exactly how much—or how little—time she has left!

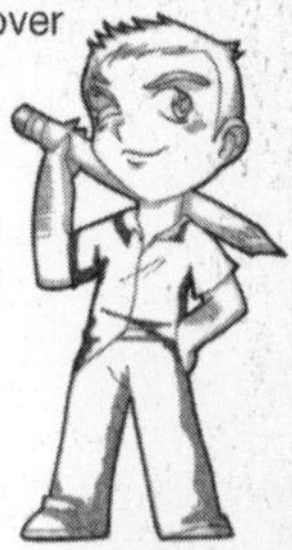

~Rob Tokar, Sr. Editor

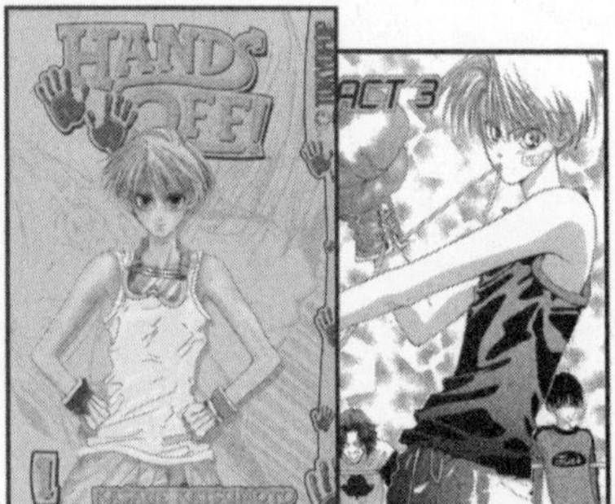
ACT 3

BY KASANE KATSUMOTO

HANDS OFF!

Cute boys with ESP who share a special bond... If you think this is familiar (e.g. *Legal Drug*), well, you're wrong. *Hands Off!* totally stands alone as a unique and thoroughly enjoyable series. Kotarou and Tatsuki's (platonic!) relationship is complex, fascinating and heart-wrenching. Throw in Yuuto, the playboy who can read auras, and you've got a fantastic setup for drama and comedy, with incredible themes of friendship running throughout. Don't be put off by Kotarou's danger-magnet status, either. The episodic stuff gradually changes, and the full arc of the characters' development is well worth waiting for.

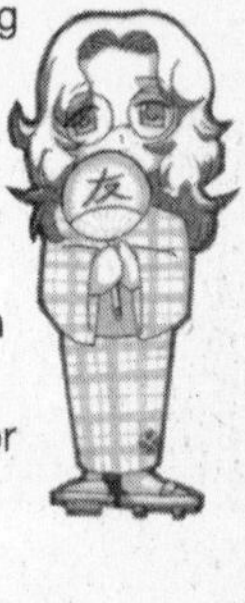

~Lillian Diaz-Przybyl, Jr. Editor